RELIGION AND SOCIETY
IN ELIZABETHAN SUSSEX

To
ANNE

RELIGION AND SOCIETY
IN ELIZABETHAN SUSSEX

A study of the enforcement of the religious settlement

1558–1603

by

ROGER B. MANNING

Associate Professor of History
The Cleveland State University

LEICESTER UNIVERSITY PRESS

1969

First published in 1969 by Leicester University Press

Distributed in North America by
Humanities Press Inc., New York

Copyright © Roger B. Manning 1969

Set in Monotype Perpetua
Printed in Great Britain by
Western Printing Services Ltd., Bristol

SBN 7185 1084 4

This volume is published
with the help of a grant from
the Marc Fitch Fund

CONTENTS

MAP

The Diocese of Chichester showing Rural
Deaneries and Archiepiscopal Peculiars   *at end*

LIST OF TABLES

LIST OF ABBREVIATIONS

Acts P.C.	*Acts of the Privy Council*
B.M.	British Museum
Cal. P.R., Eliz.	*Calendar of Patent Rolls for the Reign of Elizabeth*
Cal. S.P., Dom.	*Calendar of State Papers, Domestic Series for the Reigns of Edward VI, Mary, and Elizabeth*
C.R.S.	Catholic Record Society
DRO	Chichester Diocesan Record Office
E.H.R.	*English Historical Review*
G.E.C.	*The Complete Peerage*, ed. G. E. Cockayne
Hist. MSS. Comm.	Historical Manuscripts Commission
O.E.D.	*Oxford English Dictionary*
P.C.C.	Prerogative Court of Canterbury (Somerset House, London)
Peckham, *Act Book A*	*The Acts of the Dean and Chapter of the Cathedral Church of Chichester, 1545–1642*, ed. W. D. Peckham
P.R.O.	Public Record Office
S.A.C.	*Sussex Archaeological Collections*
S.N. & Q.	*Sussex Notes and Queries*
S.P., Dom., Eliz.	P.R.O., State Papers, Domestic Series for the Reign of Elizabeth
S.R.S.	Sussex Record Society
V.C.H.	*The Victoria County History*
WSCRO	West Sussex County Record Office, Chichester

PREFACE

THE IDEA OF doing a study on the enforcement of the Elizabethan Religious Settlement in Sussex was first suggested to me by the Reverend Professor Eric McDermott, S.J., who introduced me to Tudor England when I was a student at Georgetown University. I owe more to his patience, guidance and encouragement than words can ever repay.

My other debts of gratitude for assistance and advice are numerous. Professor Joel Hurstfield of University College, London guided my research during the year that I spent as a graduate student at the Institute of Historical Research of the University of London and was unfailingly generous with both time and encouragement. Thanks are due to him and to Professor Sir John Neale and Professor S. T. Bindoff and to all the members of their seminars who did so much to help me define my purpose and avoid pitfalls. Few men have done so much to promote Anglo-American friendship. Indeed, as Professor Neale often remarked, the Institute of Historical Research is a commonwealth of knowledge.

I remember with particular pleasure the many kindnesses of W. D. Peckham, Esq., the Hon. Archivist of the Dean and Chapter of Chichester Cathedral, whose knowledge of the ecclesiastical history of the Diocese of Chichester is unsurpassed. Not only did he give me the benefit of this accumulation of knowledge, he also showed me English hospitality at its best.

I must also acknowledge my gratitude towards those of my teachers and colleagues who have read various parts of the manuscript of this book: Fr Eric McDermott, S.J., Professor Joel Hurstfield, Dr Patrick Collinson, Dr Thomas Campbell, Dr J. S. Taylor, and especially Professor Clayton Roberts, who read the entire manuscript. Fr F. X. Walker, S.J. allowed me to profit from his research experience in the Chicester Diocesan Record Office and to use and cite his dissertation. Several former students of the Institute of Historical Research graciously have allowed me to consult their dissertations: Dr Patrick

Collinson, Dr Joyce Mousley, Fr Albert Loomie, S.J., Fr Eric McDermott, S.J., and Fr Michael O'Dwyer.

My thanks are also due to the Trustees and the staff of the British Museum, and the librarians and archivists of the Folger Library and the Library of Congress, the Institute of Historical Research of the University of London, the Public Record Office, Lambeth Palace Library, the Bodleian Library, Oxford, the Archives of Westminster Cathedral, the Cleveland Public Library, to Mr Francis Steer of the Chichester Diocesan Record Office, Chichester and the East and West Sussex County Record Offices, to the Trustees of the Sussex Archaeological Trust, Lewes, to the libraries of Georgetown University, Ohio State University, Cleveland State University, and also to the President of the Probate, Divorce and Admiralty Division of the High Court of Justice, Somerset House, London, for permission to examine the registers of wills of the Prerogative Court of Canterbury. I wish also to thank Professor A. G. Dickens, editor of the *Bulletin of the Institute of Historical Research*, for permission to reprint parts of my article "Catholics and local office holding in Elizabethan Sussex" from the May 1962 issue of the *Bulletin*, and Dr Ralph Pugh, editor of *The Victoria History of the Counties of England*, for permission to derive the map at the back of the book from *The Victoria History of the County of Sussex*, volume II.

This book could never have been written had I not been sustained and encouraged by my wife. Not only did she spend many hours proofreading the manuscript; she also typed it twice through.

ROGER B. MANNING

The Cleveland State University
28 March 1968

INTRODUCTION

THE EXERCISE OF royal control over nationalized churches was a factor of great importance in the consolidation of the New Monarchies. To an age that regarded religious dissent as the other face of sedition, an erastian church afforded an extensive establishment for preaching what every prince regarded as the Christian duty of rendering obedience to constituted authority. Yet, in England what was considered to be the most important of royal powers was at the same time one of the greatest sources of criticism because of the manner in which the powers of the royal supremacy were exercised. In the constitutional struggles that led up to the English Revolution of the seventeenth century both royalists and parliamentarians repeatedly emphasized the necessity of controlling the state church in order to secure victory for their respective programmes. The final defeat of royalist theory and practice during the Glorious Revolution of 1689 in effect transferred the royal ecclesiastical supremacy to a predominantly lay Parliament and led to a tacit admission of the futility of forcing one state religion on the people of England.

A particularly crucial period in the debate over who should control the established church was the reign of Elizabeth I. Throughout her reign the queen was obliged to defend the powers of her supreme governorship against encroachment by Puritans and parliament men. The origins and expressions of their ideas have received wide attention from scholars, but a deeper understanding of the powers of the royal ecclesiastical supremacy must await more detailed studies of the exercise of that supremacy by local agents of the Crown. This book attempts to study these local agents of the supreme governor of the Church of England and to analyse the administrative and social problems that they encountered in enforcing the Elizabethan religious settlement[1] in Sussex. These problems were many.

[1] By the term "Elizabethan religious settlement" I refer not only to the Acts of Supremacy and Uniformity of 1559 (1 Eliz. I, c. 1 & 2), but also the

The Elizabethan religious settlement was a compromise that satisfied almost no one.[1] Elizabethan England was far from being an homogeneous society. Roads everywhere were poor and hindered communication. There was no salaried, professional civil service in the provinces. Considering these difficulties, it is no wonder that a gap existed between the intent of the Acts of Supremacy and Uniformity and their actual enforcement in the counties of England.

Rural Sussex presented additional difficulties at the beginning of this period. Social conservatism was very strong. This study will attempt to demonstrate that both the government and the local governors agreed that social stability should be given primacy over the enforcement of religious uniformity. In the event, the transfer of social power from the Catholic nobility and gentry to the new Protestant aristocracy was accomplished in stages and spread over twenty-five years.

There is an inescapable complexity to the whole problem of the enforcement of the Elizabethan religious settlement. Besides the widespread craving for order and stability, other factors such as the failure of episcopal leadership, the ineffectiveness of church courts, the growth of anticlericalism among the gentry, the condition of the clergy and the character of the opposition to enforcement, all need to be explained. Under the last heading there is not only the problem of investigating the decline of Catholicism but also the survival of Catholic recusancy in so far as it did survive, not to mention the failure to suppress Puritanism in late Elizabethan Sussex.

Although the classic period of the English Reformation is sometimes thought of as being confined largely to the period before 1558,[2] the full realization of the ideas preached by the first generation of Protestant reformers was delayed,[3] and

---

various other parliamentary statutes, royal proclamations, ecclesiastical canons and injunctions which were promulgated to reinforce the original two Acts.

[1] Sir John Neale, "The Elizabethan Acts of Supremacy and Uniformity", *E.H.R.*, LX, 306ff.

[2] For example, cf. Sir Maurice Powicke, *The Reformation in England* (Oxford: 1961), p. 125.

[3] Christopher Hill, *Intellectual Origins of the English Revolution* (Oxford:

delayed more particularly in Sussex. Religious novelties did not spread as rapidly in Sussex as they did in London. True, there were pockets of Protestantism in east Sussex that dated from Edwardian times, but these were the exceptions, not the rule. When discussing the idea of the English Reformation I think it is well to distinguish between (1) the official or Henrician reformation, which broke with Rome and erected the royal supremacy for purely political considerations, (2) the theological reformation, which began under Henry VIII, but was not really under full steam until Edwardian times and continued into the middle of the seventeenth century, and (3) the popular reformation which commenced only when the people began assuming a Protestant, as opposed to a merely anti-papal attitude.

The first Elizabethan bishop of Chichester, William Barlow, was aware that outside of these few areas in one end of Sussex the popular reformation really had not begun. Barlow explained this situation by pointing to the lack of dependable lieutenants and learned preachers of a Protestant disposition. He also emphasized the fact that Catholics remained on the commission of the peace. The full ferment of the popular reformation in Sussex did not reach its peak until the episcopate of Richard Curteys in the 1570s after the universities had begun to make good the deficiency of educated Protestant clerics.

Thus, it was not until two decades after the parliamentary settlement of religion in 1559 that the conservative leadership among the Sussex nobility and gentry was finally broken. This crucial fact reminds us of Sir John Neale's observation about vigorous and revolutionary forces jostling an older tradition.[1] The slowness of Sussex in accommodating itself to a new national policy is not hard to understand in the light of the remoteness of the organs of central government from provincial Englishmen; the clergy, the officials of county and borough were the only agents of royal government they ever saw. England was still a collection—almost a federation—of communities, and English society was constructed within the framework of the county. This social importance of the county is

---

1965), p. 3; A. G. Dickens, *Lollards and Protestants in the Diocese of York, 1509–1551* (London: 1959), p. 251.

[1] *Elizabethan Essays* (London: 1958), p. 29.

difficult to grasp for those of us who live in an age of urbaniza-tion and centralization.[1] The economic situation in Elizabethan Sussex favoured the leadership of the country gentry: the Cinque Ports continued their decline while the profits of the nascent iron industry fell to the gentry rather than an urban middle class. Independence was not an attitude that flourished where influence and power lay largely in the hands of the local squire.

The leaders of this society were not of the stature of the sea-dogs and courtiers who have attracted so many biographers to the Elizabethan period. They were mostly the men of middle rank in society—the administrators and aspiring politicians. Joel Hurstfield has urged historians to spend more time study-ing these men of middle rank since effective government ulti-mately depends more upon the men who execute the laws than those who make them.[2]

The important instruments in the exercise of the royal supremacy in ecclesiastical matters were the bishops. However, Elizabethan bishops were handicapped in several ways: while their position had improved somewhat since Henrician and Edwardian times, bishops were still regarded as little more than ecclesiastical justices of the peace deriving their power of jurisdiction from the crown. Theories of divine-right episco-pacy could never have the same appeal to the Tudors as they did to the Stuarts. The careers of the four Elizabethan bishops of Chichester afford ample illustration of the decline in power and prestige of the office of bishop that had begun after the fall of Cardinal Wolsey. The episcopal courts of the diocese of Chichester could command neither sanction nor respect.

There were other forces at work, filling the void created by the decline of episcopal leadership: the age of the layman had dawned, and it was only appropriate that as a result of par-liamentary legislation the landed magnates of Sussex should be joined with the bishops of Chichester in the task of overseeing the local enforcement of the religious settlement. The resulting conflict of jurisdictions, the constant interference of J.P.s, royal judges and the Privy Council, and the execution by the

[1] Neale, *The Elizabethan House of Commons* (London: 1949), p. 21.
[2] "Conyers Read and Historical Biography", *The Listener* (28 April 1960), pp. 747–8.

bishops of temporal functions, could well lead to a crisis. The question of who could "bear rule" arose and was thrashed out when the gentry saw their dearest interests threatened by the zealous Bishop Curteys who, they felt, behaved too much like a medieval prelate. In the event, Curteys's concept of reform suffered a severe setback at the hands of the Sussex gentry. The next two incumbents of the diocese of Chichester, Bickley and Watson, proved more acquiescent to the rule of the gentry. For their part, those among the gentry who were not attached to Protestantism by fervour, were at least willing to conform for the sake of being counted among the local governors.

The ambition and family pride that impelled members of the country gentry to seek and hold local office was, in my opinion, a crucial factor in tying those who wavered in their religious professions to the new regime. Nor was such a pattern of behaviour unrelated to the Elizabethan government's desire to break the social and religious power of the rather numerous quasi-feudal nobility of Sussex. Whereas the gradual elimination of the Catholic nobility from important positions of influence and patronage, such as the lieutenancy, hardened those peers in their religious and social conservatism, the more lenient government attitude towards crypto-Catholic and even open Catholic office-holders undoubtedly contributed to the erosion of Catholic beliefs among the untitled gentry and, at the same time, assured the queen of the loyalty of this group. Thus, while there is no significant decline of Catholicism among the peers of Sussex, the proportion of Catholics among the heads of eighty-eight families who at some time during the reign of Elizabeth held an important local office fell from one-half in the 1560s to one-sixth in the 1590s.

Professor Trimble's rigid definition of Catholicism[1] notwithstanding, the Elizabethan government saw the necessity of distinguishing between differing degrees of Catholicism. Uncompromising Catholics among the gentry—never a numerous

[1] W. R. Trimble, The Catholic Laity in Elizabethan England, 1558–1603 (Cambridge, Mass.: 1964). For a more detailed criticism of Professor Trimble's methods of investigation see below p. 255 ff., and also my review of his book in the Archiv für Reformationsgeschichte, Jahrgang 55 (1965), Heft 2, p. 275.

group—were dealt with very severely; by 1580 their leaders were either imprisoned or fled into exile. At any rate they were effectively isolated. Less intransigent recusants were subjected to the economic pressure of fines and the sequestration of their lands. The crypto-Catholics were enticed away from religious disaffection by the opportunity to hold local office.

The problems of methodology, classification and quantification that an administrative and social study of the Elizabethan religious settlement raises, are manageable only where one county or a portion of a county is studied. The historian must get to know his subjects as intimately as possible by marshalling all available evidence—a technique already employed by Sir Lewis Namier and Sir John Neale and their disciples in the field of parliamentary history. To be avoided is the sort of study that seeks only crude percentages of Catholics (or for that matter Puritans) who are selected from a sampling of a number of counties. To give only one example of the problems of classification and measurement that are encountered, the latter type of study is not likely to tell us very much about this important group of crypto-Catholics who could wield far more influence than their more uncompromising cousins locked away in the Clink or restricted to within five miles of their homes.

Puritanism in Sussex presents even greater problems of delimitation than Catholicism. Separatism is quite rare during the Elizabethan period, since the great majority of Puritans had not yet abandoned hope of remodelling the established church along the lines of the Swiss churches. Furthermore, whereas the dogmatic differences between Catholic and Anglican were readily apparent, the creed of Puritanism could be distinquished from the reigning Calvinist theology among the Anglican upper clergy only by the enthusiasm with which these beliefs were preached.[1] The disagreement concerning ecclesiastical polity was closer to the real issue: here the Puritan protest grew out of a deeply felt need to make the rusty medieval ecclesiastical

---

[1] The futility of trying to estimate the number of lay Puritans in Sussex is implicit in Christopher Hill's definition of Puritanism as including "all those radical Protestants who wanted to reform the Church (but before 1640 at least) did not want to separate from it." *Intellectual Origins of the English Reformation*, p. 26.

machinery more responsive to the spiritual needs of lay people. Ultimately the Puritans were led to question the royal supremacy itself. During the episcopate of Richard Curteys, clerical Puritanism was hardly distinguishable from the reform movement which the bishop headed. It was Curteys who, like several of his episcopal contemporaries, had sponsored the prophesyings or clerical exercises in the early 1570s; they survived Curteys's overthrow, metamorphosed and reappeared as a Puritan classical movement in the early 1580s. The appointment of John Whitgift to the archbishopric of Canterbury in 1583 signalled the queen's determination to root out the presbyterians. Whitgift at first proceeded vigorously against suspected ministers; later he was forced to moderate his approach when he discovered the extent of Puritanism, not only in Sussex but elsewhere, and when he realized that he could not depend upon the Privy Council to back him up.[1] Considering the lack of support from the Privy Council for bold prelates such as Curteys and Whitgift, it is not to be wondered that the aged Bickley and the absentee Watson, the third and fourth bishops of Chichester, allowed the Puritan classical movement to go unchecked until the time of James I and Archbishop Bancroft.

No claim is made here that Sussex was a typical county during the Elizabethan period. There are certain characteristics that surely are unique among English shires; but there are others that hopefully will suggest similar lines of investigation for other counties. I did not begin this book with the intention of writing revisionist history, but only to discover how the religious settlement was actually carried out. This has not been easy, for the gaps in surviving evidence are maddeningly frequent, while what has survived will not always yield the answers to the questions that one would like to ask. Yet, I do feel that the picture of the enforcement of the Elizabethan religious settlement that will emerge in the following pages is a more convincing one than most textbooks give us because it is drawn from the lives of real people whose individuality has not been snuffed out by abstractions.

[1] P. M. Dawley, *John Whitgift and the English Reformation* (New York: 1954), p. 156 and especially pp. 168–9.

PART I

THE SETTING

I

THE COUNTY

IFFICULTIES OF COMMUNICATION and the overwhelm-
ingly rural character of Sussex society necessarily affected
the administration of Sussex by the central government.
Situated on the Channel coast due south from London and
bounded by Kent, Surrey and Hampshire, Elizabethan Sussex
displayed a wide divergence of geographical and economic
conditions. Three different geographical regions run parallel
across the county, east to west. The Weald, a forest belt
stretching across the northern part of Sussex, and the Downs,
open chalk hills cutting across the central part of the county,
were sparsely populated and inaccessible. Most of the population was concentrated along the arable coastal belt. Commerce,
not only with Ireland and the Continent, but with other parts
of England, was almost completely dependent upon maritime
transportation since the roads were impassable except during a
dry summer. The decline of the Sussex ports during the
sixteenth century only emphasized the isolation of the county.

Conservative social tendencies also help to explain the slowness of Sussex in accepting the Elizabethan religious settlement.
These tendencies arose out of the rural character of Sussex
which persisted during the latter part of the sixteenth century
because of the economic conditions. The economic activities
that prospered the most were arable farming and iron-founding,
both of which were controlled by the landed gentry. Evidence
for the prosperity of the landed classes may be seen in the rise in
land prices.[1] While the yeomanry also profited from this
appreciation of assets, Bishop Curteys observed that not
enough of them were freeholders to counterweigh the social

---

[1] G. E. Fussell gives the example of a Sussex copyhold of 30 acres that was
converted into a freehold in 1559, when it fetched a yearly rent of 10s. The
purchase price, which was £165 in 1559, had more than doubled twenty
years later, and had soared to £437 10s. in 1655. "Four Centuries of Farming
Systems in Sussex, 1500–1900", S.A.C., XC, 62. See also Sir John Clapham,
A Concise Economic History of Great Britain (Cambridge: 1963), p. 208.

influence of the gentry.[1] At the same time, maritime commerce and fishing were in decline, thus affording no opportunity for the emergence of an independent urban middle class.

Even in the seventeenth century, when iron-founding reached its zenith in the Weald, agriculture still remained the predominant occupation among the people of the county. The main crop along the arable coastal plain was corn. Wheat was raised primarily for export from West Sussex ports to Ireland and the Low Countries, while lesser folk had to content themselves in times of plenty with barley. In times of dearth the poor were reduced to eating a loaf made of beans or oats mixed with acorns.[2] Although the chalk Downs were covered with a layer of clay too thin to anchor any flora except grass or rye, it had been obvious from an early date that the Downs afforded excellent sheep pasturage. Since large amounts of land were always at hand for sheep-grazing, the Sussex coastal plain was not as troubled by the evils growing out of enclosures as were other arable parts of the southern and midland counties, although in the closing years of the reign of Henry VIII there were several armed riots aimed at enclosures, mostly in the vicinity of Pevensey in east Sussex.[3] In the sixteenth century, before the development of the Southdown breed of sheep, sheep were kept mainly for manure since their wool was too coarse to compete with the finer north country wools.[4] One fifth of the Weald was still forest in the time of Elizabeth, and its infertile sands and clays discouraged any type of agriculture except raising pigs and beef cattle. The Wealden yeomen depended upon smithing and charcoal-making for a livelihood, with subsistence farming as a secondary occupation. Since the iron forges could operate only in the winter when the Wealden streams were swollen by rain, the two activities did not conflict.[5]

Timber, sawn lumber and firewood were the next most

[1] P.R.O., S.P., Dom., Eliz., 165/22.
[2] Julian Cornwall, "Farming in Sussex 1560–1640", S.A.C., XCII, 55–6.
[3] V.C.H. Sussex, II, 170–89.
[4] Cornwall, op. cit., S.A.C., XCII, 49, 63; Fussell, "Four Centuries of Farming Systems in Sussex 1500–1900", S.A.C., XC, 60.
[5] Cornwall, op. cit., S.A.C., XCII, 67–77, 88; Fussell, op. cit., S.A.C., XC, 61.

important exports of the county. Arundel, which traded with Dieppe and other Norman ports, led in this traffic, followed by Shoreham, Rye, Winchelsea, Chichester and Lewes, which shipped to London and to French and Dutch ports. The rulers of Tudor England were very much alarmed at the depletion of timber as is witnessed by the plethora of statutes seeking to preserve forest resources for shipbuilding; however, the Sussex gentry, animated by the spirit of the new commercialism, always saw to it that these statutes expressly excluded the Weald from their provisions.[1] And so the destruction of precious timberland proceeded unchecked and nothing was done to promote systematic forestry;[2] the consequent erosion of the soil contributed to the silting up of Sussex harbours.

Since the difficulties of overland transportation made the carrying of bulk goods economically impractical, an iron ore deposit was quite useless unless there was wood for charcoal situated nearby. In the Weald all of the necessary factors were present enabling ironmasters to carry out their mining and smelting in the same location, and the iron industry flourished here for the hundred years or so after 1560. The largest concentrations of forges were at Kirdford, where there were ten foundries within a four-mile radius, and at Heathfield, where eighteen were scattered over the same area. Here, also, were located nine of the twelve glass furnaces known to have existed in Elizabethan times.[3] However small the output, iron-making was of necessity a capitalistic venture owing to the expense of machinery; the end of the fifteenth century saw the increasing use of blast furnaces while William Camden's description of iron-founding in the Sussex Weald indicates that water wheels drove hydraulic hammers in Sussex forges.[4] Not all of those

[1] Cornwall, "Forestry and the Timber Trade in Sussex", *S.N. & Q.*, XIV, 85–91; Paul Mantoux, *The Industrial Revolution in the Eighteenth Century* (rev. ed., New York: 1962), p. 281.

[2] John Norden lamented: "He that hath known the welds of Sussex, Surrey and Kent, the grand nursery especially of oak and beech, shall find such an alteration in less than thirty years as may well strike a fear lest few years more, as pestilent as the former, will leave few good trees standing in those welds." (*The Surveyors Dialogue* (1607), p. 214, quoted *ibid.*)

[3] G. H. Kenyon, "Wealden Iron", *S.N. & Q.* XIII, 234–41.

[4] *Britanniae Descriptio* (1607), II, 105, quoted in Mantoux, *op. cit.*, p. 273.

who owned forges were crass upstarts; ancient families such as the Percys, the Nevilles, the Howards and the Ashburnhams had also been infected by the new commercialism and had iron works on their own lands. Michael Drayton concurred in the view that iron-founders ruthlessly disregarded the needs of future generations when he made a chorus of oaks and ashes cry out

"Could we, say they, suppose, that any would cherish,
Which suffer (every day) the holiest things to perish?
Or to our daily want to minister supply?
These iron times breed none, that mind posterity . . .
When under public good, base private gain takes hold
And we poor woeful Woods, to ruin lastly sold."[1]

Conditions in the once thriving port towns were very distressing; trade was lost to the rising West Country ports, while their populations drifted away, except in the case of Rye and possibly Chichester. The decline of most of the Sussex ports was due to the gradual change of the coastline since medieval times; the harbours and navigable rivers were rendered useless by the accumulation of silt, a condition which Drayton's "unpitied woods" only exacerbated, and by the common practice of ships dumping ballast at anchor. The eclipse of Winchelsea came about more suddenly, through storms and high tides. At Hastings, the premier of the Cinque Ports,

". . . the towne is much decayed, the traffique of marchants thither forsaken, the fishing, by reason of the dangerous landing but little vsed, the riche and wealthy men gone thence, and the poore men yet remaining would gladly doe the like, if without offence of our lawes they might be elsewhere received."[2]

Winchelsea was sick unto death; in 1587 the town could muster neither master nor able mariner, while only one

[1] Michael Drayton, *Polyolbion*, 17th Song, in *Complete Works of Michael Drayton*, ed. R. Hooper (London: 1876), II, 226-9.
[2] Royal proclamation of 30 Oct. 1578 concerning repairs to be undertaken on the harbour pier, quoted in W. D. Cooper, "Notices of Hastings", *S.A.C.*, XIV, 84.

inhabitant qualified as a sailor.[1] The dissolution of Winchelsea's two religious houses contributed to the port's depopulation, and in 1575 William Lambarde declared that "there were not then above 60 houses standing and those for the most part poorly peopled".[2] Rye, the principal port of Elizabethan Sussex, was more prosperous, but its trade was falling into the hands of foreigners. Fishing enjoyed a revival in the 1570s but in 1630 Rye had no more than ten fishing boats.[3]

Various attempts were made to revive the waning ports. Seaford was incorporated in 1544 under a royal charter and annexed to the port of Hastings to help share the latter's burden of defence, while Hastings was granted a more favourable charter. Twice, attempts were made to repair the harbour pier at Hastings, only to see it destroyed each time by storms and spring tides.[4] Chichester, although technically a port, was not situated directly on the sea, depending instead upon various anchorages in the estuary of the Lavant and a pier at Dell Quay. However, there were no warehouses at Dell Quay, and the roads to the city were very bad. A plan to dig a canal to the suburb of Fishbourne at the west gate of the city was conceived in the 1580s, but never materialized; the estuary, which could accommodate merchantmen of 30 tons in the sixteenth century, could be navigated by ships of no more than 10 tons in 1661.[5]

[1] J. M. Baines, "The Ships of the Cinque Ports in 1586/7", *S.N. & Q.*, XIII, 241–4.

[2] Montagu Burrows, *The Cinque Ports* (London: 1888), p. 222.

[3] *V.C.H. Sussex*, II, 145; Burrows, *op. cit.*, pp. 219–20.

[4] *Ibid.*, pp. 194–225; Cooper, "Notices of Hastings", *S.A.C.*, XIV, 84; Hist. MSS. Comm., [Hastings Corp. MSS.] xiii (4), 357.

[5] *V.C.H. Sussex*, III, 100–102. One result of the economic decline of the Sussex ports was to force mariners into piracy and wrecking. With its many small inlets and harbours, the Sussex coast was a natural haven for pirates. This lawlessness had become endemic in the closing years of the middle ages, but it was checked by the strong early Tudor monarchs. However, the continuous wars of the Elizabethan period afforded an excellent opportunity for those pirates who remained to extend their activities. The task of detecting and punishing them was made more difficult by the fact that the inhabitants of the Sussex ports enjoyed a profitable trade with the pirates. Even the officials appointed to discover such offences were not wholly free from suspicion, and in order to avoid opportunities for connivance vice-

An even more important factor contributing to the rural isolation of Sussex was the impassability of the roads. Roads, of course, were bad everywhere at this time, but the mire of Sussex was legendary. Even as late as the eighteenth century the royal judges could rarely be persuaded to go beyond Horsham or East Grinstead, on the northern border of Sussex, to hold their assizes. William, first Earl Cowper, later lord chancellor, having gone only as far as Horsham as a barrister on the home circuit in 1690, came away with a poor opinion of Sussex:

"I vow 'tis a melancholy consideration that mankind will inhabit such a heap of dirt for a poor livelihood. The county is a sink of about fourteen miles broad which receives all the water that falls from two long ranges of hills on both sides of it; and not being furnished with convenient draining, is kept moist and soft by the water till the middle of a dry summer, which is only able to make it tolerable to ride for a short time."[1]

Now, judges of assize were an important means of conveying the royal will to the local agents of the central government. If, then, the judges riding out only twice a year through the shires, found Sussex so difficult to penetrate even in the eighteenth century, we can more readily appreciate the obstacles that the government had to overcome in enforcing the Elizabethan religious settlement.

While provincialism and social conservatism continued to act as centrifugal forces, the royal government was at pains to

admirals were instructed to work only in conjunction with other commissioners.

Subsidiary to piracy was the practice of "wrecking" which involved the salvage of cargo or fittings from ships wrecked along the shore by the owner of the property bordering on that particular shore. Legally, a ship was not a wreck if a man, cat or dog escaped alive from that ship, but Sussex wreckers were not over particular about points of admiralty law. A magistrate charged in 1569 with confiscating a pirate's bark and recovering stolen goods found that the mayor of Chichester had taken the ship and goods into his own custody and had not indicated a willingness to part with them. (Hist. MSS. Comm., *Salisbury MSS.*, I, 286; *V.C.H. Sussex*, II, 147–8; Folger Library, Loseley MSS., L.b. 587.)

[1] Quoted in Charles Thomas-Stanford, *Sussex in the Great Civil War* (London: 1910), pp. 6–7.

bind the loose groupings of rural England into a nation. Lacking the armies of civil servants at the disposal of twentieth-century governments, the Crown was obliged to utilize the existing social leadership of the country gentry for the enforcement of the laws. A conflict between national aspirations and local interests was inherent in such a system.

The chief official of the county was the lord lieutenant, who was sometimes a member of the Privy Council and nearly always a peer. Originally appointed in the time of Henry VIII to command the defences of the county, the lord lieutenant had come to be the eyes of the Privy Council in the county, supervising county government and wielding much patronage. The existence of rival factions among the nobility in Sussex necessitated the appointment of two and sometimes three peers to the lieutenancy for almost the entire Elizabethan period. It was unusual to issue a commission of lieutenancy to more than one person, but then the number of noblemen resident in Sussex was also without parallel among English counties, and especially southern English counties. Since the lords lieutenant could not always be present in their counties, deputy lieutenants were chosen from among the most prominent knights and esquires.

The most important figure in local government was the justice of the peace, an unpaid magistrate who was a peculiarly English figure. Chosen from among the nobility and the upper gentry, the J.P.s became more significant in local government. As the sphere of governmental activity expanded under the Tudors, they were forced to take on greater responsibility. The powers granted by the commission of the peace were both judicial and administrative. All J.P.s had the power to punish misdemeanors and to arraign and imprison persons accused of felonies pending trial. In addition to being commissioned of the peace, those J.P.s who were lawyers, or at least had some training in the law, were said to be of the quorum, i.e., they were also commissioned judges of oyer and determiner, which gave them authority to hear and determine all criminal charges.[1] The burden of administrative duties of the J.P.s increased in

[1] The trial of a felony required an indictment and the empanelment of a jury.

the century preceding the Civil War and came to include the regulation of wages and food supplies and responsibility for poor relief. The social influence of the J.P. is not to be over-looked either for it was a matter of great pride for the head of a county family to hold a commission of the peace; more ger-manely, it increased the control of a landowner over his tenants and servants.

A general assembly of the J.P.s, called the quarter-sessions, was held in each shire four times a year. At these times general gaol delivery was held, those accused of felonies being cleared out of the gaols for indictment, trial and speedy punishment. The J.P.s, when sitting under a commission of oyer and deter-miner, could mete out any punishment from a fine to death by hanging. Any unusual cases would be referred to the royal judges at the assizes. The assizes were the principal means by which the Crown supervised the judicial work of the J.P.s. In between the semi-annual assizes the Privy Council bombarded these local governors with an endless stream of directives to guide them in the administrative side of their duties.

Sussex was divided into six administrative units called rapes. The quarter-sessions for the three eastern rapes were held at Lewes, and those for the three western rapes at Chichester. Since travel from east Sussex to west Sussex was time-con-suming this arrangement was convenient for the individual justices, but it hampered the administration of the county. This administrative inconvenience was apparent to several of the justices, who sought and obtained support from the Privy Council in 1584 to unite the quarter-sessions in one town, but seventeen other J.P.s, including five noblemen, signed a petition against this move, and the quarter-sessions remained separate until the beginning of this century, when two admini-strative counties were created out of Sussex with their county towns at Lewes and Chichester.[1]

Other indications of the basically rural character of Sussex can be seen in the population figures of Sussex towns and their

[1] B.M., Harley MS. 703 fo. 16; *A Descriptive Report on the Quarter Sessions, Other Official, and Ecclesiastical Records in the Custody of the County Councils of West and East Sussex with a Guide to the Development and Historical Interest of the Archives* (Chichester: 1954), p. 199.

forms of government. Chichester and Lewes, the two county towns, were the most populous: Chichester in the 1520s contained 1,700–2,000 souls, possibly another 150 if its suburbs are included; Lewes, including its suburb of Southover, numbered between 1,500 and 1,600.[1] Moreover, some towns were legally indistinguishable from villages, being governed through courts leet and baron by the lords of the manor or their stewards. Of eight important Sussex towns studied for the period of the 1520s, several were boroughs and returned members of parliament, but Chichester was the only one of the eight that was a chartered borough and had "an active civic life".[2]

In those towns that did regulate their own affairs the corporations tended to become closed and their aldermanic classes more exclusive. At Arundel the corporation traditionally consisted of a mayor and twelve burgesses. However, the new patent of 1583 confirming the borough's powers made no mention of a limitation on the number of burgesses, and the members of the corporation used this omission to diminish, not to increase their number.[3] Lewes was a borough within the barony of Lewes and was governed by "a societye of the wealthier & discreeter sorte of the Townesmen comonly called the Twelve . . .", whose number was not to exceed eighteen members.[4] There was no mayor; instead, two constables and

---

[1] Rye was third in size with possibly 1000, although the migration caused by the religious wars on the continent later in the century may have doubled its size. Petworth had 900 or more people. Next followed Horsham and Midhurst with somewhere between 500 and 600. There is no evidence that any other town had a population of above 500. (These figures, based on the subsidy of 1524, were worked out by Julian Cornwall in his "English Country Towns in the Fifteen Twenties", *Economic History Review*, 2nd ser., XV, 54–69.)

[2] *Ibid.* The eight towns were: Chichester, Lewes, Petworth, Horsham, Midhurst, Arundel, Steyning and East Grinstead. All of these towns returned M.P.s except Petworth. Of the Cinque Ports in Sussex, Bramber, Shoreham Rye, Hastings, and Winchelsea also had parliamentary representation.

[3] M. A. Tierney, *The History and Antiquities of the Castle and Town of Arundel* (London: 1834), pp. 704–5.

[4] *The Book of John Rowe, Steward of the Manors of Lord Bergavenny, 1597–1622*, ed. W. H. Godfrey (Lewes: S.R.S., 1928), XXXIV, 170; cf. also *The Town Book of Lewes, 1542–1701*, ed. L. F. Salzman (Lewes: S.R.S., 1954), XLVII, 13ff.

two headboroughs, or petty constables were chosen from among the twelve to act as chief executives. Their powers seem to have been more custodial than executive in nature, as contrasted with the mayor of Arundel, who executed and returned all royal writs within his jurisdiction like any sheriff. The municipal government of Chichester was still in the hands of the medieval gild merchant. The gild, consisting of the mayor, aldermen and free citizens, was in effect a self-perpetuating oligarchy. In 1524 none of the aldermen or mayors was worth less than £20 in goods, while one former mayor was assessed at £200 in goods. By all odds, Chichester was the wealthiest town in Sussex. The remainder of the city's inhabitants ranked as commoners. They were not entirely divested of rights: they had the right of assembly in the gildhall, the right of selecting a mayor from among candidates nominated by the gild, and they elected one of the city's two members of parliament. However, there was discontent among the commoners which occasionally broke out into open revolt, as, for example, in 1540 and 1580 when certain dissident elements tried to seize the right of nomination of mayoral candidates from the gild.[1]

The reign of Elizabeth saw the increasing intrusion of the country gentry into municipal politics. Chichester had managed to retain control of its parliamentary representation until 1571, the gildsmen and the commoners each electing one member. Thereafter, the Chichester M.P.s were usually outsiders, such as Dr Valentine Dale, a master of requests, or members of the local gentry, such as Richard Lewkenor. Once entrenched they clung tenaciously to their seats. In 1572 a gildsman took exception to Dale's re-election, but to no avail, while in 1584 James Colbrand, a Puritan intruder, set himself up as a demagogic leader of the commoners and tumultuously, but unsuccessfully, contested Richard Lewkenor's election, though not before the former had made a Star Chamber matter of it.[2] Until 1597 the Rye M.P.s were mostly chosen by the corporation from among the jurats despite outside pressure,

[1] Cornwall, op. cit., Economic History Review, 2nd ser., XV, 54–69; Neale, The Elizabethan House of Commons, pp. 261–2.
[2] Neale, op. cit., pp. 262–72.

but by 1601 the elders of Rye had yielded and accepted two strangers.[1]

What emerges from this glimpse at the Elizabethan county of Sussex is a picture of a basically rural and conservative society. The only forms of economic activity that seem to have been prospering in Sussex, agriculture and iron-founding, were precisely those controlled by the landed aristocracy, while the economic decline and resulting depopulation of the ports and the bad roads helped to accentuate the rural character of the county and to reinforce the authority which the gentry wielded as magistrates. Here was also to be found a well-regulated society, whose leaders, entrenched in both town and country, had an inherent fear of any disruption of the established order. "Must we please the people?" asked an alderman during a stormy Chichester election. "No, no; the people must be governed not pleased."[2] This attitude of mind contributed to a feeling of conservatism that linked the interests of the country gentry and the municipal oligarchies and helps to explain the relatively peaceful acceptance of the Elizabethan religious settlement in Sussex. But, as we shall see, the local governors felt that religious disputes should not be allowed to get so out of proportion as to disrupt the commonweal.

[1] The Cinque Ports and their corporate members traditionally enjoyed special privileges and franchises, as well as freedom from taxation in return for furnishing ships and seamen to England's medieval kings. Although they were administratively independent of the counties of Kent and Sussex and possessed their own courts and a separate commission of the peace, this did not protect them against the growing influence of the country gentry in municipal politics. See Michael Reed, "The Keeping of Sessions of the Peace in the Borough of Hastings", S.A.C., CI, 46–59; Neale, op. cit., pp. 262–72; V.C.H. Sussex, IX, 53.

[2] Quoted in Neale, op. cit., p. 268.

THE ECCLESIASTICAL MACHINERY

THE EFFECTIVE ENFORCEMENT of the Elizabethan religious settlement depended, among other factors, upon the efficiency of administration and quality of personnel in both civil and ecclesiastical organs of government. While the episcopal injunctions gathered by the late Bishop Frere and Professor Kennedy have served to throw more light upon the processes of ecclesiastical administration, Professor Kennedy realized that a balanced picture would not be had until attention was focused on the records of the courts responsible for the enforcement of these injunctions.[1] A glance at the injunctions and articles of enquiry will suffice to show that the Elizabethan bishops desired to regulate the religious life of the nation to a degree that no medieval prelate could ever have dreamed of,[2] but the Elizabethan bishops of Chichester were hindered in their efforts to enforce ecclesiastical discipline and religious uniformity by constitutional limitations, the conflict of jurisdictions, and especially by the ineffectiveness of the episcopal courts. The excessive use of the sentence of excommunication coupled with an inability to sanction their penalties bred contempt for the ecclesiastical courts of the diocese of Chichester.

The diocese of Chichester had undergone no changes during the reign of Henry VIII; in Elizabethan times it continued to be coterminous with the county of Sussex except for peculiars belonging to the archbishop of Canterbury. In addition, the dean of Chichester exercised a jurisdiction that was partially exempt from the bishop of Chichester. Until 1912 the diocese of Chichester was divided into two archdeaconries: Lewes being the larger of the two and comprising all of East Sussex

[1] W. P. M. Kennedy, *Elizabethan Episcopal Administration* (London: 1925), I, xvii.

[2] E. R. Brinkworth. "The Study and Use of Archdeacons's Court Records: Illustrated from the Oxford Records (1566–1759)", *Royal Historical Society Transactions*, 4th ser., XXV (1943), 102.

and the eastern part of West Sussex, while that of Chichester included all that was left of western Sussex. Each archdeaconry was in turn divided into four rural deaneries.[1] Altogether there were 272 parishes in the diocese of Chichester, not including the cathedral church, of which 145 were in the archdeaconry of Lewes and 127 in the archdeaconry of Chichester.[2] These figures do not include dependent chapels, which did not constitute separate parishes. The number of communicants in the diocese, according to a contemporary estimate based upon the bishops' returns of 1603 on nonconformity, was 46,325.[3] Thus Chichester ranked nineteenth among 26 English and Welsh dioceses from the standpoint of population. Considering the difficulty of travel in Sussex during most of the year, the location of the seat of the bishop was especially unfortunate. Because it was situated near the border of Hampshire, the eastern part of Sussex was not readily accessible to the bishop. This made the bishop particularly dependent on his subordinates there.

As the new monarch sought more and more to control the activities of his subjects, so the Elizabethan bishops desired to regulate the spiritual lives of their flocks. But despite this desire, there still operated several medieval limitations upon the power of bishops. In the diocese of Chichester the ancient constitution of the cathedral church enjoined that no patents, acts, or other episcopal pronouncements made by a bishop were binding upon any of his successors unless they were ratified by the dean and chapter. At the same time none of the acts of the chapter were regarded as binding upon succeeding

---

[1] *A Descriptive Report on the Quarter Sessions, Other Official, and Ecclesiastical Records in the Custody of the County Councils of West and East Sussex with a Guide to the Development and Historical Interest of the Archives* (Chichester: 1954), p. 92.

[2] *V.C.H. Sussex*, II, 42–4, gives a total of 265 parishes with 120 in the archdeaconry of Chichester. The *V.C.H Sussex* bases its information on the Taxatio of 1291 and the *Valor Ecclesiasticus* of 1535.

[3] Figures were missing for fourteen parishes in the diocese, and a contemporary reader reduced the estimate to 43,197. From B.M., Harley MS. 280, art. 29, printed in J. O. W. Haweis, *Sketches of the Reformation and the Elizabethan Age Taken from the Contemporary Pulpit* (London: 1884), pp. 306–7, and in Brian Magee, *The English Recusants* (London: 1938).

chapters unless ratified by the bishop, so bargains were apt to be struck. The struggle between bishop and chapter was of long duration and seems to have reached a climax in the episcopate of Bishop Rede (1397–1415). The chapter balked at swearing obedience to the bishop, and only Rede's persistence brought compliance in this matter and reduced them to submission to episcopal visitations.[1] Although the members of the chapter, especially canons residentiary, were reduced in number from pre-Reformation times, their ability to defy the bishop had increased, as is well shown by the successful attempt of the canons residentiary in 1574 to force Bishop Curteys to exempt them from visitations even when they also held parochial benefices.[2] The Elizabethan age saw the plundering of capitular as well as episcopal revenues, which caused the canons residentiary to force Curteys to agree to a reduction in their number in order that the butter on their bread might be spread a little thicker.[3] In short, the government of the chapter was becoming vested in the hands of the dean and the four residentiaries—this number being prescribed by the statutes of 1574 —to the total exclusion of the lesser members of the chapter such as the vicars choral and the clerks. Although the bishop did have the power to fill vacant prebends and to institute to lesser benefices in the cathedral,[4] it was not likely that sufficient vacancies would occur among the resident canons during his episcopate to enable a bishop to plant a dominant faction to his liking. A lack of lieutenants hampered all of the Elizabethan bishops of Chichester in their reforming efforts. This deficiency is explained by the failure of these prelates to prevail over the vested interests of a closed capitular corporation in getting their lieutenants admitted to residence in the cathedral close.

Another serious limitation upon episcopal power was the

[1] W. R. W. Stephens, *Memorials of the South Saxon See and the Cathedral Church of Chichester* (London: 1876), p. 127.

[2] James Dallaway, *A History of the Western Division of the County of Sussex* (London: 1815), I, 106.

[3] *Statutes and Constitutions of the Cathedral Church of Chichester*, ed. F. G. Bennett, R. H. Codington, C. Deedes (Chichester: 1904), pp. 22–8.

[4] W. D. Peckham, "The Parishes of the City of Chichester", *S.A.C.*, LXXIV, 65–97.

fact that the bishop of Chichester could exercise full ordinary power in his cathedral city only during the occasion of a formal episcopal visitation of the city and, apparently, even this could be done only when the deanery was void. The rest of the time the dean acted as ordinary, and although not competent to confirm or ordain, did institute to benefices, issue mandates to induct, and pronounce sequestrations, and perform other functions deriving from the jurisdiction of an ordinary.[1] This exemption of the deanery of Chichester was to prove another serious obstacle to Bishop Curteys in his quarrels with the dean and chapter. It also afforded a certain amount of protection to the citizens of Chichester, which enabled them to play such an important part in the dispute between Bishop Curteys and the Sussex gentry in the 1570s.

By custom the manors belonging to the archbishop of Canterbury outside of his own diocese were exempted from the jurisdiction of the local bishop. In Sussex there were three such peculiars: the deaneries of Pagham and Tarring in West Sussex and the deanery of South Malling in East Sussex; also, the parish of All Saints in the Pallant, Chichester, being exempted from the dean of Chichester's jurisdiction, might be said to have been a peculiar within a peculiar. In practice, the archbishop's peculiars never posed as serious a challenge to the bishop of Chichester's power as did the dean of Chichester's privileges, because the primate usually picked a judge from one of the church courts of the diocese of Chichester as his commissary in the archiepiscopal peculiars.[2]

When the bishopric of Chichester was vacant, the temporalities were seized by the Crown, to which would accrue the income from episcopal properties. This was usually the motive for the queen delaying the appointment of a new bishop, and the see of Chichester was void for three long periods during

[1] *Ibid.*, pp. 65–7. An ordinary is one who exercises ecclesiastical jurisdiction on his own authority and not as a deputy.

[2] John Strype, *The History of the Life and Acts of the Most Reverend Father in God, Edmund Grindal* (Oxford: 1824), p. 359.

The visiting power of a commissary generally was specifically limited to a particular deanery or archdeaconry, whereas the powers of a vicar general in spirituals had the same geographical limitations as the jurisdiction of the ordinary.

Elizabeth's reign—1558–60, 1568–70 and 1582–85—all very critical periods. In the meantime spiritual jurisdiction would be exercised by the metropolitan. This was the occasion of the metropolitical visitations of 1569 and 1585. If there happened to be no archbishop of Canterbury, which was the case from November 1558 through 1559, the spiritual jurisdiction of a void see usually fell to the dean and chapter of Canterbury. However, during the royal visitation in the summer of 1559 all episcopal authority throughout England and Wales was in abeyance, and before any of the bishops of the southern province could visit their dioceses their jurisdiction was inhibited by the archbishop of Canterbury's announcement of his intention to visit all dioceses. This metropolitical visitation, with its inhibition of episcopal authority, continued, in some cases, into early 1562.

It was F. D. Price who suggested in a series of articles that the Elizabethan church courts were in decline because their sanctions were ignored and the sentence of excommunication was imposed indiscriminately for trivial matters.[1] The general thinking now is that Dr Price's detailed study of the dioceses of Bristol and Gloucester revealed an extreme and untypical example, and that the jurisdiction of church courts was not undermined by the influences of the Reformation. Indeed, the late Professor Norman Sykes went so far as to express the opinion that the courts of the Church of England actually had their jurisdiction strengthened by the legislation of the time of Henry VIII.[2] It is true that visitations were held more frequently and more regularly than was the case in medieval times.

Unfortunately, not enough dioceses have been studied to say with complete and final assurance what was and what was not typical. The studies contributed by Robert Peters[3] and the

[1] "The Abuses of Excommunication and the Decline of Ecclesiastical Discipline under Queen Elizabeth", *E.H.R.*, LVII (1942), 105–6; "An Elizabethan Church Official—Thomas Powell, Chancellor of Gloucester Diocese", *Church History Review*, CXXVIII (1939), 94–112; "Elizabethan Apparitors in the Diocese of Gloucester", *Church Quarterly Review*, CXXXIV (1942), 37–55.

[2] *E.H.R.*, LXXII, 550–1.

[3] Robert Peters, *Oculus Episcopi: Administration in the Archdeaconry of St Albans, 1580–1625* (Manchester: 1963).

late Dr H. G. Owen[1] show that in the diocese of London, visitations were well attended and the ecclesiastical courts were reasonably healthy even though the same pattern of excommunication for contumacy or failure to comply with court procedures manifests itself throughout. The Elizabethan bishops of London were far more capable administrators than their counterparts in Chichester or Gloucester. Mr Peters has noted a correlation between the quality of episcopal leadership —stronger under Richard Bancroft, weaker under George Abbott—and the administrative effectiveness of the archidiaconal court of St Albans.[2]

Christopher Hill tells us that the powers of the church courts "potentially . . . were great".[3] Yet, when all is said, few scholars would be willing to deny that the church courts found it increasingly difficult to enforce ecclesiastical discipline whether against the clergy or the laity. In all fairness, the same failing is found to a lesser degree in the temporal courts. It was "a reflection of the ineffectiveness of *all* sixteenth-century administrative and judicial processes. Quarter sessions had similar difficulties in getting offenders to appear."[4] Patrick Collinson points out that much of the trouble was due to: (1) the failure of Parliament and the crown to authorize and promulgate a revision of the body of canon law; (2) the fact that the concept of ecclesiastical discipline changed under the impact of Calvinist theology, for discipline now meant "brotherly admonition"—not penalties imposed by a mercenary judge and culled out of papal and Roman canon law; (3) the press of business and the consequent delays which litigants in instance cases (which corresponded to civil suits in the common-law courts) encountered. The last of these factors also afflicted the common-law courts and was a general manifestation of the litigiousness of increasingly prosperous propertied classes. At least part of the unpopularity of the ecclesiastical courts reflected the more sophisticated legal knowledge of a

[1] H. G. Owen, "The Episcopal Visitation: Its Limits and Limitations in Elizabethan London", *Journal of Ecclesiastical History*, XI, 179–85.

[2] Peters, *op. cit.*, p. 3.

[3] *Society and Puritanism in Pre-Revolutionary England* (London: 1966), p. 372.

[4] *Ibid.*, p. 371.

landowning aristocracy who considered a stay at the Inns of Court to be a requisite part of their education. They objected to the unfamiliar procedures of the church courts, although they did not hesitate to initiate instance causes when their own interests were at stake in the case of impropriated tithes or the probate of wills.[1]

But it is not with regard to instance or probate causes that the effectiveness of the archidiaconal and episcopal courts is to be judged. The crux of the matter concerns the *ex officio* cases initiated by the judge, which involved breaches of religious discipline that needed correction.[2] The detection and punishment of ecclesiastical offences worked well enough against the poorer sorts of people, but the system broke down when it came up against the influential and the wealthy.[3] It failed totally in its efforts to punish recusants among the gentry, and parliamentary legislation against recusancy increasingly placed the enforcement of the penal laws in the hands of the justices of the peace.[4] In the diocese of Chichester the episcopal courts failed to remove even the ministers known to be associated with the Puritan classical movement.[5] Finally, the effectiveness of the church courts was hindered by their unpopularity; they were resented by an ever-growing number of people because they were corrupt, vexatious and unfair.

By the end of the seventeenth century, the church courts had abandoned altogether the task of enforcing religious conformity and had handed over the functions of maintaining social control and regulating morality among artificers to the justices of the peace.[6]

---

[1] Patrick Collinson, *The Elizabethan Puritan Movement* (London: 1967), pp. 38–42.

[2] Peters, *op. cit.*, p. 5.

[3] Hill, *Society and Puritanism in Pre-Revolutionary England*, p. 312.

[4] See below, this chapter and Chapter 7.

[5] See below, Chapter 10, section iii. In the diocese of Chichester the non-conformist ministers were at least detected through the churchwardens. Ronald Marchant, *The Puritans and the Church Courts in the Diocese of York, 1560–1642* (London: 1960), pp. 92, 106 *et passim*, has found that in the diocese of York even the detection apparatus broke down and the judges were forced to fall back upon rumour.

[6] Hill, *op. cit.*, p. 377.

Elizabethan bishops laboured under the same administrative handicap in trying to enforce the religious settlement as did the queen's ministers in attempting to execute the royal will in temporal affairs: both were faced with the problem of trying to solve modern problems with cumbersome medieval machinery. The most important flaw in the ecclesiastical machinery, Ronald Marchant has observed, was "the practice of conducting administration through courts of law—the medieval method, and one which the church found hard to abandon. The result was that the detection of offenders was under the control of the same men who were responsible for trying and sentencing them."[1] Yet despite the fact that the ecclesiastical judges of the diocese of Chichester were better educated than many Sussex J.P.s, the latter proved themselves more flexible in dealing with the problems of local government.[2]

The chief means of discovering ecclesiastical offences were the episcopal and archidiaconal visitations. The frequency of episcopal visitations varied from one diocese to another, but in all dioceses it was customary to conduct a visitation during the first year of the bishop's episcopate.[3] In the diocese of Chichester no distinction between the episcopal and archidiaconal visitations can be discerned except, as in the visitation of 1577 when the bishop himself is present in consistory; this was because the two archidiaconal courts were, in fact, episcopal courts. The archdeacons of Chichester and Lewes had little power and did not sit in judgment in these courts, nor did they appoint deputies to do so. This power had been assumed by the bishop, and the archdeacons had no other duties than those normally exercised by prebendaries or canons residentiary of the cathedral chapter. The bishop's vicar general in spirituals, more commonly called the chancellor, sat as judge for the episcopal court of the archdeaconry of Chichester which was usually called the consistory court: when actually

[1] Ronald Marchant, *op. cit.*, p. 4.

[2] All of the ecclesiastical judges known to me were university graduates; at least three of them were civil lawyers.

[3] J. V. P. Thompson, *Supreme Governor: A Study of Elizabethan Policy and Circumstance* (London: 1940), p. 17.

presiding he bore the title of official principal. On the other hand, the judge of the court at Lewes was variously known as official principal or commissary and sequestrator. The sessions of the former were held in the cathedral; those of the latter in one of the parish churches of Lewes. The chancellor of the diocese was the more important of the two officials, since, in addition to his judicial duties, he instituted to benefices and carried out certain other functions for the diocese as a whole. More lieutenants could be temporarily empowered when necessary; in an episcopal patent issued in September 1567 for a visitation of the archdeaconry of Lewes, Bishop Barlow appointed two of his lieutenants as vicars general and a third as commissary, the latter's authority being specifically limited to the archdeaconry of Lewes.[1]

The archidiaconal visitations were conducted every six months, when the bishop's officers would proceed with their enquiries deanery by deanery. Here the clergy would appear to submit proof of ordination, university degrees, licences to preach, and titles to benefices, which were recorded with varying degrees of completeness in the *Libri Cleri*. There would also be assembled the churchwardens from the various parishes in the deanery, to whom articles of enquiry would be ministered by the *inquisitores*, usually six in number, and like the churchwardens themselves, of very humble origin.[2]

The articles of enquiry were based to some extent on the abuses found in the last visitation, but generally tended to become stereotyped, seemingly suggesting a lack of initiative on the part of the bishops. While it may be argued that the constant reappearance of some articles indicated the inability of the ecclesiastical authorities to stamp out the offence, it must also be remembered that the articles of enquiry were to a considerable degree founded on the statutes of supremacy and uniformity and on the royal injunctions of 1559 as well as upon later administrative orders of the primate.[3] By 1570 the articles were usually printed up for distribution among the churchwardens, and the expense of printing may have been a deterrent

---

[1] DRO, Ep. I/15, A 2(1).
[2] B.M., Add. M.S. 39,454, *passim*.
[3] Thompson, *op. cit.*, p. 18.

to frequent revision of the articles. However, when printed the number and scope of articles included would have tended to make frequent revision unnecessary.[1]

After the visitation, the incumbent, each curate and the churchwardens returned answers to the articles of enquiry. The churchwardens also made presentments of offences twice yearly in addition to the answers to the articles ministered at the archidiaconal visitations. The latter were copied into a register of churchwardens' presentments; in 1570–71 it was the practice to leave a space vacant after each entry, where the action taken against the individual subsequently was noted down.[2] A few years later the records of the trials of ecclesiastical offences, corresponding to criminal offences in temporal courts, were entered in Detection Books, while litigation, corresponding to civil matters in temporal courts, was recorded in the Instance Books, with the evidence briefly recorded in Deposition Books.

It must be remembered that the parish was a unit of the civil administration as well as the spiritual government. The dissolution of the monasteries, manorial decay and the alarming growth of poverty all contributed to the increasing responsibilities of the churchwardens, which already included collecting the churchmark or landscot for upkeep of the church,[3] and seeing to it that the church was kept in a state of repair. The Elizabethan government would continue to add to their administrative burdens as the years passed.

The churchwardens were chosen by a variety of methods, the most usual being election by the parishioners with approval by the incumbent. Although persons of standing were preferred, in practice the churchwardens and sidemen, or assistant church-

---

[1] E.g., cf. *Articles Ministered by . . . Anthony, Bishop of Chichester, at the visitation begun there the 6 of September 1600, and to bee enquired of quarterly within the seide Diocese* (London: 1600), Bodleian Library, B. II. 23, reproduced on University Microfilms no. 13623.

[2] DRO, Ep. I/23/1, *passim*.

[3] The scot was also used for the expense of the bailiff's court and the upkeep of drains in marshy areas. Apparently the churchwardens did not always distinguish between taxes collected for the maintenance of the church fabric and those collected for public works. Cf. B.M., Add. MS. 33,410, fo. 101.

wardens (there were usually two of each), were not only of
humble origin, but nearly always illiterate, as their marks on
letters and presentments still testify.[1] Of course, an office that
would entail presenting one's neighbours, or even the local
squire, would hardly be an enviable one: it was the practice of
the Court of High Commission never to divulge the names
of accusers in cases brought before that body for determination,
but such a precaution would hardly protect the churchwardens
in a small parish where their names were known to all. Consequently, the archidiaconal visitors found it necessary to extract
an oath from the churchwardens to present all offences
according to the articles given them. Failure to carry out their
duties to the last letter usually resulted in excommunication
and the burdensome expense for a poor man of seeking absolution. In the archidiaconal court of Lewes on 6 February 1582/3
the churchwardens of Friston were absolved of the pain of
excommunication for 2s. 6d., while the churchwardens of
eight other parishes also paid between 3s. and 4s. to have their
sentences lifted.[2] The records are full of their plaintive excuses:
at Rustington "we present that thaparitor Roger Edwards kept
our easter quarter bill and made vs the churchwardens to [be]
excommunicate and so we have wronge"; at Poling "we knowe
not what the fees ys that tharchdeacon['s] Regester or appara-
tors shold have but we have bene shrodely pinched in many
things within thies fewe yeres";[3] while at Petworth in September 1604 the churchwardens had not completed their tasks
because of the plague: "you know that by reason of gods
visitation of our towne we were not permitted to come to
your visitation, neither have we any articles nor sidemen".[4] It
does not seem too hazardous to venture the opinion that this
treatment of churchwardens contributed as much as anything
to the general unpopularity of church courts. To the poor
harassed churchwarden, who year after year had to dig into
his pocket for money to buy off an unjust sentence of excom-

[1] B.M., Add. MS. 33,410, *passim*; Sir Thomas Smith, *De Republica
Anglorum*, book 1, chapter 24.
[2] DRO, Ep. 11/9/2, fo. 88.
[3] B.M., Add. MS. 39,454, fos. 35v–36.
[4] DRO, Ep. I/15, A 2(1).

munication, the practice could suggest only one thing—widespread corruption.

Because of their humble social status the churchwardens could not always be counted upon to report infringements of law by the gentry. This was particularly true in cases of recusancy. The statute of 1581[1] made recusancy an indictable offence and placed its punishment in the hands of the J.P.s assembled at the quarter-sessions, although the detection of recusants still depended upon the churchwardens' quarterly presentments.

Another reason why punishment of cases involving the more substantial recusants was taken out of the hands of the churchwardens was the insufficient deterrent offered by the twelve-penny fine, prescribed by the Act of Uniformity in 1559. The Puritan rector of Ashhurst told of the case of one parishioner who had not received the communion in three years, and when he was warned that the churchwardens would present him, replied that "he cared not if they did present him, for it [is] but a matter of xijd".[2] The statute of 1581 raised the fine for recusancy to £20 per month.

After the churchwardens' presentments had been entered in a register, the court would send out a messenger, known as an apparitor, who would first seek to serve a citation upon the accused, but that failing he would nail a copy of it on the accused person's door. It was not necessary for the accused to appear before the judge in person, for upon payment of a fee, the apparitor would be employed to act as the accused person's proxy. (It would be interesting to know whether any of this money found its way into the hands of the judges.) Since citations were often issued to a number of people in one parish, it was found to be more convenient to have one apparitor appear for everyone, certifying obedience to injunctions, orders of the court, transmitting sentences, and even receiving absolution. Thus the apparitors, the very persons responsible for the personal appearance of offenders before the church courts, were allowed to profit from the practice of representation by proxy. This failure to demand or to compel personal appearance of accused persons before the judges contributed to the lack of respect for the ecclesiastical courts. Unless the offender

---

[1] 23 Eliz. I, cap. 1.   [2] DRO, Ep. I/15, B 1 (3) 17.

appeared personally or was represented by proxy there was often little choice of discipline left to the judge except suspension or excommunication for contumacy.[1]

There were other penalties that could be meted out by the official principal. Occasionally there would be a light fine: in the Chichester archidiaconal court in 1600 a parishioner of Iping was sentenced to pay a fine of 8d. plus a moiety for the judge for refusing to contribute his twopenny churchmark for repairs to the church.[2] Another penalty still in use for cases of incontinency, when attendance upon the court prevented an excommunication for contumacy, was public penance. Here is how one such sentence was carried out in 1592 at Sidlesham, as certified by the vicar to the archidiaconal court of Chichester:

"Thes are to certifie your worshippe thatt vpon Sonday vz the xxvjth of November last past in the forenoone in the parishe church of Sidlesham att morning prayer dunys [Denice] Maitlyn did stand att the Quyre dore in the vew and sight of all the parisshoners there assembled, having vpon her a whyte sheete & a whyte wan[d] in her hand, and so contynewed during all the tyme of divine service and sermon in poenitent and sorrowfull manner, and the sermon being ended she did peonitently acknowledge & confesse her fault with lowd voyce, in thatt shee had been incontinent with John dylmer the younger of the same parishe, desyring the people to pray for her (which they did shee repeating after me such forme of confession & prayer as was conteyned in a scedule brought thether for the purpose by the Apparitour)."[3]

It was possible for the accused to clear himself by producing several of his neighbours to take an oath of compurgation testifying to his innocence of the crime alleged against him. There seems to have been no customary number of compurgators required: in 1593 a man from Salehurst produced four compurgators who supported his denial of a charge of carnal

[1] F. D. Price, "The Abuses of Excommunication and the Decline of Ecclesiastical Discipline under Queen Elizabeth", *E.H.R.*, LVII (1942), 106–115.   [2] DRO, Ep. I/17/10, fo. 7.
[3] B.M., Add. MS. 33,410, fo. 73.

knowledge, and the judge dismissed the case and restored him to his "former reputation [*pristinae famae*]";[1] while in 1574 the defendant in a paternity case as Climping, was ordered by the official principal "to purge himself under the hands of seven of his neighbours". When he failed to do so, the defendant was convicted, enjoined to do public penance in the parish church of Climping and in the market place at Arundel, and, at the same time, he was excommunicated with absolution reserved to the bishop and in addition he would forfeit £40 should he fail to appear before the ordinary on the appointed day. It might be added that he appeared, and the will of the court was carried out;[2] but such stringency is quite rare, being found only during the episcopate of Bishop Curteys. But, if the compurgation were accepted, it was sometimes the practice to have the fact published during divine service in the parish church of the accused in case there should be anyone who would have cause to "obiect or against say the purgacyon".[3] However, since an objection to a compurgation had to be made in the consistory court in Chichester, the inconvenience of the trip or the expense of an apparitor served to make this an empty formality.

The foregoing examples of penalties all tend to be exceptions to the general rule, for the most widely used penalty was that of excommunication. It was used against recusants; it was indiscriminately meted out to churchwardens, however minor their negligence; it was decreed in well over half the cases of incontinency; and it was universally applied in cases of contumacious failure to appear in court. Taking the year 1600 as a sample, from one to a dozen people were excommunicated every term from practically every parish.[4] Since many never bothered to get absolution, there must have been a fair proportion of the population under sentence of excommunication at any given time. That such a sentence could be ignored with impunity can be attributed to the failure of the ecclesiastical

[1] W. C. Renshaw, "Notes from the Act Books of the Archdeaconry Court of Lewes", *S.A.C.*, XLIX, 47–65.
[2] DRO, Ep. I/17/3, fos. 15–22.
[3] B.M., Add. MS. 33,410, fo. 66; DRO Ep. I/15, B 1(3).
[4] DRO, Ep. I/17/10, *passim*.

officials to seek the sanction of the temporal arm. If, at the end of forty days after the publication of the fact of excommunication in the offender's parish church that person had not sought absolution, the law allowed a writ of *significavit* to be obtained against him, which when returned into Chancery resulted in the issuance of a writ *de excommunicato capiendo*, commanding, but powerless to force, the sheriff to incarcerate the person excommunicated until he saw the light of reason.[1] Despite the passage of a statute in 1563[2] to close up the loopholes relating to the execution of the writ *de excommunicato capeindo*, one rarely hears of such secular sanction being applied.[3]

The excessive use of the penalty of excommunication and the contempt of ecclesiastical authority which it bred, caused John Field and his friends, in their *First Admonition to Parliament* (1572), to ask "that Excommunication be restored to his olde former force". The *Second Admonition*, published in the same year, further entered a plea that the penalty be used only for serious offences and "after sondrye brotherly and sharp admonitions", for "Excommunication is a fearfull thing, as it is prescribed by scriptures . . .", and "the civil magistrate, the nurse and foster father of the churche, shall dve well to provide some sharpe punishment for those that contemne this censure and discipline of the church."[4] The commutation of penances for money payments, especially in seeking absolution from excommunication, became so universal, that the attempt made by the Canons of 1571 to reserve absolution from sentences of excommunication to the ordinaries, was

[1] F. D. Price, "The Abuses of Excommunication and the Decline of Ecclesiastical Discipline under Queen Elizabeth", *E.H.R.*, LVII (1942), 106–115. [2] 5 Eliz., c. 23.

[3] I know of only one case of imprisonment following excommunication, that of George Sympson, vicar of Findon in 1600. B.M., Add. MS. 33,410, fo. 96; DRO, Ep. I/17/10, fo. 20. There also existed a lesser form of excommunication reserved for beneficed clergymen, which was known as suspension *ab ingressu ecclesiae*. This penalty made it necessary for the incumbent to employ someone to serve his cure until the suspension was lifted. It was used against Puritan clergymen in the diocese of Chichester, but without any permanent effect. Cf. Chapter 10.

[4] *Puritan Manifestoes: A Study of the Origin of the Puritan Revolt, With a Reprint of the Admonition to the Parliament and Kindred Documents*, ed. W. H. Frere and C. E. Douglas (London: 1954), pp. 14, 121–2.

doomed to failure from the very beginning; these disciplinary Canons, one of many unsuccessful projects to remedy the lack of a code of canon law in the Church of England, failed to secure either the approval of the lower house of Convocation in that year or the authorization of the queen.[1]

Evidence survives of only one case where this provision was put into effect.[2] There was still no visible effort made to reform the church courts and the outcry against their abuses, coming not only from Puritans, grew more shrill, until, following one such attack in 1602, Archbishop Whitgift took the drastic step of warning his fellow prelates that there might soon be no alternative but to abolish the church courts.[3]

The conflict of jurisdictions was one of the chief problems that hampered Elizabethan bishops in the administration of their dioceses and the enforcement of the religious settlement. The increasing activity of the Court of High Commission was tantamount to official recognition of the lack of respect felt for the older church courts. Like the king's writ, the High Commission's power extended throughout the whole realm, and as in the case of the older prerogative courts, it was faster and more efficient than the dilatory diocesan courts. Intended to fill the void created by the abolition of the papal legatine courts, it exercised the royal supremacy in ecclesiastical affairs by commission. This court did not hesitate to hand down stiff fines or imprisonment. Moreover, its decrees were enforced.[4] Such severity seemed necessary in order to counterbalance the increasing contempt felt for the pronouncements of the older church courts. Furthermore, doubts persisted in the minds of both bishops and Puritan opponents of episcopacy about the exact legal authority of episcopal sanctions, and there is evidence that several bishops attempted to reinforce their own power of jurisdiction by securing the appointment of local branches of the High Commission.[5] Thus, in addition to the

[1] V. J. K. Brook, *A Life of Archbishop Parker* (Oxford: 1962), p. 270.

[2] This was the case of John Joye in 1574. DRO Ep. I/17/3, fos. 15–32.

[3] Thompson, *op. cit.*, p. 18.

[4] G. R. Elton, *The Tudor Constitution* (Cambridge: 1960), p. 219.

[5] For examples of such opinions, cf. S. B. Babbage, *Puritanism and Richard Bancroft* (London: 1962), pp. 103ff. and 121. Also see pp. 246–7 *ibid.*, and Elton, *op. cit.*, pp. 218–19.

main body sitting in London, there were also established, from time to time, general and extraordinary branches of the ecclesiastical commission for particular dioceses and localities; permanent branches were to be found in the northern province, in Marches of Wales, and in the dioceses of Bristol and Gloucester.[1] Although reference was made by Archbishop Parker to the existence in 1570 of a separate commission for the diocese of Chichester,[2] what scanty evidence survives inclines one to the belief that this was an extraordinary and temporary commission only. Every other reference to the ecclesiastical commissioners clearly refers to the body sitting in London: it was to London that the leaders of the Sussex recusants were sent in 1580; in 1594 the vicar of Iden denounced a parishioner to the High Commission in London for incest, for which offence he was fined £40, ordered to do penance in Rye and Hastings, and then to be imprisoned in Newgate Prison.[3] Bishop Curteys was of the quorum in the Ecclesiastical Commission of 1572 and had the power to hear and determine most types of offences specified in the commission of 1572. However, he appears to have exercised visitatorial powers only. He is known to have recommended in 1570 the establishment in Sussex of a branch of the Ecclesiastical Commission,[4] but whether this was the branch referred to by Archbishop Parker in the same year cannot be established with certainty; if so, it did not survive to the end of Curteys's episcopate. In asking for a local commission for ecclesiastical

[1] F. D. Price, "The Commission for Ecclesiastical Causes in the Dioceses of Bristol and Gloucester, 1574", *Transactions of the Bristol and Gloucestershire Archaeological Society*, LIX, 61–181.

[2] Brook, *op. cit.*, p. 64.

[3] Folger Library, Misc. MS. X. d. 317 (1).

[4] S.P., Dom., Eliz., 74/44. The fact that the names of four people resident in Sussex are included in the Ecclesiastical Commission of 1572 (*Cal. P.R.*, 1569–72, V, 440–2) indicates that authority existed to constitute a special court of Ecclesiastical Commission in Sussex. (Other members of the Ecclesiastical Commission resident in Sussex were William Overton, Henry Worley and Henry Marvyn. All were clerics except for the last, who was one of the few zealous Protestant J.P.s in Sussex.) Three were needed to constitute a proper court, but Worley and Overton were cautioned to use their judicial powers "only where the ordinary course of common justice is defective." (*Ibid*).

causes Bishop Curteys was recognizing two facts: firstly, that many magistrates still could not be relied upon to convict recusant neighbours, and secondly that his episcopal authority was weakening and that the episcopal courts were largely impotent.

Although the work of the High Commission certainly inspired more respect (if not love) for the queen's ecclesiastical authority, it sometimes only added to the confusion already existing among often conflicting jurisdictions. What could happen to an agent trying to execute the orders coming from these overlapping jurisdictions is amusingly, if somewhat pathetically, shown in the case of Anthony Hilton, vicar of Billinghurst. Sometime in 1592, Thomas and John Shelley of Mapledurham, Hampshire, cousins to the Shelleys of Michelgrove and Warminghurst in Sussex, had been committed to the custody of Hilton "vnder the handes and seales of the L. Bisshope [Bickley] and six other [ecclesiastical] commissioners . . ." to make them conformable in religion. The Shelleys of Mapledurham, like many other recusant gentry in eastern Hampshire and western Sussex, were closely tied together by blood and marriage, and were wont to slip back and forth over the border to elude whatever bishop or sheriff or J.P. happened to be seeking them. While burdened with the expense and responsibility of entertaining his guests, Hilton found himself in the impossible position of being summoned before the archidiaconal court of Chichester, yet forbidden to leave his charges by the High Commission; he wrote to the judge of archidiaconal court on 20 October 1592 begging to be excused appearance by reason of the fact that "diverse of her maiesties commissioners have straightly chardged and commaunded me . . . with the safe keping of mr Thomas Shelley." Evidently the court still persisted in its summons, since on 26 October Hilton again pleaded with the judge of the archidiaconal court to be excused from appearing because Sir Henry Goring, a Sussex J.P., had told him that he should stay with Thomas Shelley.[1] The result was that Hilton was "excommunicated by his Ordinarie . . . for not makinge his appearance, and since hath bene absolved from the sentence of

[1] *Acts P.C.*, XXIII, 368; B.M., Add. MS. 33, 410, fo. 47.

that excommunication by the moste reverand father in God the Lo. Archbishop of Canterburie; and hath submitted himself desiring absolucon . . ."; the condition being that he was compelled to make bond to be forfeited to the queen should he not in future obey his ordinary.[1]

Operating in an atmosphere of such rigid legalism, it is little wonder that the episcopal courts in the diocese of Chichester were not equal to the task of enforcing the Elizabethan religious settlement,[2] nor were they capable of effecting the reforms looked for by the more zealous Protestants. Furthermore the corruption and blind blundering of the bishops' officers were such that the scathing denunciation in *The Admonition to the Parliament* of 1572 would have struck a sympathetic chord in many non-Puritan as well as Puritan hearts:

"As for the commissaries court, that is but a pettie little stinking ditche, that floweth oute of that former great puddle, robbing Christes church of lawfull pastors, of watchfull Seniors and Elders, and carefull Deacons. In this court . . ., one alone doth excommunicate, one alone sitteth in judgement, and when he will, can drawe backe the judgement which he hath pronounced, having called upon the name of God, and that for money which is called the chaunging of penaunce. In this courte, for non paiment of two pence, a man shall be excommunicated if he appeare not when he is sent for. . . ."[3]

It was the medieval practice to create new bodies, such as the ecclesiastical commissioners, to serve needs to which older institutions were no longer equal, or to transfer to them already existing responsibilities, but not to abolish the older organs of government. Besides, episcopacy was the framework of the religious settlement, and an attack upon the power of the

[1] Lambeth Palace Library, MS. Carta Misc. IV/154.

[2] H. G. Owen's assessment of the episcopal visitations in Elizabethan London concludes that the diocesan visitation was far from being an out-dated instrument of ecclesiastical discipline, and actually commanded more respect in the latter years of the reign, yet he admits that the visitation could be no more effective than the church courts which constituted the permanent instrument of administration. "The Episcopal Visitation: Its Limits and Limitations in Elizabethan London", *Journal of Ecclesiastical History*, XI, 179–85.   [3] Frere and Douglas, *op. cit.*, p. 33.

bishops' officers might easily be construed as an attack upon episcopacy. Since the bishops were the principal agents of the royal supremacy in matters ecclesiastical, this could only undermine the powers of the royal control over the Church of England. Elizabeth and the early Stuarts were only too well aware of what would follow upon any successful attempt to abolish bishops.

3

THE RELIGIOUS SITUATION IN THE 1560s

THE MOST SIGNIFICANT fact about the enforcement of the Elizabethan religious settlement in Sussex during the first twenty years of the queen's reign was the slowness of change. This reflected not so much the desire of the queen and her Privy Council to move slowly as inability to move any faster until the local agents exercising the royal ecclesiastical supremacy were sufficiently reliable to permit the central government to impose a uniform Protestantism on the people of Sussex. The many shifts in official religious policy in the 1540s and 1550s and the rapid turnover of bishops in the diocese of Chichester in those years combined to reduce episcopal administration to a state of chaos. At the same time, the deprivation of those among the cathedral clergy who would not swear the oath of supremacy left Bishop Barlow in the 1560s without sufficient lieutenants to accomplish anything beyond a grudging acceptance of the Book of Common Prayer. A spiritual vacuum necessarily existed until the universities made good the deficiency of a learned Protestant ministry in the 1570s. The first two decades of Elizabeth's reign were taken up with attempts to supply the pulpits of Sussex with an educated clergy and to fill the temporal magistracy with reliable members of the gentry.[1] To these factors, then, more than to Catholic resistance, must be attributed the slowness of Sussex to accept the popular Reformation.

That the transition from official Marian Catholicism to official Elizabethan Protestantism was effected peaceably within the established Church of England is commonplace. Nor is this gainsaid by what is known about the religious life of Sussex parishes in the 1560s. The absence of any untoward events within the county was noted in October 1560, by Anthony, Viscount Montague, the only temporal peer who consistently

[1] See Chapter 12 on the Gentry.

opposed the ecclesiastical bills of 1559[1] and a man who was well-informed through his contacts at court and his position in county affairs. In a letter to a Catholic friend, Francis Yaxley, he reported that "This barrayne countrey bringeth forth no newes & I thinke itt not therefor the more unhappye, for that where smalle newes be there is comminelye a quyett commine welthe".[2] The only known instance of violence occurred in March 1559 when Protestant rioters desecrated the parish church in the east Sussex market town of Hailsham.[3]

Despite the relative tranquillity of Elizabethan Sussex it must not be supposed that there was no resistance to change: a stubborn, although not very vigorous variety of Catholicism persisted in many parts of the county, and the rather feeble efforts on the part of the bishops of Chichester before the time of Richard Curteys to propagate official Protestantism did very little to alter habitual piety or indifference to the *volte-faces* of official religious policy. An examination of the provisions of last wills and testaments in Sussex at the beginning of the reign indicates to what extent traditional piety ignored not only official attempts to discourage praying for the dead but also the spreading spirit of social utilitarianism. The episcopal and metropolitical visitations of the 1560s reveal official concern at the strength of Catholicism in the diocese of Chichester and also convey to us an idea of the quality of Catholic piety.

(i) *The Battle for the Parish*

The first decade of Elizabeth's reign was dominated by a struggle for the parish. The royal commissioners encountered delays in depriving those clergy who refused to swear the oath of supremacy, but with the exception of a handful of remote parishes, acceptance of the Book of Common Prayer was secured before the end of this period. The greater part of the

---

[1] Sir John Neale, *Elizabeth I and her Parliaments, 1559–1581* (London: 1953), p. 120.

[2] S.P., Dom., Eliz., 14/32. The following February Lord Montague again told Francis Yaxley that he had no news with which to "quyte your advisis [quit your advisoes, i.e. to pay him back for his dispatches]". *Ibid.*, 16/12.

[3] *Acts P.C.*, VII, 76.

Catholic gentry had by that time abandoned the parish, finding it safer to worship privately within their manorial households. Yet, popular acquiescence in the use of the Protestant Prayer Book did not constitute popular acceptance of the Reformation. Traditional Catholic piety still persisted until the coming of a learned Protestant ministry in the 1570s.

The resistence to religious change in early Elizabethan Sussex was generally more pronounced in rural parishes than those in the towns. This can be seen in the execution of officially-decreed liturgical changes. In the rural parish of Tarring the Mass books were not discarded until 1569, while an inventory of church plate and vestments taken in 1562 revealed that the parish still possessed all of the equipment necessary for saying Mass.[1] On the other hand, the demolition of the altar was the first act recorded after the proclamation of the queen in the churchwardens' accounts of Rye.[2] But Protestant Rye was an exception.

The problem of getting the missionaries of Protestantism into each parish was even more difficult than persuading rural parishes to yield up their Mass books. While the 1560s saw one-sixth of the clergy of the diocese of Chichester deprived of their cures, most of the parish clergy who conducted services according to the Book of Common Prayer in the 1560s were the same men who had offered Mass in the same church under Mary. Moreover the squire who turned recusant in the 1570s generally was still sitting in his accustomed pew in the parish church in the early 1560s.[3] Later, the more intransigent

[1] Churchwardens' Accounts of Tarring, in J. Dallaway and E. Cartwright *A History of the Western Division of the County of Sussex: The Rape of Bramber* (London: 1832), II. 2, 13015.

[2] William Holloway, *The History and Antiquities of the Ancient Town and Port of Rye in the County of Sussex* (London: 1847), pp. 500–1.

[3] As John Bossy observes in "The Character of Elizabethan Catholicism", *Crisis in Europe, 1560–1660*, ed. Trevor Aston (London: 1965), p. 226: "For the first twenty years of the reign the minimum of conformity was almost universally observed by men who within their own households continued to live as Catholics; and this with no sense of strain or moral discomfort. All that was implied was a distinction in the order of society between what was the Queen's and what was one's own. . . . The Government, at least provisionally, accepted the distinction, and conflict either interior or exterior was minimal."

Catholics among the gentry either withdrew voluntarily from parish life, turning inward and confining their activities to their Catholic households, or were forcibly removed from the scene by imprisonment. In the 1560s their conservative influence may have slowed the process of liturgical transition, but at the same time their presence in the parish church helped to maintain social stability during the time of religious changes.

Little is known concerning the survival of Edwardian Protestantism in Sussex during the reign of Mary. It would appear that in the 1560s Protestantism was largely confined to a few towns of east Sussex, and that apart from Rye and Lewes, the Protestants still formed only a minority. The evidence concerning the geographical distribution of Protestantism in Sussex during the Marian persecution is based upon the locations of public executions, since heretics usually were burned only in towns where the spread of heterodox doctrine caused particular alarm. Philip Hughes argues that some doubt exists as to how valid such statistics are as an index to the strength of Protestantism in a particular locality;[1] but that the existence of Protestantism in these particular Sussex towns is not to be doubted is borne out by figures that will be presented elsewhere concerning the geographical distribution of Puritan ministers in the 1580s and 1590s.[2] A total of 27 convicted heretics were burned during the four years of the Marian persecution, 1555–58, at five different towns in Sussex: two were burned in Chichester, one in Steyning, three at East Grinstead, four at Mayfield and seventeen at Lewes.[3] The greater number—24 out of the 27—were put to death in east

[1] Fr Hughes thinks that the figures in Essex and Kent are misleading because a sizeable portion of the many heretics burned in these counties may have been anabaptists, who were greatly feared by Protestants as well as Catholics. If this is true of Kent and Essex, it may be true of Sussex (especially east Sussex) where the figure of 27 heretics out of a national total of 273 seems disproportionate to what is known of the strength of early Elizabethan Protestantism in Sussex from other sources. *The Reformation in England*, II, pp. 261–2.

[2] See Chapter 9 on Puritanism, Table I.

[3] Hughes, *op. cit.*, II, 260–4. John Foxe's *Book of Martyrs* lists the residences of 11 of the Sussex martyrs: East Grinstead, 4; Woodmancote, 2; Wythiam, 2; and one each from Ardingly, Brighton and Rye. All of these towns are in east Sussex; three are in the deanery of Lewes.

Sussex towns. Being closer to the continent than west Sussex, east Sussex was more open to the influx of new ideas, and several Flemings were included among those who suffered death for heresy in the diocese of Chichester under Mary. Protestantism is known to have existed in Winchelsea and Rye as far back as the reign of Henry VIII. In the latter town the Protestants were especially vociferous, but even here the reactionary party apparently remained more numerous for some time. When the papalist curate of Rye was removed in the early 1540s, Bishop Richard Sampson warned his replacement to go slowly and to avoid arousing his parishioners.[1]

The evidence concerning the extent of Protestantism in Sussex at the beginning of the Elizabethan period is scanty and by itself would be inconclusive. But taken together with evidence of the continuing strength of Catholicism gleaned from wills and visitation returns, the argument that the spread of the popular Reformation in Sussex was retarded during the 1560s becomes much stronger.

One way of estimating the persistence of Catholicism in Sussex at the beginning of Elizabeth's reign is to examine the provisions of last wills and testaments. The method here has been to select certain towns and parishes between 1552, when the Second Book of Common Prayer was issued, and 1560.[2] From the selected towns and parishes all recorded wills between 1552 and 1560 are studied to ascertain how many testators, in making obits (and nearly all did in every parish), explicitly requested that their souls be prayed for,[3] and how

[1] V.C.H. Sussex, II, 18.

[2] The former date may be taken as beginning the first concerted official action both to promulgate and enforce a Protestant liturgy. One of the purposes of the Second Prayerbook was to discourage praying for the dead. While there had been earlier attempts to discourage this practice they were only sporadically enforced. Since the same could, to a lesser extent, be said about attempts to enforce usage of the First Book of Common Prayer, it is seen that my selection of the date 1552 is arbitrary. The terminal date 1560 is dictated by the fact that the published excerpts from Sussex wills do not go beyond 1560. The source throughout this section is *Transcripts of Sussex Wills*, ed. R. G. Rice (S.R.S., vols. XLI–XLIV). The entries are arranged alphabetically by parish.

[3] This is a good example of a traditional Catholic obit, from the will of William Lyttelton, vicar of Chiddingly, dated 1 October 1558: "I will vj

many did not specify prayers for their souls, but instead chose
to provide only for the distribution of alms at the time of
burial.[1] The first type of obit indicates that the testator
is Catholic; the second type is doubtful and neither proves that
the testator was Protestant nor precludes the possibility that the
testator was Catholic.[2] For example, the figures for Chichester
classify the Edwardian treasurer of Chichester's obit as doubtful
yet his bequests to the cathedral include a silver pix, a silver
cross and a pair of silver censers—hardly the accountrements of
an Edwardian reformer! While the analysis and tabulation of the
provisions of obits is an indication (though not a completely
accurate one) of the persistence of Catholic attitudes in particular parishes, this method can be a misleading index of the
reception of Protestantism in such parishes unless corroborated
by independent evidence. Beyond the fact that about half of the
wills sampled in selected rural and urban parishes between
1552 and 1560 indicate that the testators were Catholic, it is
difficult to generalize too much.

As might be expected, an analysis of the provisions of obits
argues that the persistence of Catholic attitudes was very strong
in rural parishes. In the parish of West Firle, Catholic obits

---

prestis to Synge or saye dirige and masse to praye for my soule and all
chrysten soules everye preyst to have xij^d and bestowe at my buryall amongest
the povertye xl^s in monye to pray for my soule and Chrysten Soules Item I
will Lyke wyse to be done at my monethes daye . . . I will to twentye of the
pourest howseholders within the paryshe of Chetynglyghe xij^d apece." Ibid.,
XLII, 4.

[1] Here is an example of what I classify as a doubtful obit from the will of
Harry Brydger of Cuckfield, dated 6 March 1558/9: "I wyll that ther be
geven and dystributed amonge the poore people in the day of my buryall to
the value of x^s and my monethes day iij^s iij^d." Ibid., XLII, 59–60.

[2] This classification of obits as either Catholic or doubtful is admittedly
faulty, being based entirely upon attitudes toward purgatory and the efficacy
of praying for the dead. It says nothing about attitudes toward papal power.

Two further objections regarding the usefulness of wills for estimating the
survivals of Catholicism must be answered: (1) While it might be objected
that wills would tend to express the religious opinions only of the older
generation, one must remember that death struck more indiscriminately in
former times. (2) What proportion of the population made wills it would be
difficult to say. However, they were executed by small property owners as
well as big ones.

outnumber doubtful provisions twelve to four; Seddlescombe
had seven Catholic testators and another three whose obits are
inconclusive, while during the same period four wills from the
parish of Boxgrove were probated of which three are definitely
Catholic. A preponderance of Catholic wills could be due to
either of two factors. Firstly, the presence within the parish of
influential families of the gentry, whose own beliefs were
strongly Catholic: this was the situation at West Firle, the seat
of the Gages, who later became important leaders of the recusant gentry. Yet the Carylls of Warnham did not exercise this
sort of influence within their parish, where only one of the ten
wills probated during this period can be classified as Catholic.
Secondly, a pronounced number of traditional obits might have
been due to a persuasive curate, since parish priests quite often
were called upon to witness wills. This seems especially evident
in several parishes where the obits in a number of wills are
almost exactly the same with regard to both provisions and
wording. On the other hand, there were a few rural parishes
where the practice of testators making provisions for prayers
for their souls had completely died out, such as Horsham
where none of the eighteen testators between 1552 and 1560
left money for masses, requiems or dirges. A large proportion
of doubtful wills from a particular parish can be attributed to a
curate too indifferent or too ignorant to instruct his parishioners
rather than to any preference for Protestantism on the part of
the people of the parish. Perhaps, the example of Battle might
help one to understand the danger of placing too much stress
upon the number of doubtful obits within a given parish. The
fact that between 1552 and 1560 only nine of the twenty-one
wills probated from the parish of Battle have provisions for
Masses etc., might lead one to the conclusion that Catholicism
was not especially strong at Battle. However, all other evidence
concerning the religious views of the people of Battle force one
to the conclusion that Battle must have been one of the most
Catholic towns in all of Sussex.[1] For good reason too. Battle
Abbey was the principal seat in east Sussex of the Lords
Montague, a family among the Catholic nobility of Sussex whose

[1] See S.P., Dom., Eliz., 60/71, printed *V.C.H. Sussex*, 24–6, and B.M.,
Lansdowne MS. 82, fos. 103–103v.

social influence weathered the storms of religious change remarkably well.

The paucity of Catholic obits among the testators of such towns as Rye, Steyning or Arundel is not surprising in the light of what is known about these places from other sources.[1] The fact that half the testators in Chichester were Catholic is consistent with both the observations of contemporary witnesses and with the amount of opposition encountered by Bishop Curteys in the cathedral city. Yet, the extent to which Catholic practices still persisted in Lewes and Cuckfield is remarkable considering the amount of Puritan activity emanating from these towns at the end of the reign. Twelve of the twenty-nine wills probated from Lewes between 1552 and 1560 can be described as Catholic; in Cuckfield Catholic testators actually predominated ten to six.

The second body of proof for the continuing tenacity of Catholic practices in Sussex in the 1560s is derived from the return to the Privy Council made by Bishop Barlow in 1564 and from the metropolitical visitation of 1569.

In 1564 the Privy Council called upon the bishops for an assessment of conditions in their sees. In his reply,[2] Bishop Barlow stressed the great scarcity of educated clerics who could be trusted to preach good doctrine and the lack of reliable men among the upper clergy from whom he could draw the officers who staffed the church courts and otherwise assisted the bishop in details of administration. Bishop Barlow explained to the Privy Council that if only he had a few learned preachers he might hope to attract a small following among the "men of hounour" in the shire. He quite despaired of winning over the common people until more members of the gentry had been persuaded to support the religious settlement.[3] Among educated members of the upper clergy there

[1] For Rye see Chapter 10 on Puritanism; both Arundel and Steyning had Puritan ministers later in the reign of Elizabeth. Cf. Table I.

[2] "A Collection of Original Letters from the Bishops to the Privy Council", ed. Mary Bateson, Camden Society Miscellany, IX, 8.

[3] For Barlow's estimate of the number of gentlemen who were not considered to be loyal to the Protestant establishment and a discussion of the difficulties encountered in attempts to purge Catholics from the commission of the peace in the 1560s, see Chapter 12 on the Gentry.

were only two holding benefices in his diocese whom Barlow felt that he could trust as commissaries or vicars general.[1] And one of these two was non-resident! As for the rest of the upper clergy, Barlow added: "I refrayned to communicate so franckly with others because I doubted of their secretness that retinue and alliance beinge so great in theis partes". Neither of these two deficiencies really began to be made good until the episcopate of Richard Curteys in the next decade.

The consequence of this was that the Reformation made no significant progress in securing popular support in Barlow's time beyond a grudging acquiescence in the liturgy of the Book of Common Prayer. Indeed, this first of the Elizabethan bishops of Chichester was thankful that so far his diocese was "fre[e] from all violent attempts eyther to affi[c]te the godlye or to distourbe the [e]stablisshed good orders of this Realm". Barlow confessed to the Privy Council that it was only because of "feare of your Lordshippes vigilante Aucthorite" that "open violence" was avoided in Sussex.

That this was all that the agents of the royal supremacy were able to accomplish during this period can be seen in the metropolitical visitation of 1569. Bishop Barlow had died in 1568 and the see lay vacant for two years until the appointment of Richard Curteys in 1570. In 1569 a visitation of the diocese of Chichester *sede vacante* was made by commissaries of Archbishop Parker of which a detailed report sent to the Privy Council still survives.[2] Although this summary of the state of the diocese of Chichester is not always as precise as one could wish, it does draw a vivid picture of the degree to which Catholic piety still found popular expression in many parishes and leaves little doubt of the official dismay which this caused.

[1] The two were the brothers Austin and William Bradbridge. Austin died in 1567 and William, who was also a prebendary of Salisbury, did not live in Chichester after 1567. Barlow seems to have relied increasingly upon his son-in-law, William Overton, who became treasurer of Chichester Cathedral in March 1566/7. The names of two other lieutenants also appeared in episcopal commissions for the visitation of 1567. Peckham, *Act Book A*, nos. 744 & 696; DRO, Ep. I/15, Box A 2 (1).

[2] S.P., Dom., Eliz., 60/71, printed in *V.C.H. Sussex*, II, 24–6. This is the source for the discussion of the 1569 visitation unless otherwise indicated.

Yet the defiance of Catholic squires or the passive resistance of Marian priests still clinging to their benefices ten years after the first attempts to enforce the religious settlement is actually ironical, for their actions reveal to us (although this was not apparent to the author of the visitation report) that Catholicism was losing the battle for the parish and was already in the process of retreating into the seigneurial household.[1] Thus the embryonic form of later Elizabethan recusancy is already beginning to display certain recognizable characteristics.

Efforts to maintain traditional Catholic piety in the life of the parish were still being made in 1569 by those who continued to hope that the present religious settlement would prove no more durable than those of the preceding 35 years. At Arundel the altar still stood in the parish church "to the offence of the godly", while at Battle and Lindfield the parishioners were very "blind and superstitious" and everything was held in readiness "to set up the Mass again within 24 hours' warning. . . ."

Sometimes the resistance to religious innovations was led by the lord of the manor; elsewhere it was the parish priest or schoolmaster. At Racton the squire, Arthur Gunter, had prevented the election of churchwardens and ruled "the whole parish". In the parish of Findon the vicar, who also doubled as the schoolmaster, fortified this resistance; but in the parish of Arundel the schoolmaster taught within the safe precincts of the Lodge, where the earl of Arundel's comptroller resided.

"In the town of Battell, when a preacher doth come and speak anything against the Pope's doctrine they will not abide but get them out of the church. They say that they are of no jurisdiction, but free from any bishop's authority [i.e. a liberty]; the schoolmaster is the cause of their going out, who afterwards in corners among the people doth gainsay the preachers. It is the most popish town in all Sussex."

Seven Marian priests are described as opposed to the Protestant Settlement of religion though still clinging to their benefices. Four appear to have been offering only passive

[1] On the Catholic household see the very suggestive sociological analysis in John Bossy's essay, *loc. cit.*

resistance; they had been licensed to preach under Mary but "now do not nor will not, and yet keep their livings". The remaining three offered more active resistance; two of them kept for the use of their parishes copies of a book by the Catholic exile and controversalist Nicholas Saunders, entitled *The Rock of the Church* (Louvain: 1567), which "doth not account the bishops now to be any bishops". One of these, David Spencer, parson of Clapham, was looking after the property of Thomas Stapleton, and sending him money at Louvain.[1] Another of the seven unreformed Marian priests, Richard Gray, rector of Withyham, was among the four beneficed clergymen summoned by Bishop Curteys to the episcopal visitation of 1577.[2] Most of the seven seem to have

[1] Spencer died in 1573. His will (P.C.C., 11 Peter) was witnessed by William Shelley of Michelgrove, head of one of the most important Catholic families in Sussex, and his two executors included Mr Story, the schoolmaster-vicar of Findon, who had been cited as an unreformed Marian cleric along with Spencer in 1569, and Mr King, parson of "Clapham by London [Clapham, Surrey]", who possibly could be the same Mr Kinge parson of Stanmer, accused along with Spencer of keeping the book by Nicholas Sanders.

The testaments of faith prefixed to the wills of suspected Marian clerics are usually vague and inconclusive. After the 1560s only powerful members of the nobility, such as Lord Montague, dared to flaunt bold Catholic testaments of faith in their wills, but sometimes one does find other and more mundane details that provide a clue to the testator's religious outlook. Another Marian priest cited in the metropolitical visitation of 1569 was Nicholas Hickett, parson of Pulborough. An ex-chantry priest, he had been receiving a pension of £4 p.a. since early in the reign of Edward VI (*Sussex Chantry Records*, ed. J. E. Ray (S.R.S., XXXVI), pp. 47, 61, 144). His will, dated 15 May, 1585, begins with a simple testament: "I comende and bequeathe my soule to the omnipotent god the father, the sonne & holie ghoste my maker my Redeemer and comforter". (DRO, Archdeaconry of Chichester, Registers of Wills, STC 1/13, fos. 205v–207.) So far no clue to Hickett's religious convictions, but the very last item in the will reads: "I give and bequeathe to Mr doctor Langdale my beste gowne". Alban Langdale was the deprived Marian archdeacon of Chichester, who was Lord Montague's chaplain until his death sometime between 1587 and 1589 (*D.N.B.*, sub Alban Langdale; Richard Smith, *An Elizabethan Recusant House, Comprising the Life of the Lady Magdalen Viscountesse Montague (1538–1608)*, ed. A. C. Southern (London: 1954), p. 19).

[2] Either Richard Gray showed himself sufficiently conformable, or else Bishop Curteys was unable to have him deprived, for he was still rector of Withyham in 1581. In that year he was excommunicated for failure to appear

been acquainted with one another, and it is not unlikely that there was a degree of organization behind their opposition. That even a bare handful of suspected Catholics remained among the clergy of the diocese of Chichester as late as Bishop Curteys's episcopate is amazing. How much greater were the problems of enforcing the religious settlement in Sussex may be seen when contrasted with London: Dr Owen's study of Elizabethan London reveals that only one suspected Catholic remained among the parish clergy of that city in 1561.[1]

The beginnings of Catholic recusancy are becoming evident in Sussex in 1569. The visitation report mentions ten families of the gentry whose households were becoming little islands of Catholic worship. More and more they refuse to come to church, especially at Easter when all were required to communicate; instead they "get them[selves] out of the country until that feast be past [in order to avoid the penalties for not receiving the sacrament at their parish churches] . . ." or "receive Communion at home in their chapels, and choose priests from a distance". Six of the ten families listed were jointly or individually maintaining deprived Marian priests as chaplains—four of whom are mentioned by name. These chaplains travelled across Sussex and Hampshire, building up the communications system that was so essential to the survival of Catholicism a decade later when the English colleges on the continent began sending forth their missionary priests. One of them, "Father Moses, sometime a friar in Chichester, . . . runneth about from one gentleman's house to another with news and letters". Books on apologetics printed abroad were already being smuggled into the country to hold Catholics in their faith until the seminary priests arrived. Four people were known to be sending money to Thomas Stapleton to support his work at Louvain, where he was beginning to build

---

at the visitation but he subsequently petitioned for and received absolution on condition that in the future he would respect the authority of the church (DRO, Ep. II/9/2, fo. 34).

For a discussion of the visitation of 1577, see chapter 4.

[1] H. G. Owen, "The London Parish Clergy in the Reign of Elizabeth I" (London Ph.D. thesis, 1957), p. xix.

his reputation as an able polemicist and the most learned English Catholic of his time.[1]

Summing up the state of the diocese of Chichester, the archbishop's commissary concluded pessimistically "Except it be about Lewes and a little in Chichester, the whole diocese is very blind and superstitious for want of teaching . . ."; even in "the city of Chichester few of the aldermen are of good religion".

"They use in many places ringing between morning and the litany, and all the night following All Saints' day, as before in time of blind ignorance and superstition taught by the pope's clergy.

Many bring to church the old popish Latin primers, and use to pray upon them all the time when the lessons are being read.

Some old folks and women used to have beads in the churches, but these I took away from them but they have some yet at home in their houses."

The contemporary explanations by Bishops Barlow and Curteys of this failure of the Reformation to win popular support in Sussex in the 1560s all agree with that expressed in the report of the visitation of 1569:

"Many churches there have no sermons, not one in seven years, and some not one in twelve years, as the parishes have declared to the preachers that of late have come thither to preach.

Few churches have their quarter sermons according to the Queen's Majesty's injunctions.

In many places the people cannot yet say the commandments, and some not the articles of their belief, when they be examined before they come to the communion, and yet they be of the age of forty and fifty years. The ministers there for the most part are very simple."

Of course, the habitual Catholic piety of old men and women who could neither recite the commandments nor confess the

[1] *D.N.B.*, *sub* Thomas Stapleton; see also Eric McDermott, "The Life of Thomas Stapleton, 1535–1598" (London M.A. thesis, 1950).

creed was not the sort of religious tradition that could continue long without priests to offer the Mass and minister the sacraments. The mere passage of time would favour a party of reform that could fill the spiritual void created by the failure of the Catholic clergy to catechize the laity. The advent of Bishop Curteys's vigorous reforming leadership would bring learned Protestant clergymen from the universities into Sussex to combat both religious ignorance and Catholic resistance.

(ii) *The Disruption of Episcopal Administration*

In the first part of this chapter the conditions have been described which warrant the assertion that the popular Reformation still had not prevailed in Sussex during the 1560s. In the remainder of this chapter I will explain this situation in terms of the disruption of ecclesiastical government since the Henrician breach with Rome. This in turn was due to the rapid turnover of bishops at Chichester under Henry VIII and Edward VI and to the want of educated clergy who were disposed to support the religious innovations by preaching or to assist the bishops in the execution of religious settlements that never seemed to last very long.

The lack of effective leadership and continuity in episcopal administration in the diocese of Chichester grew out of the failure of the government to secure episcopal sanction for doctrinal or liturgical changes from three out of four Henrician and Edwardian incumbents of the diocese of Chichester. The first Henrician bishop of Chichester, Robert Sherburne (episcopate, 1508–36), reluctantly proclaimed Henry VIII's supremacy over the Church of England and then wrote to Thomas Cromwell, the king's vicegerent in spirituals, asking to be allowed to resign his mitre in consideration of his "age and impotency".[1] He formally resigned before Convocation on 9 June 1536. Sherburne was immediately replaced by Richard Sampson (episcopate, 1536–43), who was a reformer in the Erasmian sense but certainly no radical. Training as a canonist

[1] W. R. W. Stephens, *The Memorials of the South Saxon See and the Cathedral Church of Chichester* (London: 1876), p. 206.

had bred caution in this prelate.[1] Although Sampson had written a pamphlet defending the royal supremacy, he incurred the enmity of his former patron Cromwell for the part that he played in putting the theologically conservative Act of Six Articles of 1539 through Parliament and especially for his close association with Bishops Gardiner and Tunstal, who led the opposition against Cromwell. Cromwell accused Sampson of being a papalist and had him locked up in the Tower of London on a charge of treason. He was not released until after Cromwell's fall.[2] The third Henrician bishop of Chichester, George Day (episcopate, 1542–53, 1554–57), was another conservative who dragged his feet even more than Sherburne or Sampson. Day survived well enough during the conservative reaction in the last years of Henry's reign, but in the next reign soon ran foul of the Privy Council for continued opposition to the radical Edwardian reforms. Day was finally imprisoned and formally deprived for his refusal to order the altars of his churches to be demolished. Thus it was not until 1552 that the see of Chichester was held by a Protestant reformer, John Scory; he remained only two years until turned out after Mary's accession. George Day was restored to the bishopric of Chichester in 1554.[3]

John Christopherson, who succeeded George Day upon the latter's death in 1557, was appointed to the see of Chichester by a papal provision.[4] One of the first of the Louvainists, Christopherson had fled Cambridge upon the accession of Edward VI.[5] Although Christopherson was given little time to make much of an impression on the administration of his diocese Thomas Fuller considered him a persecutor and said that "had he sat long in that see, and continued after that rate, there would have needed no iron mills to rarefy the woods of this county, which this *Bonner*, junior would have done himself".[6] But an earlier writer—an Anglican bishop—thought Christo-

---

[1] On Sampson's career see L. B. Smith, *Tudor Prelates and Politics* (Princeton, N.J.: 1953), *passim*.

[2] Stephens, *op. cit.*, pp. 290ff.

[3] *Ibid.*, pp. 221ff.

[4] John Le Neve, *Fasti Ecclesiae Anglicanae* (Oxford: 1854), I, 249.

[5] *D.N.B.*, *sub* John Christopherson.

[6] *The History of the Worthies of England* (London: 1840) III, 244.

pherson was "a man very learned, whereof hee hath left many testimonies behind him".[1] Within three weeks after Elizabeth came to the throne Christopherson was placed in close confinement because of a sermon that he had preached at Paul's Cross attacking another sermon preached a week earlier by the Edwardian Protestant, William Bill.[2] Christopherson's death, after a month of imprisonment, saved Elizabeth the trouble of depriving him, but did nothing to remedy the increasing lack of continuity in episcopal administration in the diocese of Chichester.

Apart from the lack of dependable lieutenants, the re-establishment of firm episcopal leadership in the diocese of Chichester was delayed by several political factors and by the confusion about just who was exercising ecclesiastical jurisdiction in Chichester diocese during the first four years of Elizabeth's reign.

The diplomatic situation—the necessity of not offending the Spanish ally while France still retained a foothold in Scotland—dictated a religious settlement that could be neither hasty nor radical. Already having lost the initiative to Parliament in the making of a statutory religious settlement, the Elizabethan government continued to be too distracted for at least two years to undertake enforcing religious uniformity. Priority was given to the enforcement of the royal supremacy. There was also the task of finding 25 new bishops—partly from among a handful of Edwardian prelates, but mostly from among the Marian exiles—and the choice was neither wide nor to the queen's liking. Once Elizabeth had nominated new bishops they remained unconsecrated until they had consented to the alienation of episcopal lands,[3] which was authorized under a recent act of Parliament[4] permitting the Crown to exchange

[1] Francis Godwin, *A Catalogue of the Bishops of England* (London: 1615), p. 474.

[2] Joseph Gillow, *A Literary and Biographical History or Bibliographical Dictionary of the English Catholics from the Breach with Rome to the Present Time* (London: 1885), I, 485–6.

[3] S.P., Dom., Eliz., 7/19.

[4] 1 Eliz. I, cap. 19. For a discussion of this statute, see Christopher Hill, *The Economic Problems of the Church from Archbishop Whitgift to the Long Parliament* (Oxford: 1956), pp. 14–15.

impropriated rectories for episcopal manors. By the time that Barlow and the other bishops elect had consented to this royal plundering and were consecrated, almost every diocese in England and Wales had been without episcopal leadership for over a year. The queen finally signified her assent to Barlow's election to the bishopric of Chichester on 18 December 1559 but he does not seem to have taken up residence at Chichester until early in the summer of 1560.[1]

Thus, from the death of Bishop Christopherson in December 1558 until the summer of 1560, episcopal authority had been in abeyance in the diocese of Chichester. Of course, this was generally true of all English and Welsh dioceses. At the very least, all episcopal authority was suspended from May to November 1559 by royal writ while the royal visitation was being conducted for the purpose of ministering the oath of supremacy. Bishops of the southern province were further inhibited from visiting their dioceses after May 1560 by the archbishop's announcement of his intention to conduct a metropolitical visitation. Since Chichester diocese still had not been visited in August 1561, Bishop Barlow, in all probability, could not have conducted his first visitation until, at the earliest, the spring of 1562. Now, neither the royal visitors of 1559 nor the ecclesiastical commissioners of 1559–62 concerned themselves with anything but the ministration of the oath of supremacy. It was not until the spring of 1559, when the Treaty of Cateau-Cambrésis, in effect, recognized her as queen, that Elizabeth felt secure enough to reveal her true religious policy. No effort was made to enforce the Act of Uniformity until the metropolitical visitation of 1560–61, and it is not at all certain that the diocese of Chichester was even visited by the archbishop.[2]

Hence, it was not until three years after the enactment of the Elizabethan religious settlement that William Barlow came to exercise full episcopal authority. Almost nothing had been done to spread the new religion in Sussex; nor were Barlow's

[1] Bishop Barlow did not commission a chancellor until July 1560. *Act Book A*, no. 612.

[2] Henry Gee, *The Elizabethan Clergy and the Settlement of Religion, 1558–64* (Oxford: 1898), pp. 158, 249.

efforts very auspicious, hampered as he was by an under-
standable inability to reform the whole diocese of Chichester
by himself.

A former Henrician prelate and a Marian exile, William
Barlow already had a long and chequered career behind him
when he became bishop of Chichester. Thomas Fuller's biographical sketch called him a man "of much motion and promotion". Since Fuller's time Barlow's career has generated
heated historical and theological controversies. Historians have
long puzzled over his pre-episcopal career and generally have
succeeded only in conflating the lives of three, or possibly four
men.[1] Some theologians have been exercised with attempts to
prove or disprove the validity of Barlow's consecration
because for a long time all Anglican orders were reckoned to
descend from this peripatetic prelate;[2] others have been

[1] Probably few men in English religious history have had so many offices
attributed to them as William Barlow. The mistake of telescoping the careers
of several men of the same name was begun by the seventeenth-century
antiquarian Anthony á Wood, *Athenae Oxoniensis* (Oxford: 1813), I, 364–6;
continued by C. H. and T. Cooper, *Athenae Cantabrigienses*, (Cambridge:
1858), I, 276, and T. F. Tout's article in the *D.N.B.*; and compounded by A.
Koszul, "Was Bishop William Barlow Friar Jerome?", *Review of English
Studies*, IV (1928), 24–5. M. M. Knappen, *Tudor Puritanism* (Chicago: 1939),
pp. 21–2, follows Koszul in identifying Bishop Barlow with Friar Jerome, a
friar observant of Greenwich and a friend of Tyndale and William Roy.
L. B. Smith, *Tudor Prelates and Politics, 1536–1538* (Princeton: 1953, pp.
10–11, 107–8, leans toward the view that Bishop Barlow was the Austin
canon who subsequently pursued a diplomatic career. Professor Smith has discovered the existence of two William Barlows who were cousins.

The most successful attempt to get the details of Barlow's career straight is
found in E. G. Rupp, "The Early Career of Bishop Barlow", *Studies in the
Making of the English Protestant Tradition* (Cambridge: 1949), pp. 62–72.
Professor Rupp uses evidence of an indirect nature to argue that Bishop
Barlow was not the Friar Jerome who wrote the virulent *Burial of the Mass*.
Rupp feels sure that Bishop Barlow was the same man as the prior of Haverfordwest and adds that if the future Bishop Barlow were in the royal diplomatic service during the few years of Friar's Jerome's known career, then the
story would make better sense. After all, most of Henry's bishops were
diplomats by background.

[2] Barlow participated in the consecration of Matthew Parker as archbishop
of Canterbury at Lambeth Palace on 17 December 1559. None of Mary's
Catholic bishops could be persuaded, and since Barlow was the only Henrician
bishop in the group, Anglican orders were descended from him. Although

content to accept the fact that if Barlow was not the father of the Anglican hierarchy in the spiritual sense of the term, he was in a physical sense.[1]

The first reference to Barlow of which one can be absolutely certain is his promotion to the Welsh bishopric of St Asaph in 1536.[2] Apparently still unconsecrated, he was translated to

---

Barlow had held several bishoprics under Henry VIII and Edward VI, a Catholic historian, A. S. Barnes, in *Bishop Barlow and Anglican Orders* (London: 1922), pp. 18–19, claims that he was never validly consecrated. But Claude Jenkins, "Bishop Barlow's Consecration and Archbishop Parker's Register: with some new documents", *Journal of Theological Studies*, XXIV (1922), 1–32, has discovered documents which speak as if Barlow had been validly consecrated.

[1] Sometime prior to his translation to Bath and Wells, Barlow married Agatha Wellesbourne, who bore him two sons and five daughters. One of the sons, William, later became bishop of Lincoln, and all five daughters were eventually married to bishops. The five daughters and their husbands were: (1) Anne, who married Augustine Bradbridge, chancellor of Chichester, whose brother William was bishop of Exeter. After Augustine's death she married Herbert Westphaling, bishop of Hereford. (2) Elizabeth, who married William Day, bishop of Winchester, whose brother George had been Mary's first Catholic bishop of Chichester. (3) Margaret, wife of William Overton, treasurer of Chichester Cathedral and later bishop of Coventry and Lichfield. (4) Frances, who, after burying her first husband Matthew, a younger son of Matthew Parker, was married to Toby Mathew, archbishop of York. (5) Antonine or Antonia, who married William Wickham, successively bishop of Lincoln and Winchester (Edward Marshall, "Bishop William Barlow", *Notes and Queries*, 6th series, VIII (1883), 33–4; Wood, *Athenae Oxoniensis*, I, 364–6). The fact that two of Barlow's daughters found husbands for themselves from among the Cathedral dignitaries of Chichester may explain why Bishop Barlow had so much difficulty in recruiting others to join his party of reform.

[2] Marshall, *loc. cit.* I am accepting Professor Rupp's argument that Bishop William Barlow was the same man as the diplomat and not Friar Jerome. Professor L. B. Smith's explanation (*op. cit.*, p. 108) of how he obtained his mitre would thus seem to be the most plausible one: Barlow's opportunity for advancement was apparently due to his elder brother John, who as chaplain to Sir Thomas Boleyn, the father of Anne Boleyn, was much employed as a personal representative of the family throughout Europe. While that unfortunate queen's star was still in ascendancy, Barlow was granted the Welsh priory of Haverfordwest and the management of the queen's earldom of Pembroke. His advancement was then hastened by his appointment to be one of the ambassadors to Scotland.

St David's in April of the same year.[1] Barlow's behaviour during his residence in this small Welsh Cathedral City reveals that he was possessed of more zeal than tact. His views were considered excessively radical by the canons and citizens, who complained to Roland Lee, bishop of Coventry and Lichfield and lord president of the Council of the Marches of Wales, that their new bishop preached most heterodox doctrine, denouncing purgatory and confession and proclaiming that when two or three persons, even "cobblers and weavers were in company, and elected, in the name of God, that there was the true Church of God". Nothing was done about these complaints until Barlow unjustly imprisoned one of his vicars-choral. When commanded to restore the imprisoned vicar-choral to liberty under pain of forfeiting a surety of £500, Barlow simply refused. He further angered the canons and citizens of St David's by calling the city a place of detestable "anti-Christian superstition" and conceiving a plan for moving the seat of the bishopric to Caermarthen, where he hoped to be free of "barbarous rural persons".[2] By this time, Barlow had become a protégé of the duke of Somerset and through his favour was translated again in 1547—this time to Bath and Wells, where his alienation of church land is legend.[3] The accession of Mary in 1553 brought imprisonment; eventually, Barlow escaped and made his way into exile in Germany and Poland.[4]

[1] Arguing that his fellow prelates would not have yielded precedence to Barlow were he unconsecrated, Claude Jenkins places Barlow's consecration between 11 June and 2 July 1536. *loc. cit.* in n. 41.

[2] L. B. Smith, *op. cit.*, pp. 113–14.

[3] Christina Garrett, *The Marian Exiles* (Cambridge: 1938), p. 80.

[4] *Ibid.* Barlow's first attempt at escape in April 1554 miscarried and he was recaptured. His name was conspicuously absent from the "declaration" of the imprisoned Protestant bishops on 8 May, probably because he did not want to risk continued imprisonment or the fate that awaited Cranmer, and he was released two days later. He attempted to flee abroad again only to be re-arrested and committed to the Fleet in November 1554 (*The Diary of Henry Machyn*, ed. J. G. Nichols, Camden Soc. XLII (1848), p. 75). This time he was compelled to sign a written recantation before Bishop Gardiner on 22 January, 1554/5 (printed in Wood, *Athenae Oxoniensis*, I, 364–6; see also Stephens, *Memorials of the South Saxon See and the Cathedral Church of Chichester*, p. 249). Subsequently, Barlow was released and made his way into Germany with his family and attached himself as chaplain to the Protestant household

Barlow did not find Chichester much more to his liking than St David's. He soon fell to quarrelling with the citizens of Chichester,[1] and he found it necessary to continue the purge of papalist clergy[2] that had been begun by the royal visitors of 1559 and the Ecclesiastical Commission before he could undertake more positive reforms. To some extent, the difficulty that Barlow had in finding committed Protestants among the clergy of his diocese can be explained by the disproportionately high number of clerics who had to be purged in Chichester diocese as compared to the much lower figures for most other dioceses. Henry Gee's pioneering study[3] of the deprivations of Marian

---

of Catherine, dowager duchess of Suffolk and her husband Richard Bertie. The Bertie household went to Poland at the invitation of the reformer, John á Lasco. Barlow was back in England by at least 28 May 1559 (Ralph Churton, *The Life of Alexander Nowell, Dean of St Paul's* (Oxford: 1809), p. 395).

[1] S.P., Dom., Eliz., 36/50–51.

[2] Even though removed from his cure by ecclesiastical authorities, a Marian cleric was not necessarily deprived of his spiritual influence. Alban Langdale, archdeacon of Chichester and chancellor of Lichfield, was stripped of all his benefices in 1559 and committed to the custody of Lord Montague. Technically a prisoner, Landgale was actually Lord Montague's chaplain and ministered to a large Catholic household until his death in the 1580s (Richard Smith, *op. cit.*, p. 19. The *D.N.B.*, *sub* Alban Langdale, is in error about Langdale escaping abroad). Thomas Stapleton and his fellow Louvainist, Edward Goddeshalfe, were able to hold on to their prebends in Chichester Cathedral until 1562 or 1563. Meanwhile, to Bishop Barlow's dismay, they represented the cathedral chapter at the Council of Trent (S.P., Dom., Eliz., 11/24, printed in Birt, *op. cit.*, p. 425; see also *ibid.*, p. 425 n.).

Oddly enough one of the canons of Chichester deprived in 1559 was an Elizabethan and not a Marian appointment. William Tresham, canon of Christ Church, Oxford and vice-chancellor of the university, was chosen to represent the university in offering congratulations to the new queen. His reward was the chancellorship and a canonry of Chichester cathedral. This onetime Henrician had adhered to Gardiner's conservative reaction and now was removed for refusal to swear the Elizabethan oath of supremacy (*D.N.B.*, *sub* William Tresham).

[3] *The Elizabethan Clergy and the Settlement of Religion, 1558–64* (Oxford: 1898), especially pp. 248ff. The returns of the royal visitation of the province of Canterbury in the summer of 1559 are missing, although the lists of those who actually subscribed the oath of supremacy do survive for five dioceses (but not for Chichester). In these dioceses only about half of the clergy bothered to attend the royal visitation. The Ecclesiastical Commission also began to look into cases of refusal to swear the oath of supremacy in the

clerics shows that in the diocese of Chichester there were 35 deprivations or institutions after deprivation between 1559 and 1564,[1] and another 9 between 1564 and 1570.[2] At the same time, Gee estimates that no more than 200 were deprived in both provinces of the Church of England. Most historians today consider this figure too low and would place it at closer to 300.[3] But even using Gee's figures it can be estimated that about one-sixth of the Marian clergy of the diocese of Chichester were formally deprived during the 1560s.[4] This certainly points

autumn of 1559. In none of these instances, nor in the metropolitical visitation of the province of Canterbury during 1560–61, were the powers of the royal supremacy used with any rigour. Gee concludes from an examination of episcopal registers that only about 200 were actually deprived for refusal to swear the oath of supremacy in both provinces out of an estimated total of 9,400 clergy (p. 217). H. N. Birt took exception to both of Gee's estimates in his *The Elizabethan Religious Settlement* (London: 1907), arguing that between 370 and 600 out of 1130 clergy in the northern province alone refused to swear the oath of supremacy. He also says that there were only 8,731 benefices in England (but this figure would not include curates) and that pluralism must be taken into account because of the scarcity of priests. Moreover, there were instances where Edwardian clergy displaced Marian priests without formal deprivation or institution. Birt claims that he possessed the names of 700 who were formally deprived before 1565 (p. 197). To this he adds a minimum figure of 1175 disappearances from the records that cannot be explained and where Marian priests probably abandoned their livings to avoid the oath of supremacy. Birt finally arrived at the conclusion that 1,875 out of 8,000 clergymen refused the oath of supremacy (p. 203).

[1] Thirteen were canons of the cathedral and twenty-two were incumbents of parochial benefices. Gee, *op. cit.*, pp. 274–5.

[2] *Ibid.*, p. 288.

[3] See, for example, G. R. Elton, *England under the Tudors* (London: 1962), p. 276, and Sir Maurice Powicke, *The Reformation in England* (London: 1961), p. 145, both of which accept the 300 figure.

[4] Bishop Barlow certified in 1563 that there were 287 livings in the diocese of Chichester, including curacies as well as unimpropriated rectories and vicarages. The number of parishes was 272. In addition there were 27 benefices in the Cathedral chapter. Of these canonries, some were held by parish clergymen of Chichester diocese or even by clerics outside of the diocese. The number of canons who were actually resident (usually 5 or 6 including the dean) was about half the number of instances where two parish churches or chapels were served by one priest. Thus, the number of beneficed clergymen could not have exceeded 290 even if all benefices were filled, which they were not. Using Gee's figures for the number of deprivations or institutions after deprivation for Chichester diocese, it can be seen that 44

to more widespread clerical resistance to the Elizabethan religious settlement in Sussex than in most other English counties, especially southern counties. But, more pertinent to my argument is the fact that over a decade passed before Protestant replacements could be found.

Further support for this interpretation comes from Bishop Barlow's survey[1] of the diocese of Chichester, probably undertaken in the spring or early summer of 1563, which shows the difficulty in finding suitable candidates for the void cures. In that year the Privy Council had directed every bishop in England to make a return on the state of his diocese, specifying the names of all incumbents of benefices and curates and how many cures were unserved. Barlow listed 287 parish churches and chapels of ease in his jurisdiction.[2] In 102 parishes both vicarages and parsonages were void of clerical incumbents, although the cures were served by curates. Six parishes had non-resident parsons, but they had endowed vicarages with vicars to serve the cures; four other non-resident rectors had failed to appoint either vicar or curate. There were eight parishes consisting of two or more churches and dependent chapels where the combined cure of souls was served by only one incumbent or curate. In addition there were 49 churches and chapels for which absolutely no provision had been made. In other words one-sixth of the cures in the diocese of Chichester were still unserved in 1563. Large village churches such as those at New Shoreham and Winchelsea had neither rector, vicar, nor curate; while the unusually large church at Rye had only one curate to take care of a thousand souls. At Boxgrove there had stood lately a magnificent double church of noble proportions

out of about 290, or about one-sixth, of the Marian clergy lost their livings during the 1560s. Of course, not all of these Marian clerics were resident, but they were obliged to find curates.

In addition, Mr W. D. Peckham very kindly has given me the names of two Edwardian incumbents who were deprived of their benefices under Mary and reinstated in their livings under Elizabeth without reinstitution. In one case, the Marian incumbent was removed without formal deprivation.

[1] B.M., Harley MS. 594, fos. 109–115v. See also V. J. B. Torr, "An Elizabethan Return of the State of the Diocese of Chichester", *S.A.C.*, LXI (1920), 104.

[2] Three parishes were missing from the return.

of which one side had served as the monastic church of the Benedictine priory of Boxgrove. After the dissolution the parish church was torn down and the priory church given over to the use of the parish, but where there had once been a whole chapter of monks, no money could be found for even a curate.[1]

These vacant livings and inadequately-served cures are not to be explained only by the deprivation of Marian priests. The universities did not become Protestant overnight, and it was not until the 1570s that they even began to graduate sufficient learned preachers to fill the better benefices. Even then the economic problems still remained, for learned men could not be attracted to country livings that would not maintain even a carpenter or a cobbler. The problem was partly alleviated when Bishop Curteys consolidated several of the less remunerative benefices; but even after his episcopate, many of the parish clergy were tradesmen and still plied their trades.[2]

The removal by deprivation of most of the university men among the upper clergy and the apparent tepidity of those who had accommodated themselves to the new regime left Barlow with no choice but to look outside of the diocese for lieutenants to help him carry out his reforms. Some of them were, like himself, Marian exiles; the others were either his own relatives or relatives of his lieutenants. The two men upon whom Bishop Barlow chiefly depended were two brothers born in Sussex, Augustine and William Bradbridge.[3] Augustine, Barlow's first chancellor, had been a member of John Knox's congregation in Geneva and was also his son-in-law. He stayed

[1] At the archidiaconal visitation of 1579 the churchwardens of Boxgrove certified that they had not had a vicar or even a sequestrator for over thirty years, although they had finally obtained a curate, who was also vicar of another church in Chichester. The curate testified that "there is no incumbent there nor hath bene of long time by reason of the smallness of the lyvinge" and between the two benefices he made no more than £13 6s. 8d. a year. B.M., Add. MS. 39, 454, fos. 3–3v.

[2] See Chapter 9 on the Clergy. An excellent discussion of the changing relationship between the supply of graduates of Oxford and Cambridge and the availability of benefices is found in Mark Curtis's "The Alienated Intellectuals of Early Stuart England", Crisis in Europe, 1560–1660, ed. Trevor Aston, p. 295.

[3] Bateson, loc. cit.; D.N.B., sub William Bradbridge; Garrett, op. cit., p. 96.

only two years at Chichester before becoming dean of Sarum. His brother William, later bishop of Exeter, succeeded him as chancellor of Chichester in April 1562.[1] William's more moderate views had permitted him to retain his several benefices under Mary. He was in constant conflict with Richard Tremayne, another Marian exile, who apparently represented a more radical faction in the cathedral chapter.[2] Marriage to one of Barlow's daughters brought William Overton increasingly into prominence in Barlow's episcopal administration as a vicar general, and led Overton to believe that he might succeed to his father-in-law's mitre.

As it turned out, it was the new dean of Chichester, Richard Curteys, who was to become the second Elizabethan bishop of Chichester. Capitular politics were becoming extremely factious in the cathedral close. The bitter rivalries among the canons residentiary, which were to contribute materially to Curteys's undoing, and which lived on into the time of Bishop Bickley, only added to the other problems which hindered or distracted Barlow's and later Curteys's enforcement of religious uniformity.

Although the Elizabethan government had shown that it could sanction the Act of Supremacy, the enforcement of religious uniformity was another matter. The queen had found it necessary to fill her coffers before she could begin a vigorous exercise of the royal supremacy. For this reason, she was forced to accept a compromise in the enactment of the parliamentary religious settlement of 1559, and for the same reason she was forced to sacrifice the continuity in episcopal administration upon which the enforcement of religious uniformity principally depended. Thus, for three and a half of the eleven and a half years from December 1558 to June 1570 the diocese of Chichester was without episcopal leadership. But even after Bishop Barlow came to possess full ordinary authority in his diocese, he discovered that without educated Protestant missionaries he could not expect to overcome the rural

[1] Peckham, *Act Book A*, no. 641.

[2] For more on William Bradbridge as bishop of Exeter and his disputes with Tremayne, see A. L. Rowse, *Tudor Cornwall* (London: 1941), pp. 144, 323–4, 334.

traditionalism of Sussex. These missionaries were simply not forthcoming in the 1560s.[1] Barlow's episcopate had seen the passing of the old order, but it remained for his more vigorous successor to fill the spiritual vacuum that seems to have prevailed in Sussex in the 1560s.

[1] See J. I. Daeley, "Pluralism in the Diocese of Canterbury during the Administration of Matthew Parker, 1559–1575", *Journal of Ecclesiastical History*, XVIII (April 1967), 33–49, for a discussion of the difficulties that Archbishop Parker encountered in the diocese of Canterbury in the 1560s in filling parochial benefices and finding competent and dependable administrators who were not non-resident pluralists.

PART II

THE FAILURE OF EPISCOPAL LEADERSHIP:
BISHOP CURTEYS, 1570–82

4

THE ATTEMPTED SPIRITUAL REFORMS
OF BISHOP CURTEYS

BISHOP BARLOW HAD complained that there were almost no learned Protestant preachers in Chichester diocese, and by his own account he was unable to remedy the situation. It is during the episcopate of Richard Curteys (1570–82) that the full impact of the popular reformation is felt in Sussex. To overcome Catholic resistance and to counteract spiritual lethargy, Curteys brought preachers down from Cambridge, the intellectual hothouse of English Protestantism. In a theological dissertation which Curteys published in 1577, there is a preface written and signed by some forty clergymen, who were helping Curteys spread the reformed religion in the county of Sussex. They substantiated what Barlow had said and testified in glowing words to the great changes wrought by Richard Curteys:

". . . Whereas it was a rare thing before his [Curteys's] time, to heare a learned sermon in Sussex, now the pulpittes in moste places sounde contynually with the voyce of learned and Godly Preachers, he himselfe as *Dux gregis*, geuing good example vnto the rest in so graue & learned manner, that the people with ardent zeale wonderfull reioycing, & in great number take farre and long jorneyes, to bee partakers of his good and godly lessons."[1]

Curteys was convinced that the only way to extirpate "strange and irronious opynyons" was through diligent preaching and teaching, and he sought to set the best possible example himself in this regard. Besides his ordinary preaching on Sundays and holy days, his supporters testified that he had "gone three times

---

[1] . . . *The Truth of Christes naturall body*, By Richard Cortesse, Doctor of Divinitie, and Bishop of Chichester ([London:] 1577), unpaginated. Most of this preface is quoted, with a few errors, in Sir Henry Ellis, "Notices of Richard Curteys, Bishop of Chichester, 1570 to 1582", *S.A.C.*, x, 52–8.

through this whole diocesse of Chichester . . . preaching him-self at the greatest townes . . ." and taking many other learned preachers with him. This was certainly a tribute to Curteys's vitality, considering the difficulty of travel in Elizabethan Sussex. Altogether, it was thought that Curteys had been well received in Sussex—"Notwithstanding that there wanted some, though not many, which priuily both by fayre meanes & foule, laboured the contrary". But, it was asserted, not even "the most irreligious and backwarde persones" could deny that Curteys had rooted out ignorant and unworthy curates and had gone to great expense to bring more learned men into the diocese. In six years he himself had preferred to livings, or been the means of preferring, some 20 clerics, who were "well able to preache in any learned audience in this realme"; by person-ally training them in preaching and instructing them in Sacred Scriptures, the bishop had trained 40 more clergymen, so that they were considered "sufficient ynough to preach to any ordinary audyence". It was boasted that almost every incum-bent was now so well-versed in the Scriptures that he could instruct the simpler sort of people in the catechism so com-petently "that euen children can now geue a better accoumpt of the true fayth, then in times past suche as were reputed great clearks could haue done".[1] By the end of his twelve-year tenure of the bishopric of Chichester Curteys had succeeded in isolating the most stubborn members of the recusant gentry from their followers;[2] and his efforts to plant Protestantism in Sussex were beginning to bear fruit.

But the methods that Curteys used to enforce religious uni-formity sowed the seeds of social discord. His efforts to instil a new zeal in his clergy generated a restlessness that took the form of clerical Puritanism in the 1580s.[3] At the same time the reckless way in which Curteys attempted to secure religious conformity among the Sussex gentry raised fears of a revival of arbitrary prelatical power. Not only did Curteys fail to distin-guish between intransigent papalists and outwardly-conforming crypto-Catholics, but his exercise of the temporal magistracy was seen by the gentry as a threat to their social influence and economic interests. The struggle between Curteys and the

[1] *Ibid.*   [2] See Chapters 7 and 8.   [3] See Chapter 10.

Sussex gentry and his subsequent overthrow suggest comparison to the battle waged by Archbishop Laud's detractors to impeach that overmighty prelate and to discredit the methods and assumptions for which Laudianism stood. While the issues in Sussex in the 1570s were not as sharply distinguished as they were to become at Westminster in 1640, it is not too fanciful to say that the former struggle anticipated many of the grievances that later led to that bold attack by Parliament on the tyranny of government by base-born prelates.

The fact that Richard Curteys's zeal was mixed with equal parts of quarrelsomeness and tactlessness provoked factiousness and feuding wherever he went. This tendency can be seen in his university career as well as in his episcopal career. A native of Lincolnshire,[1] Curteys was a scholar at St John's College, Cambridge in 1550, where he was incorporated M.A. in 1556, elected senior fellow in 1559 and university proctor in 1563.[2] As president of St John's at the height of the vestments controversy in 1565 he had been selected by Sir William Cecil, secretary of state and chancellor of the University of Cambridge, to attempt a reformation of abuses at St John's College during the temporary absence of the master of St John's, Richard Longworth, with the help of the vice-chancellor of the university. Curteys assured Cecil: "I doe . . . nothing doubt but to reforme all"; but he feared that the return of Longworth would reverse everything. Apparently, Longworth was away pleading his side of the case with the bishop of Ely. Curteys had hoped that if John Whitgift, who was at this time Lady Margaret professor and chaplain to the bishop of Ely, heard about the matter, he would throw his influence on the side of Curteys's faction. But the future archbishop's sympathies were with the other side at this time.[3]

[1] Like most Elizabethan prelates, Curteys's social origins are shrouded in mystery.

[2] Lower, *The Worthies of Sussex*, p. 114; *D.N.B.*, *sub* Richard Curteys. The name was pronounced Curtis, but I have retained the *D.N.B.* spelling.

[3] S.P., Dom., Eliz., 38/11. A fuller account of this controversy will be found in H. C. Porter's *Reformation and Reaction in Tudor Cambridge* (Cambridge: 1959), pp. 108–35. See also Patrick Collinson's "The 'nott conformytye' of the young John Whitgift", *Journal of Ecclesiastical History*, XV, 192–200.

In the charges which Curteys drew up against Richard Long-worth and sent to Cecil, the master of St John's is accused of having been elected by irregular means, taking bribes, oppress-ing tenants of the college, and of corruption in the handling of leases. Furthermore, Longworth attended the college chapel "withowte his surplesse and hood agreeable to his degree", and he allowed others to do the same.[1] This cleavage of the college fellows, which created factions extending among the students, was part of the controversy over vestments and communion bread. Curteys's chief antagonist among the fellows was the brilliant Puritan scholar, William Fulke, who, possessing the confidence of the master and a following among the under-graduates, emerged as a leader of the extreme Puritan faction in the vestiarian protest. Fulke was accused of diminishing "the laws of the realme [by] referinge all things to conscience. . . . In all his doings he dothe Innovaet all things as well of common prayer as of orders, and exercises in learninge". Fulke also did a lot of hunting which Curteys thought "a great reproofe of the mynisterie".[2]

The next month, in January 1565/6, the harried turned on the harrier, and the zealous but now persecuted Curteys wrote to Cecil that he was "more than half discoraged with these straunge dealinges, for the which I was fully purposed to have left Cambridge". Longworth had feigned to amend his ways, according to Curteys, but was taking every opportunity to get back at him.[3] Cecil failed to back Curteys, who was driven out of St John's by his enemies.[4]

His usefulness at Cambridge now ended, Richard Curteys was consoled with the deanery of Chichester. It was Cecil's influence that in 1567 obtained the deanery for Curteys, but Cecil's choice met with the full approval of the archbishop of Canterbury, Matthew Parker, who wished in addition to give Curteys a prebend of Canterbury Cathedral for "his better furniture".[5]

---

[1] S.P., Dom., Eliz., 38/11. 1.   [2] *Ibid.*, 38/11. 11.   [3] *Ibid.*, 39/19.

[4] Fulke, as chaplain to the earl of Leicester, continued to prosper, and was elected master of Pembroke College in 1578.

[5] S.P., Dom., Eliz., 41/26, printed in *Correspondence of Matthew Parker*, ed. T. T. Perowne (Parker Soc., XXXIX), p. 290.

The cathedral chapter of Chichester stood in need of reform at least as much as St John's. But, the underhanded tricks to which Curteys resorted in his efforts to reform the chapter, especially after he became bishop of Chichester, again provoked the same bad feeling; an anti-Curteys faction within the chapter formed itself around Bishop Barlow's son-in-law and sometime deputy, William Overton, who became treasurer of Chichester Cathedral in 1567. The treasurer was nearly always a canon residentiary and in dignity yielded precedence only to the dean. That the politics of the capitular corporation were to be characterized by such rancour was not entirely the fault of Curteys. The factiousness was also due to the ambition of William Overton who seems to have coveted the bishopric for himself[1] or at least hoped to procure the bishopric for a relative.[2] Overton, later to become bishop of Coventry and Lichfield after years of scheming for a mitre, was a thorough scoundrel, capable even of shocking a man like Lord Burghley, who said of him to Queen Elizabeth in 1584: "The Bishop of Lichfield and Coventry . . . made seventy ministers in one day for money, some tailors, some shoemakers and others craftsmen. I am sure the greatest part of them are not worthy to keep horse".[3] During the "Martin Marprelate" controversy, the anonymous Puritan author of those tracts attacked Overton as an "unlearned prelate", perhaps the only unjust charge that could be made against him.[4]

As dean of Chichester, Curteys found that the cathedral statutes were not being observed, and that the handling of capitular property was irregular. A typical example of the laxity that had been permitted in the chapter in the 1560s is the case of Francis Coxe. Coxe, prebendary of Wittering, was called before the dean and chapter on 22 September 1569 to answer certain articles objected against him. It was charged that he was not "an actual regent in theology" (i.e., he had not qualified at one of the universities) when he was collated to his

[1] S.P., Dom., Eliz., 46/9.
[2] B.M., Add. MS. 6246, fo. 45.
[3] Conyers Read, *Lord Burghley and Queen Elizabeth* (London: 1960), p. 303.
[4] *D.N.B.*, *sub* William Overton. He was also noted in 1575 as being a pluralist with an annual income of £127. S.P., Dom., Eliz., 96/p. 185.

prebend, nor had he lectured on theology as prebendaries were bound to do, nor had he preached in Wittering Church as he was obliged to do.[1] Coxe answered that he had preached except when sick, but when he was again pressed to specify how often he had preached in the cathedral close in the last two years, he answered that he did not know. When asked if he had farmed out his prebend he replied that he had leased it for 40 years at £20 per year. Farming out benefices for long-term leases, which would be binding on the succeeding incumbent, was a widespread abuse in the chapter, and in actuality Coxe had put his prebend out to farm for 61 years in return for an unspecified fine and a rent of £20 per year. Thus, in return for a substantial fine or first payment, Coxe reduced the income of his benefice for probably two or three lifetimes to practically nothing. He was subsequently reprimanded, but evidently not because of his long-term lease, a practice of which the whole chapter was guilty.[2]

In the religious sphere, the new dean of Chichester found that traces of Catholicism still lingered about the cathedral close. In another disciplinary matter William Weaye, holder of one of the clerkships endowed by the Henrician Bishop Sherburne, was convented before the dean and chapter on 13 October 1569, when it was charged that he had in his possession certain Catholic theological and devotional books and a portable altar. Weaye admitted that the articles specified had been in his possession, and when asked what he thought of purgatory, the veneration of the saints, the Mass and transubstantiation, he "lyketh of these". "He believes as the Catholic church does, whereof he thinks the Pope to be the head, or else there should be many heads if every prince were supreme governor in their [sic] own realm." The dean and the residentiaries ordered the deprivation of Weaye and decreed that he be paid 30 shillings "out of hand".[3]

It was Bishop Barlow's death that appears to have heightened

---

[1] Peckham, *Act Book A*, no. 729.

[2] *Ibid.*, Gee, *op. cit.*, p. 288. William Overton had farmed his prebend out for sixty years, while another canon had leased his for eighty years. Peckham, *Act Book A*, no. 668.

[3] *Ibid.*, no. 730.

the feud between Overton and Curteys. Barlow had died on 13 August 1568, and William Overton lost no time in writing to Sir William Cecil to warn against entrusting the bishopric of Chichester to anyone "who might be either weak in judgment or not steady in mind, or more slack in painstaking"—most likely a reference to the dean of Chichester. The diocese of Chichester was everywhere "full of Papists & Popism", and Overton felt that the best man to succeed his father-in-law was his brother-in-law, William Day, provost of Eton College and later Bishop of Winchester, whom Overton acclaimed as "noted among all for learning & piety".[1] Archbishop Parker also wrote to Cecil of Barlow's death and took the opportunity to put forward the name of Richard Curteys, whom he felt to be the best qualified cleric available among a very limited group of candidates.

". . . When the Queen's pleasure shall be to appoint another [bishop of Chichester], I pray you remember her chaplain Mr. Curteys to that office. The choice is not great other where and he being an honest learned man, I would trust that he should well supply it, to God's honour, and to the Queen's contentation."[2]

It would be sheer folly, Parker continued, to appoint another man like Bishop Richard Cheyney of Gloucester, who, although he desired to reform his sheep, saw that he was too old ever to live to accomplish the task and consequently did nothing "and wisheth he were discharged". Curteys, on the other hand, was of "competent" age.[3]

Curteys was selected to replace Barlow, but he had to wait nearly two years to take possession of his bishopric during which time the crown enjoyed the income deriving from the bishopric—£676 per annum.[4] One writer has maintained that Curteys was highly thought of by both Archbishop Parker and

[1] B.M., Add. MS. 6346, fo. 45.

[2] S.P., Dom., Eliz., 47, printed in *Correspondence of Matthew Parker*, p. 331.

[3] *Ibid*. It is not certain whom Parker had in mind when he says that he was "loth it should fall upon one such body as, I am informed by his friends, make[s] suit for it". This individual could well have been William Overton.

[4] S.P., Dom., Eliz., 96/p. 175.

the queen,[1] but such esteem was probably based upon his reputation as a preacher rather than his abilities as an administrator. Curteys was a well-known and popular preacher even at Cambridge, where his eloquence was sufficient to move Matthew Parker to appoint him as his chaplain, while the queen made him her chaplain in ordinary. He was a frequent preacher at Paul's Cross in the city of London, which was an appointment nominally made by the bishop of London, though usually reflecting the opinions of some powerful personage of the court or the Privy Council, and he continued to preach there after he became bishop of Chichester, when several of his sermons were printed. In a letter to Sir William Cecil written on 3 June 1569, Archbishop Parker spoke of his hesitation to remove Curteys's influence from court and to replace him with lesser divines. "Mr. Curteys might do better to be nigher to serve the Court, than as yet to be removed far; it is hardly thought of, so mean chaplains to be towards the prince & c."[2]

It would be well to examine the sermons of Richard Curteys before going on to analyse his work in the diocese of Chichester, for his actions there may not seem quite so erratic once one understands his theological position. In a sermon[3] preached at Paul's Cross during the Lenten season of 1575, Curteys took as his theme a quotation from *Revelations*:

"There was a great wonder in heaven, a woman was clothed with the Sun, and the Moon was under her feete, and upon her head was a Crown of xij starres, as she was with childe, and she cried & was payned to be delivered."[4]

Curteys explained to his audience that the woman was the Church, which consisted of the "people of God chosen to saluation".[5] He claimed that the English Church was truly clothed with the robe of Christ "and yet it is a wunder to see

[1] W. R. W. Stephens, *Memorials of the South Saxon See and the Cathedral Church of Chichester* (London: 1876), p. 255.

[2] B.M., Lansdowne MS. 11, art. 57, printed in *Correspondence of Matthew Parker*, p. 350.

[3] *Two Sermons Preached by the reverend father in God the Bishop of Chichester, the first at Paules Crosse on Sunday beeing the fourth day of March. And the second at Westminster before the Queenes maiestie the iij Sunday in Lent last past* (London: 1576).   [4] *Ibid.*, p. 73.   [5] *Ibid.*, p. 75.

howe colde the zeale of it is, how little hate of sinne it hath". The English Church "travailed and payned to bring forth her child the Gospel of Christe", and like the Reformation in Germany, Switzerland, Denmark, Poland and Scotland the Reformation in England would triumph despite adversity.[1] For "God hath fed his Daniels, Luther, Zuinglius, Caluine, and infinit others in the Lyons den of persecution and trouble".[2] Having already spent seven years in Sussex, Curteys wanted to remind his audience that the popular reformation had not yet begun or at least was not finished in some parts of England.

In another sermon preached before the queen at Westminster Palace, Curteys asked a very curious question for a bishop:

"What . . . should these Preachers doo with Lordships and Mannours and Tithes: they hinder them from their bookes and study. It were better for them to have a pention [pension] quietly paid them, and they they might go quietly to their bookes and to their preaching."[3]

Thus it can be seen that Richard Curteys, like most of his fellow reformers among the English clergy, was a Calvinist in theology, holding views which were not entirely acceptable to the queen. He was also a "Grindalian". As such he believed in encouraging prophesyings in order to build up a preaching ministry, although he steadfastly maintained an imparity of ministers and thus could not be classified as a presbyterian.[4] Within the context of Christopher Hill's definition of Puritanism before 1640 as encompassing those who wanted to reform the English Church, but not to separate from it,[5] Curteys was a Puritan. His links with other Puritans are many.[6] His concern to see his parish churches all served by

---

[1] Ibid., p. 87.

[2] Ibid., p. 98.

[3] Ibid., pp. 118–19.

[4] Patrick Collinson, The Elizabethan Puritan Movement (London: 1967), pp. 171, 173, 179–80.

[5] Intellectual Origins of the English Revolution, p. 26.

[6] His brother Edmund was certainly a Puritan and he gave benefices to several other Puritans who ran into trouble with the diocesan courts under his more conservative successors. At least one of Curteys's protégés was deprived by Archbishop Bancroft in 1605. See Chapter 10.

learned preachers and his pains to train preachers himself all
are characteristically Puritan. Of course Curteys was a conforming Puritan, and he obliged others to conform as well. Nevertheless, although upholding episcopacy and the supreme governorship and exacting observance of the *Prayer Book*, Curteys
held views and employed methods of reform which, of their
very nature, tended to lessen respect for episcopal government
and, indeed, to undermine the royal supremacy itself.

Curteys's attempts to reform the cathedral chapter were
continued after his elevation to episcopal rank. In the early
months of 1570 an effort was made to obtain better preachers
and to enforce the rules of residence on the canons residentiary, who, besides their duties of conducting services and
preaching in the cathedral and several of the other Chichester
churches, were also bound to supply quarterly sermons in
parishes where the dean and chapter collectively or one of the
prebendaries individually owned an impropriated rectory. In
January 1569/70 Thomas Drant, the poet,[1] was given a prebend and, because of his reputation in learning, was admitted to
residence within the cathedral close almost immediately. It
was unusual for a canon to win the privilege of residence so
soon, and the reason given was "because there were not
enough in residence to make a full chapter and for lack of
preachers in the Church". For the first year the greedy canons
refused to allow Drant any claim to the money shared yearly by
the residentiaries above the individual prebendal incomes
except that he would be allowed a share of the common bread.
However, he was granted a house in the cathedral close for
life.[2]

If the addition of Thomas Drant made a full chapter on
paper, it was quite another matter actually to get the residentiaries to observe the statutes governing the required period of
residence. At a chapter meeting on 7 May 1571 it was asked
whether Thomas Drant, Henry Worley and Thomas Willowby
had "resided according to the statutes". It was found that none
of them had done so. Francis Coxe, who had already been cited
for questionable practices in leasing his prebend and for

---

[1] *D.N.B.*, *sub* Thomas Drant.
[2] Peckham, *Act Book A*, nos. 734–9.

negligence in preaching, was this time also cited for non-residence. He pleaded that he had been detained in "distant parts" and promised to take up residence in June; "on account of his morals and virtues, and of his gifts as a preacher", his excuse was accepted by the chapter.[1] At another meeting a week later, it was decided that a residentiary might share in the common bread only on those days when he or his vicar choral had actually attended morning prayer.[2] In July 1571 it appeared that Thomas Drant still was residing in the cathedral close only a small portion of the year. He asked that he might receive part of the chapter dividend in proportion to the number of days that he had actually been present and living in the close during the previous year and further proposed that in the future he should receive the common bread and yearly dividend for eighty days a year only, or for that period of time when he was actually present. Evidently an infrequent preacher was considered better than no preacher at all, and Drant's plea was acceded to "in consideration that he is a preacher, and may do much good abroad in the country thereby".[3]

Now that he was no longer a member of the chapter, Bishop Curteys's task of capitular reform depended upon his supporters having a majority among the canons residentiary. Moreover, he had to find benefices for his administrative lieutenants; both comfortable benefices and housing could be found for them in the chapter. At the same time, Curteys was faced with the continuing enmity of William Overton and his faction within the chapter, and the bishop resorted to the unscrupulous means of packing the chapter with his followers, who then tried to dominate the chapter and to exclude Overton's party from the conduct of chapter affairs.

The quarrel between the factions led by William Overton and Bishop Curteys came to the surface at a chapter meeting on 20 July 1573. Overton, as treasurer and president of the chapter, Francis Coxe and Richard Kitson held a "rump" meeting of the chapter to protest against certain actions of Anthony Rushe, the new dean, and Henry Worley, who were members of the bishop's party. Apparently, Rushe and Worley had held their own extraordinary chapter meeting in the

[1] Ibid., no. 751. [2] Ibid., no. 752. [3] Ibid., no. 756.

treasury on 20 April, where certain protestations for residence, leases and patents had been confirmed "with the consent of certain persons summoned, though having no right to complete the quorum". They specifically objected to Henry Blaxton, another of Curteys's men, being admitted as a residentiary without their consent, and probably they were attacking indirectly Curteys's grant to Worley of the offices of chancellor and commissary.[1] Ralph Barlow, the chapter registrar, another member of Overton's faction and who himself was to become involved in a quarrel with Bishop Curteys at a later time, wrote this account of the transaction of business when Rushe and Worley held their meeting:

"In the absence of the majority of the residentiaries who should compose a just and lawful chapter, Worley forced the Chapter chest open, or picked their locks with the help of a blacksmith, took out the seal, and sealed the leases and confirmed patents and grants of next presentation, regardless of their admission oath to keep the statutes and approved customs which forbid bringing novelties into the church without general consent."[2]

The result of this affair was that the chapter, or at least the Overton faction, forced Bishop Curteys to promulgate new statutes, which would prevent a repetition of these abuses in the future. That it was this particular incident that caused the dissident residentiaries to press for satisfaction of their grievances in general is clearly revealed by the statutes themselves. The first statute stated that no lease, patent, confirmation, grant or any act was to be confirmed and sealed with the chapter seal except at four specified times a year, when the dean "and most part of the Residentiaries [should] then be present besides

[1] *Ibid.*, no. 777. Quite possibly Overton's faction were also resentful of the grant to Curteys's brother Edmund of the next presentation of Cuckfield vicarage. Since Edmund had already been instituted to the vicarage in 1571, this means that he could pick his own successor. This was one of the methods by which Curteys intended to perpetuate his reforms. See J. H. Cooper, *A History of the Parish of Cuckfield* (Haywards Heath, Sussex: 1912), p. 38.

[2] Peckham, *Act Book A*, no. 777.

the Dean".[1] The second statute prescribed that no one was to be admitted a residentiary

"except he do first severally ask the good will of the Dean and every one of the Residentiaries for the time being, and also have the consent of the Dean and more part of the Residentiaries beside the Dean."

The third statute was intended to prevent a recurrence of Worley's lock-picking activities. This incident still had not been forgotten when, some seventeen years later, Bishop Thomas Bickley complained that these statutes were hampering business, and the chapter were quick to recall that

"the late Dean, Dr. Rush, before the making of the statutes, having anything to be confirmed or granted under Chapter Seale for his own private commodity was wont to watch his time and take opportunity, when most of the Residentiaries were from home, and drawing one or two of his Faction, to grant and confirme with Chapter Seale what hee would, not making an Act of record in writing what was passed or done."[2]

On 20 October 1573 Henry Worley and Henry Blaxton were compelled to swear an oath to observe the recently decreed statutes, and William Overton, Francis Coxe and Richard Kitson "promised to do so as soon as the Dean is in Chapter to do the like".[3] Blaxton's name was the first on the list of those who wrote and signed the testimonial to Bishop Curteys in 1577. Another signer, and member of the bishop's party, was Thomas Gillingham, prebendary of Firles, who sought permission to become a residentiary on 2 May 1575 and was accepted forthwith. A few days later he was installed as archdeacon of Chichester on a mandate of the bishop.[4] Thus Curteys continued to pack his friends into the chapter, but if he had gained a temporary advantage from this struggle, it would be little

[1] *Statutes and Constitutions of the Cathedral Church of Chichester*, ed. F. G. Bennett *et al.* (Chichester: 1904), pp. 22–8, statute 1. The statutes were promulgated 15 October 1573.

[2] DRO, Chapter Statute Book B., fo. 26v, quoted in Peckham, *Act Book A*, no. 777n.

[3] Peckham, *Act Book A*, no. 796.

[4] *Ibid.*, no. 790.

comfort when his enemies among the residentiaries had allied themselves with the gentry of Sussex and the citizens of Chichester and when his friends began to desert him.

Similar methods were sometimes used in gaining control of the parish churches of Sussex. Curteys was able to confer benefices on most of his clerical supporters in Sussex, but in several cases he had to resort to a stratagem often used by Puritans—that of intruding these clerics as lecturers into a parish where the incumbent could not be dislodged. Most of the parish clergy held benefices that had been endowed with land since medieval times, and it was extremely difficult for a bishop to pry an incumbent loose from his benefice, which was considered a freehold at law. Since the common law courts did not even recognize a connection between title to the tithes attached to a benefice and performance of spiritual duties pertaining thereto, episcopal courts could hardly deprive an incumbent for mere lack of zeal. The more zealous of Protestant reformers hit upon the idea of endowing a lectureship in such cases, which would bypass the authority of the parson or vicar, and enable a worthy preacher to spread the gospel. It has been found that at least three and possibly four of the clergymen who signed the testimonial to Curteys in 1557 possessed extraordinary lectureships of this type[1]—probably endowed by wealthy London merchants.

One such lecturer was Richard Fletcher, member of a gifted literary family, who became "minister", or more properly lecturer of Rye about 1574.[2] Fletcher was very popular

[1] This information is based on a list very kindly given to me by Mr W. D. Peckham, who is currently engaged in compiling an exhaustive *Fasti*, or list of all clergy in the diocese of Chichester from early times to 1845. One of these extra-parochial lecturers, Samuel Norden, a presbyterian, was later beneficed, but deprived in 1605.

[2] Richard Fletcher, the father of the dramatist John Fletcher and the brother of Giles Fletcher the elder, who is perhaps best remembered for the description of his travels in Russia, was ordained by Bishop Ridley in 1550. He was educated at Trinity College, Cambridge, and became a fellow of Corpus Christi College, a veritable hotbed of radicalism in 1569. In 1595, as bishop-elect of London, he was a member of the group, headed by archbishop Whitgift, that was instrumental in drawing up the Lambeth Articles, which effected an accommodation of Calvinist doctrines with the official articles of faith of the Church of England. Queen Elizabeth was most dis-

with the mayor and jurats of Rye, who wrote to Bishop Curteys on 20 September 1576 complaining that there was such confusion over who should exercise ecclesiastical jurisdiction within the town that spiritual chaos prevailed. They themselves were loath to act in the matter "lest it shuld be laid to our charge we ponishe suche crymes as merely dothe apperteyne unto the spirituall jurisdiction".[1] As one of the Cinque Ports, Rye technically was not a part of the county of Sussex and came under the jurisdiction of the lord warden of the Cinque Ports rather than the lord lieutenant of Sussex, but no one was sure who should exercise the spiritual power in these crosscurrents of jurisdiction.[2]

In his reply to the corporation of Rye Bishop Curteys acknowledged that "you made request unto me that the ecclesiasticall jurisdiction might be exercysed within your Porte of Rye". In order to make Fletcher's status somewhat more regular, Curteys had made Fletcher a "chapleyne", but he asked for a "helpynge hande so to sett forwarde the matter as that he maye as well have the lyvynge and vycaridge as he have the troble and charge of your towne".[3] There is no explanation why there was difficulty in obtaining the vicarage for Fletcher, and one must fall back on surmises: very likely a vicar was there already, although he may have been non-resident, or the patron of the

---

pleased and very severely reprimanded the authors and condemned their doctrines. Before this rather rash act, Fletcher had been a royal chaplain, enjoying the queen's favour and rapidly gaining advancement. Sir John Harrington wrote of him that "he could preach well and speak boldly, and yet keep decorum. He knew what would please the queen and would adventure on that though that offended others." *D.N.B.*, *sub* Richard Fletcher.

[1] Hist. MSS. Comm., [Rye Corporation MSS.] xiii (4), 45–6.

[2] According to a list of ecclesiastical divisions of Sussex printed in the *V.C.H. Sussex*, II, 42–4, based on the *Taxatio* of 1291, Rye was in the rural deanery of Hastings, which was within the archdeaconry of Lewes. The bishop of Chichester certainly exercised jurisdiction there as late as 1538, when Bishop Sampson placed a certain Mr Welles in charge of Rye parish church. *Ibid.*, II, 18. That the elders of Rye could not remember who possessed ordinary authority in Rye certainly lends substance to my argument that the continuity of ecclesiastical administration was disrupted between the episcopates of Bishops Sherburne and Curteys. See Chapter 3.

[3] Hist. MSS. Comm., [Rye Corporation MSS] xiii (4). 45–6.

living had no liking for the zealous Mr Fletcher. Unfortunately, Rye does not appear in any of the Elizabethan visitation returns for the archdeaconry of Lewes, which are very incomplete. In May 1576 the mayor and jurats of Rye sent a rather vague certificate to the bishop of Chichester testifying that

"Richard Fletcher, M.A. . . . being called hither of such as have the dealing in that behalf, to preach in the church of Rye, both administered the sacraments as becomes a good minister of Jesus Christ and no less in the other life amongst us visiting our sick with diligence and doing his duty to the good example of the people."[1]

The joint endeavours of Bishop Curteys and the jurats of Rye to build a little model Christian commonwealth offer quite a contrast to the hostility that Curteys's reforming efforts aroused among the gentry of Sussex and the citizens of Chichester. Whereas Rye was apparently already a Protestant town even before the arrival of Fletcher, the social influence of the Catholic gentry of Sussex still had not been broken when Curteys's reforming zeal began to be felt nor had the commission of the peace been thoroughly purged.[2] Technically not a part of the county of Sussex, the municipal oligarchy of Rye, unlike the ruling classes of Chichester and Sussex, had nothing to fear from Curteys's exercise of the temporal magistracy.[3]

The main task facing Curteys as bishop of Chichester was to enforce religious uniformity among the gentry. Put very simply, his plan of action was to delay an encounter between himself and the gentry until he felt that his position was sufficiently strong. Picking a time when the threat of invasion seemed imminent, all of those even remotely suspected of being Catholic, whether they conformed outwardly or not, were to be summoned together before the bishop in a specially-staged consistory in the cathedral where Curteys naively hoped

---

[1] *Ibid.*, xiii (4), 52. Fletcher was still preaching at Rye in May 1582, when a similar certificate was sent to the bishop of Chichester. *Ibid.*, xiii (4), 81.

[2] See Chapter 12.

[3] For a discussion of Curteys's activities as a temporal magistrate, see Chapter 5. Curteys was on the commission of the peace for the county of Sussex. Rye and the Cinque Ports had separate commissions.

that they would be overawed. At the same time the bishop and his ecclesiastical lieutenants would use their authority in executing their commissions of the peace and other temporal commissions from the crown to destroy the economic power of those among the gentry who opposed Curteys and to counteract their social influence.[1] That the reaction of the gentry would be violent, that they would complain to the Privy Council and win a sympathetic hearing, in short, that the whole business would blow up in his face, would not have surprised a more realistic man than Richard Curteys.

This excessively dramatic showdown between himself and the Sussex gentry was postponed by Curteys until the spring of 1577. The delay was not due to want of energy, since Curteys seems to have set the machinery in motion for conducting his first visitation very shortly after his installation.[2] Getting control of the chapter was the most immediate task not only because of the necessity of finding benefices and housing for Curteys's chief lieutenants within the cathedral close but also because of the constitutional relationship between the bishop and the chapter. Curteys seems to have attempted to have his showdown with the gentry in 1573, but the move was premature and resulted only in the Privy Council appointing a special commission of enquiry to investigate some unspecified charges against Curteys made by Sir Thomas Palmer the elder and George Goring.[3] Curteys appears to have contemplated another attempt to bring about complete conformity among the Catholic and crypto-Catholic gentry in 1575 when he

---

[1] See Chapter 5.

[2] Bishops were required to hold visitations of their dioceses within the first year of their episcopates. Curteys certainly wasted no time in preparing for his first visitation: he was installed as bishop of Chichester on 30 May 1570; the Register of the Stationers Company records that a licence was issued before 22 July to have Curteys's visitation articles and injunctions printed. B.M., Add. MS. 39,355, fo. 168v. Unfortunately there are no visitation returns until 1572 for the archdeaconry of Chichester, and there is a gap from 1575 to 1579; in the archdeaconry of Lewes there are no returns until 1580. Those that do survive for the 1570s tell us very little. The possibility is not to be discounted that earlier ones for the reign of Elizabeth never existed because of the chaos in episcopal administration.

[3] Acts P.C., VIII, 166. It was only the intercession of the earl of Leicester that saved Curteys from total disgrace on this occasion.

sought and received a letter from the Privy Council authorizing him to confer individually with the recusants and suspected crypto-Catholics. But Curteys was admonished that difficult cases should be left for the Privy Council to deal with.[1] If his detractors are to be believed, Curteys did nothing until March 1577, when instead of conferring with the suspected recusants or crypto-Catholics individually, he chose to confront a good part of the Sussex gentry all at once in a series of two consistories held in Chichester Cathedral on 2 and 17 March.[2]

Curteys's tactlessness had already been revealed in the abortive attempt to reform St John's College and in his relations with the Cathedral Chapter, but his reckless way of holding the consistory of 2 March 1577 surpassed all of his previous indiscretions. The response of those whom Curteys had summoned was so indignant that Richard Curteys and his party of reform found themselves forced back onto the defensive and faced with the necessity of justifying their actions to the government. The preface to Curteys's *Christes Naturall Body*, published in 1577, sought to give the impression that Curteys's enemies were nothing more than "Machevils, Papistes, Libertines, Atheists, and other erronious persons . . .", but it did not try to hide the fact that the opposition was very extensive.

". . . Most bitter and bad speeches are throwne out against hym [Curteys]; yea, and certayne [men] hyred and suborned to go from Noble man to Noble man, from Justiciaries, to Justiciaries, from common table, to common table, and to be briefe, from place and person, to place and person, to carry such tales & surmises as the enformer knoweth to be false, and the reporter is mere ignorant of."[3]

The summoning of some thirty-five people, the greater part of them members of the gentry, to appear before the bishop himself in an open consistory in the cathedral before all the

[1] S.P., Dom., Eliz., 112/13. I.
[2] *Ibid.* Actually, Curteys's enemies admitted that some of them had conferred with the bishop, but had found his terms unacceptable, and were therefore obliged to attend the consistory. *Ibid.*, 112/35.
[3] Curteys, *Christes Naturall Body*, unpaginated.

people of Chichester not only seemed calculated to embarrass those summoned, it also smacked of an attempt to revive medieval prelatical power. What were the reasons that led Curteys to proceed against the accused persons in such an extraordinary way? Curteys's explanation to the Privy Council was that the people of Sussex were generally "backward in religion" and grew worse upon hearing the report that Don John of Austria, the bastard half-brother of Philip II, was now in the Low Countries, and an invasion was rumoured. Moreover, recusants from Kent, Surrey and Hampshire had been seeking refuge with friends and relatives in Sussex to escape harrassment in their own counties. Curteys complained that he particularly had trouble with crypto-Catholics, those who "pretende well, and yet be not sound in relligion", who were the leaders of the faction which beset him. He wished to have these individuals, who feigned to be well-affected in religion, "cleane putte owte of the Commission of the Peace", or at the very least he desired that writs of Dedimus Potestatem be issued to compel these individuals to take oaths affirming the queen's supremacy at the next quarter sessions. Local office-holders, such as sheriffs and J.P.s, had been required by law to swear the oath of supremacy since 1563,[1] but Curteys stated that it was "comonly and crediblye thoughte, that some of them never tooke that othe, although it be otherwise returned".[2]

Bishop Curteys's assessment of the religious situation in Sussex was essentially correct, although the danger of Catholic disloyalty was very much exaggerated. Catholics still remained in the commission of the peace,[3] but only at the price of occasional conformity. That most of the thirty-five or so people[4] summoned to attend the consistory of 2 March 1577 were recusants is not to be doubted. Their names were returned time and time again as recusants. Everyone agreed

[1] 5 Eliz. I, cap. 1.
[2] S.P., Dom., Eliz., 111/45, 112/7.
[3] See Chapter 12 section i for a discussion of this problem.
[4] Bishop Curteys's list (S.P., Dom., Eliz., 111/45) has 32 names, of whom one was a knight, two were yeomen, four were clergymen, and the rest were esquires and gentlemen. The list submitted to the Privy Council by Sir Thomas and the gentry (Ibid., 112/13. I) gives 33 names, of whom one was a knight and the remainder were esquires or gentlemen.

that intractable papists had to be removed from public office. Where Curteys went wrong was in his treatment of crypto-Catholics who conformed for the sake of retaining public office and their positions of influence in the community; for it was semi-official government policy that such persons were to be encouraged to conform by the lure of public office. As it turned out, three of the men whom Curteys accused of feigning conformity commanded a great deal of influence among the Sussex gentry and were to become the leaders of the opposition to Curteys. These three were: Sir Thomas Palmer of Parham (d. 1582), Thomas Lewkenor of Selsey (c. 1538–95), and Richard Ernley. All were J.P.s during the 1570s and also executed other commissions of the crown.

In 1564 "Sir Thomas Palmer of Gadwode, knight" was listed by Bishop Barlow among the justices of the peace favourably disposed to the religious settlement, although the bishop felt obliged to qualify his statement by saying that Sir Thomas was "a fainte furtherer" of the Protestant religion.[1] In the 1569 metropolitical visitation it was found that he had harboured a deprived Marian priest as chaplain, who also frequented the homes of other Catholic gentry, and that he refused to receive communion except at home in his own chapel.[2] Both Sir Thomas Palmer of Parham and his son-in-law, Sir Thomas Palmer of Angmering, were prominent among the Sussex magistracy: besides serving a term as sheriff, the elder knight was one of the three deputy lieutenants of Sussex from November 1569, presumably until his death in 1582, while the younger knight was sheriff in 1572–73 and was also a deputy lieutenant after 23 July 1585.[3] But so far as can be determined,

[1] "A Collection of Original Letters from the Bishop to the Privy Council", ed. Mary Bateson, *Camden Society Miscellany*, IX, 8–11. There is no confusion about Palmer's identity, because Parham was not built until later and was completed only in 1577. He was also called at a later date Sir Thomas Palmer the elder to distinguish him from his son-in-law and cousin, Sir Thomas Palmer of Angmering, sometimes called Sir Thomas Palmer the younger, who was not knighted until 12 August 1573. P.R.O. *List of Sheriffs*, List of sheriffs for Sussex and Surrey.

[2] S.P., Dom., Eliz., 60/71, printed in *V.C.H. Sussex*, II, 24–6.

[3] Joyce E. Mousley, "Sussex Country Gentry in the Reign of Elizabeth" (London, Ph.D. thesis, 1955), pp. 279–80.

Sir Thomas of Parham's only son, William Palmer, was never in the commission of the peace—a very difficult thing to explain, unless it was on account of his religion. For, in 1571 a writ of Dedimus Potestatem was issued out of Chancery to force William Palmer to receive the sacrament.[1] It is very curious that the government should feel it necessary to issue a special commission to force a private person to communicate according to the established rite. Evidently, the whole family were under great pressure to conform. At the archidiaconal visitation of 1579 the churchwardens of Parham parish presented over twenty parishioners for communicating infrequently. "Sir Thomas Pallmer the elder and my ladie receved but once last yere & that [was] at eastar." William also received only once while his wife communicated twice.[2] Equally revealing is the fact that Sir Thomas the elder had several connections with other prominent Catholic families.[3] Sir Thomas Palmer of Parham was a weak man for whom the lure of public office proved irresistible, but yet he did not want to sever his remaining ties with the old religion.

The evidence that Thomas Lewkenor and Richard Ernley were crypto-Catholics is not as strong as that which has been presented in the case of Sir Thomas Palmer of Parham, but it is still convincing—at least in the case of Thomas Lewkenor. Thomas Lewkenor was first mentioned by Bishop Barlow in

---

[1] P.R.O., Chancery 202/144, 26 June, 12 Eliz. So far as can be ascertained, this document is unique; in this same box of documents are to be found many certificates testifying that sheriffs had sworn the oath of supremacy, but all other individuals concerned were office holders except William Palmer. (I owe this reference to the kindness of Professor S. T. Bindoff.)

[2] B.M., Add. MS. 39,454, fos. 42–3v.

[3] Sir Thomas Palmer of Parham's first wife was Griselda Bridget, the daughter of John Caryll of Warnham, while his sister Elizabeth had married the same John Caryll. His daughter Elizabeth married John Leedes of Wappingthorne in Steyning parish, who was a lifelong recusant and for some time a Catholic exile. While John Leedes was still in exile overseas, his wife —probably very homesick, if not physically ill—returned to the home of her father, who, hounded by the bishop of Chichester, dared not receive her without permission from the Privy Council. *Parham in Sussex*, ed. J. W. Fitzwilliam, (London: 1947), pp. 40–1; Eleanor Lloyd, "Leedes of Wappingthorne", *S.A.C.*, LIV, 37 ff.; *Acts P.C.*, X, 50.

1564 as a "myslyker of godlie orders";[1] yet, although he was not then a justice of the peace he subsequently became one in 1575 and remained in the commission until the year of his death—and this despite the fact that it was known that he maintained close connections with Catholic relatives.[2] In 1586 he was returned as a member of parliament for Midhurst. His brother, Sir Richard of West Dean, an eminent lawyer who later became chief justice of Chester, was also at this time a Sussex J.P. as well as being recorder of Chichester; he had sat in the 1572 Parliament as the junior citizen for the city of Chichester. The Lewkenors pretty well ran things in the rape of Chichester, and their influence was becoming increasingly felt within the city of Chichester.[3] Whatever the religious beliefs of Thomas Lewkenor were, it does not appear that he or his family conformed to the established church with marked enthusiasm, for at the visitation of 1579 the parish church-warden of Upmarden wrote: "I present that Mr Thomas Lewkner Justice hath never bene at Church but foure times and at Eastar he received the comunyon".[4]

These were the men who Curteys believed were only feigning conformity. Their indignant reaction to being per-sonally summoned to appear at a visitation held in consistory had so alarmed the bishop that he felt compelled to explain his actions to the Privy Council even before Sir Thomas Palmer and his friends had drawn up their complaint. In a letter written on 6 April 1577,[5] Curteys admitted that he had threatened them by mentioning certain letters from the Privy Council and by reminding them that he was an ecclesiastical commissioner,

---

[1] Bateson, *loc. cit.*, pp. 8–11. He was described here as "Thomas Lewknour of Tangmer"; he did not acquire his lease of part of the episcopal manor of Selsey until 1578. John Comber, *Sussex Genealogies* (Cambridge: 1931), Lewes Centre, 153.

[2] See Chapter 12.

[3] Neale, *The Elizabethan House of Commons* (London: 1949), pp. 263ff.

[4] B.M., Add. MS. 39,454, fo. 5. At the same time the churchwardens of Westwittering reported that Richard Ernley had a certain Mr Nevell staying with him as a guest for several weeks at Eastertime. Nevell had married Thomas Lewkenor's daughter Mary, and neither husband nor wife came to church the whole time they were staying with Ernley. *Ibid.*, fo. 14.

[5] S.P., Dom., Eliz., 112/9.

yet he maintained that he had convoked the visitation entirely on the basis of his ordinary authority. That much of the trouble was due to the bishop's tactlessness is candidly revealed in his own words: "Thinckinge with my selfe I mighte be both blamed & charged yf I called some & lefte oute others, I thoughte good to ryte them all." Yet Curteys stoutly denied that those summoned had to appear if they were innocent: there were several alternatives. A man who felt himself wrongly accused could be discharged from the necessity of attending the consistory in Chichester Cathedral if he could obtain a certificate from the curate and churchwardens of his parish testifying to his soundness in religion. Or, if "notwithstandinge anie thinge paste" he promised in writing that he would conform in the future, then the bishop would give his assurance that the individual would be released from the necessity of appearing. If such person would only "admitte charitable & learned conference" and see the bishop personally before the day appointed for the consistory, then Curteys promised all the "tyme & respytte, which they could reasonably desier". Only those who had refused these alternatives had to appear. Curteys said that he realized that most of the people summoned, being uncompromising Catholics, would leave the county if they had not already done so, and that others would take advantage of the opportunity to come see him privately. Only a dozen of those summoned actually showed up at the consistory, of which six "did not well lyke and reedely [readily] obey the proceedings". Of these latter six discontented individuals, three were Palmer, Lewkenor and Ernley; the other three seem to have been citizens of Chichester.[1]

The visitation articles of enquiry which Curteys put to the accused persons sought to determine how often they had attended common prayer in their parish churches since 1 January 1576, how often they had communicated and how many sermons they had attended. Curteys then went on to enquire whether any of them possessed books by Catholic

[1] *Ibid.*, 112/30. Two of these men were Thomas Andrewes and Richard Lyne, who, Curteys says, had been presented by the churchwardens at a recent visitation, and the other was probably Ralph Chauntler. For the opposition of the citizens of Chichester to Curteys see Chapter 5.

polemicists, or whether any of them had sent letters or money to Catholic exiles. The remaining articles sought to ascertain how many members of their households were religiously disaffected.[1] Curteys stated that these articles had been drawn up four years previously by the earl of Leicester, who ordered that they be asked at all visitations.[2]

When Sir Thomas Palmer, Thomas Lewkenor and Richard Ernley complained about Curteys's actions to the Privy Council,[3] they charged that the bishop's motive for summoning them was based on malice rather than any failure to conform in matters of religion. The bishop of Chichester was accused of trying to discredit them in the eyes of the common people, of whom they felt themselves the natural leaders as justices of the peace, and in the eyes of the Privy Council. They maintained that they did come to church for common prayer and to hear sermons and occasionally received the communion, and that they had sworn the oath acknowledging the queen's supremacy in spiritual matters.

They further felt that the bishop's method of conducting the visitation was not only tactless, but showed a total want of discretion—that it was a "great oversighte of the saide Lord Byshoppe to appointe so great a number of gentellmen of such worshippe and callinge to appeare in suche an open place all at one daye, tyme, and instante". This was at the session of the consistory court held on 2 March. Yet Curteys apparently did not think that he had made his point by summoning the better part of the gentry of Sussex to appear before him on that day, and he ordered them to assemble again at another consistory on the 17th of the same month. Palmer and his fellows pointed out the great danger of quarrels and fights that might arise when so many servants and retainers were assembled in a small market town and cathedral city with nothing to do but await the pleasure of their masters. Nor had the bishop allowed this

[1] Ibid., 111/45.
[2] Ibid., 112/33.
[3] Ibid., 112/13, 112/13. I. This first verbal attack against the bishop of Chichester, dated 13 April 1577, was sent to the earl of Arundel, a leading Catholic and eventually found its way into the hands of the Privy Council. The authors asked Arundel to secure for them an impartial hearing of their dispute with Curteys before the Privy Council.

situation to go unexploited: his own servants had offered unwarranted provocation to the assembled serving-men of the gentry, hoping to discredit the accused persons by the quarrels that would naturally follow. Another complaint told of how two of the accused gentlemen, who were justices of the peace, had been handed a summons by one of the bishop's men as they sat conducting the quarter sessions in the city of Chichester.

The bishop's enemies told of how, on 2 March, the day appointed for the first consistory, he had ridden into Chichester from his house at Aldingbourne

"with manie more servants the[n] he was accustomed to ride withall well weaponed, which with theire weapons stode aboute the consystorie all the tyme of his Lordship's sittinge, and a servante of his Lordship being regestor [registrar] had his sworde holden in the consistory by him by a somner, which heretofore hath not binne seene."

Upon appearing at the consistory, the first act of the gentlemen summoned was to ask to see the letters from the Privy Council that the bishop had so vaguely alluded to in support of his action in summoning them. Sir Thomas maintained that the letter read to them was dated sometime in November 1575 and conveyed the queen's pleasure that the bishop of Chichester should call before him such gentlemen as refused to conform themselves, where conference should be used to persuade them to come to church. However, the queen's instructions were that "no rigor or hard dealinges should be vsed", and where the bishop concluded that conference was of no avail in dealing with recalcitrant Catholic gentry, their names were to be certified to the Privy Council, after which the matter would be withdrawn from episcopal jurisdiction. Yet Bishop Curteys in the year and a half since the letter was received from the Privy Council had not summoned any of them for conference or warning until the day when he summoned them all, although some of them lived right in Chichester or very close by, and had been "divers & sundrie tymes in his companie, both in his owne howse and ells where".

There is no doubt that Curteys, as the ordinary of the

diocese of Chichester, had the authority to summon these people before him. That would be in conformity with both parliamentary legislation and canonical usage. But, of course, a naked display of power, however legitimate its source of authority, always breeds resentment. Sir Thomas Palmer and his friends felt that the letter from the Privy Council in 1575 had temporarily superseded Curteys's authority in this matter. That Curteys bothered to mention the letter at all shows that he feared that his authority alone would not have been sufficient to command obedience and that otherwise no one would have appeared at the consistory of 2 March. The bishop's enemies said that it was common knowledge that Curteys had been severely reprimanded by the Privy Council for his methods after the abortive attempt of 1573 to get the gentry to conform, and that only the intercession of the earl of Leicester had saved him from total disgrace.[1]

Since that time, Sir Thomas Palmer and his associates among the Sussex gentry maintained that Curtey's methods had become more inquisitorial than ever. When some of their number had gone to see the bishop of Chichester prior to the consistory of 2 March to clear themselves, he had insisted that they swear that they "kepte no companie with anie that were backward in religion". The gentry found this most objectionable and told the bishop that they could swear no such oath, maintaining that "we cannott take knowledge of everymans religion and conscience that cometh into our companie".[2] At the consistory of 2 March they had promised to reform any points of error that arose from ignorance.

"And if for lacke of knowledge we have omytted anie thing that we should have don we promysed to amend it hereafter to the best of our powers wisheing all other to do the like, yet his Lordship woulde not discharge vs but verie rigorouslie woulde have enforced vs vpon paine of the lawe to have sworne to aunsweres to a number of hard and captious articles by his Lordship devised and some of them being suche as his Lordship had no aucthorite to enquire of."[3]

The essence of the problem was that Curteys's fanaticism and

[1] *Ibid.*, 112/34.   [2] *Ibid.*, 112/35.   [3] *Ibid.*

inquisitorial methods clashed with the attitude of practical tolerance that the Sussex gentry felt was dictated by the special conditions of local politics in Sussex. Tudor social policy was conservative: Elizabeth's government was always reluctant to disturb the existing social order. The central government was obliged to select its local agents from among the natural leaders of society. Since religious attitudes were still very traditional among many of the Sussex gentry during the 1570s, the government had to be satisfied with outward conformity from men like Sir Thomas Palmer, Thomas Lewkenor and Richard Ernley. Time favoured the success of a moderate religious policy that could be content with a public display of religious loyalty in the classical Roman sense.

When the complaint about Curteys's methods reached the Privy Council the matter was turned over to Sir Francis Walsingham and Sir Walter Mildmay, a pair of Puritans who were not likely to be well-disposed towards a bumbling bishop. The letter in which the Privy Council notified Curteys of their action has not been found, but its contents were sufficient to induce a more humble tone in the bishop of Chichester, who, although he denied the charges made by Sir Thomas Palmer and his friends, wrote that he was very sorry his "dealynges have breadd great offence".[1] Although not bound to do so by law, he offered "recompence . . . according to the judgements" of the Privy Council, and, like a chastised schoolboy, he promised to amend his demeanour in the future. Implying that his enemies were attacking him for other than religious reasons, Curteys asked to be relieved from the many temporal duties that he had been performing.

"As I perceyve my dealynge in temporall causes hath bredd greater offence then I supposed it would, I most humbly beseeche your Lordships that I may be hereafter excused from hauyng to doe in such businesse, that I may the better entende my proper office of preaching and prayer."

Apparently Curteys misunderstood the letter that the Privy Council had written to him, or else his tone was not sufficiently humble. The next letter from the Council to Curteys—which

[1] S.P., Dom. (Add.) Eliz., 25/14.

unfortunately has not been found—must have been quite vitriolic, for it certainly appears to have frightened Curteys. It would seem that Curteys had been ordered to appear as quickly as possible before the Council to answer the complaints made about his behaviour. Curteys either conveyed the impression to the Council that he did not intend to hurry or else he chose to ignore their command completely, for in his reply he felt compelled to swear an oath that he meant no disrespect: "Before God I speake it, it never entered my thought, and God forbyd I should lyue the howre, that I should not appeare vpon your Lordships' pleasures".[1]

From this time to the end of his career, vexed as he was by attacks from all sides as his enemies began to unite against him, Richard Curteys's influence was to decline as he became enmeshed in a web of intrigues. Although his efforts to provide better preaching in the diocese of Chichester were bearing fruit among the common people, the protracted struggle with the chapter, and later with the Sussex gentry and the citizens of Chichester, increasingly wasted his time and energy. If the struggle between Bishop Curteys and the Sussex gentry were studied only in terms of the actual enforcement of religious conformity, it would remain a puzzle as to why Curteys put off dealing with the gentry for so long. It has been seen that Curteys was not content with mere compliance with the Acts of Supremacy and Uniformity—outward conformity could never satisfy a zealot such as Curteys who wanted to convert the inner man as well. The next chapter will suggest that both Curteys and the gentry viewed this struggle in broader terms than religion alone; and that Curteys had already been at work to undermine the social and economic influence of the Catholic and crypto-Catholic gentry even before the dramatic confrontation that occured on 2 March 1577. The fact was that Richard Curteys acted under the assumption that those who could not be converted entirely were adversaries who must be destroyed. Only a study of the economic and social aspects of this struggle can explain the vehemence with which Curteys's enemies attacked him.

[1] S.P., Dom., Eliz. 112/20.

5

BISHOP CURTEYS AND THE
TEMPORAL MAGISTRACY

THE INTENSE ANTIPATHY towards Richard Curteys was caused not only by his aggressive religious policy as displayed in the episcopal visitation of 1577, but also by his exercise of temporal powers and the threat which his exercise of these temporal powers offered to vested economic interests. Indeed, as Curteys's enemies among the gentry and the citizens of Chichester mounted their attack upon him, it became increasingly obvious that the religious issue was fading into the background. The conflict had become basically social in nature: this was a struggle to see who would "beare rule".[1] In an arrogant mood, Curteys, according to his detractors, had once boasted that he would be "Aut Caesar aut nullus".[2] For their part, Sir Thomas Palmer and his allies among the ruling oligarchy of the county of Sussex and the city of Chichester were equally determined to defend, if not actually to increase, the social leadership and economic power which they wielded both as property owners and as justices of the peace.

Besides his spiritual jurisdiction as bishop of Chichester and member of the Court of High Commission, Richard Curteys also had many temporal powers granted him by his commission of the peace and by other special commissions from the crown. Moreover, Curteys's exercise of the temporal magistracy was thought to be even more arbitrary than the reckless way in which he had used his spiritual powers. Curteys admitted his own ignorance of the common law, and he made many mistakes in procedure, which his enemies were quick to point out. On several occasions, it was said that he had caused individuals to be summoned before the lord treasurer without "any iust cause".[3] If he desired to arrest someone for a temporal offence, he would serve the warrant through his own servants rather than through the sheriff or the bailiffs appointed for that purpose. Presumably, forgetfulness entered into some of these

[1] S.P., Dom., Eliz., 112/37.   [2] *Ibid.*, 112/32.   [3] *Ibid.*, 112/31.

negligences such as when he forgot to certify the recognizances that he had taken or when he bound over certain persons for appearance at the quarter sessions and assizes, but forgot to exhibit any charges against them when they appeared.[1]

As a member of the commission of the peace, the bishop of Chichester held precedence above the rank of baron, but below that of viscount. As such, Curteys outranked all of the members of the untitled gentry on the commission of the peace, for the role of peers was nominal and the real work was done by the knights and esquires. In a rural society where social rank was so important, Curteys's own obscure social origins caused him to be held in contempt. A house full of penurious relatives and bad management of episcopal lands strained the finances of the bishopric of Chichester (already weakened by the plundering of episcopal revenues) to the utmost, and when Curteys died the bishopric was impoverished. Living in a decaying house at Aldingbourne, just outside Chichester, Bishop Curteys was in no position to cut a figure among the gentry by providing abundant hospitality.[2] Never accepted by the gentry, he appears to have chosen his friends from among a half-dozen or so citizens of Chichester.

All of this made Curteys very sensitive about his standing in the community. It led him to denigrate the men whom he had claimed he was trying to convert. Sir Thomas Palmer relates that after the first complaint made by him and his friends concerning Curteys in 1573, the Privy Council had heard the case and dismissed it hoping that the "Lord Bishop woulde . . . have reformed in himselfe all faults and disorders . . ." and would in the future show a "charitable Mynde" towards the complainants, but instead Curteys returned to Chichester and "caused to be spred abrode by his servants" the rumour that Palmer had been greatly rebuked by the Privy Council, who took him to be "but an olde foole".[3] On another occasion Curteys had called Thomas Lewkenor of Selsey "a proude

---

[1] Ibid.

[2] The episcopal manor house at Aldingbourne, which served as the bishop's palace because of the lack of a residence in Chichester, was in such a bad state of repair that it had to be pulled down in the seventeenth century.

[3] S.P., Dom., Eliz., 112/30.

arrogante foole"; and he admitted to the Privy Council that he had propagated the rumour that Lewkenor "hath no landes nor lyvinge and is of very simple credite in his countrie" and was very much in debt to London merchants and money-lenders.[1] Again, although the three citizens of Chichester, who were summoned to the consistory of 2 March 1577, were described on the list drawn up by Sir Thomas Palmer and his associates as gentlemen, Curteys maintained that they were "no gentlemen, or at le[a]st some of them are nothing in the subsidy book".[2] If the Sussex gentry considered these three to be gentlemen—a matter about which they were better informed than Curteys, who was not a native of Sussex—then Curteys's remarks can only be considered a calculated affront.

These were the factors that caused Sir Thomas Palmer and his friends to take the side of all "other people in that countie fynding themselves greeved"[3] and to attempt to have Curteys removed from the commission of the peace. This they undertook to do by charging Curteys with offences of such magnitude that the Privy Council would be compelled to take action against him. When Curteys maintained that Palmer and his friends had no right to make complaints for other people unless they possessed proxies or power of attorney, the latter retorted that they, as justices of the peace, had a general right to seek redress of such injuries.[4]

In a series of letters to the Privy Council in the spring of 1577, Sir Thomas Palmer, his friends and their allies set forth a long list of articles specifying instances of misconduct by Bishop Curteys. Besides the general charge of using his powers deriving from both the temporal and the spiritual magistracies to further his own ambition and to discredit his enemies, Sir Thomas Palmer and his friends accused Curteys of disregarding the proper procedures under common law;[5] of abusing his powers as a commissioner for regulating the grain trade in

[1] *Ibid.*, 112/29.I. Although Lewkenor must have possessed freehold land somewhere—possibly at Tangmere, his principal seat was the episcopal manor of Selsey which he held by leasehold.

[2] *Ibid.*, 112/30. Two of these men were Thomas Andrewes and Richard Lyne, who, Curteys maintained, had been presented by the churchwardens at the visitation, and the other was most certainly Ralph Chauntler.

[3] *Ibid.*, 112/29.   [4] *Ibid.*, 112/34.   [5] *Ibid.*, 112/31.

order to ruin his opponents economically;[1] of similar misconduct in executing a commission for assessing subsidies;[2] and
with misuse of ecclesiastical sanctions.[3] Other, more particular
charges included: six counts of bribery involving sums
totalling £132,[4] eight counts of extortion,[5] four counts of
simony in the granting of benefices and ecclesiastical offices,
one count of cozenage based on the evidence of his own letters
patent,[6] three counts of wrongfully detaining money or goods,[7]
that he kept benefices without incumbents so that he could
enjoy the profits, and that he made "leases and advowsons with
antedates".[8]

Some of the charges were greatly exaggerated, for Curteys
was no worse than most of his fellow bishops in the early part
of Elizabeth's reign, but there was enough truth in them to
damn Curteys. Added to this was the supercilious attitude that
he displayed in the face of such accusations. When Richard
Ernley complained that the bishop had written him "sharpe &
tauntinge letters vndeservedly" accusing him of illegally trans-
porting corn out of Sussex, Curteys replied that he was
inclined to doubt that Ernley could be injured by a letter
written by "hym self alone". When he was charged with
"defacinge, alteringe and [e]racinge some wrytings acts and
mvnuments[9] contrarie to lawe and conscience", Curteys chose
to evade the question with a pun: he did not know what the
plaintiffs could mean unless it was the order he gave that "the
Images & supersticiouse monuments in the Church of Chy-
chestre should be razed & defaced, as they were in the tyme of
king Edward [VI]".[10] It was for this reason that Curteys's

[1] *Ibid.*   [2] *Ibid.*, 112/34.   [3] *Ibid.*, 112/29.I.
[4] *Ibid.*, 112/44. Elsewhere, S.P., Dom., Eliz., 112/29.I, alleges that
Curteys accepted bribes to set aside ecclesiastical punishments. Actually, the
commutation of sentences of excommunication by fines was a very widespread abuse in ecclesiastical courts. See Chapter 2.
[5] *Ibid.*, 112/43, 112/32. Curteys and his servants were accused of extor-
ting excessive fees, presumably for securing episcopal confirmation of grants
of patents and leases.
[6] *Ibid.*, 112/44.   [7] *Ibid.*, 112/43.   [8] *Ibid.*, 112/31.
[9] Muniments or monuments in the sense of a legal document.
[10] S.P., Dom., Eliz., 112/30. Fewer than half of the complaints against
Bishop Curteys have survived in their original documentary form. Thus the
details of half of these charges cannot be obtained. The substance of the

detractors resorted to a vicious campaign of slander charging the bishop with "Toleration of Incest, Pride, Contentiousness, Gaminge and Idleness, Incontinencye and Dronkennes".[1]

Bishop Curteys did not appreciate the seriousness of the charges made against him. After nearly a decade at Chichester he remained an outsider, spurned by the greater part of the gentry and scorned by all but a handful of the citizens of Chichester. Ignorant of the law and poorly advised about how he should defend himself against the charges lodged against him before the Privy Council, Curteys, in effect, condemned himself with his own testimony.

To the local governors Bishop Curteys's actions seemed irresponsible and his attitude incorrigible. Not only were they determined to have his name stricken from the commission of the peace, they would not rest content until they had pulled down that overmighty prelate altogether.

In order to understand the hostility that the ruling oligarchy of Sussex and Chichester felt towards Bishop Curteys, and to assess the truth of the charges that they hurled against him, it is necessary to study the temporal aspects of Curteys's power as bishop of Chichester and as a civil magistrate and to ascertain to what extent they disturbed the vested interests of these rulers of town and county.

The bishop of Chichester's temporal power derived from three sources: the various crown commissions granting him authority as a civil magistrate, the *potestas jurisdictionis*, which empowered him, as the ordinary of the diocese, to impose ecclesiastical sanctions of a temporal nature, and lastly, the proprietary rights that he possessed as lord of several episcopal manors and liberties and as a patron of benefices. Considering the illegality of some of his opponents' economic activities, a vigorous and alert exercise of these powers could not but cause deep resentment.

Take for example Curteys's attempts to detect and punish infringements of admiralty law. Elizabethan shippers and

---

charges is epitomized in a series of lists to guide the Privy Council through the volume of evidence. These lists are found in S.P., Dom., Eliz., 112/29.I, 32, 43, 44.

[1] *Ibid.*, 112/43.

mariners did not draw a precise distinction between piracy and legitimate maritime commerce. The many inlets and estuaries that fell within the jurisdiction of the port of Chichester provided a haven for pirates, smugglers and wreckers. Since admiralty law is derived from Roman civil law rather than from English common law, special training was required for dealing in these matters which the ordinary justice of the peace did not have. Minor cases of piracy and other offences pertaining to the law of the seas along the Sussex coast were tried in special vice-admiralty courts staffed by the same judges who sat in the two archidiaconal courts, and the responsibility for the running of the vice-admiralty courts belonged to the bishop of Chichester. The preface to *Christes Naturall Body* emphasizes that one of Curteys's duties was "the withstanding of robbers and Pyrates".[1]

One individual accused of trading with pirates was George Fenner. A ship's captain and a merchant firmly established in the aldermanic class of Chichester, Fenner was among those citizens of Chichester actively working for Curteys's overthrow in 1577.[2] Since piracy was such a serious offence, however widespread it was, Curteys sometimes deemed it safer to make his accusations against his opponents' servants rather than against the principals in the crime. For example, Thomas Lewkenor's henchman, William Grover, deputy searcher for the port of Chichester at the time of the dispute between Lewkenor and Curteys concerning the regulation of the grain trade, was accused by Curteys of being an accessory to piracy.[3]

Another of Curteys's less popular duties was that which required him to act as a commissioner for assessing subsidies and loans to the government. In this capacity Curteys was responsible, for example, for rating the clergymen of his diocese for the purpose of equipping soldiers for service in Ireland and the Low Countries.[4] Curteys was also called upon

---

[1] Curteys, *Christes Naturall Body* (1577), unpaginated.

[2] *V.C.H. Sussex*, II, 148; DRO, Ep. I/15, Box A 2 (1).

[3] S.P., Dom., Eliz., 112/37.

[4] See S.P., Dom., Eliz., 188/58 for a certificate by Bishop Thomas Bickley of the clergy of the diocese of Chichester who refused to contribute to the war in the Low Countries. In 1595 the rating of the clergy of the diocese of Chichester for equipping soldiers for service in Ireland was apparently

by the government to determine the ability of lay people to contribute towards subsidies voted by Parliament, and at least one complaint was made that he used this power vindictively.[1] Because Curteys exercised this power unfairly he was not always successful in collecting the subsidies; when he died in 1582 he was in debt to the crown to the extent of 100 marks for uncollected subsidies and tenths dating back to 1570.[2]

But the temporal duty that bred the most offence was "the restrayning of such as vnnaturally carry away grayne, victuals and other commodities of the Realme".[3] The office of commissioner for the grain trade was the sphere of temporal responsibility that Curteys first thought of when he replied, in a letter to the Privy Council, to the charges made by Sir Thomas Palmer and his allies:

"I was very desyrouse to go on in the matters of Religion, and did make my most humble peticion to some of my especiall good Lords [of the Privy Council] to be [a] meanes to aunswere the matter of embarking of certayne grayne into Ireland by my learned counsayle, because I am not skylled in the common lawes of this realme."[4]

Because of the heavy speculation of Thomas Lewkenor and Richard Ernley in grain and their consequent vulnerability in anything touching the grain trade, Curteys seems to have decided to use his powers as a commissioner for regulating the grain trade to bring economic ruin to his opponents. Nor, it would appear, did Curteys's intentions go unnoticed by Lewkenor and Ernley. This particular controversy came to a head when Curteys granted a licence to James Hoare, a victualler and merchant in the Irish trade to export 80 quarters of corn. When Hoare arrived at Chichester with his ship in February 1577, he brought a special appeal from the lord

---

entrusted to lay commissioners rather than to the incompetent and aged Bishop Bickley, since the certificate is found in the letter book of Sir Walter Covert, deputy lieutenant of Sussex (Harley MS. 703, fos. 89–95).

[1] P.R.O., Star Chamber 5/C43/10.
[2] John Strype, *Annals of the Reformation* (Oxford: 1824), V, 481–3.
[3] Curteys, *Christes Naturall Body*, unpaginated.
[4] S.P., Dom., Eliz., 112/37.

deputy of Ireland stressing the great dearth of corn in that land.
Hoare had brought from Ireland a load of cured herring, which
was much needed in Sussex because Lent was just beginning,
and the current price for herring in Chichester was so dear that
Bishop Curteys feared that "the poore people should be dryven
to great extremity".[1] When Hoare came to Curteys to get
permission to transport the grain he also brought a special plea
from the corporation of Chichester to be allowed to buy the
herrings as well as a letter from the Privy Council authorizing
the shipment of the grain. Although Curteys was the only
other commissioner resident in the rape of Chichester at this
time, he instructed Hoare to get another signature besides his
own. When Hoare failed to locate another commissioner, the
bishop's chancellor, Henry Worley, obligingly added his
signature, although he does not appear to have been a commissioner.

Acting on orders from Richard Lewkenor, William Grover,
the deputy searcher for the port of Chichester, refused to let
Hoare sail. The deputy searcher said that he had ordered the
sails from James Hoare's bark taken into custody because he
suspected that the ship contained more corn than the bill of
lading stated.[2] Worley had ordered the sails to be returned
when he signed Hoare's licence. The deputy searcher was
furious when he discovered this, and again he confiscated the
sails and this time locked them up in his own house, but the
"sayde house was broken open by one of the Bishops servants
and . . . the sayles taken awaye in ryotous order". When the
deputy searcher obtained a warrant signed by two J.P.s to
measure the grain, he was violently resisted and then "appre-
hended and carryed to the sayde Bisshopp & ther imprysoned
by the space of two dayes in the Bisshopps house sufferynge no
man to speake with him except his owne servants".[3]

Curteys maintained that Richard Lewkenor, Thomas's
brother, had instructed the deputy searcher to obstruct the
bishop's order to allow Hoare to sail because the bishop had
previously refused to allow Thomas Lewkenor to ship large
quantities of grain out of Chichester rape as he had been doing
in Arundel rape. The implication, of course, was that the

[1] Ibid.   [2] Ibid., 112/36.   [3] Ibid.

Lewkenor brothers were shipping grain illegally.[1] Curteys charged that the deputy searcher had admitted to Hoare that his sailing was being delayed only in order "to trye who should beare rule there".[2]

Thomas Lewkenor replied by making serious accusations concerning Curteys's conduct as a commissioner for the grain trade. He charged that Curteys had allowed his own servants to transport corn illegally. Furthermore, when persons desiring to ship grain were unable to get licences from the other commissioners, they could count on obtaining them by "givinge some of the saide Lord Bishops servants money for the same".[3] It was Curteys's custom to issue licences to badgers on his authority alone, despite a request by the other commissioners not to issue licences until all were assembled. Not without cause for alarm, Lewkenor told of how Curteys was trying to bring about his financial ruin: although Lewkenor possessed letters from the Privy Council granting him permission to transport a hundred quarters of wheat to London, Curteys had refused him a licence, leaving Lewkenor with "twyce so moche wheat" as he could sell.[4]

This controversy with Thomas and Richard Lewkenor about shipments of grain out of Sussex was not an isolated incident. Curteys was carrying on this same sort of economic warfare with a number of citizens of Chichester, who were also shipping large quantities of grain out of west Sussex.[5] It was more than just a personal vendetta: like the Laudians who followed two generations later, Curteys had no use for profiteers and engrossers who exploited public misery for private gain. Curteys's complete disregard for property rights and the procedures of common law would inevitably lead to disaster just as the same attitudes would stir property owners against meddlesome prelates in the 1630s.[6]

The complaints made to the Privy Council about Richard

---

[1] *Ibid.*, 112/29.I.   [2] *Ibid.*, 112/37.

[3] *Ibid.*, 112/31.   [4] *Ibid.*

[5] The names mentioned in this connection were Ralph Chauntler and Thomas Fenner. *Ibid.*, 112/33.

[6] See also Hugh Trevor-Roper, *Archbishop Laud, 1573–1645* (2nd ed., London: 1962), pp. 166–70.

Curteys's abuse of the temporal powers pertaining to the bishopric of Chichester were in a similar vein: he used the ecclesiastical courts to harrass his opponents; imposed ecclesiastical sanctions for personal motives or to interfere with the processes of temporal courts; he was indifferent to the existence of bribery and corruption among his lieutenants and servants; he was said to have sold ecclesiastical offices and benefices; he was accused of being a harsh landlord. But most of all he disturbed vested interests.

As an illustration of Curteys's abuse of ecclesiastical sanctions, Sir Thomas Palmer and his associates cited the case of several persons to whom the bishop had ordered communion to be denied because they had testified in a common-law court against Thomas Mansbridge, a servant of the bishop, on an action of trespass. The incumbents of the parishes in which these individuals lived were ordered not to minister the sacrament to them until they asked forgiveness of Mansbridge, which was, as Palmer and his friends pointed out, undisguised interference with the administration of justice.[1] Curteys's excuse was that "they did openly brawle, fight, & revile one another & were not in charity".[2] "To revenge his private displeasure", Curteys would often summon a person who lived in east Sussex to appear at the archidiaconal court in Chichester, while those in west Sussex would be summoned to Lewes. He had imprisoned several people in the episcopal palace, where "some of his servants have taken money of the persons so imprisoned for fees of the saide imprisonment".[3] Curteys replied that he and his predecessors had always maintained a prison in their houses. He doubted that his servants had taken money from the prisoners, but "if it be, it concerneth not hymself".[4]

[1] S.P., Dom., Eliz., 112/29.I.

[2] Ibid., 112/30.

[3] Ibid., 112/31.

[4] Ibid., 112/33. Thomas Lewkenor complained that Bishop Curteys had harassed him in his own parish of Selsey. The bishop had set the curate of Selsey upon him (there was no incumbent because Lewkenor had apparently impropriated the vicarage), who went up to London and accused Lewkenor of being a "notoryous Papiste" before the Privy Council and the High Commission (S.P., Dom., Eliz., 112/19.I). Curteys explained that when the curate

The charge of venality in the sale of offices to the highest
bidder was made by William Coverley, bailiff of the episcopal
liberty and hundred of the Manwood, who certified that he had
purchased the bailiffwick from Bishop Curteys paying

"the value of x pounds viz iij fatt baren kyne, and one fatte
steere for which he the saide Walter paide vij^{li} x^s which by the
said Lord Bisshopps appointments were delyuered in his Lordships parke of Aldingborne to his Lordships vse."[1]

Coverley asserted that he also paid one of the Bishop's servants
by the "Comaundment of the said L. Bisshoppe in consideration
of the saide office . . ." a further 50s. after which Curteys
refused to pay part of the customary fee due to Coverley and
prevented him from exercising the office. Curteys demurred
explaining that he had removed Coverley from exercising the
bailiffship because Coverley had refused to apprehend two
pirates who were hiding in the Manwood; he had fraudulently
sold and delivered titles for parcels of Manwood Common to
Sir Thomas Palmer and Eton College; and he had refused to
serve a warrant out of the Court of King's Bench against one
William Kitchin of Aldingbourne.[2] Coverley's replication
denied the first two points of Curteys's demurrer. As for the
serving of warrants, he attempted to serve a process in an
action of trespass against Thomas Mansbridge, a servant of the
bishop, "which the said Lord Bishop dyd take from hym
againste his will, and wolde not suffer hym to serve it".
Coverley admitted that he had not served the warrant against
Kitchen: after incurring the bishop's displeasure for attempting
to deliver the summons to Mansbridge he was afraid to do so,

(according to Lewkenor, a "very simple and vnlearned mynister and a man
very contentious", previously deprived for "euell and lewde behavior" and for
being infected with a "lothsome disease") reported discovering "some books
and monuments of superstition" in Selsey, Lewkenor, in a furore, had turned
his bailiff and servants loose on the curate to abuse him in "word & deede".
The inhabitants of the Isle of Selsey had asked the bishop to allow the curate
(who apparently had fled in terror) to come back again, but Lewkenor
threatened violence to anyone who should give the curate food, drink or
lodging, or even keep company with him (*Ibid.*, 112/30).
[1] *Ibid.*, 112/39.
[2] *Ibid.*, 112/38.

"knowinge that the said Kyttchyn had maryede the sister of the Lord Bishop, and was in greate favor with his Lordship".[1]

Another complaint against Curteys shows that he was sometimes inclined to squeeze too much out of his manorial rights. One of the individuals brought forward by Sir Thomas Palmer to blacken the reputation of Bishop Curteys was William Faires, who lamented that his horse had been confiscated by Thomas Mansbridge, the deputy bailiff of the liberty of the bishopric of Chichester, on the disputed part of Manwood Common. Either Faires or Sir Thomas Palmer had attempted to prosecute Mansbridge for the trespass alleged to have been committed on the disputed ground. Curteys argued that Manwood Common had been part and parcel of the liberty of the Manwood since before the Norman Conquest and ancient custom permitted the lord of this liberty to confiscate all horses above a certain size found running loose on the common. William Faires had been one of those to whom Bishop Curteys had forbidden the reception of communion, and Curteys had the audacity to defend this action in the document in which he admitted confiscating the horse, because Faires and the others involved had "reviled on[e] another openlye, and fought one with another".[2]

That Curteys was guilty of venality and of being a grasping landlord was true. But these were also common enough failings among his opponents in the ruling class of county society. The real issue here was that Richard Curteys persisted in flagrantly disregarding the doctrine of property rights commonly held by the property-owning classes of Sussex. This group included not only landlords but also office holders, who considered their offices to be species of property. This conflict can be seen very clearly in Curteys's dealings with the petty officials, drawn from among the citizens of Chichester, who clustered around the cathedral close, earning a living as notaries, solicitors and tithe-farmers by attending to the details involved in running

---

[1] *Ibid.*, 112/40. If Walter Coverley actually was removed from his bailiff-ship, he was again reinstated, for he held the bailiffship of the liberty and hundred of the Manwood in 1582 at the death of Bishop Curteys and was listed as receiving an annuity of £4. DRO, Fp. I/44/1.

[1] S.P., Dom., Eliz., 112/40.

the episcopal courts, transacting chapter business, and leasing and farming ecclesiastical property and parcels of tithes. They were small fish, indeed, but they had come to hold an exalted view of their tenure of these minor offices as freeholds which did not admit of their being removed for irregularities.

The case of Edward Amyers illustrates the irregularities practised by these minor ecclesiastical officials. Amyers was a notary public, who had been registrar to the dean and chapter, later holding a similar office in the archidiaconal court of Chichester. Amyers complained that he had been removed illegally from the latter office. Curteys explained that Amyers had been deprived of the registrarship of the dean and chapter "for his fowle dealinges, and euell misdemeanour in the same office . . .", and subsequently bought the second office from the previous registrar, but that this had never been confirmed by an episcopal patent.[1] Although Curteys claimed that this was illegal, he had allowed Amyers to exercise the registrarship of the archidiaconal court of Chichester for three years until complaints were made about his lack of learning and skill and accusations of "falsefijng and [e]rassing the recordes of the same Court". Curteys then prosecuted Amyers in the Court of Star Chamber and obtained a conviction, after which Amyers was dismissed from office.[2] In his answer to the Privy Council, Amyers denied that he had been dismissed from the registrarship of the dean and chapter for misconduct. The only offence of which he was guilty was that he had secured the installation of the bishop's brother, Edmund Curteys, in a prebend by mandate of the bishop "agaynste the mynd of the deane and certayne of the chapiter". This caused such a storm that he chose to forbear exercising his office. He claimed that he did have a patent from Bishop Curteys to hold the registrarship of the archdeaconry of Chichester but that the bishop had become angry with him because he refused to certify falsely that a will had been proved in the archidiaconal court in order to help obtain a false title to a house in Chichester for one of the

---

[1] *Ibid.*, 112/41. The Chapter Acts for 7 May 1571 record that Amyers had been dismissed for "misconduct" sometime prior to this date. Peckham, *Act Book A*, no. 751.

[2] S.P., Dom., Eliz., 112/41.

bishop's friends. The bishop, being angry with him, had him prosecuted on perjured evidence in Star Chamber.[1]

Even when Bishop Curteys succeeded in depriving an ecclesiastical office holder, he could not remove him from the cathedral close, where such individuals thrived on the shady transactions that characterized the leasing and farming of church property. Although Curteys never wanted imagination in harrassing his opponents, he generally failed to pry them loose; most of them were still clinging like lampreys to their offices, reversions to offices, advowsons and long-term leases long after he was gone. Curteys's encounter with two citizens of Chichester, Ralph Barlow and Thomas Hills, showed the futility of a mere bishop trying to deal with these vested interests. The story of Barlow and Hills and their friends is of further significance because it reveals evidence of just how widespread the opposition to Curteys was in and around the cathedral close. William Overton's faction within the chapter had linked up with Hills and Barlow and other citizens of Chichester to plot the ruin of Bishop Curteys.

It was during the year 1575 that the growing disenchantment with Bishop Curteys, already manifested in the chapter and cathedral close in previous years, spread to the citizens of Chichester. Hills and Barlow seem to have taken a lead in voicing criticism of Curteys and his lieutenants, for they were the ones that Curteys went after; in February of 1576 the Privy Council appointed a special committee to examine "Thomas Hilles, Ralph Barlowe and others, informed to be contrivers of certein libells to the infamye of the Buisshop of Chichester".[2] Tantalizingly, we are never told of just what the libel consisted. The Privy Council granted the commission the power to settle the matter themselves, but the discontent was so widespread that the commissioners were apparently unable to accomplish anything. The libel was not an isolated incident, but rather it was an external symptom of widespread dissatisfaction with Curteys's rule.

Thomas Hills, yeoman and citizen of Chichester, was a petty official who symbolized the close connection between the cathedral close and the city of Chichester. At the time of the

---

[1] *Ibid.*, 112/42.   [2] *Acts P.C.*, IX, 87.

controversy about the shipment of grain in 1577, he was comptroller of the port of Chichester, but he made his living principally as a farmer of ecclesiastical benefices.[1] Ralph Barlow of the Close, yeoman, was a notary public and what would now be considered a solicitor. His income seems to have been derived mainly from legal transactions dealing with ecclesiastical property, and he specialized as a dealer in advowsons and reversions to minor offices. In 1573 he was made deputy to the chapter registrar and clerk; in 1574 he jointly held the registrarship and acted as secretary, keeping "all acts and registers" in his own custody.[2]

Bishop Curteys and several of his faction pressed the charge of libel against Barlow and Hills and prosecuted them in the Court of Star Chamber.[3] The defendants were charged with uttering, printing and publishing slanderous speeches against the plaintiffs, making them the butt of jests and rhymes, and also counterfeiting letters showing them in an unfavourable light.[4] Unfortunately, the only document that has survived among the records of the Star Chamber concerning this interesting case is the answer of Thomas Hills to the original charge by the plaintiffs, in which Hills admitted the charge of libel by the bishop. Hills' defence was based on undue provocation on the part of Bishop Curteys who, he charged, in a recent subsidy to be paid to the crown had assessed him far above any other citizen of Chichester. In his own inimitable style, Hills paints a vivid picture of how the bishop had "daunted" him

"by setting his seruant to assalt & skale the dweeling house of this defendant, and to pull the same downe as it weare vppon his hed, and to challenge to fight with hym and beate hym, and

[1] S.P., Dom., Eliz., 112/37; Peckham, *Act Book A*, nos. 645, 657, 671.

[2] *Ibid.*, nos. 767, 783.

[3] Also acting as plaintiffs were Thomas Gillingham, archdeacon of Chichester, Henry Blaxton or Blackstone, chancellor of Chichester, and John Sherwyn, citizen and alderman of Chichester and customer of the port of Chichester. Blaxton and Gillingham were the first two clerics to sign the testimonial to Bishop Curteys in *Christes Naturall Body*, and had been beneficed by him at the time of the bishop's quarrel with the chapter. S.P., Dom., Eliz., 112/37; see above, p. 74.

[4] P.R.O., Star Chamber 5/C43/10, 30 May 1576.

also to anoy the said defendant the more, to pull [down] a Rowe of buyldings about CC foote longe situate in one of the Chiefest streets of Chichester and adioyning to the said dwelling house of this defendant in place whereof by the space of twoo yeres past hath bene and yett is a most contagious donghill adioyning to the Buttereye and dwelling house of the said defendant y[i]elding daylie an horryble & most vnholsome savour."[1]

Provoked by these actions and an attempt by the bishop to serve on him a process under the authority of the Ecclesiastical Commission because he was friendly to certain clerics whom the bishop did not like, Thomas Hills confessed that in a fit of anger he had sat down and composed and printed an eclogue holding Curteys and two of the bishop's lieutenants up to ridicule. The speakers in the short poem had names very similar to those of the bishop and his two lieutenants, and certain abuses, of which Hills thought them guilty, were satirized. Hills maintained that he had never intended to publish the printed poem and when his anger had passed, he had resolved to destroy it, but somehow it was misplaced. Several months later he awakened one morning and was startled to find that the archdeacon of Chichester and the bishop's chaplain, with several servants, were searching his home armed with a warrant from the Ecclesiastical Commission. They found much manuscript material of an incriminating nature, including a rhyme written ridiculing a blazon of arms fraudulently claimed by the bishop's friend, John Sherwyn, yeoman, who was seeking to become John Sherwyn, gentleman. As a result, Hills was imprisoned in the Counter in London, where he was examined in the presence of Bishop Curteys. Since the evidence was so overwhelming, he decided to confess everything and ask for mercy.[2]

Apparently nothing could be proved against Ralph Barlow, but Thomas Hills was sentenced to pay a fine of £50 and to stand in the pillory with one ear nailed flat and overhead a placard proclaiming his offence.[3] But Curteys was not to have

[1] *Ibid.*   [2] *Ibid.*
[3] B.M., Harley MS. 2143 ("Sentences in Star Chamber"), fo. 31v.

his revenge, for the Privy Council wrote to the bishop instructing him "to remitte the fault committed against him by Thomas Hilles, touching the matter of a libell or eglogue [eclogue]. . . ."[1] However, Curteys had the comfort of knowing that certain powerful men were on his side, and he wrote to the earl of Sussex, thanking him for "countenancing, comforting, and defending of me, and certain learned Preachers, in the Star Chamber, against the Libellers and their co-actors".[2]

Although Ralph Barlow had gone free temporarily, that did not mean that Bishop Curteys had forgotten about him. During the time of the consistory on 2 March 1577 two of the bishop's servants pursued Barlow into a church near the cathedral and forcibly tried to carry him away. Sir Thomas Palmer charged that the bishop's servants refused to show a warrant until a justice of the peace, spying the tumult, ordered them all in the queen's name to keep the peace and demanded that the bishop's servants show a warrant.[3] According to Curteys, Barlow had to be arrested in that particular church or churchyard because that was the extent of the bishop's liberty within the city of Chichester. All else in the city of Chichester was in the dean's peculiar, and the dean, Anthony Rushe, was no longer a member of the bishop's party. The regular bailiff had tried to arrest Barlow three weeks before in the same place, but Barlow

"did violently take awaye his warrant, and drewe the sayd Balyff out of the Churcheyard into a garden, where he taking a pitchforke runned at the sayd Balyff in such sort, as he had kylled or maymed hym, if one Rychardson had not reskewed the sayd Balyff."[4]

Curteys explained that the sheriff decided to appoint as special bailiffs two sturdy men, who were ordered to take Barlow by

[1] *Acts P.C.*, IX, 199, 5 Sept. 1576.
[2] *A Collection of Letters from Original Manuscripts of Many Princes, Great Personages and Statesmen, together with some Curious and Scarce Tracts, and Pieces of Antiquity, Religious, Political and Moral*, ed. Leonard Howard (London: 1753), pp. 293–4.
[3] S.P., Dom., Eliz., 112/13. The warrant was from the chief baron of the Exchequer and the sheriff, according to Curteys, and Barlow had previously resisted having it served upon him. [4] *Ibid.*, 112/30.

surprise, seizing him before he could resist, but Sir Thomas
Palmer and his friends charged that the warrant was surmised
and made without the knowledge of the sheriff or his deputy,
while the two bailiffs were simply servants of the bishop and
had not been sworn in properly.[1]

Another fellow conspirator of Barlow and Hills was Thomas
Andrewes, gentleman. A lay singing man of Chichester
Cathedral, he had been among those summoned to the consistory held on 2 March 1577.[2] A very decayed manuscript lists
charges drawn up against Andrewes and presumably exhibited
in the Chichester episcopal court sometime in 1576 or 1577.[3]
It was specified that Andrewes had been guilty of adultery,
failure to receive communion according to "the lawes of the
Realme", and with failure to reform himself after being
presented for the same. But to the bishop's party, the other
charges were more serious:

"Item you spend much of your tyme revilyng and spekyng ill of
the godly ministers and p[rea]chers of this dyoces and namely of
Henry Blaxton and Thomas Gillingham, Daniell Gardyner and
other[s] that preach in the Cathedrall church of Chichester . . .
[I]tem you have spoken ill of your ordynary the Buisshop of
Chichester."

This interesting document reveals very clearly the extent of the
opposition to Bishop Curteys in both the cathedral close and
the city of Chichester. It tells of how Andrewes, Hills and
Barlow and others were in the habit of gathering at suppers to
discuss their grievances against the bishop and his lieutenants.
On one such occasion their wives were overheard to describe
Curteys as a "useless man" and certainly "noe Buishop". A larger
group of those "that vngodly railed on the Buishopp" often
frequented a house near the old Friary in Chichester; besides
Barlow, Hills and Andrewes, this group included at least four
other leading citizens of Chichester, plus William Overton,

---

[1] *Ibid.*, 112/29.I. Credence is lent to Palmer's charge by Curteys's
admitted reluctance to send his men beyond the extent of the episcopal
peculiar. If they were properly sworn bailiffs of the city of Chichester,
ecclesiastical jurisdictions would have been irrelevent.
[2] *Ibid.*, 112/30, 112/13.I.   [3] DRO, Ep. I/15, Box A 2(1).

leader of the clerical faction against Curteys, Anthony Rushe, dean of Chichester, and several other canons residentiary and vicars choral.[1]

Although Curteys did not give up trying to pack his own supporters into the chapter, it was becoming obvious that his opponents among the chapter members were securely established in benefices that were considered freeholds before the common law. Even the petty officials like Ralph Barlow were safely entrenched behind vested interests that proved far more durable than the rule of a mere mortal bishop. Despite the fact that Barlow was a mortal enemy of the bishop, Curteys was unable to remove Barlow from the offices that he held. Barlow was still chapter registrar in 1592, long after Curteys had passed out of this world, and at the time of Bishop Curteys's death in 1582 he was still custodian of the mansion belonging to the episcopal manor of Amberley.[2] Thomas Hills continued for many years to deal in ecclesiastical property, and in 1585 he managed to obtain an episcopal patent granting him for life the office of receiver of the chapter with an annual income of £10.[3]

The commissioners appointed to decide the dispute between Richard Curteys and his many enemies submitted to the Privy Council a decision embodying recommendations to settle some of the points at issue. The decision was a humiliating defeat for the bishop of Chichester, and he agreed to only one of the six articles contained in it:

"That he shall forbere to deale in thexecution of the comission of peace or any other temporall Jurisdiction vntill the Lords

[1] It was apparently members of this group that started the rumour sometime in April of 1577 that Bishop Curteys while "dininge the sixtyne daye of April Laste paste the generalle sessyons days at the howse of Mr Jhon Sherewyn citizen and Alderman of the Cittie of Chechester was soe ffar overcome with drincke, as was too vnseamelye to beholde and especiallie in a man of his callinge" (S.P., Dom., Eliz., 114/8). Six of the bishop's party, who claimed to have been present at the dinner at John Shervyn's, came forward to testify under oath that Bishop Curteys had "behaved hym selffe and talked then and there both wisely, soberly, gravely, and Lernedly, and that he nether spake nor dyd ani thyng wherebye anye well meaninge man could coniecture anie such thinge in hym" (Ibid.).

[2] Peckham, Act Book A, no. 915; DRO, Ep. I/44/1.

[3] DRO, Ep. II/24/1; Peckham, Act Book A, nos. 645, 657, 671.

[of the Privy Council] shall soe cause to revoke their inhibition."[1]

But when it was ordered that he should draw up a written submission acknowledging his "disorderlye manor of proceedings in his diocesse", Curteys balked, saying that he felt that his previous letters to the Privy Council had already supplied a submission. Richard Curteys may have accepted defeat, but he still was not ready to admit that he was at fault.

Nor can one blame Curteys for his resentment at these farcical proceedings. When it was suggested that further points of difference should be decided by two arbiters—one of whom was his arch enemy, Thomas Lewkenor of Selsey, Curteys objected, and they were replaced by Sir Francis Walsingham and Sir Walter Mildmay. Ordered to make satisfaction to, and reconcile himself with, his enemies among the gentry and clergy, the bishop arrogantly answered that he was "content to such as wyll [do likewise]", but that he would not be "driven to travell to any his inferiors to offer hit under the degre of nobillitie". Bishop Curteys was also ordered to remove "such inferior officers . . . as have byne noted to have bine ministers of the vexations he is charged withall", but he maintained that he could not remove those who possessed lawful patents.[2]

For the time being, the Privy Council were content to let the matter rest. Although they most likely thought Richard Curteys a foolish, arrogant and indiscreet prelate, the members of the Privy Council probably did not believe all of the charges against Curteys. Otherwise, they would have felt compelled to take more drastic action. Besides, the most pressing religious problem was still the extirpation of Catholicism, and Curteys was a zealous man in that regard. For this reason a note of caution was appended to the commission's recommendations:

"That sum convenient way be thought on by the Lords [of the Privy Council] aswell for the satisfaction of the cuntrie [i.e. the county of Sussex] as also that the Bishop's discharginge his dutie may not bee hadd in contempte."[3]

The Privy Council could not have it both ways: to treat a

[1] S.P., Dom., Eliz., 112/49-50.   [2] *Ibid.*   [3] *Ibid.*

bishop in such a shabby manner could not but expose him to contempt. Henceforth until his death, Curteys effectively enforced religious uniformity only against those recusants who had withdrawn voluntarily from participation in local government and had secluded themselves within their seigneurial households.[1] As for the families of those crypto-Catholics who had caused Curteys so much trouble, they were either drawn into the established church by the passage of time and concern for their social prestige and economic position, or for reasons of conscience became recusants.[2] But the efforts of the bishop of Chichester had no discernible influence on these events. In the meantime the gentry of Sussex were simply waiting for a chance to humiliate Curteys completely and to have him deprived of his spiritual functions as well.[3] It was the controversy stirred

[1] See Chapters 7 and 8.   [2] See Chapter 12.

[3] In order to put Bishop Curteys's feud with the Sussex gentry into better perspective it would be as well to take note of other instances of conflict between Elizabethan bishops and the gentry of their dioceses.

Edmund Sandys was another prelate, who, like Curteys, made trouble for himself wherever he went. Less than a year after Sandys was made bishop of Worcester in 1559, a quarrel developed between him and Sir John Bourne. Sandys accused Bourne of Romanist practices. Bourne complained that the bishop was seeking personal revenge because Bourne, as Queen Mary's principal secretary of state, had tried to dissuade the queen from pardoning Sandys saying "he was the greatest heretic in Cambridge". An exchange of insults between the retainers and servants of Sandys and Bourne led to actual fighting in which several persons were wounded. When Bourne complained to the Privy Council, he was reprimanded, imprisoned and forced to apologize to Sandys (Strype, Annals, I.2, 15–42).

In 1581, after Sandys had been translated from London to the archbishopric of York, another dispute occurred with Sir Robert Stapleton of Yorkshire. That gentlemen attempted to blackmail Sandys by conspiring with an innkeeper of Doncaster to plant the innkeeper's wife in bed with his grace of York. Sandys attempted to keep the affair quiet for some time, but finally he revealed all to Lord Burghley. The result was that Stapleton and the innkeeper were punished in the Court of Star Chamber and made to confess their sins before the York Assizes (Strype, Annals, III.1, 142–58).

The evidence would seem to indicate that in both of these quarrels, a desire on the part of Bourne and Stapleton to alienate episcopal lands and patronage was an important contributing factor. These two cases, together with that of Richard Curteys and the Sussex gentry would seem to indicate that economic rivalry was at least as important a source of contention in disputes between the bishops and the gentry as religious differences. [Cont.

up by his brother Edmund Curteys, vicar of Cuckfield that gave them that opportunity.

A far more interesting clash occurred in Norwich diocese during the episcopate of Bishop Edmund Freake (1575–1584). Here, the Puritan gentry directly challenged episcopal authority by joining together with certain ministers and attempting to exercise ecclesiastical discipline as justices of the peace through the quarter sessions. Edmund Freake belonged to the second generation of Elizabethan prelates, who were in reaction against the episcopal Puritanism of Grindal. Patrick Collinson observes that "These appointments led to a rift between the episcopate and the Protestant nobility and gentry which was scarcely more marked in the years of Archbishop Laud's ascendancy". (*The Elizabethan Puritan Movement*, p. 201. See also pp. 187–8, and pp. 201–5.) In Freake's case, as in Curteys's, the opposition gentry obtained a sympathetic hearing before the Council.

6

THE VICAR OF CUCKFIELD CONTROVERSY AND THE SUSPENSION OF BISHOP CURTEYS

THE VICAR OF CUCKFIELD CONTROVERSY is important to our present study of Bishop Curteys's enforcement of the religious settlement because it helps to illustrate the extent of the opposition to Curteys among the Sussex gentry and certain privy councillors, and because it was this incident that brought about Curteys's suspension from the spiritual functions of his office.

The vicar of Cuckfield controversy had begun at the parochial level as a feud between the squire of Cuckfield Park and the Puritan vicar of Cuckfield. Henry Bowyer, a successful ironmaster who had purchased Cuckfield Park in 1564, was an overbearing upstart trying to establish ascendancy in the parish. His ambitions had been thwarted by Edmund Curteys, the vicar, who seems to have possessed the same tendencies to quarrelsomeness and tactlessness as his brother, the bishop of Chichester. All the parishioners had taken sides in the feuding, which was intensified by the interference of outsiders. When Bowyer made certain accusations of improper conduct against Edmund Curteys, the enemies of the bishop exploited the opportunity to convince the Privy Council that a prelate, who refused to deprive so unworthy a minister, was not himself fit to exercise episcopal jurisdiction.

Ever since 1577, when Sir Thomas Palmer and his friends had complained to the Privy Council about the bishop of Chichester's arbitrary actions, Curteys's authority to execute any but the most routine duties had, in effect, been suspended. As a result of the charges against his brother, even these routine duties were taken away. From this time on, the interference of the Privy Council in the affairs of the diocese of Chichester grew more frequent.

None of the members of the Privy Council was more active in the vicar of Cuckfield controversy than Sir Francis Walsingham. Deceived by the bishop's enemies, he was outraged that the bishop of Chichester would tolerate such a man as Edmund Curteys to remain in charge of the spiritual welfare of the people of Cuckfield. Later, when he had learned the truth, he did everything possible to make amends to Edmund Curteys. Moreover, he continued to take a personal interest in the parish of Cuckfield, and acted as a sort of protector of the Puritan party of that parish, which flourished in subsequent years.

Edmund Curteys had been granted the vicarage of Cuckfield in 1571 by his brother, the bishop of Chichester, who was the patron of the benefice.[1] A St John's man like his brother, Edmund had previously served as a minister in the diocese of Ely.[2] Cuckfield was a market town in east Sussex with eight hundred communicants who were favourable to the established church.[3]

The quarrel with Bowyer had started not long after Edmund came to Cuckfield, apparently arising out of attempts by the latter to reform the squire's conduct. Wishing to be rid of the meddlesome vicar, Bowyer had sworn

"That as longe as he had a hart to thinke, or a tonge to speake, or a groat to spende, he wolde neuer giue him ouer. And that he wold spend fyue hundrethe pounds but he wolde depriue [Edmund Curteys] . . . of the mynisterie."[4]

The dispute flared up again in the early months of 1578 when Edmund Curteys accused Bowyer of dallying with one of the latter's maidservants. While employed by Bowyer, the girl had become pregnant and was delivered of a still-born child. Some of the vicar's supporters had accused Bowyer's wife of inducing an abortion after she discovered the maidservant's embarrassing

[1] J. H. Cooper, *A History of the Parish of Cuckfield* (Haywards Heath, Sussex: 1912), p. 38. Bishop Curteys also collated his brother to the prebend of Thorney in the same year. Peckham, *Act Book A*, p. 76n.

[2] S.P., Dom., Eliz., 131/18; J. H. Cooper is in error when he states that Edmund Curteys attended Clare Hall. "The Elizabethan Vicars of Cuckfield", *S.A.C.*, XLIV, 13 and *A History of Cuckfield*, p. 38.

[3] John Strype, *Annals*, IV, 277.

[4] S.P., Dom., Eliz., 129/16, Edmund Curteys to the lord chief justice of the Court of Queen's Bench, Jan. 1578/9.

condition. In order to clear this wife's name, Bowyer had called in a couple of justices of the peace, Walter Covert and Walter Bartlett of Stopham, to investigate the charges.[1] In a letter to his brother, Simon Bowyer, but clearly intended for the eyes of Sir Francis Walsingham, Henry Bowyer said: "the matter that tocheth my wife is so vntrew and odyous that I must neds [needs] bryng him to his answer therein to his vtter overthrowe".[2]

Bowyer sought his revenge in kind by countercharging Edmund Curteys with misconduct. As Edmund complained in his defence, when he later appealed to the lord chief justice of the Court of Queen's Bench, Bowyer and his faction then drew up articles "both forged and false" against him and

"exhibited the same to the Quenes maiesties Iustices of peace at the quarter Sessyons holden at Lewis . . . the third daye of October last past [1578]. And therof haue accused your said orator beinge a lame man to be faultie, and him indicted as a common Barretor,[3] vpon the othes [oaths] or not othes of the procurers of this matter, and their sa[i]de partakers. Certainlie persuadinge them selues of the countenance of certaine of the Justices of the benche then sittinge namelie Sir John Pelham, George Goringe esquyer,[4] Henrie Barkleye esquyer, and

---

[1] The factionalism that rent Cuckfield parish can be seen in the investiga- tion of this case. Rival coroner's juries, each made up exclusively of women, sought to determine the cause of the infant's death. One jury, presided over by Bowyer's wife, declared the maidservant, Mercy Gold, to be innocent of the baby's death and explained that the baby was born dead because of a prenatal illness of the mother (S.P., Dom., Eliz., 123/27). A second jury, empanelled a year later, was composed of the vicar's supporters, including his wife. This jury exonerated Bowyer of being the cause of Mercy's pregnancy, but sought to shift the blame for the infant's death to Bowyer's wife. Mrs Bowyer was accused of administering a potent draught to the maidservant, which caused her to have an abortion (Ibid., 131/26. I). Bowyer maintained that the potion given Mercy by his wife was brewed especially for the plague, to which Mercy had been exposed recently (Ibid., 131/26).

[2] Ibid., 131/26.

[3] A barrator is one who sells ecclesiastical preferment.

[4] George Gorings's term as receiver-general of the Court of Wards from 1584 until 1594 was marked by such widespread corruption and embezzle- ment of crown funds that even his contemporaries—all accustomed to their generous "perquisites"—were shocked. See Joel Hurstfield, The Queen's

Doctor [William] Ouerton who are knowne to be enymies to the right reuerend father in God Richard Bushoppe of Chichester, your sayd orators naturall brother."[1]

Edmund Curteys was declaring that he had been tried by a bench packed with his brother's enemies who were trying through his own ruin to accumulate more damning evidence against Bishop Curteys. Nor was Edmund making wild charges. George Goring had been an enemy of Bishop Curteys since 1573 when he and Sir Thomas Palmer had first complained about Bishop Curteys to the Privy Council; William Overton's enmity had been unremitting since the time when Curteys was still dean of Chichester; and Henry Barkeley, a civilian, was one of those gentlemen who had been indiscriminately summoned by Bishop Curteys to the consistory of 2 March 1577. Predictably, a conviction was obtained and Edmund was sentenced to pay a fine, but he felt that to have done so would have been an admission of guilt, and he chose instead to appeal to the lord chief justice.

To support his appeal, Edmund obtained a testimonial signed by several gentlemen and numerous yeomen of his parish. They testified that, although Edmund Curteys had been greatly handicapped by lameness and sickness ever since he first came to Cuckfield, he had caused the parish "so well to be serued that we haue good cause to thinke well of the zeale and behavioure of the sayd Mr Edmunde Coortesse in discharginge his dewtie in his callinge". He had preached "bothe godlie & zealouse" sermons, and their only complaint was that he did not preach more, which they felt that he was inclined to do but for his handicap.

Meanwhile, Bowyer also had made formal complaint to the Privy Council about Edmund Curteys, and Sir Francis Walsingham wrote to Bishop Curteys on 6 March 1578/9 asking him to remove his brother from the vicarage of Cuckfield and to deprive him of all ecclesiastical functions whatsoever.[2] In the

---

Wards: Wardship and Marriage under Elizabeth I (London: 1958), pp. 116–17, 208–9, 226–8, 270.

[1] S.P., Dom., Eliz., 129/16.

[2] *Ibid.*, 130/1. This letter is an unsigned draft copy written in Walsing-

strongest of language, Walsingham bluntly informed Bishop Curteys that Edmund's ignorance was so great and his life "so vyle" that modesty would force him to "spalw [spawl] to name some particularities delivered . . . for the p[roo]ffe of the same". He felt that the matter was even worse when one considered the fact that the vicar of Cuckfield was the bishop's own brother, but he trusted that Bishop Curteys would put duty before blood and remove the cleric who was so offensive to the "good gentlemen and people of that parish . . ."[1] Walsingham was not without a remedy for the situation: in the same letter in which he asked Bishop Curteys to deprive his brother, Walsingham proposed his own candidate to fill the vicarage of Cuckfield when it should become vacant. Walsingham added that this alternative would save Curteys's reputation and that it would prevent the spread of rumours that Curteys habitually suffered unworthy men to discharge the cure of souls in the diocese of Chichester.

In his answer to Sir Francis Walsingham,[2] Bishop Curteys explained that certain charges against Edmund (presumably made by Bowyer or one of his friends in an attempt to deprive Edmund) had been brought before the ecclesiastical commissioners several years previously and the case was still pending.[3] He promised Walsingham that he would not let ties of blood interfere with the performance of his duty, but as an "inferior iudge" he could not well recall the case from the Court of High Commission.

---

ham's hurried handwriting. The handwriting is not that of the lord treasurer, Lord Burghley, as is stated by Strype, *Annals*, IV, 277–8.

[1] There is a scribbled note in the State Papers, probably dictated by Walsingham to an assistant, which described Edmund Curteys as the "Lewd vicare of Cuckfield" and then went on to paint this picture of him as a "pastor now Idolum, voyd of all learning & discretion, for reading insufficient, a prophaner of the Sacraments, a deprauer of preachers, a scoffer at singing of psalmes, a co[mmo]n alehowsehunter, accused of Incontinency, a mainteyner of strumpetts cawses, a seeker to wiches, a dronkerd, a quarreller & fighter, convicted for a co[mmo]n barratter, infected with a lothsome & contagius disease, his talke is of ribaldry, consignatus a natura, & a contemner of her majesty's Lawes & Justices." S.P., Dom., Eliz., 130/2.

[2] *Ibid.*, 130/22.

[3] From internal evidence, it would seem that Edmund Curteys's case first came before the High Commission in 1575.

By this time, however, the government had already decided to take strong action against Bishop Curteys himself. The discontent with Curteys's methods had become so widespread among the gentry that a way had to be found to remove the bishop of Chichester; yet, as in the case of Edmund Grindal, archbishop of Canterbury, the government could not afford the scandal of a formal deprivation.[1] There is an allusion in Curteys's letter to Walsingham to the existence of an unwritten agreement between him and the Privy Council—probably made sometime in 1578—whereby Curteys would not be deprived of the bishopric of Chichester if he would forego the actual spiritual administration of the diocese of Chichester and entrust it to John Becon, at that time chancellor of Norwich.

". . . By order of the counsaill I was contented to my great charge to referr ouer all the dealings in Iurisdiction to Mr D[octor] Becon a man as verie well liked of mee, so speciallie commended and named by your Honor, [and] I moste Humblie beseech your goodnes, that following my preaching I maie neither herin, now in anie like matter be troubled herafter. . . . I lyve to my books, praiers and preachinge, my Iurisdicion and disposicion of other lyuings in my guyfte grauted ouer to others."[2]

Richard Curteys's letter to Walsingham attempted to convey the impression that, in effect, he was now reduced to the status of a cathedral canon—studying, praying and preaching. Yet, Curteys still retained a voice in the administration of the diocese. He was able to force a compromise with his enemies whereby his own chancellor, Henry Worley, who had been at his side since 1573, was to exercise the office of chancellor jointly with Becon.[3] Evidently, Curteys's informal suspension

---

[1] Grindal was under suspension from 1577 until his death in 1583 for refusing to carry out the queen's order to suppress Puritan "prophesyings". For two other examples of prelates disciplined by the queen, see R. E. Head, *Royal Supremacy and the Trials of the Bishops, 1558–1725* (London: 1962), p. 23 ff. Fletcher of London's suspension was only temporary, but Middleton of St Davids seems actually to have been deprived following conviction for civil and ecclesiastical crimes.

[2] S.P., Dom., Eliz., 130/22, 30 March 1579.

[3] On 1 August 1579 the dean and chapter confirmed a commission of

was at least partially lifted towards the end of his life: during the summer of 1580 he is found dealing with cases of recusancy,[1] and in 1582 he was busy assessing the reliability of the commissioners of the peace for Sussex and reporting to the Privy Council the names of those who were sympathetic towards recusants.[2] However, he does not appear ever to have been restored to the Ecclesiastical Commission.

Although Bishop Curteys spoke well of John Becon in his letter to Walsingham, Becon had already acquired the reputation of being contentious.[3] Shortly after Becon's arrival in Chichester, William Overton took steps to assure himself of the new chancellor's friendship by promising future preferment when he should receive "some good Bishoprick".[4] It seems likely that Overton succeeded in his attempt to win Becon over to his side, since Becon was later appointed chancellor to Overton when the latter finally obtained his bishopric.[5]

The Privy Council had allowed the Sussex Gentry to humble Bishop Curteys to the point where the respect for the royal ecclesiastical supremacy could not but be diminished. And this was at a time when Puritan attacks upon episcopacy were growing more shrill. Still the bishop's enemies pressed for Edmund Curteys's removal as well. Whether the Privy Council believed the charges against the vicar of Cuckfield any more than they accepted those against his brother at face value, is not clear. At any rate it looks as if the Privy Council were trying to

---

Bishop Curteys dated 12 September 1578, granting the office of chancellor or official principal jointly to Becon and Worley for the duration of their lifetimes. Becon did not begin residence in the cathedral close until 13 October 1579. Peckham, *Act Book A*, nos. 819 & 821.

[1] DRO, Ep. I/37, no. 48.

[2] See Chapter 12.

[3] As chancellor of the diocese of Norwich, Becon had become embroiled in a quarrel with the bishop of that diocese, and it was several months before he could extricate himself from his difficulties and take up his new duties in Chichester. *D.N.B.*, *sub* John Becon.

[4] S.P., Dom., Eliz., 137/31.

[5] Overton became bishop of Coventry and Lichfield in 1579. Later, after the two had fallen out, Becon was obliged to defend himself against accusations that he charged excessive fees as a judge in the ecclesiastical courts of the diocese of Chichester. *Ibid.*, 158/42.

appease the Sussex gentry. One possible explanation for this appeasement is suggested by the action of Lord Buckhurst, the lord lieutenant of Sussex and a member of the Privy Council, who had, according to Edmund Curteys, offered Edmund a sum of money to resign his benefice.[1] Buckhurst, at this time, was trying to build up his power in the county and therefore depended on the goodwill of the gentry.[2] Edmund told Walsingham that he could not resign under such circumstances without committing simony.

Although he must have known that he was powerless to counter the influence wielded by his enemies with the Privy Council, Edmund continued to make appeals to Sir Francis Walsingham. In all the parishes where he had served, his behaviour had never been called into question until he came to Cuckfield and "sought the punyshment of certaine wicked men, which hath two wyues a pece nowe alyve".[3] He asked Walsingham if his enemies would accept a compromise whereby he would appoint "a learned preacher" to serve under him as curate, but still retain his benefice.[4] In another letter to Walsingham Edmund complained of the persecution that he had suffered at the hands of his enemies. The commission set up by Walsingham at the request of Edmund (and composed of three members of the Sussex gentry) had done nothing to determine the truth of the accusations. Although his guilt had not yet been proved, Edmund lamented that his vicarage had been sequestered by Giles Fletcher, the official principal of the archidiaconal court of Lewes; his prebend had also been sequestered and was currently being farmed by his brother's arch enemy, Thomas Lewkenor.[5] Edmund was in dire financial condition and probably was dependent on his brother and his friends for help.

Edmund Curteys pleaded in vain with Walsingham, for when the Privy Council acted it was to remove him. On 5 February 1580/1 the Privy Council ordered the ecclesiastical commissioners to proceed to the deprivation of Edmund Curteys not only from his vicarage, but also from the exercise of "any function ecclesiasticall in the ministerie elsewhere" in

---

[1] *Ibid.*, 131/18.   [2] See Chapter 11.

[3] S.P., Dom., Eliz., 131/18.   [4] *Ibid.*   [5] *Ibid.*, 146/22.

order to avoid "further offence and slander".[1] The actual deprivation was carried out on 21 February, but Edmund refused to leave the vicarage house.[2]

The deprivation of Edmund Curteys represented the final victory of the Sussex gentry over Richard Curteys and his policy of reform. Perhaps the final blow of Edmund's deprivation was too much for Bishop Curteys. He died sometime late in August 1582.

The deprivation of Edmund Curteys did not end the feuding in the parish of Cuckfield. Two members of Edmund's faction, Ninian Challoner and Thomas Mitchell, had preferred certain charges against Henry Bowyer and John Hussey[3] and others had secured indictments at the assizes sometime in the first months of 1581.[4] Upon hearing of what had happened, the Privy Council summoned Challoner and Mitchell to present themselves and explain their contempt of a previous council order forbidding them to "deale anie further in the matter of the Vicaridge of Cuckfelde".[5] At the same time the Privy Council ordered the justices of assize to stay all indictments preferred against the squire of Cuckfield and his friends and transferred the matter to the jurisdiction of the Council.[6] Challoner and Mitchell were locked up in the Marshalsea Prison for ten days until they thought better of defying the Privy Council. They were set at liberty "uppon their submission and promise not to enter meddle hereafter in the matter of the Vicaredge of Cuckfelde . . . with some good lessons to behave themselves more dutifully hereafter."[7]

[1] *Acts P.C.*, XII, 324.

[2] Cooper, "The Elizabethan Vicars of Cuckfield", *S.A.C.*, XLIV (1901), 20.

[3] In 1564 John Hussey was the owner of the impropriated rectory of Cuckfield. As the lay rector, he was entitled to the greater tithes of the parish, a practice much condemned by the Puritans. Cooper, *History of Cuckfield*, p. 38.

[4] *Acts P.C.*, XII, 125.   [5] *Ibid.*   [6] *Ibid.*

[7] *Ibid.*, XIII, 130 & 140. While he was away in London, Thomas Mitchell was presented by the churchwardens of Cuckfield for not attending church. At a session of the archidiaconal court in Lewes on 14 November 1581, presided over by Giles Fletcher, official principal, Mitchell certified through his apparitor that he was in London on business, but Mitchell nevertheless was sentenced to pay a fine of 7s. and a moiety for his recusancy (DRO, Ep.

Edmund Curteys was still occupying the vicarage house a year after his deprivation. He had been allowed to remain there for that length of time because of his poverty, but now the Privy Council determined that he was to be paid £40 "by wage of charitye" out of the tithes and other fruits of the vicarage, which had been sequestered while the enquiry into the charges against him was still being carried out, and he was ordered to vacate the vicarage house by 5 March 1582. If he failed to be out by that day, the local magistrates were commanded to see that he was bodily ejected.[1]

There is a surprising sequel to the story of Edmund Curteys. On 17 July 1585, Edmund walked into the Chapter House in Chichester and produced to the residentiaries there assembled letters that had been written by none other than Sir Francis Walsingham himself[2] directing his reinstatement in his old prebend of Thorney. So radical a change of heart is difficult to explain in the man who had done so much to have the "lewd" vicar of Cuckfield deprived. Possibly Walsingham always knew that Edmund was innocent but was forced to give in to the overwhelming opposition of the powerful and influential gentry of Sussex to Edmund's brother, the bishop of Chichester. The letter ordering Edmund's reinstallation in the prebend of Thorney could thus be interpreted as a salve to Walsingham's conscience. Although the pressure from the Sussex gentry may have appeared to warrant a scapegoat in Walsingham's eyes, it seems more likely that Walsingham committed the act in ignorance, after which his Puritan friends probably pointed out that he had been fighting on the wrong side for the wrong cause in the vicar of Cuckfield controversy. Edmund was reinstated by Henry Worley, who was still chancellor.[3]

II/9/2, fo. 35). However, Mitchell appealed against the sentence on the 29th of the same month, when Thomas Underdowne, a notorious Puritan (see Chapter 10), was substituting for Fletcher, and the churchwardens were ordered to pay back the fine to Mitchell (DRO, Ep. II/9/2, fo. 70). The feuding in Cuckfield between the squire of Cuckfield and the Puritan party, including later vicars of Cuckfield, continued into the late 1580s, when Bowyer ironically enough appears to have been converted to Puritanism.

[1] MSS. Acts of the Privy Council, 28 Feb. 1581/2, printed in Cooper, "The Elizabethan Vicars of Cuckfield", S.A.C., XLIV, 20–1.

[2] Peckham, Act Book A, no. 861.   [3] Ibid.

Walsingham did not stop after he had secured Edmund's reinstatement in his old prebend; he deluged the chapter with letters demanding that Edmund be made a canon residentiary. The chapter proved adamant in their refusal to admit Edmund to residence, and Walsingham replied that he was "vexed" that his former letters were of no avail, because he was very sorry for the poor man's plight. He knew that the admission of another canon would reduce their annual dividends derived from fees charged by the cathedral chapter for burial and sealing documents,

"but this is so small a matter as in reason not to be respected, especially considering the great penurie of the man, his charge of children, and the quietnesse which might growe to so great and poore a parish as is now burthened with him."[1]

Walsingham asked them to reconsider his request.

The Chapter's reply to Walsingham listed several reasons why Edmund Curteys could not be admitted to residence: the Statutes of 1574 decreed that there were to be only four residentiaries besides the dean, which number was already supplied;[2] he was not considered a sufficiently able preacher to supply "that dutie of a Residensarie necessarilie required . . . in this end of the diocese where are so few preachers besydes the Residensaries . . . who are, and ought to be preachers."[3] It was also objected that Edmund Curteys was "thought to be very contentious and unquiet. . .";[4] but probably the real reason that the chapter refused to admit Edmund was that they

<hr />

[1] *Ibid.*, no. 867.

[2] B.M., Egerton MS. 1693 (Letters of Robert Beale, Clerk of the Council), fo. 128. This is an unsigned and undated letter from the chapter evidently written to Bishop Bickley, which appears to have been passed on to the Council. The letter in DRO, Cap. I/4, printed in Peckham, *Act Book A*, no. 867, gives almost the same reasons for refusal, and I have combined the substance of the two letters here.

[3] Peckham, *Act Book A*, no. 867. A complaint was made in 1586 by the churchwardens of Thorney that Edmund had not preached in the church. He was obligated to preach quarterly sermons there because the rectory of Thorney was appropriated to prebend of Thorney. DRO, Ep. I/23/7, fo. 24.

[4] B.M., Egerton MS. 1693, fo. 128; Peckham, *Act Book A*, no. 867.

thought that the parish of Cuckfield should bear the burden of relieving their own poor rather than the residentiaries.[1]

Sir Francis Walsingham had made a startling about-face in regard to Edmund Curteys, but viewing Cuckfield from some distance, he was forced to evaluate the situation through the eyes and ears of other people, who were often prejudiced, and actually, it was only natural that he would eventually side with the struggling Puritan faction. But if Henry Bowyer, the squire of Cuckfield were to join the Puritan party, that would be simply astonishing. Yet, apparently, that is what happened. In his will he bequeathed two gold angels to John Waterhouse, the Puritan vicar of Cuckfield with whom he had previously quarrelled, and he made an unusually long and profoundly fervent testament of faith strongly smacking of Puritanism.[2] His son, the younger Henry Bowyer, whom his father charged to "faiethfully feare and serve god [and to] love and earnestly imbrace the religion of the most glorious gospel of Jhesus Christe crusified . . .", was one of the signers of the Puritan petition presented to James I in 1604.[3]

The vicar of Cuckfield controversy underlines the growing tendency of the Privy Council to treat once lordly prelates as social inferiors and as mere agents of the queen's royal government in matters religious. Richard Curteys's removal from the actual spiritual administration of the diocese of Chichester was the penalty he paid for presuming to be other than the government's obsequious servant. His policy of reform was defeated because it failed to take into account the rising influence of the gentry, and was based exclusively on the leadership of a small clerical faction.

---

[1] Beyond their prebendal incomes, six residentiaries had received £20 15s. each at Michaelmas 1585, and they had no desire to reduce this income by the addition of another residentiary (Ibid., no. 867).

Edmund Curteys continued to live in Cuckfield as an accepted member of the parish until his death in 1605. He continued to take an active part in the parish quarrels, but was negligent in his prebendal duties, apparently because of his lameness (Cooper, "The Elizabethan Vicars of Cuckfield", S.A.C., XLIV, 23; Peckham, Act Book A, nos. 865, 950, 982).

[2] P.C.C., 74 Leicester, proved 30 Oct. 1589.

[3] "Extracts from the MSS. of Samuel Jeake", ed. T .W. W. Smart and W. D. Cooper, S.A.C., IX, 45–9; see also Chapter 10.

Henceforth, the leadership of the popular reformation in Sussex would lie with the country gentry, especially that segment of the gentry which co-operated with the presbyterian ministers in the classical movement of the 1580s and 90s.[1] Recusant affairs would increasingly be entrusted to this small group of earnest aristocrats, some of whom had been Marian exiles.[2] Consequently, those bishops of Chichester who followed Curteys (until Lancelot Andrewes heralded the *de jure divino* conception of episcopacy upon his accession to the see of Chichester in 1605) were little disposed to play as leading a role in the religious life of Sussex as Richard Curteys had done.

[1] See Chapter 10. There is irony in the fact that although Richard Curteys's leadership was rejected by the gentry, yet the Puritan classical movement in Sussex owes as much to his sponsorship of the clerical "excerises" as to any other factor.

[2] See Chapters 7 and 12.

PART III

OPPOSITION TO THE ENFORCEMENT
OF THE RELIGIOUS SETTLEMENT

7

METHODS AND PROBLEMS OF
ENFORCING THE PENAL LAWS

"ALMOST ALL PLACES in our part of the world are full of Papists and Popishness", wrote William Overton, the chancellor of Chichester to Sir William Cecil in August of 1568.[1] Overton's father-in-law, Bishop Barlow, and Overton's antagonist, Bishop Curteys, had both, in varying degrees, expressed the same feeling of alarm. Certainly, the situation was potentially dangerous. Possibly half of the Sussex gentry of the local office-holding class—certainly no less than about 39 per cent—were known to be Catholic in the 1560s.[2] They still dominated the local magistracy in the mid 1560s, and only towards the end of that decade was any progress made in replacing them with dependable Protestant magistrates. Although there were no signs of political disaffection among the gentry, the danger existed as long as the disgruntled Henry Fitzalan, earl of Arundel and his son-in-law, Lord Lumley, still retained any influence in the county.[3]

Actually the Catholics in Sussex in the 1560s were no great cause for alarm, because the spiritual force of the Catholic Reformation had not yet reached the shores of England (the theological pronouncements of the Council of Trent did not begin to become generally known until the arrival of the first missionary priests in 1574), and most Catholics still attended their parish churches. Even Lady Montague, a very pious woman who later became such an exemplar to her fellow Catholics, sometimes attended common prayer during this interim, which her chaplain, Bishop Richard Smith, later "imputed to the defect of instruction [rather] than want of zeal".[4] As for the influence of quasi-feudal noblemen such as

[1] S.P., Dom., Eliz., 47/4, quoted in Philip Hughes, *The Reformation in England* (London: 1954), III, 129–30.

[2] See Chapter 12, section ii.   [3] See Chapter 11

[4] Richard Smith, bishop of Chalcedon, *An Elizabethan Recusant House, comprising the Life of the Lady Magdalen, Viscountess Montague (1538–1608)*,

Arundel or, at a later period, the earl of Northumberland, they dragged very few of the Sussex gentry into their conspiracies; most of the Catholic gentry seemed to have looked to Lord Montague for guidance. Ever a devout Catholic, his loyalty to the queen was, at the same time, unswerving.

It was after 1570 that the attitude of Catholics concerning attendance at common prayer began to change. For in that year the Papacy took a less temporizing position when Pope Pius V published the Bull excommunicating Elizabeth. Catholic resistance began to stiffen and to take the form of recusancy—the refusal to attend the parish churches. In a sermon delivered at the opening of the assizes in East Grinstead, William Overton told of the change that had come over Catholics in Sussex:

"I wis, I wis, there are many cursed Calves of Basan abroad, which since they sucked the bull that came from Rome, have given over all obedience and allegiance both to God and the queen; for before that time they could be content to come to the church and hear sermons, and to receive the sacraments, and to use the common prayer with the rest of the congregation of Christ, and so forth. They were conformable in all respects, and content to do anything that beseemed good Christians to do; but since they sucked that mad bull, they are become even brain sick calves, froward, stubborn, disobedient, in word and deed, not to be led or ordered by any reason."[1]

Overton exaggerated the reaction of Catholics in order to make a pun, but there can be no doubt that the "Bull of Basan" had placed Catholics in an uncomfortable position. As a result of retaliatory legislation passed by Parliament, pressure increasingly was placed upon Catholics to conform; while at the same time their consciences bade them to absent themselves from their parish churches. To persist in recusancy required courage on the part of a recusant's whole family and household as well as himself.

---

translated into English from the Original Latin of Dr Richard Smith . . . by Cuthbert Fursdon, O.S.B. in the year 1627, ed. A. C. Southern (London: 1954), p. 44. Hereafter cited as Smith, Lady Montague.

[1] J. O. W. Haweis, Sketches of the Reformation and the Elizabethan Age taken from the Comtemporary Pulpit (London: 1844), p. 193.

The first concerted effort to deal with recusancy in Sussex did not come until the period after 1577. The delay was due to the inefficiency of the episcopal machinery in detecting and punishing recusancy and to the troubles encountered by Bishop Curteys during this episcopate. Although the proportion of Catholic families among the greater gentry dropped during the episcopate of Bishop Curteys from perhaps a half to a sixth, this was due not to the enforcement of the penal laws, but to other factors. By 1580 about 15 recusants families among the greater gentry and about 30 among the lesser gentry are seen to have emerged as hardcore recusants. Despite the more stringent recusancy laws of the 1580s their numbers do not diminish during the remainder of the Elizabethan period. The few instances where Catholic families are known to have become Protestant are attributable to other factors: to the lure of public office or to the influence of Puritanism.[1]

The execution of the Act of Uniformity was entrusted to the bishops and their lieutenants at a time when they were ill-prepared to assume the burden.[2] Even more unrealistically, the detection and punishment of recusancy was placed in the hands of the parish churchwardens, who were very much the social inferiors of the gentry. Until 1581 the chief weapon against recusancy was a weekly fine of 12d.; mild as it was compared to the heavier fine imposed by the statute of 1581,[3] it was levied only sporadically. This was because the church-wardens, whether out of loyalty or fear of reprisal, often felt that they could not afford the luxurious independence of pre-senting their betters for recusancy. In 1579 the sidemen of Racton stated that Geoffrey Pole and his household had not been to church in two years; no recusancy fines had been collected because there were no churchwardens to collect them. There were no churchwardens because Arthur Gunter, another recusant gentleman "who rules the whole parish", had prevented their election for over ten years.[4] In the parish of Clapham, where William Shelley of Michelgrove was squire and patron, the 1579 archidiaconal visitation revealed that the

1 See Chapter 12.   2 See Chapter 3, section ii.   3 23 Eliz. I, c. 1.
4 B.M., Add. MS. 39, 454, fos. 20–1; S.P., Dom., Eliz., 60/71, quoted
V.C.H. Sussex, II, 24–6

churchwardens of the previous year had failed to present those who did not communicate. The churchwardens of Clapham presented two persons for recusancy and three for failure to communicate in 1579; one of the erring churchwardens the previous year was a sideman at the time of the 1579 visitation, but still refused to sign the presentments.[1] Although the Shelleys' schoolmaster was cited by the churchwardens in 1573 and 1579, it is worth noting that none of the Shelleys appear in churchwardens' presentments until after 1580, by which time Bishop Curteys was already well aware of their activities from other sources.

Because the churchwardens proved so unreliable in the detection of heresy, it became common practice to require presentments at the time of visitations to be submitted by the incumbent and each curate as well. This system of verifying the churchwardens' presentments yielded slightly better results but still did not escape the problem. Like the churchwardens the parish clergy were usually of inferior social origin and often were in an economically vulnerable position. In more than a few cases incumbents owed their benefices to Catholic patrons, whom they could hardly denounce as recusants. In the 1603 return of recusants in the archdeaconry of Lewes, the rector of Catsfield complained of how his involvement in a dispute with Lady Montague over leases and tithes had hampered him and the churchwardens in reporting cases of recusancy. Two gentlemen, who had been presented as recusants by the parish authorities, had sought refuge with Lady Montague at Battle Abbey. There were also "two house holders in the said parish which neyther usually resorte to church nor receyve the holy communion and yet [are] not suspected for recusants but they depend upon the Lady Viscountesse Montague['s] protection."[2] Altogether, very few of the cases of recusants known to us in the diocese of Chichester in the 1570s were reported by the parish officials; of these only a handful were members of the gentry. Information concerning recusancy among the gentry during this period comes mostly from higher ecclesiastical officials.

Where the parish officials were unable to collect fines from

[1] B.M., Add. MS. 79, 454, fo. 37v.   [2] DRO, Ep. II/24/1.

a recusant or where the accused person had failed to heed a warning from the curate or the churchwardens, the case could be called before the archidiaconal court.[1] Of the cases of religious disaffection tried before the archidiaconal courts, only a few dealt with actual recusancy; these usually involved recusants who had refused to pay the fines levied by the church-wardens. Most of the cases were concerned with people who refused to communicate at Easter in their parish churches. If the accused chose to appear before the archidiaconal court, he might be admonished by the judge to bring a letter from his curate before the next Whitsunday certifying that he had communicated. He might also be placed under a bond to insure that the judges admonition was heeded.[2] Or the individual might be sentenced to pay a fine. When a parishioner of West Hampnett was ordered to pay a fine of 7s. and a moiety for the judge for failure to communicate, he appeared in person and maintained that he had offered himself for communion, but the curate had refused to minister the sacrament to him. The curate himself was cited before the court to explain his actions, and the parishioner was ordered to receive communion before the next feast of the Epiphany.[3] In the seaside parish of Selsey another individual was cited to appear before the archidiaconal court of Chichester under suspicion of hiding a mass book in his house. In an area where religious disaffection often escaped with impunity, he had no trouble securing a certificate of compurgation from sufficient of his neighbours to exonerate himself of the charge.[4]

More commonly, in cases involving a violation of the Act of Uniformity, a Catholic who defied the parish authorities was likely to ignore a summons from the archidiaconal court as well. When the accused person failed to present himself he was nearly always placed under sentence of major excommunication for contumacy. A fairly typical case is the one involving an

[1] The enforcement of the Act of Uniformity was also entrusted to justices of oyer and determiner, justices of assize and municipal officers (1 Eliz., I., cap. 2, §§ 5 and 10). Unfortunately, none of the quarter sessions rolls that have survived for the late 1590s throw any light upon the problem.
[2] DRO, Ep. I/17/4, fo. 12.   [3] DRO, Ep. I/17/10, fo. 9.
[4] DRO, Ep. I/23/1, fo. 13v.

inhabitant of Selmeston who in the spring of 1583 was twice summoned to appear before the archidiaconal court on charges of recusancy. Failure to appear on the second occasion brought excommunication. Subsequently he appeared with letters certifying that he had cleared himself of the offence, and his penalty of excommunication was lifted. Within three months the same individual was again excommunicated.[1] In Chichester as in other dioceses, the indiscriminate use of the penalty of excommunication bred contempt and the authority of episcopal courts no longer carried much weight. At any given time during the reign of Elizabeth we find large numbers of people under sentence of excommunication for contumacy; rarely do they ever incur the wrath of the secular arm as in medieval times.[2] Obviously, the regular parochial and diocesan administrative machinery was inadequate for dealing with the problem of recusancy.

The inability of the parish churchwardens to deal with the problem of recusancy—especially among the Catholic gentry— and the failure of the older ecclesiastical courts to sanction their decrees in such cases led to the more extensive use of the Court of High Commission to supplement, or in some cases supplant, the bishops' ordinary authority.[3] The excuse for the Ecclesiastical Commission to extend its jurisdiction in cases of recusancy was provided by the general deterioration of the international situation in 1580: a Papal expedition had actually landed in Ireland in 1579 to begin the execution of the "Enterprise of England" by Pope Gregory XIII. Most Englishmen saw a link between these two separate events, and this was all the excuse that was needed by Lord Burghley to take stronger action against the English Catholics. On 22 July the Court of High Commission directed Bishop Curteys personally to secure more conformity in his diocese. Having compiled lists of recusants, Curteys issued summonses to at least sixty

[1] DRO, Ep. II/9/2, fo. 98v. ff.   [2] See Chapter 2.

[3] See G. W. Prothero, *Select Statutes and other Constitutional Documents Illustrative of the Reigns of Elizabeth and James I* (4th ed., Oxford: 1913), p. xxvii. For a detailed study of the use of the Northern High Commission to combat recusancy, cf. F. X. Walker, "The Implementation of the Elizabethan Statutes against Recusants, 1581–1603" (London Ph.D. thesis, 1961), *passim*, but esp. pp. 36–111, 389.

recusants to appear before him.[1] Some of those summoned, including such important recusants as William Dawtrey of Petworth, John Apsley of Pulborough and John Leedes of Steyning, obtained certificates of conformity from their parish officials and writs of supersedeas from the ecclesiastical commissioners.[2] In each case mere conformity was not sufficient; the individual in question also had to communicate. The documents pertaining to the bishop's proceedings are nearly all without date, but apparently Curteys tried first to secure attendance at the episcopal palace at Aldingbourne by sending letters out to local constables and parish curates summoning the recusants for informal conference where a warning would be given. Despite his promise that all would go away free, very few seemed to have showed up. This failing, the recusants were summoned before a formal session of the episcopal consistory court sitting in the cathedral church, where a sterner line was taken. In order to seek out those who still remained contumacious, justices of the peace were called in and posses organized to search the homes of the recalcitrant recusants. Geoffrey Pole, charged with "Maintaynyng couenticles . . . and keeping preistes to say them masses", was one gentleman who had refused to appear, and Bishop Curteys complained to the justices of the peace that "no constable not aided by some[one] of estimacon dare venter to apprehende hime".[3] Despite the help of the J.P.s and search parties the bishop told the ecclesiastical commissioners that

"only syke women are taken. For either they are fled out of the country or harbored in woods & dens or otherwies intertayned in houses of such as have the disposycyon of theyr lyvinge or are of like disposycyon which they favor their opynyons although they com[eth] to churche."[4]

Bishop Curteys felt that there was nothing more that he could do with the remaining recusants, except to hand their names over to the High Commission and to urge that some sort of action be taken against those who had been helping the

---

[1] DRO, Ep. I/37, *passim*.   [2] *Ibid.*, no. 3.
[3] *Ibid.*, no. 42.   [4] *Ibid.*, no. 48.

recusants in question by hiding them or holding their property to prevent sequestration.[1]

Nine of the recusants on the bishop's list were bound over to appear before the Court of High Commission in London in early August of 1580. By the 11th of that same month John Gage of Firle, Edward Gage of Bentley, William Shelley of Michelgrove and Richard Shelley of Warminghurst were lodged in the Fleet and Marshalsea prisons as a result of action taken by the Ecclesiastical Commission.[2] These four men provided a large measure of the leadership of the more uncompromising members of the Catholic gentry. Several others were also imprisoned at the same time, and Bishop Curteys had hopes that this would put an end to Catholic resistance. The increased pressure for conformity in 1580 was, of course, nationwide. But when a number of leading Catholics from other counties throughout England, who also had been under close imprisonment, were released in May 1581 under bonds,[3] the two Shelleys and the two Gages were excepted. Richard Shelley of Warminghurst was not out of the Marshalsea until early 1584; Lord Montague secured the temporary release of Edward Gage in December 1581, but he was back in the Marshalsea in March 1583; William Shelley was soon back in prison on an additional charge—treason.[4]

The threat of confinement to prison might well have been a deterrent to weaker Catholics when they were summoned before the High Commission, but actual imprisonment was unlikely to bring about the rehabilitation of zealous Catholics like the Shelleys and Gages. Prison conditions were harsh, but close supervision of the prisoners was lacking and the prison officials were utterly untrustworthy. It was actually safer and more convenient for a Catholic to hear mass in a London prison than in a Sussex country house. In 1582, when Richard Shelley of Warminghurst was in the Marshalsea, he was able to

---

[1] *Ibid.*   [2] B.M., Harley MS. 360, fo. 1.

[3] These recognizances specified that the person under bond was to remain within three miles of his home until conformity was certified by the ordinary of the diocese. B.M., Add. MS. 11, 402, fo. 30.

[4] See my "Richard Shelley of Warminghurst and the Catholic Petition for Toleration of 1585", *Recusant History*, VI (Oct. 1962), 265–74.

invite five friends to join him in assisting at a mass said by Fr Thomas Hartley.[1] Catholic prisoners in the Clink made that prison an important link in the communications system that Catholics had built up in the south of England.[2] The government was also aware of the corruption and bribery of guards and the general mismanagement in the Tower of London where mass was also being said by imprisoned priests, who were given food and money by the earl of Arundel.[3] In December 1594 Lord Burghley received a letter from a certain William Lee, who claimed that because he had sat on the jury that convicted the Jesuit, Edmund Campion, several Catholics had procured his imprisonment (probably for debt). Evidently trying to bargain for his release Lee informed Burghley that Lord Buckhurst had recommended as subwarden of the Fleet a Sussex gentleman, who "purposethe to anymate the Recusants (beinge of his owne sort) and to affict the Queen's faythfull subiects."[4]

The same factors which had led in 1580 to the more stringent enforcement of the laws against recusancy by the High Commission also brought forth more severe financial penalties from Parliament when it was called back into session in 1581. The proposal to bleed the recusant gentry white by stiff fines was an old one and had long been backed by the episcopal bench. A bill embodying this approach to the problem had been vetoed by the queen in 1571.[5] The idea of impoverishing recusants by heavy fines was revived again in 1577 when John Aylmer, bishop of London, wrote to Sir Francis Walsingham of his new plan for crushing Catholicism. Aylmer reasoned that fines would sap the strength of recusants, who were beginning to increase in numbers, whereas imprisonment had proved ineffective because "by sparing their housekeeping [it] greatly enricheth them".[6] The Privy Council thought this an excellent idea and wrote to all the bishops instructing them to list the

[1] S.P., Dom., Eliz., 155/27.
[2] Joel Hurstfield, *Liberty and Authority under Elizabeth I* (London: 1960) p. 9.
[3] *Cal. S.P. Dom.*, 1581–90, p. 555.
[4] Hatfield MS. 29. fo. 20.
[5] Neale, *Elizabeth I and her Parliaments*, 1559–1581, pp. 192–3, 386.
[6] *Cal. S.P., Dom.*, 1547–80, p. 549.

names of persons who refused to attend the services of the established church, with the value of their lands and goods.[1] Accordingly, on 26 October 1577 Bishop Curteys certified the names of 22 recusants, almost all of whom were quite substantial. Aylmer's plan was subsequently put aside because of the French marriage negotiations.

The renewed concern of Parliament and the government about the international danger of a revived Catholicism resulted in the Act of 1581 (23 Eliz. I, c. 1). This statute extended the law of treason to include anyone who sought to reconcile any of the queen's subjects to the Church of Rome and raised to £20 per month the fine for those who persisted in their recusancy. The most important of the penal laws after the two Acts of Supremacy and Uniformity, the Recusancy Act of 1581 also provided that once a court of law had certified conviction for recusancy to the Exchequer, the fine would automatically be assessed at the rate of £20 a month until the recusant made formal submission and became conformable. Actually, even among the more substantial recusant gentry very few were able to pay the £260 in recusancy fines due every year (the year was divided into thirteen lunar months); and, in fact very few did so.[2] Peers were exempted from the penalties of this act, and, of the leading Catholic gentry in Sussex, John Gage of Firle was the only one who came close to paying the full amount year in and year out. The Carylls escaped these fines by a sufficient show of conformity, while Richard and William Shelley were imprisoned most of the time that the statute was in force.[3]

John Gage II of Firle (c. 1539–1595) was consistent in his recusancy from the 1570s when the records of this offence were first kept. In 1577 his goods were valued at £500 and his income was said by Bishop Curteys to be 400 marks a year; in 1587 his goods were valued at £2000 and his yearly income at £800.[4] John Gage began accumulating recusancy fines in

[1] *Ibid.*, p. 558, 15 Oct. 1577.

[2] Walker, *op. cit.*, pp. 226–9; Michael O'Dwyer, "Catholic Recusants in Essex, c. 1580–c. 1600" (London M.A. thesis, 1960), pp. 195, 202, 224.

[3] William Shelley was attainted of treason in February 1585/6 and consequently forfeited his property to the crown.

[4] S.P., Dom., Eliz., 117–15, printed C.R.S., *Miscellanea* XII, pp. 80–1; B.M., Lansdowne MS. 53, no. 69, printed *S.A.C.*, LIII, 69.   [*Cont.*

1581. He was unable or unwilling to pay all of the fines between 1581 and 1585, and in 1593 he still owed £460 to the government. In 1593 he paid all but £280 on the latter sum.[1] Between 1585 and 1595 John Gage is definitely known to have paid the full sum of fines due for those years; in 1603 his heirs were able to get a court order remitting part of the full sum for the last year of his life because he died before the end of the year.[2] In March 1594, when sums of £140 were due into the Exchequer from recusants for a period of seven lunar months, John Gage was the only Catholic from Sussex who paid the full amount. Edward Bannister paid £67; Thomas Pounde £38; the five remaining Sussex recusants on this list paid less than £10 each.[3]

The Recusancy Act of 1581 also specified that continued failure to pay fines twice yearly could result in seizure by the Exchequer of the goods and two-thirds of the lands of the defaulting recusant, although this provision was not uniformly enforced. However, this penalty was applied in the case of John Gage II's mother, Elizabeth, Lady Gage. She had accumulated fines of over £1000 for a four year period. Consequently, the Exchequer sequestrated lands belonging to her in Alciston and Maresfield which had a total income in 1593 of £253 13s. 4d. While the penalty of sequestration was carried out in Lady Gage's case, the Exchequer made partial compensation by granting the farm of her two manors in Maresfield to her son, Edward Gage of Bentley. The total income from her lands in 1593 is not known, but the Exchequer's share was £226.[4] The

---

Although Dr J. E. Mousley's researches indicate that the Gages of Firle were not prospering during the reign of Elizabeth ("The Fortunes of Some Gentry Families of Elizabethan Sussex", *Economic History Review*, 2nd ser., XI (April 1959), 467–83), John Gage II did leave an estate that was still sufficient for his nephew and heir, John III, to maintain the dignity of a baronetcy.

[1] *Recusant Roll, no. I, 1592–93*, ed. M.M.C. Calthrop (London: C.R.S., 1916), XVIII, 336.

[2] Sussex Archaeological Trust (Barbican House, Lewes), "Calendar of the Sussex Muniments of Viscount Gage" (Typescript, 1931), III, 16, 19. Hereafter cited as "Cal. Gage MSS".

[3] B.M., Harley MS. 7042, fo. 310v.

[4] *Recusant Roll no. I, 1592–93*, XVIII, 325, 329.

amount of property actually confiscated must have accounted for at least the full two-thirds which the Exchequer might sequestrate under the statute of 1581, because in 1577 Lady Gage's income had been estimated at £100 a year, and in 1587 at £200.[1]

The confiscated lands of recusants provided a source both of profit and patronage to members of the court. One of the queen's *valets de chambre* obtained through the influence of Lord Burghley a lease of lands confiscated from Thomas Gage of Alciston, another of Lady Gage's sons.[2] Gage's lands appear to have been sequestrated early in 1590, and the Exchequer was still seized of them in 1601. After the attainder of William Shelley of Michelgrove for treason and the forfeiture of his lands to the crown, Burghley promised the lease of a pasture to Sir Thomas Palmer of Angmering; but Lord Buckhurst tried to persuade Burghley to grant the lease to Harry Shelley, a cousin to both William Shelley and Buckhurst. Buckhurst stated that his reason for recommending the suit of Harry Shelley was because of the latter's zeal "in religion . . . being so rare a thing in that name".[3]

Confinement to prison, the levying of ruinous fines and sequestration of property did not exhaust the legal means of harassing recusants. The government also resorted to the imposition of extraordinary forms of taxation, the taking of recognizances to insure good behaviour and the supervision of wardships involving the children of recusants.

Elizabeth's government attached great importance to economic pressure, as a means of securing religious obedience, and recusants were commonly subjected to additional and extra-ordinary forms of taxation. In the seventeenth century it was not unusual for recusants to be put on the subsidy roll to pay twice the normally-assessed subsidy. In the Elizabethan period they were called upon to equip light horsemen for service in Ireland. In August 1584 the sheriff and justices of the peace or commissioners of muster were given the power to assess each

[1] S.P., Dom., Eliz., 117/15, printed C.R.S., *Miscellanea XII*, pp. 80–1; B.M., Lansdowne MS. 53, no. 69, printed *S.A.C.*, LIII, 69.

[2] Sussex Archaeological Trust, "Cal. Gage MSS", III, 16017.

[3] M.B., Lansdowne MS. 50, fos. 39–40 v.

recusant according to his ability to pay. Since the government had not had too much success in collecting recusancy fines, the Privy Council instructed local officials to inform the recusants that if they co-operated in the matter of furnishing light horse-men, the government would "qualify some part of the extre-mity of the punishment that otherwise the law doth lay upon them".[1] In the event that it was not convenient for a recusant actually to furnish a light horseman, he might compound for £25 in place thereof, but that was the minimum sum that he could pay.

However, the government discovered that justices of the peace could not be depended upon to carry out the assessments with anything like rigour. In 1584 the J.P.s returned a schedule with only three names on it. The Privy Council returned the list, telling those responsible to add more names. In October of 1587 the job of assessing the ability of recusants to contribute was entrusted to special commissioners and this time 13 Sussex recusants were rated to furnish light horsemen. In each case the assessment was for one or two horses or their monetary equivalent. But in each case Thomas Bishop, the sheriff, reduced the sum.[2] John Leedes was charged with two light horses or £50 but he actually paid only £20; Edward Gage of Bentley and John Shelley of Michelgrove paid £25 each where they had been assessed at £50 each; Nicholas Wolfe and George Britten paid £10 each, and John Delve £5. Another recusant had died recently; another had conformed and was removed from the list while three others currently were imprisoned. Two of those imprisoned were found to be of "verye meane abilitie"; the sheriff excused them from paying altogether. One of the latter pleaded with the sheriff that "since my last commitment into the Marshalsey, I have loste upon the statute of Recusauncie all my leases and goods; and nowe have not [the means] to supply the necessitie which my poor olde wife

[1] In February 1585/6 the Privy Council undertook to fulfill their promise to allow recusants to compound for recusancy fines according to their ability to pay, but the deterioration of the international situation in 1587 appears to have brought this scheme to naught (B.M., Harley MS. 703, fos. 19–20, printed in "Sussex Religious Houses and Recusants, Temp. Hen. VIII and Elizabeth", S.A.C., XIII (1860), 197–202).
[2] S.P., Dom., Eliz., 183/38. I–XIII; 184/45.I.

and I have and much more by means of my long imprisonment".[1]
A more zealous Protestant than Thomas Bishop might have
extracted more money from these recusants, but, as Bishop
Curteys had complained in 1582, Thomas Bishop was very
liberal towards Catholics.

Recognizances were frequently taken of recusants to provide
security for good behaviour or to compel them to listen to
arguments by Protestant divines intended to convert them.
George Britten of Northchapel, who was under suspicion
because he had served in the household of the eighth earl of
Northumberland, had to put up security in 1597 guaranteeing
that he would remain in England. In 1596 two other Sussex
recusants were under bond to attend conferences with the
archbishop of Canterbury intended to persuade them of their
error.[2] It was common for troublesome Catholics to be confined to houses of trustworthy Protestants. Both Edward
Banister and his hosts Henry and George Goring of Burton had
to post large bonds guaranteeing that Banister would not try to
escape, and that he would "confer with such learned men as
they shall think meet for him to confer withall".[3] Banister
was given ten months in which to satisfy the bishop of
Winchester that he had conformed or else to return himself to
the White Lion Prison in Southwark.

More than one Puritan in Parliament had been led by fanati-
cal zeal to suggest that children be taken from their recusant
parents and raised in foster homes as Protestants. A fear often
expressed by Puritans was that these children of Catholic
families would be sent to one of the new continental Catholic
seminaries to be educated for the priesthood, and it was for
this reason that the government was doubly careful to keep
track of grants of wardship involving children of Catholic
parents, especially during the war years of the 1590s.[4] Yet even
during these troubled years the Court of Wards was still
granting wardships to Catholic relatives, although they were

[1] *Ibid.*, 183/38. VII.
[2] Lambeth Palace Library, MS. Carta Misc., IV, 171 & 85.
[3] Loseley MSS., vol. V, printed in St G. K. Hyland, *A Century of Persecution under Tudor and Stuart Sovereigns* (London: 1920), pp. 121–2.
[4] Joel Hurstfield, *The Queen's Wards* (London: 1958), pp. 119–20.

probably expected to compete in the bidding with everyone else. When Thomas Gage of Firle died in 1590, the guardianship of his son John III (later the baronet) was particularly valuable because he was also the heir apparent to the estate of John II of Firle, who was childless. Another uncle, Edward Gage, who was a well-known lawyer in London, stepped in and obtained by letters patent the grant of the wardship and marriage of John III. Within six months the wardship was assigned by Edward Gage to John Gage, who apparently was a younger brother of John II. The deed of grant was signed by Lord Burghley and specified that the guardian must produce the body of the ward before the Court of Wards every four years, at which time questions would be asked concerning the education of the ward.[1]

The laws penalizing recusancy were mild compared to those enacted against missionary priests and those who aided and abetted them. By the 1570s the old Marian priests were dying off, and legislation was enacted by Parliament to cut off the source of candidates for the priesthood who were beginning to be educated at the English College at Douai, founded by Cardinal Allen in 1568. A law of 1571 (13 Eliz. I, c. 3) forbade English subjects to go overseas without a licence beyond the duration of one year under pain of confiscation of property. The Act of 1581 (23 Eliz. I, c. 1) specified that missionary priests, once ordained, were to be adjudged traitors if it could be proved that they had sought to withdraw any of the queen's subjects from their natural obedience to her as sovereign or supreme governor of the church. Such overt acts were found difficult to prove in a court of law, and the statute of 1585 (27 Eliz. I, c. 2) made it necessary only to prove that a man was a Jesuit or a seminary priest in order to secure a conviction for high treason.

The government had been unable to prevent English Catholic youths from making their way overseas to the continental seminaries;[2] and it was physically impossible to prevent the

---

[1] Sussex Archaeological Trust, "Cal. Gage MSS.", III, 8 & 12.

[2] Two sons of the Poles of Racton and two sons of the Shelleys of Michelgrove are known to have been at Douai (*The First and Second Diaries of the English College Douay*), ed. T. F. Knox (London: 1878), pp. 190, 199; *The*

missionary priests from landing in England. It was the alarm caused by the mission of the Jesuits Campion and Parsons that prompted the Privy Council to order the bishops and the High Commission to bring more conformity into their dioceses in the summer of 1580. The new seminary priests were hunted down, and the most notorious Catholic leaders among the gentry were imprisoned by the end of that summer.

If the government could not prevent these seminary priests from landing in England, it could make it very dangerous for Catholics to harbour them. The statute of 1585 (27 Eliz. I, c. 2) which proscribed as traitors all Jesuits and seminary priests caught within the realm, also made it a capital felony to provide aid or comfort for such a priest. John and Margaret Gage of Haling, Surrey, cousins to the Gages and Shelleys of Sussex, were condemned under this law, but were later reprieved, although never pardoned.[1] Edward Shelley of Warminghurst was hanged, drawn and quartered at Tyburn Hill in August 1588 for helping a priest.[2] His brother Richard died a lingering

---

Douay College Diaries, Third, Fourth, and Fifth, 1598–1654 (London: C.R.S., 1911), I, 110, 112. John Darell of Scotney was imprisoned in London *c.* 1597–1598 evidently for sending his children overseas to be educated (Hist. MSS. Comm., *Salisbury MSS.*, IV, 69).

[1] The letter respiting their execution arrived while the Gages actually were being drawn in a cart to their place of execution. The queen never pardoned the Gages or restored their property, and Margaret's brother, John Copley, was of the opinion that Lord Howard of Effingham, who had obtained a lease of the Gages' property from the queen, did not want to have the Gages executed, because their property would then be forfeited to the crown. Copley was apparently confused, because the Gages' property would have been forfeited to the crown when they were convicted of a capital felony and sentenced. The execution by hanging was only part of the sentence and should not have affected Howard's tenure of his lease. It seems possible that Howard's motives may not have been as base as Copley supposed (*Chronicle of the English Auugstinian Canonesses Regular of the Lateran, at St Monica's in Louvain, 1548–1644*, ed. Adam Hamilton (Edinburgh: 1904), I, 90; John Gage, *The History and Antiquities of Hengrave in Suffolk,* (London: 1822), p. 231; Henry Foley, *Records of the English Province of the Society of Jesus* (London: 1877), I, 186–8).

[2] *Lives of the English Martyrs*, ed. E. H. Burton and J. H. Pollen (London: 1914), I, 416–20; *Unpublished Documents Relating to the English Martyrs*, ed. Pollen (London: C.R.S., 1908), pp. 105–6; B.M., Harley MS. 7042, fo. 209v.

death in the Marshalsea for having the temerity to present to Queen Elizabeth the Catholic Petition for Toleration which had been drawn up by a group of gentlemen led by Lord Vaux and Sir John Arundell. They had presented the petition in an attempt to prevent the royal assent from being given to the parliamentary bill that subsequently was enacted as the Act against Seminary Priests (27 Eliz. I, c. 2).[1] The recusant family which kept a priest as a chaplain lived in constant terror of being betrayed by a servant. A house once known to have harboured a priest was apt to be repeatedly searched by armed posses. If it was suspected that the priest had hidden himself away, which was the case when a posse hunting down the Jesuit Richard Blount was searching Scotney Castle in the late 1590s, the pursuivants would simply move into the house until the priest was starved out or the wine cellar depleted.[2]

Only on one occasion was a sentence of death under the Act against Seminary priests ever carried out in Sussex. That was in 1588, a year of bloody persecution brought about by the threat of a Spanish invasion. Evidently the government felt that Sussex was a place where those inclined to religious disaffection might need to be recalled to their loyalty by means of exemplary executions. Therefore, four priests, who had been arrested after landing in Sussex and sent up to London for imprisonment, were brought back down to Chichester for execution. Ralph Crockett, Edward James, John Owen, and Francis Edwards were tried and condemned as traitors at the Chichester sessions. Three were sentenced to be executed just outside Chichester on Broyle Heath by the presiding justice Richard Lewkenor, whose own brother was a recusant. John Owen escaped execution by publicly swearing the oath of supremacy, while Francis Edwards lost courage and was reprieved after witnessing the execution of Crockett and James that same afternoon.[3]

The rigour with which the statutes against recusants and

[1] See my "Richard Shelley of Warminghurst and the English Catholic Petition for Toleration of 1585", *Recusant History*, VI (Oct. 1962), 265–74.

[2] The visit of the pursuivants to Scotney Castle was terminated by Fr Blount's daring escape, of which two separate and detailed contemporary accounts survive (Foley, *op. cit.*, III, 481–6; John Morris, *The Troubles of Our Catholic Forefathers Related by Themselves*, (London: 1872), I, 212–15).

[3] S.P., Dom., Eliz., 60/18. I.

missionary priests were enforced in the 1580s and 1590s depended upon the enthusiasm of the officers entrusted with executing the statutes and the Privy Council's judgment as to how dangerous the international situation was.

Some of the justices of the peace were known to have made false returns certifying that other J.P.s had sworn the oath of supremacy.[1] Many were very lax in reporting cases of recusancy. Moreover, the Privy Council had been very dissatisfied with the leniency shown by the Sussex J.P.s in the rating of recusants for the levy of light horses in 1584. After that recusant affairs were entrusted to special commissioners who were known to be staunch Protestants. These special commissioners were armed with broader and broader powers as the international situation became more tense.

The inquisitorial methods employed by these special commissioners were thought to be illegal and too extreme by some of the Sussex gentry. Led by Lord Buckhurst, the more active of the two lord lieutenants, and including such magistrates as Thomas Bishop, this group of politiques showed themselves very reluctant in carrying out the stricter directives concerning recusants that were sent out by the Privy Council in the 1580s. Even during the excitement of 1588, when a Spanish invasion was rumoured, Lord Buckhurst never lost his sense of decency or his respect for legal process. In the early part of 1588 the Privy Council began taking precautions against the possibility of a Spanish landing in Sussex. They ordered the deputy lieutenants of Sussex to draw up accurate lists of recusants and to determine which of them should be restrained. If clergymen or trusted members of the gentry could not be found who were willing to receive these reluctant guests into their houses then they were to be locked up in the common gaols.[2] When three of the deputy lieutenants proposed to imprison one such recusant gentleman, Anthony Kempe of Slindon, another deputy lieutenant, Sir Thomas Shirley, wrote to Lord Buckhurst vouching

[1] See Chapter 12, section i and my article "Catholics and Local Office Holding in Elizabethan Sussex", *Bulletin of the Institute of Historical Research*, XXXV (May 1962), 47–61.

[2] B.M., Harley MS. 703 (Letter Book of Sir Walter Covert of Slaugham), fo. 52.

for Kempe's loyalty and good character. Obviously finding the whole business very distasteful, Lord Buckhurst questioned the authority of the deputy lieutenants in imprisoning Kempe, and asked that the charges against the accused be sent to the Privy Council before proceeding any further. In rebuking the three deputy lieutenants Buckhurst wrote: "Albeit your dooings may seeme to proceede of zeale in you, yet I could have wished that it had been joyned with some better consideracon."[1] In practice a letter from the Privy Council was usually considered a sufficient warrant for taking someone into custody, but Buckhurst wrote again to warn the deputy lieutenants not to exceed their orders because of zeal, and enclosed another warrant spelling out the limitation of their powers in restraining recusants.[2] Buckhurst stated that it was his opinion that the deputy lieutenants had no "warrant or authoritie" for a general ministering of the oath of supremacy to recusants; referring to the case of Anthony Kempe again, he thought it very "injurious" to assume that a recusant was a dangerous man "before his cause be first harde [heard] and tryed."[3] However, the moderate Buckhurst did not represent the prevailing view of the Privy Council; most of the other councillors placed a higher value on such zeal and broader powers subsequently were conferred on the deputy lieutenants and special commissioners dealing with recusancy.

The idea of a separate commission, vested with extraordinary powers for dealing with recusancy, was not new. Bishop Curteys had always been distrustful of the J.P.s in their handling of recusancy cases; as far back as 1570 he had recommended that such matters be withdrawn from their jurisdiction and entrusted to special "commissioners for causes ecclesiastical". Evidently, what Curteys had in mind was a special branch of the High Commission sitting in Sussex.[4] Later, Curteys had proposed that townsmen from the Protestant Cinque Ports be brought into rural areas to serve in the magistracy and to keep an eye on those magistrates among the gentry who were reluctant to persecute their relatives and neighbours. It is not until 1585 that we come across special commissioners for

[1] Ibid., fos. 52–52v. [2] Ibid., fos. 52v–53.
[3] Ibid., fo. 52v. [4] See Chapters 2 and 12, section i.

disarming recusants. The letter[1] mentioning the existence of these special commissioners also refers to them as holding separate commissions for discovering recusants and seminary priests. These commissioners in the 1580s were found to be too lax in their job of detecting recusants, and the commission was later reconstituted and strengthened by the addition of several magistrates of pronounced Puritan sympathies.[2]

The war years of the 1590s brought sweeping powers to these commissioners. In December 1592 the four deputy lieutenants, whose names were always included in the commissions for dealing with recusants and seminary priests, were given a general warrant to search the houses of recusants for priests, forbidden books or seditious writings and to commit suspicious persons to prison.[3] Since Sussex was so close to the Continent the commissioners for recusants and seminary priests were authorized to work with the vice-admiral, port officers, mayors and "gentlemen that you shall assuredlie knowe to be discreete and well affected" in order to aid in the discovery and interrogation of people disembarking in Sussex ports or proceeding overseas.[4] The interrogators of suspected persons were also their judges, for the commissioners for recusants and seminary priests also appear to have been commissioned as justices of oyer and determiner. In 1597 Lord Burghley authorized the sheriff of Sussex and Surrey to pay commissioners for recusants and seminary priests an allowance of 5s. for each case brought to trial. To make sure that nothing was left to chance, Lord Burghley further specified that when such suspects were to be tried, the commissioners were to select the juries very carefully: "fforeseeing that you Retourne and warne [i.e., summon] verie sufficient freeholders . . . well affected to that service". At the time that the jury received their charge, they were to be paid an allowance of 13s. 4d., "allwayes p[ro]vided that the same allowance be not made but where hir ma[jes]tie is to re-

1 B.M., Harley MS. 703, fo. 68v.

2 *Ibid.*, fo. 69. In 1592 the commissioners for dealing with recusants and seminary priests included the bishop of Chichester, Lord Buckhurst, Sir Thomas West, Sir Thomas Shirley, Sir Walter Covert, Sir Henry Goring, Sir Nicholas Parker and Robert Sackville, Esquire.

3 *Ibid.*, fos. 73–73v.

4 *Ibid.*, fo. 73v.

ceive a Benefitt by the said service", cautioned Lord Burghley.[1] Thus, when the government finally did work out effective methods of enforcing the recusancy statutes, it was at the price of resorting to questionable legal procedures such as general warrants and tampering with juries.

Administrative inefficiency had plagued the government in the enforcement of the penal laws until late in the reign of Elizabeth. The ecclesiastical machinery had proved unequal to the task of administering the Act of Uniformity. Indeed, nowhere is the inadequacy of episcopal administration more strikingly revealed than in its failure to deal with the recusancy problem. It was not for want of zeal that the bishops failed to deal with early recusancy through their episcopal courts; they were as animated against Catholics as any of the Puritans in Parliament. But the machinery for detecting recusancy, as far as it depended upon churchwardens, simply did not work, and even where it did the church courts ultimately lacked sanction. From the very beginning only the Court of High Commission of all ecclesiastical courts was effective against important Catholics. But Parliament, biased as it was against prerogative and ecclesiastical courts, could hardly be expected to bolster the Court of High Commission with additional powers; and so, when stricter laws were enacted against recusants and seminary priests in the 1580s, Parliament was for this and other reasons impelled to place the execution of the newer statutes in the hands of officers drawn from the gentry.

It was presumed that the gentry commanded sufficient respect to qualify for the task of enforcing religious uniformity with vigour. As it turned out, many of the gentry did not feel as detached from their recusant neighbours as did an outsider such as Bishop Curteys, and eventually it became necessary to restrict recusant affairs to hand-picked Protestant magistrates who were known to be reliable.

The effectiveness of the penal laws was hampered further because the penalties provided were unrealistic. The Act of

[1] *Ibid.*, fo. 113. For letters from Lord Buckhurst giving the same instructions to the commissioners for recusancy in Sussex in 1598 and in Dorsetshire in 1600, see St G. K. Hyland, *A Century of Persecution under Tudor and Stuart Sovereigns from Contemporary Records* (London: 1920), pp. 223–6.

Uniformity of 1559 imposed a fine that was too low to penalize wealthy recusants, while the Recusancy Act of 1581 prescribed a fine that was too high for most recusants to pay. However, in the case of the later law there are indications that the government may have been more interested in the sequestration of the recusants' lands than in collecting the £20 fine.[1] At the same time, it must be kept in mind that the government intended to enforce the full penalties of the law against lay Catholics only when the international situation seemed to warrant it. Regardless of the weight of such fines, there is no conclusive evidence that they ever secured anything more than temporary conformity.

[1] O'Dwyer, *op. cit.*, p. 224.

8

THE SOCIAL INSTITUTIONS
OF RECUSANCY

ALTHOUGH ABOUT HALF of the Sussex gentry appear to have been Catholic at the beginning of Queen Elizabeth's reign, only about one-sixth of the greater gentry can be classified as recusants during the 1580s and 1590s.[1] It is generally agreed that Elizabethan Catholicism could survive only where there were social institutions to support it.[2] A picture of the background of the recusant gentry, their status, and their efforts to keep alive their faith, will afford an idea of the nature of these social institutions and will help to explain why so many of the recusant gentry ultimately became isolated from the county society in which they lived.

The leadership of the recusant gentry tended to be drawn from the proud old county families, usually established in Sussex since the fifteenth century or earlier. It almost goes without saying that their political and social views leaned towards the conservative as did their religious views. But one must not stereotype the conservatism of this group, for several of these families that later became recusant had refounded their fortunes as barristers or by service to the Tudor monarchs. Indeed most of them had been Henricians; some had helped to execute commissions for suppressing the monasteries of Sussex; and

---

[1] See Chapter 12, section ii.

[2] John Bossy, "The Character of Elizabethan Catholicism", *Crisis in Europe, 1560–1660* (London: 1965), pp. 223–46; A. G. Dickens, "The Extent and Character of Recusancy in Yorkshire, 1604", *Yorkshire Archaeological Journal*, XXXVII (1951), 40–2. In the West Riding of Yorkshire, although recusants probably comprised less than 1 per cent of the population, they constituted something like 25 per cent of the nobility and the gentry (Hugh Aveling, "The Catholic Recusants of the West Riding of Yorkshire, 1558–1790", *Proceedings of the Leeds Philosophical and Literary Society*, Literary and Historical Section, X, vi (1963), 191). Catholicism in Yorkshire survived in isolated, but concentrated pockets. On the other hand Fr O'Dwyer ("Catholic Recusants in Essex, *c.* 1580–*c.* 1600" (London M.A. thesis, 1960), pp. 229–230) found that in Essex recusants remained widely distributed throughout the whole county until the end of Elizabeth's reign.

none, when presented with the opportunity, had held back in the matter of monastic spoil.[1] Although not noted for the careful management of their estates,[2] faced with heavy fines for recusancy after 1581 or even possible sequestration of their estates, a surprising number of recusant families appear to have maintained or even improved their social position. Members of the Shelley, Gage, Caryll, Ashburnham and Leedes families were knighted by Queen Elizabeth or made baronets by James I. The Gage and Ashburnham families moved up into the peerage in the late seventeenth century.

It is striking how many of the families of Sussex gentry which became recusant under Elizabeth had buttressed their position in society by service to the early Tudor monarchs. Sir John Gage, K.G., of Firle was a soldier, diplomat and member of the Royal Council under Henry VIII. A protégé of the duke of Buckingham, he had caught the eye of the king in the French campaigns. From vice-chamberlain and captain of the royal guard, he rose to be comptroller of the royal household, chancellor of the duchy of Lancaster, and constable of the Tower of London. Sir John was one of the sixteen executors of Henry VIII's will and the dead monarch bequeathed £200 to him. Although no Protestant, Sir John Gage had accepted the Henrician supremacy; later he was identified with the conservative party of Gardiner and Norfolk that came into power after the fall of Thomas Cromwell. Like his relatives, Edward Shelley of Warminghurst and Sir Anthony Browne, he was the progenitor of a staunchly Catholic family, but Sir John Gage made his share out of the suppression of the monasteries.[3] The ascendancy of the Protector Somerset sent him into temporary retirement, but he was recalled as a royal councillor by Mary.[4]

[1] See G. W. O. Woodward's *A Short History of 16th Century England* (New York: The New American Library, 1963), p. 110 ff., which shows the connection between the conservative reaction of the 1540s and Elizabethan recusancy.

[2] Joyce E. Mousley, "The Fortunes of Some Gentry Families of Elizabethan Sussex", *Economic History Review*, 2nd ser., XI (April 1959), 467–83.

[3] Sir John Gage was joined with Richard Layton as a coadjutor in the commission for receiving surrendered monastic properties. He had received as a reward several choice pieces of monastic property.

[4] The principal sources of information on the Gages are: the *D.N.B.*;

The Brownes and the Shelleys had also been Henricians. Sir Anthony Browne, K.G. was a soldier, diplomat and a favourite of Henry VIII, and was also active in carrying out the suppression of the monasteries. Sir Anthony's son, the first viscount Montague, became perhaps the greatest beneficiary of the monastic spoliations in Sussex when he inherited not only his father's properties but also those of his half-brother, Sir William Fitzwilliam, earl of Southampton.[1] Sir William Shelley of Michelgrove was a well-known lawyer who became a judge of the court of Common Pleas. His son, Sir Edward, served the Protector Somerset as a soldier and was killed at the Battle of Pinkie-field in Scotland. Edward, a younger brother of William Shelley, refounded his fortunes at Warminghurst with the lands of the dissolved monastery of Sion and sired a fiercely Catholic family that included two martyrs to the cause of the old faith under Elizabeth.[2]

The Brownes and the Gages were the keystones of Queen Mary's regime in Sussex. Sir Anthony Browne's son and heir

M. A. Lower, *The Worthies of Sussex* (Lewes: 1865), p. 279 ff.; John Gage, *The History and Antiquities of Hengrave in Suffolk* (London: 1822), pp. 231–9; Thomas Gage, *The English American: A New Survey of the West Indies, 1648*, ed. A. P. Newton (London: 1946), pp. xii–xv. More useful information on the Gages can also be found in Phillippa Revil and F. W. Steer, "George Gage I and George Gage II", *Bulletin of the Institute of Historical Research*, XXXI (1958), 141–53.

[1] *D.N.B.*, *sub* Sir Anthony Browne and Anthony Browne, first viscount Montague. See also Chapter 11.

[2] The principal sources of information on the Shelleys, except where otherwise noted, are: the *D.N.B.*; Lower, *Sussex Worthies*, pp. 128–9; Edmund Cartwright, *The Rape of Bramber* (London: 1819), II. 2, 77. The Shelleys also had links with the old order: three members of that family were members of the Knights of St John's of Jerusalem, otherwise known as the Knights of Malta. A younger brother of Sir William had died defending the island of Rhodes against the successful Turkish siege; Sir Richard was the turcopolier and last English grand prior of the order; his younger brother Sir James was a commander in the same order. When the Reformation came, Sir James apparently conformed and accepted an annuity of £40 from the government (*Cal. P.R. Eliz.*, II, 507, dated 23 May 1563). Sir Richard preferred exile to giving up his faith (For Sir Richard's Career, see *D.N.B.*, *sub* Sir Richard Shelley; *The Letters of Sir Richard Shelley* (n.p.: 1774); Strype's account of Sir Richard in his *Annals*, V, 183–92, is full of errors).

was raised to the peerage by Queen Mary; Sir John Gage's son, Edward was made a Knight of the Bath and licensed to keep thirty retainers in his household. As sheriff of Sussex Sir Edward Gage underservedly incurred odium for the part that he was compelled to play in carrying out executions for heresy in Sussex during the Marian persecution.

The Catholic gentry were well entrenched among the local governors at the beginning of Elizabeth's reign, but unless they were flexible like the Carylls, they found themselves displaced from the commission of the peace during the late 1560s and the early 1570s, although sometimes still saddled with the financial burdens of the sheriffdom.[1] For a time, they still retained an indirect voice in county affairs—although that voice was progressively diminishing from 1569. Lord Montague shared the lieutenancy of Sussex and Surrey with Lord Buckhurst and William West (later Lord De La Warr) despite his known Catholic opinions, and occasionally could be counted upon to intercede with the Privy Council on their behalf. In return for providing Lord Buckhurst with the help that he needed in breaking the influence of the Arundel-Lumley faction, Lord Montague could sometimes find a place for a recusant as undersheriff or captain of the local trained bands, or secure an imprisoned recusant's release so that he might attend to pressing private business. But Lord Montague was permanently dropped from the commission of lieutenancy in 1585.[1]

Most of the leaders of the recusant gentry were imprisoned by the High Commission in the early 1580s.[1] After their release from prison they were often placed under restraint in times of international tension. Their sense of isolation was further increased by the Act of 1593 (35 Eliz. I, c. 2), which compelled recusants to remain within five miles of their homes unless licensed to travel outside those limits.

Turned out of the offices that they considered to be their birthright and increasingly subjected to legal penalties for nonconformity, they gradually withdrew from participation in county and parish affairs, leading lives that were filled with heroism and sacrifice, but living in a world that was turned in upon itself. This was a most unfortunate result of the English

[1] See Chapter 12, section i.   [2] See Chapter 11.   [3] See Chapter 7.

government's anti-Catholic religious policy, since most of the Catholic gentry were unreceptive to the dark political over-tures of the Catholic Reformation that originated in Spanish fanaticism or in the minds of embittered exiles. The govern-ment's purpose in enforcing religious uniformity was to promote social and political unity and to avoid the civil wars of the Continent, but this policy succeeded only at the cost of alienating a not unimportant segment of society.

Increasingly cut off from political power or even an indirect voice in the affairs of the county and parish, the natural reaction of the recusant gentry was to draw closer together to preserve their faith in the face of persecution. This they did by the quasi-feudal devices of marital alliances and economic inter-dependence. The Shelleys of Michelgrove were the most aristocratic of these recusant families in Sussex outside of the peerage. The heads of this family were allied by marriage with the Fitzwilliams and the Wriothesleys, successive holders of the earldom of Southampton, who were seated at Titchfield in Hampshire. A strong relationship also existed between the Brownes and the Gages of Firle. The Elizabethan Gages of Firle were cousins by marriage of the first and second Lords Montague and also leased land from them; the second Lord Montague was an overseer of the will of John Gage II.[1] The Gages, the Shelleys and the Copleys of Gatton, Surrey and Roffey, Sussex were extensively intermarried with one another. Moreover, both the Shelleys and the Gages had numerous cadet branches; the other branches of the Gages were located at Bentley, Sussex and Haling, Surrey while the Shelleys of Michelgrove had cousins at Warminghurst, Sussex and at Buriton and Mapledurham in Hampshire. Marriages contracted by the family heads of the cadet branches and the daughters of both senior and cadet branches linked the Shelleys and the Gages to families of the lesser Catholic gentry such as the Kempes of Slindon, the Thatchers of Priesthawes and the Apsleys of Pulborough.[2] Together the Brownes, the Shelleys,

[1] P.C.C., 43/4 Kidd.

[2] John Comber, *Sussex Genealogies*, IV, 247; Sir W. St J. Hope, *Cowdray and Easebourne Priory in the County of Sussex* (London: 1919); Smith, *Lady Montague*, p. xii; Christopher Devlin, *The Life of Robert Southwell, Poet and*

the Gages and the Copleys formed a tightly-knit clan of recusant families, who provided much of the Catholic leadership in Sussex, Surrey and Hampshire, and maintained a communications network that smuggled priests from south-coast ports up to London.

The social isolation of the recusant gentry from their Protestant neighbours was not only a consequence of the government's anti-Catholic policy, it was also a necessary precaution from their own point of view. The whole household could be endangered if the presence of a priest were reported to the authorities. There are instances of Protestants such as Sir Thomas Bishop and Lord Buckhurst, who maintained very cordial relations with their recusant neighbours and did them favours, but they tended to be exceptional.

The new seminary priests who began making their way into England after 1574 were needed by the English Catholics to replace the Marian priests who had been dying off. Without the spiritual sustenance which could only be provided by the priesthood, Catholicism might well have faded away completely within a couple of generations, as was the case in the Scandinavian countries. The Catholic gentry played a major role in preserving Catholicism because the missionary priests were absolutely dependent on their hospitality. Only the houses of the gentry could provide the protective seclusion that their dangerous missions required. Furthermore, the homes of the Catholic gentry in Sussex were, by reason of their geographical location, a particularly strategic link between the continental seminaries and London, where the wealthier gentry had townhouses or relatives established as lawyers among the Inns of Court, from whence these priests could spread out into the other counties of England. Robert Southwell, the Jesuit poet and martyr, is known to have used this communications system; the Shelleys, the Gages and the Copleys were his cousins.[1] William Shelley of Michelgrove and Edward Gage of Bentley both had houses in London: Edward Gage's was in the parish of St Andrew's, Holborn; William Shelley's was in

Martyr (New York: 1965), _passim_. See also above pp. 152–3 n. for other references.

[1] Devlin, _op. cit._, p. 15.

Trinity Lane. Lady Montague had two "goodly mansion houses" in London, the most important being the former priory of St Mary Overy in Southwark, not far from the south end of London bridge.[1] There were two main routes for smuggling priests up to London. One led up to London by way of Battle Abbey, where Lady Montague lived after the death of her husband in 1592, the Gages' seat at Bentley, and the Copleys' house at Gatton, Surrey. The infamous priest hunter, Richard Topcliffe, discovered another route that ran from the houses of the Shelleys at Buriton and Mapledurham in Hampshire to the house of George Cotton, at Warblington on the Hampshire-Sussex border, and then across the border to Lord Montague's seat at Cowdray; from there priests and their assistants were sent on to the Shelleys at Michelgrove in the rape of Bramber, and then up to London to Southampton House. On one occasion John Shelley of Buriton and a friend, both gentlemen retainers of Lord Montague, were accused of accompanying a priest through Sussex, whom they had disguised in Lord Montague's livery.[2] In the early 1590s a government spy reported that there were always three priests residing at Bentley and another at Michelgrove. William Shelley's house in Trinity Lane was full of secretly hidden books and papers, while George Cotton maintained a Jesuit at his house in Fleet Street.[3] In 1594 an apostate Catholic turned spy reported to the lord keeper that the Shelleys were keeping "a collidge of preests" at Mapledurham. Sir Thomas Bishop, himself a J.P. and a commissioner for discovering recusants and seminary priests, had living under his own roof a recusant gentleman whose son was a priest and who had smuggled two priests into London from Cornwall.[4]

The houses of the Catholic gentry had to be ready at a moment's notice for a visit from priest-hunters, and the most common practice was to hide the fugitive away in a priest hole. Sussex and east Hampshire had several examples of this intriguing Elizabethan architectural device. At Mapledurham the

---

[1] Smith, *Lady Montague*, pp. 41–2.

[2] Devlin, *op. cit.*, pp. 218–19, 128; *Cal. S.P. Dom.*, 1582–90, p. 352; *Acts P.C.*, XIV, 224–5.

[3] *Cal. S.P., Dom.*, 1591–1594, p. 176.

[4] S.P., Dom., Eliz., 248/116.

Shelleys had provided a vault under a table with an opening for light and air provided by a grate of iron placed behind the garden and covered up by rosemary.[1] Scotney Castle astride the Kent-Sussex border seems to have had several hiding places for the Jesuit chaplains who resided there beginning in the 1590s.[2] Sir Thomas Leedes of Steyning was another harbourer of priests and fancier of priest holes. Leedes, who was in the service of the lord chamberlain, kept one priest as a chaplain in London and a second at his country seat, Thorne House. Living nearby was Nicholas Wolfe of Washington House, described as a great companion of Leedes. Wolfe kept "an alter and other massing stvff" hidden away beneath the false top of a large cupboard. The Caryll family of West Grinstead and Harting were inveterate constructors of secret chapels and priest holes. When forced to dismantle the church that was attached to their home at West Grinstead, they used the stone to put up another house with a secret chapel and a hidden retreat for the priest. The Caryll house became the centre of Catholic worship at West Grinstead and John Caryll made a small endowment towards providing a chaplain there.

The Catholic gentry of Sussex were able to maintain centres of Catholic worship in their houses with relative impunity during the 1560s and 1570s. Many of them sheltered Marian priests as chaplains during those years. But after the High Commission assumed the task of punishing religious disaffection in the summer of 1580, the Catholic leaders among the untitled gentry were either under restraint or under constant surveillance. From this time forward the recusant gentry found it more and more difficult to keep priests in their domestic establishments for any space of time. Some few did maintain more or less permanent chaplaincies for the members of their households and their tenants, and we can only marvel at their courage and ingenuity. But more and more, many of the gentry were compelled to seek their spiritual nourishment in the privileged households of the nobility. There appears to be a very definite connection between the continuing strength of Catholicism among the gentry in certain parts of Sussex and the proximity and accessibility of those noble households, which

[1] *Ibid.*   [2] See above, p. 145 n.

were able to maintain internal autonomy with regard to religious worship because their heads were careful to maintain a distinction between the spiritual aspects of post-Tridentine Catholicism and its political overtones.[1]

The households of Philip Howard, earl of Arundel and Surrey and Henry Percy, eighth earl of Northumberland were destroyed because of the political indiscretions of those noblemen. The influence of Lord Lumley was certainly diminished because of his father-in-law, Henry Fitzalan, earl of Arundel.[2]

But as long as a nobleman was considered loyal, his household continued to enjoy, for all practical purposes, complete exemption from the jurisdiction of local magistrates. Thus, a large noble household, such as that of the first two Lords Montague at Cowdray in the rape of Chichester, or, after the death of the first Lord Montague, the dowager Lady Montague's household at Battle Abbey in the rape of Hastings, could exert a powerful influence in maintaining Catholicism by reason of the freedom of worship that it could offer to so many people. The spiritual needs of each of these domestic establishments were continuously supplied by several resident chaplains throughout the whole reign of Elizabeth.

A vivid impression of the vigorous religious life in the Browne households can be gained from Bishop Richard Smith's biography of Lady Montague.[3] A chapel had been built at Battle Abbey complete with "a very fair altar of stone" enclosed with rails, a choir for singers, and a pulpit, "which perhaps is not to be seen in all England besides". A sermon was preached every week and on solemn feasts, Mass was celebrated "with singing and musical instruments", and sometimes with deacon and subdeacon. Lady Montague took pride in the great number of Catholics who resorted to her chapel. On special occasions it was not unusual for as many as one hundred and twenty people to attend mass with perhaps sixty communicating.[4]

---

[1] See Chapter 12, section ii.
[2] See Chapter 11.
[3] *Op. cit.*, p. 43–4.
[4] The second Lord Montague's household at Cowdray Park, near Midhurst, may well have drawn as many worshippers from the household proper as from among guests. In 1595, 37 different classes of household

The relative freedom of worship that existed in these two households is attributable to several factors. Anthony Browne, the first viscount Montague, was a large landowner and his economic influence was extensive. He was allied to the lord lieutenant, Lord Buckhurst, both politically and by marriage, his grandson and successor, Anthony Maria, having married Buckhurst's daughter, and thus he retained a friend at court and on the Privy Council even after he had been dropped from the commission of lieutenancy in 1585.[1] But the most important factor was Lord Montague's character.

Lord Montague's unique position as the most important Catholic in Sussex and perhaps the most influential Catholic in England derived from his unquestioned loyalty to the queen and his scrupulous moderation in religious matters. His father, Sir Anthony Browne, had been a Henrician Catholic, but Lord Montague came to accept the religious principles of the Catholic Reformation while rejecting the aggressively political overtones that blew out of Philippine Spain with the "Enterprise". Bishop Richard Smith, later vicar apostolic, who personally knew some of the chaplains that had been at Cowdray in Lord Montague's day, says that Montague occasionally had attended Protestant services, which Bishop Smith blamed on Alban Langdale, "a learned and pious man indeed, but too fearful".[2] When Langdale died,[3] his place was taken by Fr Robert Gray, a priest of the Catholic Reformation who did not hesitate to reproach Lord Montague in no uncertain terms

---

officials and male servants were required to staff Cowdray, a splendid mansion that any sovereign would have been proud to own ("'A Booke of Orders and Rules' of Anthony Viscount Montague in 1595", ed. Sir S. D. Scott, *S.A.C.*, VII, 180–1).

[1] See Chapter 11.

[2] Smith, *Lady Montague*, p. 19. After his deprivation from the archdeaconry of Chichester, Langdale came to live at Cowdray and probably was Lord Montague's chaplain. A pamphlet saying that it was not wrong "to give to the time" and to attend Anglican services occasionally was mistakenly attributed to Alban Langdale. Joseph Gillow says that the treatise was written by Alban's nephew, Thomas Langdale, a Jesuit who later apostatized (*Biographical Dictionary of English Catholics* (London: 1885), IV, 117–18).

[3] Langdale died sometime between 1587 and 1589. Robert Gray was in Lord Montague's service at least as early as 1589.

about the error of attending heretical services. This is how Bishop Smith, to whom the story was related by someone actually present, describes Lord Montague's reaction.

"Instantly putting off his hat and falling on his knees, both with a gesture of his whole body and tongue, he most humbly submitted himself to the censure and piously promised never thence-forward to be present at heretical service which all the rest of his life he exactly observed."[1]

Both Lord and Lady Montague drew a careful distinction between what they considered to be legitimate means of preserving their faith and what could only be construed as treason. This distinction was not based upon what could be done safely and what might bring ruin; it arose from an attempt to draw a line between what was God's and what was rightfully the Queen's. For example Lady Montague twice offered to let Bishop Smith set up a printing press in her household, yet she consistently refused to be drawn into any plots, even those engaged in by her brother, Francis Dacre, who was caught up in the Essex conspiracy. When, in September 1597, a messenger arrived at Battle Abbey with a packet of letters for her daughter and another to be conveyed to the earl of Essex, Lady Montague promptly turned him over to a magistrate. She then related all she knew to Lord Buckhurst, the lord lieutenant, sending her niece along as a witness.[2]

Lord Montague died in 1592. His grandson, Anthony Maria, who succeeded him as second viscount, was at that time still only a boy,[3] so the dowager Lady Montague attempted to carry on her husband's role as protector of Sussex Catholics.[4] Lady

[1] Smith, *Lady Montague*, p. 20.
[2] Hist. MSS. Comm., *Salisbury MSS.*, vii, 396–402; B.M., Lansdowne MS. 82, fos. 103–103v. Buckhurst forwarded the information to Lord Burghley and asked to be excused from further dealing with the matter, "the Lord Montague having married my daughter".
[3] In 1602, John Ellis, an apostate Catholic turned informer, said that the English Catholics depended more on the second Lord Montague than any other person in England (Hist. MSS. Comm., *Salisbury MSS.*, xii, 367).
[4] This is Lord Montague's second wife, Magdalen, daughter of the third Lord Dacre of Greystoke and Gilsland. They had met at the court of Queen Mary and were married in 1556. Lord Montague's first wife, Lady Jane

Montague, in whose veins coursed the blood of the Talbots and Dacres of the North, was a woman noted for her remarkable strength of character and for the fact that distressed Catholics and hounded priests could always look to her for protection or shelter.

After Lady Montague went to live at Battle Abbey following the death of her husband, it was noted that "Religion in that countrey, especially in that towne, is greatly decayed".[1] Battle had been an abbey of royal foundation and an ecclesiastical peculiar exempt from the ordinary authority of the bishop of Chichester. Lord Montague had succeeded in preventing episcopal visitations from taking place in Battle, and in 1583 it was described as a place "much infected & [a] great resort of papists thither specially of late strangers in companies resorting thitherward & soom suspected as they went to be priests".[2] The archbishop of Canterbury was the only ecclesiastical officer with the authority to visit Battle and he had forgotten about the place.

In 1596 an anonymous informant told Lord Burghley that the situation had grown more alarming. The dean of Battle was the one who exercised ecclesiastical jurisdiction in that town, and he had gone over to the side of the papists and had ceased ministering according to the Book of Common Prayer. Not only had the dean and his whole family failed to communicate for two years, they were observed to keep company largely with recusants. One of the dean of Battle's companions was Robert Gray, the priest who earlier had reprimanded Lord Montague for his occasional conformity; another was Lady Montague's Catholic schoolmaster, who "had the bringing up of most of the gentlemen in that country". The dean no longer made any pretence of enforcing religious uniformity and Lord Burghley's informant reported that the people of Battle "doe what they list. There

---

Ratcliff, daughter of Robert, earl of Sussex, died in childbirth after bearing three children. Lord Montague had eight children by his second marriage (Smith, *Lady Montague*, pp. 6, 39, 43; *G.E.C.*, IV, 22).

Bishop Richard Smith was Lady Montague's chaplain from 1603 until her death in 1608. His biography of her was written shortly after her death.

[1] B.M., Lansdowne MS. 82, fos. 103–103v.

[2] S.P., Dom., Eliz., 165/22.

are many in the towne that never receive the communion & come very seldome at church."[1]

The local commissioners of the peace were equally reluctant to enforce the penal laws against Lady Montague's household. The presiding justice of the peace in Hastings Rape, Edmund Pelham, was very slack in attending church and had not received communion in over a year. His wife was a known Catholic and "Many recusants" were seen frequenting his house. Pelham was described as "chief of my La[dy] Montague's counsel . . . and a great man with the Deane of Battle". Another J.P., Henry Apsley, appears to have been equally under Lady Montague's influence.[2]

By reason of the laxity of local magistrates and the almost complete immunity of her household, Lady Montague was able to make Battle Abbey a particularly important link in an underground communications system that channelled priests coming from overseas to other parts of England. Lady Montague was aided in this enterprise by the searcher of Pevensey harbour; he and his wife dwelled in a lone house at the edge of Battle manor that was equipped with a subterranean passage. Another accomplice was a tavern keeper whose house also had an escape tunnel. The tavern keeper and all his servants were Catholics, and since he delivered provisions and barrels of beer over a wide area, he had ample opportunity to convey people secretly.[3]

The dependence of the Sussex recusants upon the Catholic nobility was an important social characteristic and did much to shape their political attitudes and behaviour. From the government's point of view this social dependence could produce good or bad results depending upon the particular views of the nobleman to whose faction they adhered. The discontent of recusants, whether arising from religious persecution or exclusion from public office, could feed upon the vague

---

[1] B.M., Lansdowne MS. 83, fos. 103–103v. Bishop Smith tells us that Lady Montague "endured no other persecution for matter of religion than that she was once accused to the pretended Bishop of Canterbury, her house twice searched, and her priest once taken and imprisoned . . ." (*Op. cit.*, pp. 41–2; see also *Acts P.C.*, XXIV, 328 and *Cal. S.P.*, *Dom.*, *1591–94*, p. 379).   [2] B.M., Lansdowne MS. 82, fos. 103–103v.   [3] *Ibid.*

promises of ambitious noblemen who conspired against the queen. William Shelley of Michelgrove, having thrown in his fortunes with those of the erratic Henry, eighth earl of Northumberland, was ultimately tried and convicted for the peripheral and unenthusiastic part that he played in the Throckmorton plot to place Mary, Queen of Scots on the English throne.[1] Fortunately, William Shelley's behaviour was exceptional. More representative of the recusant gentry of Sussex were the Gages of Firle or the Ashburnhams of Ashburnham, who whether tied by marriage or economic dependence, or whether simply sharing the religious and political views of the first Lord Montague and his wife Magdalen, were loyal and quiescent.

Another important social pattern among the recusant gentry that became evident by the middle of the Elizabethan period was their increasing isolation from parish and county life. Their exclusion from public office and their withdrawal from participation in parish affairs meant that the recusant gentry had less contact with their Protestant neighbours who were magistrates.

[1] When the eighth earl of Northumberland was released in 1573 after confinement for intriguing with the Scots queen, he was forbidden to return to the north of England where his name might still command a following, so he took up residence at his house near Petworth, Sussex. During his residence in Sussex Northumberland developed Catholic sympathies and tried with little success to involve members of the Sussex gentry in the execution of a plan to place Mary Stuart on the English throne. Northumberland and Shelley were arrested after being visited by Mary Stuart's agent, Charles Paget, who had come to sound out Northumberland on the duke of Guise's plan to invade England by way of Scotland.

Although Shelley was sentenced to death after his trial for treason in Westminster Hall, it was evident that he had been cool to the whole scheme, and his uncle, Sir Richard Shelley, writing from exile in Venice, actually was able to persuade the queen to suspend the execution of the sentence. Shelley was eventually released from prison and his estates were restored. (For details of this plot insofar as it affected the gentry of Sussex, see the following: Gerald Brennan, *A History of the House of Percy* (London: 1902), II, *passim*; *The Ven. Philip Howard, Earl of Arundel, 1557–1595*, ed. Pollen and MacMahon (London: C.R.S., 1919), pp. 127–8; *Letters and Memorials of Father Robert Persons, S.J.*, ed. L. Hicks (London: C.R.S., 1942), I, 286–9; Hist. MSS. Comm., *Salisbury MSS.*, xiii, 277–9; S.P., Dom., Eliz., 163/86, 167/59, 178/11, 182/17, 228/24; B.M., Egerton MS. 2074, fo. 73; B.M., Lansdowne MS. 51, fo. 20.).

Cut off from the sources of influence and driven to the wall by ruinous recusancy fines and the sequestration of their lands, the sons and daughters of the recusant gentry offered less attractive prospects for marriage alliances in the eyes of the Protestant local governors. An even greater obstacle to intermarriage with Protestant magisterial families was the problem of worship. There were too many difficulties in the way of the Catholic wife of a Protestant practising her faith and rearing the children in her own religion. And so recusant families among the gentry were forced to intermarry with one another not only because there were fewer alternatives available, but also because closer social relationships facilitated the preservation of their ancient faith.

9

THE CONDITION OF THE CLERGY
AND THE SPREAD OF PURITANISM

W HETHER THE FORTUNES of the gentry were rising at the expense of the peerage or falling in relation to the value of money is a question that is still being debated. But that the economic status of the clergy declined in the sixteenth century, no scholar doubts. The monasteries and chantries had already been disposed of when Elizabeth came to the throne, and, having plundered episcopal and capitular revenues for herself and her courtiers, little remained to be acquired by the enterprising investor save impropriated parish tithes and advowsons. Traffic in this variety of church plunder continued to be vigorous. The queen alone sold or granted title to tithes in 2,216 parishes.[1] With the possible exception of the confiscation of chantries, none of the previous raids on ecclesiastical lands and revenues had directly affected the parish clergy, but at the end of the reign Sir Thomas Wilson observed that the wings of the clergy were "well clipped of late by courtiers and noblemen, and some quite cut away, both feather, flesh and bone".[2]

Pluralism, non-residence and a generally inadequate ministry were consequences of the economic decline of the clergy. It was upon these abuses that clerical Puritanism throve. In the absence of modern means of shaping public opinion, the clergyman in the pulpit was potentially a major influence in winning or losing support for the established church. Yet the worsening economic and social state of the clergy cut away at what little independence remained to them, promoted pluralism, non-residence, and other abuses, and left many parishes served only by ignorant curates who were forced to neglect their

[1] Henry Grove, *Alienated Tithes in Impropriated Parishes, Commuted or Merged under Local Statutes and the Tithe Acts: Together with all Crown Grants of Tithes, Henry VIII to William III* (London: 1896), part III, *passim*.

[2] Quoted in Christopher Hill, *Economic Problems of the Church from Archbishop Whitgift to the Long Parliament* (Oxford: 1956), p. 1.

duties in order to grovel for their bread. In an age that attached so much importance to external signs of affluence the condition of the clergy bred only contempt.

Bishops Barlow and Curteys both saw the need to provide more preachers as the most pressing problem facing them in their administrations. Because of the general unavailability of sufficient learned Protestant preachers in the time of Bishop Barlow, little could be done to remedy the defect, but in the last year of his life Bishop Curteys, who accomplished more to supply the lack of preachers than any other Elizabethan bishop of Chichester, told the Privy Council that a further solution of the problem was wrapped up with the necessity of economic reform.

"By increasing the number of preachers to have the people better grounded in religion. The help whearof consisteth in the Bishop & his Chauncellour who assisted by your honours may very muche mend it partly by vniting partly by making vp stipends for these my parishes & allowing soom large portions owt of ye benefices whear vnlearned men or non residensaries bee."[1]

Bishop Curteys had already amalgamated several benefices, where the distance was not so great that the incumbent could not take charge of the services in two churches in one day, but even where two benefices were united, the total income resulting was often still insufficient to attract a learned man.

Had the bishops been able to use impropriated tithes in lay hands for supplementing meagre livings, the problem might have been solved. But, although there was an ineffectual movement in the next century to restore tithes to spiritual uses, stimulated by Sir Henry Spelman's tales of horror concerning the punishments visited upon the sacrilegious, the Elizabethans looked upon property rights as something sacrosanct in themselves. It was not just a question of the property rights of patrons of benefices or lay impropriators, but also of the property rights of clergyman, for the incumbents of benefices also had freehold rights. If an attack were made upon the property rights of impropriators, the property rights of

[1] S.P., Dom., Eliz., 165/22.

ministers would not be safe. Archbishop Whitgift felt that clergymen had little enough independence without removing their security of tenure: "If the minister were but tenant at will, or of courtesy (as you would seem to have him) his state would be most slavish and miserable, and he and his family ready to go a-begging whensoever he displeaseth his parish".[1]

Realizing the dilemma facing the bishops, what kind of men were the clerics of the diocese of Chichester and how did they gain entrance into their benefices?

Those who aspired to the choicest benefices—cathedral deaneries, chancellorships, archdeaconries—were chosen from among university graduates and, as often as not, enjoyed the patronage of a prominent courtier. Anthony Rush, D.D., who succeeded Richard Curteys as dean of Chichester in 1570, began his career as a chaplain to the powerful Thomas, third earl of Sussex, who introduced him to Archbishop Parker and the queen. Parker thought that Rush might "do good service" in the church, and he told Sir William Cecil that he did not mind helping such men to good benefices.[2] Installed in the faction-ridden chapter at Chichester, Rush at first supported the bishop's party, but was later persuaded to turn against Curteys. His tenure of the deanery of Chichester was marked by lock-picking, forgery, and continued alienation of capitular property.[3] In 1591 the chapter found it necessary to modify the terms of a lease of capitular property dated 1570 and granted to a servant of Rush's for a term of eighty years.[4] The number of long-term leases made by Rush cannot be determined, because it was not his habit to keep a written record of these transactions. Such long term leases, yielding large entry fines for the lessor to the diminution of his successors' income, were typical of the widespread spoliation that necessitated the Parliamentary statute of 1571,[5] which limited leases of capitular and episcopal property to 21 years or three lives.

The contentious William Overton, whose conduct as bishop of Coventry and Lichfield later aroused such contempt in Lord

---

[1] Quoted in C. Hill, op. cit., p. 51.
[2] C. H. and T. Cooper, Athenae Cantabrigienses, I, 363–4; D.N.B., sub Anthony Rush; S.P., Dom., Eliz., 40/3.   [3] Cf. Chapters 4 and 5.
[4] Peckham, Act Book A, nos. 910 & 777.   [5] 13 Eliz., c. 10.

Burghley, owed his preferments to the patronage of the earl of Leicester. The arrangement was materially beneficial to both patron and client as a letter from Overton, while treasurer of Chichester, to Leicester clearly reveals:

"Consyder with yourself I besech you what I am and what I have been towardes your Lordship. I am your chapleyn of olde; I have been plyable to your letters and suytes; I have ben and am in case both able and ready to do you honour if you will use me."[1]

An argument between Overton and Thomas Drant, poet and prebendary of Firles led the latter to denounce Overton from the pulpit for pride and hypocrisy.[2]

The bishop of Chichester had a large number of livings in his gift, and while he was under pressure from courtiers seeking advowsons to sell or give to clients, the bishop's episcopal officials usually owed their promotion to him. One of Bishop Curteys's staunchest supporters was Henry Blackstone or Blaxton, D.D., who had been at Clare Hall, Cambridge, and subsequently was a schoolmaster at Higham Ferrers, Northamptonshire, where Sir George Buck, poet and master of the revels in Shakespeare's time, was his scholar, later to become his brother-in-law. Blaxton became prebendary of Highleigh, rector of West Thorney and vicar of Cocking, and master of the school attached to Chichester Cathedral. Blaxton's scholastic qualifications lend support to the boast made by Curteys's supporters that the bishop beneficed many learned men in his diocese. Blaxton also served as vicar-general and commissary from 1572 until his death in 1606. The price of such a man as Blaxton was extensive pluralism and non-residence. Blaxton and his wife Joan had nine children for whom to provide, and it comes as no surprise that at least two of them became clerics: Godfrey Blaxton held the three rectories of Eastergate and Yapton, West Thorney, and St Peter the Great, Chichester and was a vicar-choral from 1594 to 1633.[3]

---

[1] "Letters of Thomas Wood, 1566–1577", ed. Patrick Collinson, *Bulletin of the Institute of Historical Research Special Supplement no. 5* (November 1960), p. xxxv.   [2] *D.N.B.*, *sub* Thomas Drant.

[3] W. H. Challen, "Henry Blaxton, D.D.", *S.N. & Q.*, XLV (May 1957), 221–5.

The pluralism, non-residence and alienation of capitular property of the canons residentiary were, however, nothing when compared with the conduct of the vicars-choral—a source of scandal to even the residentiaries. The problem originated in medieval times with the non-residence of canons, who were obliged to appoint *canonicorum vicarii sive chorales* to perform their duty of singing the office in the cathedral church. The position of the vicars-choral was institutionalized in the fourteenth century when they had a collegiate organization imposed upon them and were provided with separate endowments.[1] Originally they were usually priests or at least in minor orders, and while in Elizabethan times some were impoverished curates, most were laymen. There can be no doubt that their standard of conduct was worse than that of the average cleric, deteriorating still more after the beginning of the Reformation. Their numbers were also reduced after the breach with Rome: whereas in 1521 there had been 14 vicars-choral, their number never exceeded five during the reign of Elizabeth and was permanently fixed at four in 1596. During this time the vicars also ceased to live and eat in common—a reflection of the breakdown in corporate discipline: in 1568 three of the vicars were reprimanded for not eating in their commons hall, but by 1583 this requirement had been relaxed to the extent that a vicar need dine in commons only once a month.[2]

Their singing in the cathedral was apt to be accompanied by the yelping of a "dogge or bytche" brought into the church by one of the vicars, while in 1598 they were given to circulating "slanderous reports of one another and such tale-bearing as caused brawls", and had to be admonished not to bring suit against one another until the dispute had been submitted to the dean and chapter.[3] The vicars-choral did not enjoy the same security of tenure as the prebendaries; their frequent deprivation argues a rapid turnover of their membership. In 1587 James Williams was deprived "for matter of incontinencye, and

[1] J. Dallaway, *A History of the Western Division of the County of Sussex* (London: 1815–1830), I, 113–14.

[2] Peckham, "The Vicars Choral of Chichester Cathedral", *S.A.C.*, LXXVIII, 126–59.

[3] Peckham, *Act Book A*, nos. 1015 & 965.

for dyvers other things"; William Legat was deprived in 1569 and imprisoned on an unspecified charge awaiting general gaol delivery.[1] James Williams had already been deprived from the same office once before along with Edmund Medowcrofte on 7 May 1571 because of a drunken midnight brawl which took place between these two scoundrels in Canon Lane, when Williams was saved from Medowcrofte's naked dagger only through the intervention of another vicar. Also deprived on the same day was a third lay vicar, William Payne, who was charged with assaulting the verger and threatening to "fill his skinne full of hayleshotte".[2] These two incidents were the occasions that prompted the cathedral statute of 1573 enjoining "that none of the Vicars Choral, Lay Vicars, Singing men, or Sherborne's Clerks, shall be a fighter, a common brawler, quarreller, or drunkard, either within the Close of the same Church or . . . the City of Chichester".[3]

Very little evidence survives concerning the social origins of the clergy. Even the background of the four Elizabethan bishops of Chichester is clouded with obscurity, although Bickley seems to have claimed some kinship to the Bagots, a leading county family of Staffordshire. A few of the lower clergy were of gentle birth: a family benefice was a handy way of supporting a younger son or of relieving an impoverished cousin. John Culpepper of Wakehurst was rector of the family parish of Ardingly from 1564 until his death in 1589, where, no doubt, he preached to his Culpepper kin every Sunday.

His nephew, Nicholas Culpepper, was vicar of Alciston in 1612, and became rector of Ockley, Surrey—a parish belonging to the family manor of Ockley.[4] Lord Buckhurst presented a relative, Maurice Sackville, the son of Richard Sackville of Callis, to the rectory of Withyham, valued at £60 in 1597. Lord Buckhurst's seat, from which he took his title, lay within that parish; Buckhurst had obtained the advowson from King's

[1] *Ibid.*, nos. 871 & 723.

[2] *Ibid.*, no. 751.

[3] *Statutes and Constitutions of the Cathedral Church of Chichester*, ed. F. G. Bennett, R. H. Codrington, C. Deedes (Chichester: 1904), pp. 22–8.

[4] F. Attree and J. Booker, "The Sussex Colepeppers, Part II", *S.A C.*, XLVIII, 65–98; Will of Thomas Culpeper of Wakehurst, P.C.C., 45 Holney.

College, Cambridge in 1569 along with a grant of the manor of Withyham. Maurice Sackville was detected in 1593 for preaching without a licence from the ordinary, and when the judge of the archidiaconal court of Lewes ordered him to desist, Maurice felt bold enough of defy the judge's admonition.[1]

Of the educated clergy, one suspects that the background of Henry Blaxton, who came of Huntingdonshire yeoman stock, was more typical.[2] The bulk of the uneducated clergy, not so clever at disguising their origins, came from the humblest classes.

Conflict between incumbents and their parishioners was frequent, and even as upright a Puritan as John Frewen, rector of Northiam, was abused by a parishioner who "threatened to pull Mr Frewen out of the pulpit and spit in his face . . . and threatened that songs should be made of him".[3] The last threat amusingly enough was a real cause of uneasiness to the Elizabethan in a scurrilous age. A quarrel between the vicar of Rudgwick and a female parishioner became so bitter in 1592 that the latter requested permission to attend a neighbouring parish church. She told the judge of the consistory court of Chichester, "I woulde wishe to god that wee had a minister that had some [small] honestye and not a common drunkerde a lier a swearer & a quarreller".[4] The parson of Elsted was a good example of the unworthy clergyman who alienated his parishioners and gave proof to the charges of the Puritans. He habitually said "divine service at such vncertaine times and houres that the parisheoners do not knowe at what time they shall come to heare the same", although he had many times been requested to use regular hours. As a result many came too late to attend common prayer, and so much confusion resulted that the churchwardens ceased altogether to levy the twelve-penny fine for absence. The parson was a pluralist who also held a vicarage in Hampshire and the two livings together were worth £80 whereas many other clerics had to subsist on less than £10 a year. Not only was it suspected "that he came to the

---

[1] D.N.B., sub Sir Thomas Sackville; B.M., Add. MS. 39,444, fo. 73.

[2] Challen, loc. cit., XIV, 221–5.

[3] C. Thomas-Stanford, Sussex in the Great Civil War and the Interregnum, 1642–1660 (London: 1910), pp. 24–5.

[4] B.M., Add. MS. 33,410, fo. 97.

parsonage of Ellsted by symonye", but he neither preached nor instructed the children and servants in the catechism, nor visited the sick, nor did he read the homilies or the queen's injunctions. He was "drunk very often" and the parsonage house and chancel were in decay. Edmund Lewkenor and his wife avoided going to the parish church of Trotton after the parson had refused him communion; "the parsone hath so mysvsed her and him that theie have made a vowe never to receue at his hands."[1]

Clerical marriage was a cause of offence to conservative-minded parishioners and the occasion for bitter exchanges. In 1583 a female parishioner of Beding was charged before the archidiaconal court of Lewes with calling her minister's wife "the mistress of a Redyng prists trull" to which she added "that all prists wyvs were counted trulls".[2] The same parisiohioner who had threatened John Frewen with ribald ballads, was of the opinion that "it was a merrier world when ministers might not marry; that now they ought not to marry, and that their children are illegitimate".[3] The social status of clerical wives was not merely low; it was anomalous. The clergyman was lucky, indeed, who could make as advantageous a marriage as Henry Blaxton's son Godfrey, who married the daughter of a Chichester alderman.[4]

The quality of the clergy was partially a reflection of the astoundingly low incomes of the parish clergy of the diocese of Chichester. £30 per year was considered the minimum remuneration needed to maintain even a mediocre minister, and more was thought necessary to secure a man of learning.[5] Only four parochial benefices in the whole diocese of Chichester were worth £30 a year or more; of the four incumbents of these benefices, three were non-resident and one was known to be a pluralist in addition.[6] Meagre incomes necessitated the twin

[1] *Ibid.*, 39, 454, fos. 27v–28.
[2] DRO, Ep. II/9/2, fos. 106v–107.
[3] Thomas-Stanford, *loc. cit.*, pp. 24–5.
[4] Challen, *loc. cit.*, XIV, 221–5.
[5] C. Hill, *op. cit.*, p. 205.
[6] The rectory of Winchelsea was worth £30 in 1603; the rectory of Broadwater was valued at £30 in 1585; the rectory of Barnham £40 in 1579; and the rectory of Withyham at £60 in 1597.

evils of pluralism and non-residence, but adequate incomes certainly did not eliminate those evils: if anything, the proportion of pluralist and non-resident clerics to resident clerics tended to increase in the higher income groups (as the figures in Table I will show). For a clergyman to achieve a substantial income it was a *sine qua non* that he be a pluralist. It was only by pluralism that Anthony Rushe, dean of Chichester, could enjoy an annual income of £243 18s. 10d. or William Overton, treasurer of Chichester, an income of £127 3s. 4d.[1] As long as a benefice was thought of primarily as a piece of freehold property entitling the incumbent to an income from tithes, rather than as a cure of souls necessitating performance of duties, the abuses of pluralism and non-residence were due as much to moral attitudes as to economics. While diminished clerical incomes were a proximate result of lay appropriation of tithes, the whole problem was as much a reflection of a decline in public morality.

The visitation returns for the archdeaconry of Chichester in 1579 are illustrative of the evils arising from pluralism and non-residence. At West Thorney, Henry Blaxton, the absentee parson, "hath fellid timber in the churchyard and hath not bestowyd it nether vpon the chaunsell nor vpon the bodie of the church". Blaxton was also vicar of Cocking, where he "letith his benefice to his reder but what he giveth we knowe not, but the vicarage hous ys in ruyn. The churchyard is vnrepayred."[2] However, Blaxton did discharge his quarterly sermons, which is more than most non-residents did. The name of the parson of Barnham, whose income of £40 was the highest of any parochial benefice in archdeaconry of Chichester, was not even known to the churchwardens. The vicarage was long void, and instead the parson hired a curate at £6 a year, which was increased to £8 in 1585. Both the church and the chancel were badly in need of repairs; "as for the vicarage yt is so decayed in all respects that a man wold be loth [to go] therein".[3]

The Puritans were always alert for flagrant cases of non-

[1] S.P., Dom., Eliz., 96/p. 175.
[2] B.M., Add. MS. 39,454, fos. 9v & 22v.
[3] *Ibid.*, fo. 33v; Lambeth Palace Library, MS. Carta Misc. XII/6.

TABLE I

Pluralism and Non-residence

The Benefices and Curacies of the Archdeaconry of Chichester in 1579 (B.M., Add. MS. 39,454; Lambeth Palace, MS. Carta misc. XII/6).

Stipend in £ of Benefices

	1–5	6–10	11–15	16–20	21–25	26 or over	stipend unknown	total
Resident rectors	5	21	8	1	1	—	2	38
Partially non-resident rectors*	—	4	2	—	—	—	—	6
Non-resident rectors	—	4	2	5	2	2	3	18
Pluralist rectors	2	13	4	2	3	1	3	28
Status of rector unknown	1	1	2	—	—	—	—	4
Resident vicars	3	26	7	—	—	—	2	38
Partially non-resident vicars	1	1	1	—	—	—	—	3
Non-resident vicars	—	5	1	—	—	—	—	6
Pluralist vicars	2	5	2	—	—	—	—	9
Status of vicar unknown	—	2	—	—	1	—	—	3
Resident curates**	5	7	8	1	—	—	15	36
Partially non-resident curates	1	1	—	—	—	—	1	3
Non-resident curates	—	1	—	—	—	—	—	1
Pluralist curates	1	2	—	—	—	—	1	4
Status of curate unknown	—	1	—	1	—	—	—	2
Benefices void	4	6	—	1	—	—	3	14
No information available	—	—	—	1	—	—	11	12

* Partially non-resident clerics were those serving amalgamated parishes where the churches were within half a day's journey of one another.

** The term 'curate' here includes readers.

residence to feed to their propagandists. Sometime before Sir Edward Lewkenor presented his petition to Parliament in February 1585,[1] a survey was made in East Sussex of "such ministers . . . as are impossible to be framed to any good in Gods ministerie, so farre as in any equitie can be conceyved of them".[2] The vicar of Eastbourne and Burwash, which were twenty miles apart, was "one Bane a subcanon [vicar choral] at Chichester & vseth not to see his people in thes places once in two years. His curat at Burwash is vnlearned, and of a base occupacon." At Herstmonceux the parson was "one Iones who cometh so seld[om]lye ther, that it is thought ther be verie fewe of the people that knowe his face"; while the vicar of Rye was

"one whose name is not knowine to many in the contrie nor in that place, he came not ther of many yerres. The tythes are taken vpp by such as he or his appoynteth, and in that place, ther is appoynted for the minister [curate] 20*l* by the yeare."

Self-rightous as they were, Puritan clergymen were not entirely blameless: it was charged that John Frewen had once absented himself from his church for six months.[3]

The town parishes were apt to be more inadequately served than rural parishes. Stipends of urban benefices were generally lower because of the greater difficulty of collecting tithes; cash profits and the wares of craftsmen were easier to conceal than the produce of the land. Also, life for an urban clergyman was made more difficult by reason of the fact that his parishioners were better organized and their criticism more vocal. Let us begin with Chichester in the early 1580s. The vicar of the Sub-deanery church was the only university graduate in Chichester, although he was not even licensed to preach; he was a resident pluralist and, with an income of £15 from the Subdeanery vicarage alone, he was far better off than any other parish cleric in Chichester. At St Peter's the parsonage, worth £4 a year, was held by a servingman, who also possessed a second benefice. The parsonage of St Pancras, yielding £8 a year was held by a vicar choral, as were the rectories of suburban Fishbourne and

---

[1] Cf. below p. 199.   [2] B.M., Add. MS. 38,492 fo. 91.
[3] Thomas-Stanford, *op. cit.*, pp. 24–5.

Rumboldswyke, worth £5 and £4 respectively. The parsonages of St Olave's, St Andrew's, and St Martin's had long been void and were all sequestered to readers or curates, none of whom received a stipend of above £5. The same lamentable conditions were to be found in parishes nearby to Chichester: at Boxgrove the vicarage of the former Benedictine priory church was void and impropriated in 1579; in 1585 it was held by a husbandman for £9 a year.[1] Considering such a situation the following Puritan description of Chichester in 1586 does not seem surprising.

"In the same citie are manie which are greatlie agrieved at the grievous abhominations and sinnes committed . . . dailie against the glorie of God by reason of the want of good and able ministers there to do the L[ord']s message faithfullie. For it is much to be lamented to see the state and condition of the same citie, which hath in it viij parish churches, and never a minister in anie of them that is able to teach and exhort the people, but most alehouse haunters, idle persons, enemies to the professors of the gospell, and such as have no care or conscience at all to performe anie dutie belonging to them: and the common people are overgrowne as it were a wildernes for lack of instruction."[2]

In the large port town of Rye, which was served by only one parish church, a battle had long raged between the town corporation and the successive vicars of Rye. In January 1580 the mayor and jurats carried their complaints to the High Commission.

"Whereas our towne of Rye cituat vppon the coast and peopled to the nombre of 1800 or 1900 communicantes and for that cause requiringe a lernid and sufficient mynister and preacher; the vicaridge thereof hath longe tyme ben entangled to one John Rolf by leace, who, reapinge the fruite of the same yerely to a greater value then the rent yeldid, hath therout made small allowaunce to our minister and preacher, and also in very dissolute sort paid the same, wherethroughe we have ben

[1] Lambeth Palace Library, MS. Carta Misc. XII/6; B.M., Add. MS. 39,454, passim.   [2] Peel, Seconde Parte of a Register, II, 190–1.

constreynid to contribute out of our common treasureye a yerely stipend for the better mainetaynaunce of our mynisterye. The which John Rolf, beinge a very lewd disposed person and a common disturber of the quiet and christian peace in our towne, by makinge himself an instrument of contention betweene party and partie, an enemye to our preacher and one that dispendith the frutes of our vicaredge in actions of common quarell to the detriment and offence of so many of the place, and allso hath incurred forfeyture of his leace as to us semith, for that it is demised to another, which notwithstandinge Rolf doth still by sute prosequut, wherthroughe our people are wonderfullye drawen unto doubte and dainger of payenge or repayenge the common duties troblesome to the people, not beinge in tymes past so delt with, and allso our great care (not without our singuler detriment) leike to be utterlye lefte destitute of so sufficient a man as hath these five yeres and more labored painefully amonge us. In regarde of the premisses we humbly and hartely beseche your good Lordshipp with the rest to graunt unto one Robert Jacson, one of the Jurates of our towne, who hath the leace in reversion, the sequestration of our vicaredge fruites till suche tyme as the sute, now dependinge betwene Rolf and the lesye and on[e] Mr. Wigmore the leasor, be determynid. So that therby both our precher and mynister maye duely receave for his travaill, and allso our people maye knowe unto whome they maie without daunger paie ther accustomed duties."[1]

Considering the miserably low incomes of Sussex benefices, it is surprising how many university graduates were to be found among the parish clergy. Of the 118 clerics in the archdeaconry of Chichester in 1585, 34 possessed university degrees and another 21 had attended a university but had left without degrees. Another five had a grammar school education (cf. Table II). Of the 67 incumbents and curates about whom we have information from the visitation of 1603 in the archdeaconry of Lewes, 29 held university degrees.[2] However, one cannot conclude that those with education were generally more

[1] Hist. MSS. Comm., [Rye Corporation MSS.] xiii (4), 67.
[2] DRO, Ep. II/24/1, *passim*.

TABLE II

Educational Background of the Clergy in Archdeaconry of Chichester in 1585 (Lambeth Palace, MS. Carta Misc. XII/6)

Incumbent	Stipend in £ of individual benefices						Amount un-known	Value of Impropriations			
	1–5	6–10	11–15	16–20	21–25	26–50		£1–25	£26–50	£51–100	Over £100
B.D.: preacher	—	—	1	2	2	—	—	—	—	—	—
B.D.: non-preacher	—	—	—	—	—	—	—	—	—	—	—
M.A.: preacher	—	8	1	1	1	—	—	2	2	—	—
M.A.: non-preacher	—	—	2	—	1	—	—	1	—	—	—
B.A. preacher	—	3	1	1	—	—	1	—	—	—	—
B.A.: non-preacher	—	6	4	1	—	—	—	1	1	—	—
At univ.: preacher	—	4	4	—	—	—	—	3	2	—	—
At univ.: non-preacher	—	8	4	1	—	—	—	2	3	—	—
Grammar sch.: preacher	1	—	—	—	—	—	—	—	—	—	1
Grammar sch.: non-preacher	—	2	1	1	—	—	—	1	2	—	—
No schooling: preacher	—	2	1	1	1	—	—	1	2	—	—
No schooling: non-preacher	—	21	7	2	1	—	—	6	3	2	—
Tradesman: preacher	—	1	—	2	—	—	—	—	—	—	—
Tradesman: non-preacher	5	13	5	—	1	—	1	4	2	2	—

Total preachers: 35   Total non-preachers: 85   Total univ. graduates: 34   Total impropriations: 43

successful in securing the choicest benefices than those with no education at all.

The one striking conclusion that can be drawn from an attempt to correlate the income of benefices with the educational background of the incumbent is that apparently no effort was made to discourage artisans and servingmen, all but one of whom held benefices worth less than £15 per year, from plying their trades. The vicar of Preston, a pluralist, "receueth the fruyts to his oune vse but he servith not the cure himself at all times". He had appointed another cleric to serve in his place as curate, who found it necessary to follow the fishing trade for a living.[1] The vicar's predecessor was discovered to have concealed lands from the Exchequer.[2] Elsewhere, we find incumbents described as merchants and curates who were tailors, drapers, clothiers, mercers, glaziers, weavers, husbandmen, shoemakers; another was a surgeon; the parson of Racton cum Lurdyton was "a sheareman"; Anthony Hobson, vicar of Lyminster and curate of Warningcamp Chapel, who was among the Sussex ministers at Lambeth Palace in 1583, was a servingman.[3]

Towards the end of the reign there were more Protestant university graduates available to serve as clergymen, and the lay readers, to whom the authorities earlier had turned out of sheer desperation to fill the many void benefices, became a source of embarrassment. Yet, when their removal was sought, extenuating circumstances could often be found by ecclesiastical officials, who had not the heart to turn these poor men out to beg. When Bishop Watson's vicar general sought to remove William Chaunceler as the lay reader of Earnly in 1597, the parishioners interceded on his behalf with the bishop, who wrote the following to his vicar general.

"I am moved . . . in compassion of the man, beeinge poore and aged, as also in regarde of the comendation which he bringith from that parishe, to recomende him to the seruice thereof in readinge of Divine service onelie, wherein you maie giue him toleration (a Licence verie sparingelie to be given in the like

---

[1] B.M., Add. MS. 39,454, fo. 35.
[2] P.R.O., E. 178/2269/4, printed in S.R.S., *Sussex Chantry Records*, XXXVI, 160–4.   [3] Lambeth Palace Library, MS. Carta Misc. XII/6.

cases, for avoydinge of clamor and offence) if there be no iuste cawse knowne vnto you to the contrarie, to whose toleration or reiection I muste therefore refer him . . . requiringe you to deale fauorablie with him, and not to depriue him of that place withowte good cawse."[1]

Before Watson sent this letter off, he was informed that Chaunceler was not in orders. The bishop's tone became less insistent, but he still could not bring himself to order Chaunceler's deprivation (which offered no legal problem since curates and readers lacked security of tenure), and instead the responsiblity for deciding the case was passed on to the vicar general. In a postscript to the foregoing letter Watson added,

"When I caused this lettre to be written, I thought the party had bene a decaied minister, which drewe me to more comiseracon: now perceaving that he is only a lay reader, I pity his condition, and wish his wants any honest way to be relieved, which I referr to you. . . ."

The Puritans of east Sussex were well aware of the indulgence which ecclesiastical officials displayed in their hesitation to deprive unworthy ministers, and as they explained to Sir Edward Lewkenor,

"because some of them have a little latyne, and other some have a little more indigenns [indigence], they are spared in hope, that if they might well sett to schoole, they might be framed to some small good."[2]

The visitation of the archdeaconry of Chichester in 1585 shows that there had been a substantial increase in the number of preachers since 1564, when Bishop Barlow had surveyed the state of religious life in his diocese. There were 35 licensed preachers in the archdeaconry of Chichester in that year, of whom 29 had been at one of the universities. Despite the possession of licences to preach by six ministers lacking a university background, among them the Puritan servingman, Anthony Hobson, one forms the opinion that such licences were not easily procured. Two M.A.s and 11 B.A.s were without such licences, as were 13 others with university backgrounds.

[1] DRO, Ep. I/15, A12(2) 15.   [2] B.M., Add. MS. 38,492, fo. 91.

The probability is that those who were licensed to preach but had not attended a university, had obtained their licences a number of years before: it seems certain that Hobson secured his from Bishop Curteys.

Archbishop Parker's *Book of Advertisements* of 1566 required that sermons be preached quarterly in every parish church, but in practice this injunction was faithfully observed only rarely; most parish churches had only one a year, and some only one in three years. There were a number of cases where individual prebendaries as rectors or the dean and chapter jointly as ecclesiastical appropriators were remiss in their obligations to provide quarterly sermons, as, for example, at West Dean in 1570 and 1571, and at Singleton in 1570. Moreover, in both parishes the dean and chapter also had allowed the chancels to fall into disrepair.[1] The person or corporation seized of the rectory was generally held to be responsible for preaching the quarterly sermons or hiring a substitute preacher. The parson of Petworth, Nicholas Smyth, although an Oxford M.A. and licensed to preach, was possibly too old to give the sermons himself; but he obtained another preacher and also paid for "several" curates to serve his parishioners.[2] Bishop Curteys was the non-resident rector of Coldwaltham, but his curate was a university graduate who preached every month. Curteys's brother John, the parson of Eastergate, did not preach "for lak of knowledge", the churchwardens reported, and this despite his university background. The sermons were preached by the bishop or his chaplain.[3] There were also numerous cases where the homilies were not read, nor were the children instructed in catechism. At Midhurst there had been no "monethly nor quarterly sermons thies iij yeres by the vycars meanes"; during this same period he had read the homilies only four times, and "he doth not enstruct the children".[4] In 1600 it was complained that the vicar of Yapton did not read the homilies distinctly, had read the Queen's Injunctions only once in three years, and was "very negligent in visitinge the sicke".[5]

The problem of inadequate incomes for the parochial clergy

[1] DRO, Ep. I/23/2, fos. 11v, 13, 80v.   [2] B.M., Add. MS. 39,454, fo. 25.
[3] *Ibid.*, fo. 30v.   [4] *Ibid.*, fo. 22; DRO, Ep. I/17/4, fo. 7.
[5] DRO, Ep. I/17/10, fo. 16.

was medieval in origin, arising out of attempts by ecclesiastical corporations to appropriate parochial tithes to their own use. In medieval times the parson or *persona* was the holder of the parochial benefice, in full possession of its rights and dues; he was the individual having title to the parish tithes at common law and entrusted with the responsibility of discharging the cure of souls.[1] Various reforms had been promulgated ordaining that where the rectory was appropriated, there should be appointed by the rector a vicar, who was to reside in the parish and exercise the cure of souls. It became customary for the rector to retain the greater tithes, while the vicar received legal title to the lesser tithes. Where monasteries had appropriated tithes they usually appointed deputies to discharge the cure of souls, but when appropriated tithes passed into the hands of lay impropriators along with other monastic properties, the spiritual responsibility became neglected despite the fact that grants of impropriated tithes specifically stated that recipients were "charged with all payments for services" in parishes where the rectories were impropriated.[2]

It is not rare to find all of the tithes impropriated as Lord Buckhurst had done at Appledram Chapel; only £3 was provided for a curacy, which in 1579 was void. Thomas Mychell of Rudgwick collected impropriated tithes from the parish of Goring worth £100 a year; only £7 remained for the vicar. A partial impropriation of the rectory of West Dean reduced the income of the rector from £15 to £9; he was able to obtain only another £1 from preaching and ministering the sacraments. The inequities that arose from impropriations were sometimes more extreme than might appear from the paper valuations of tithes. At Eastbourne in 1603 it was said that "The vicaridge is Excessively valued in the kings Books viz at 40 marks, it not beinge worth yearlye the said value by reason of the great decay of ffishinge which to the vicar within the

---

[1] *O.E.D.*; A. H. Thompson, *The English Clergy and their Organization in the Later Middle Ages* (Oxford: 1947), p. 102. William Lynwood (1375?–1446), a civilian and canonist, felt that in the ecclesiastical usage prevailing in England, the word "parson" was synonmous with "rector". Cardinal Gasquet, *Parish Life in Medieval England* (5th ed.; London: 1922), p. 71.

[2] See, for example, *Cal. P.R., Eliz.*, I, 303.

memory of man hath ben yearely worth xx*li* but now is not worth xx*s*". The impropriate parsonage was valued in the King's Books at £6 yearly, but actually it was worth "tow hundreth pounds yearely over & aboue the Rent which the farmers pay."[1]

The consequences of impropriations were apparent to all. At Burpham where there was a partial impropriation of the vicarage as well as an impropriated rectory—"our vicarage ys verie poore and the parsonage a verie rich thinge", said the churchwardens—the roof of the chancel was partly uncovered. The rectories of Lyminster and its dependent chapel of Warningcamp were impropriated to Eton College, which had apparently farmed them out with the understanding that the chancels of the two churches would be kept in repair. The churchwardens of both churches continually reported that chancel fabric badly needed repairs; at Warningcamp they complained in 1579 that the

"chaunsell of our chapell ys mervailous ruynous and in grete decay in so much that we cannot doo as other parishes doo for we cannot laie any thinge in yt, yt is in such sort, and wee the poore inhabitants haue diuers times p[rese]nted the defallt therof but no remedy we can haue or gett."[2]

In 1585 Henry Worley, Archbishop Whitgift's commissary for the archdeaconry of Chichester, was able to discover 43 impropriated rectories within his jurisdiction (and this did not include partial impropriations of other rectories or vicarages); earlier in the same year the Puritans had calculated that there were 32 impropriations in east Sussex, giving a total of 75 for the whole diocese.[3] During the seventeenth century the number grew to 137 parcels of alienated tithes in lay hands and 16 in religious hands.[4] Table II shows the extent and approximate value of impropriations in the archdeaconry of Chichester in 1585 and the direct relationship between impropriations and the presence of inadequately educated incumbents of parochial

[1] DRO, Ep. II/24/1, fos. 19v & 20v.
[2] *Ibid.*, Ep. I/23/4, fo. 39v; B.M., Add. 39,454, fo. 36v.
[3] Lambeth Palace Library, MS. Carta Misc. XII/6; B.M., Add. MS. 38,492, fo. 91, 39,454, fo. 34v.   [4] Grove, *op. cit.*, pp. cxvi–cxix.

benefices. There are only six impropriations in parishes where the incumbent was a university graduate, and 12 more where the incumbents had been at a university but failed to take a degree. But 25 of the impropriations are found in parishes where the incumbent possessed a grammar school education or less.

As might be expected, the most important owners of impropriations in the county of Sussex were the very same ones who had profited the most from the division of monastic spoils. Sir William Fitzwilliam, earl of Southampton held title to 17 impropriations in Sussex alone, which were inherited by his half brother, Anthony, Lord Montague, along with six impropriations in the same county left to Lord Montague by his father, Sir Anthony Browne. The Fitzalan family had collected 15 parcels of impropriated tithes. Two other important beneficiaries of the scramble for impropriations were Sir John Baker, chancellor of the Exchequer under Edward VI and Mary, and Sir Richard Sackville; the marriage of Sir John's daughter Emily to Sir Thomas Sackville formed an alliance between two families which had thriven in the service of the Tudors and the spoliation of the church.

The dissolution of the monasteries also brought a good many advowsons on to the market, which, when divided up, served only to increase the influence of the gentry in the patronage of parochial benefices, becoming even more preponderant in the next century. Thus would the subjugation of vicar to squire be completed, and a familiar pattern in English society established. Of 81 advowsons listed in the archdeaconry of Chichester in 1579, 42 still remained in the possession of the queen or of ecclesiastical persons or corporations.[1] The retention of so many advowsons in royal or ecclesiastical hands may have been a factor in keeping west Sussex relatively free of Puritanism. By contrast the visitation answers for the archdeaconry of Lewes in 1603 give a different picture: of 79 patrons of benefices enumerated 63 were laymen.[2]

[1] 12 were held by the dean and chapter; 14 by the bishop of Chichester; 11 by the queen; and 5 by other ecclesiastical corporations or persons. The patrons of only 81 benefices are listed for 127 parishes. B.M., Add. MS. 39,454, passim.

[2] The returns for the archdeaconry of Lewes are about 50 per cent complete;

There was little the bishop could do when he found unacceptable a cleric presented to him for institution by the patron. When Bishop Bickley tried to forestall Lord Buckhurst's efforts to have Maurice Sackville, a relative, inducted into the vicarage of Westfield, he found himself hauled before the court of Common Pleas on a writ of *quare impedit*. Despite the fact that Bickley was able to show evidence that the advowson had been alienated to his predecessor, who had actually presented to the vicarage, the court awarded the rights of patronage to Lord Buckhurst as the owner of the impropriated rectory of Westfield.[1]

The exalted view of the freehold rights of the owner of an impropriation taken by the common-law courts was symptomatic of the increasing subservience of the clergy to the gentry, while by the same token the common-law courts stood to protect the possessor of a clerical freehold, such as a parsonage, against arbitrary deprivation by church courts. From the point of view of those prelates who wished to strengthen clerical discipline, the security of the parson in his freehold or the patron in his advowson posed a problem where the bishop was seeking to eliminate nonconformity or misconduct. Thus a bishop desiring to effect reforms amongst the clergy was apt to be damned if he did anything and damned if he did not.

As for the parson, his freehold gave him tenure, but since so many advowsons had come into the hands of the gentry, it did not necessarily afford him independence. Toadyism and not outspoken support of reform was the course of action most likely to secure presentation to a fat benefice. When one considers this situation, coupled with the miserable economic status of bulk of the English clergy, it was small wonder that men of talent began increasingly to seek outlets for their talents in more secular pursuits. Those who did seek orders found their ambitions frustrated and became men seething with discontent.

The deplorable state of the Elizabethan clergy only served

---

they reveal six advowsons in the hands of the bishop of Chichester, another 10 in the possession of other ecclesiastical persons and corporations, while the king held title to only three. DRO, Ep. II/24/1, *passim*.

[1] *Les Reports du Teserudite Edmund Anderson . . . Seigniour Chief Justice del Common-Bank* (London: 1664), pp. 269–70.

to confirm the Puritans in their conviction that the Reformation remained to be completed in England. Yet, the evidence presented in this chapter indicates that there was a remarkable improvement in the level of education of the clergy of the diocese of Chichester during the twenty-year period from Bishop Barlow's visitation of 1564 until the visitation of the archdeaconry of Chichester in 1585.[1] However, except in the case of Bishop Curteys it cannot be said that the ecclesiastical officials were in anyway responsible for this improvement in the educational qualifications of the clergy. Rather, it appears to be more likely that this was primarily the result of an increased number of university graduates competing for vacant benefices. The most learned men seem to have enjoyed the patronage of laymen rather than ecclesiastics. This was especially true of those lay patrons who were sympathetic to the Puritan party of clerical reform. But because there was no increase in the remuneration of the clergy to correspond to the rise in their educational level, pluralism, non-residence and what Mark Curtis[2] sees as a growing feeling of alienation among university graduates remained grave problems. The root of the problem was the wholesale spoliation of the revenues of parochial benefices, and no solution could be looked for as long as the courts held such an exalted view of the rights of lay impropriators.

Although the bishops of Chichester were very careful about whom they licensed to preach, with the exception of Bishop Curteys they were very lax in enforcing the canonical obligation placed upon every incumbent to see that quarterly sermons were given in every parish church. The ineffectiveness of the Anglican clergy, together with the scandalous state of the church courts and the offensiveness of the Book of Common Prayer, continued to be the chief source of discontent among the Puritan clerical party down until the time of the Civil War.

[1] See also Mark H. Curtis, "The Alienated Intellectuals of Early Stuart England", *Crisis in Europe, 1560–1660*, pp. 295–316, especially p. 298 ff.
[2] *Ibid.*

10

CLERICAL PURITANISM AND THE FAILURE
OF ECCLESIASTICAL DISCIPLINE

THE SEEDS OF PURITANISM were first sown in Sussex during the episcopate of Bishop Curteys. The first adherents of clerical Puritanism were drawn from among the learned preachers that Bishop Curteys brought down from Cambridge in the early 1570s to instill new zeal in the clergy of the diocese of Chichester and to evangelize a county that contemporary observers agreed was backward in religion.[1] During that decade "prophesyings" or exercise conferences were employed by Bishop Curteys to improve clerical morals, raise the level of theological knowledge and to improve the quality of preaching. As long as Curteys's restraining influence was felt, the imparity of ministers was maintained and the Puritan movement was indistinguishable from the bishop's party of reform.

The queen ordered the prophesyings suppressed in 1576, but the order was never carried out in the diocese of Chichester —apparently because of the trouble that Bishop Curteys was having with the gentry at this time.[2] Indeed, as a result of the disruption of ecclesiastical administration caused by the suspensions of both Archbishop Grindal and Bishop Curteys, and the three-year vacancy in the see of Chichester following the death of Bishop Curteys, the exercise conferences continued to flourish. By the early 1580s the exercise conferences in the diocese of Chichester had evolved and reformed themselves as embryonic presbyterian classes. These classes later became part of a "classical" movement, which aimed at laying the foundations of a more tightly organized system of provincial and national synods. This, of course, represented an attempt to displace the bishops or at least to bypass their authority, and, ultimately, it represented a challenge to the royal supremacy over the church.

The appointment of John Whitgift to the see of Canterbury in 1583 resulted in an immediate attempt to root out the

[1] See Chapters 3 and 4. [2] See Chapters 4, 5, and 6.

leading Puritan clergy in Sussex and subsequently in other parts of England. But, when Whitgift had ascertained the extent of presbyterianism, he retreated, having realized that he could not count upon the queen to stand behind him in depriving all of the clergy who were involved in the classical movement. There was a general decline of Puritanism in the 1590s, which has been attributed to the appointment of Richard Bancroft to the Ecclesiastical Commission and to the lack of enthusiasm for a stronger presbyterian association among many of the classes. In Sussex, however, there is no indication that any effective action was taken to break up the Sussex classes or to remove the clerical leaders from their benefices until after Richard Bancroft succeeded Whitgift as archbishop of Canterbury. Indeed, there is not even evidence to show that any of the Puritan clergy in Sussex were deprived of their benefices during the period between 1583 and 1605. In 1605 ten of them were deprived by order of Archbishop Bancroft.

The reasons why the Puritans among the clergy of the diocese of Chichester escaped with relative impunity during the 1580s and 1590s are obvious. Effective episcopal leadership was completely lacking in the diocese of Chichester between the suspension of Bishop Curteys in 1578 and the beginning of Lancelot Andrewes' episcopate in 1605. Moreover, the ecclesiastical courts proved even more ineffective in dealing with Puritan ministers than had been the case with the Catholic recusants.

(i) The Puritan Classical Movement in Sussex

That the prophesyings which were widely employed by several bishops of the province of Canterbury in the 1560s and 1570s were nurseries of Puritan zeal is not to be doubted. Stressing godly instruction rather than mindless devotion, they appealed to those clerics who had already begun to feel alienated from the sterile formalism of the Prayer-Book services and who felt that the Church of England must be completely purged of all remaining popish practices. Frustrated in their attempts to secure reform through Convocation and Parliament, Thomas Cartwright and other intellectual leaders of Puritanism called for an alteration of church government to conform to the Helvetic pattern.

While the bishops of the southern province had intended to use exercise conferences only for securing clerical reform, the restless presbyterians saw in them the perfect instruments for laying the foundations for a new ecclesiastical discipline. At first the religious instruction at these exercises was confined to the prophesyings in which two or three of the most learned divines would expound upon a particular passage of holy writ before the assembled faithful; after the laity had departed each cleric would be examined upon an assigned passage of sacred scripture. But it was not long before certain ministers of advanced views ventured upon novel interpretations or digressed from their assigned texts, by which time the more forward members of the laity would be chafing at the passive role which had originally been assigned to them. This the queen could not allow and she ordered Archbishop Parker to suppress these "vain prophecyings" in 1574, but the queen's order was countermanded by the Privy Council.[1] When Grindal assumed the primacy in 1576 he allowed the exercises to continue since he was anxious to remedy the scandal of clerical ignorance, but he did write to his suffragans seeking ways of restricting the exercises to this end.

Bishop Curteys, in his reply,[2] reported that he had introduced the clerical exercise into his diocese at the beginning of his episcopate. There was an exercise conference in each of the eight rural deaneries and each met six times a year. Either the bishop himself or his chancellor acted as moderator at the exercises in the western deaneries; his commissary at Lewes acted in the same capacity in the eastern part of the diocese. Here is the order and purpose of the exercises as explained by Curteys himself:

"The speakers be 3 at a time, all Learned & discreet: The other Ministers either be set to learn some part of the Scrip-

[1] *Select Statutes and other Constitutional Documents, Illustrative of the Reigns of Elizabeth and James I*, ed. Sir G. W. Prothero (4th ed., Oxford: 1913), p. 199; M. M. Knappen, *Tudor Puritanism* (Chicago: 1934), p. 256.

[2] B.M., Add. MS. 29, 546, fos. 50v–51v, 15 July 1576 (I owe this reference to Dr Patrick Collinson).

tures abridg'd without the book, or to write their minds of some common place of Scripture, & to repeat it without book, before four of the best learned Ministers, or more of that Deanery, privately wh[en] the People be departed. Within my Jurisdiction Artificers be not suffer'd to deal but with their occupations, neither is any Lay man permitted to intermeddle with any Ecclesiastical matter.

"For the which, such as favour & fancy innovation, afford me & my officers many ill words . . .

"The continuance of the Godly Exercise among the Ministers in good order, is . . . necessary . . . to stay the Ministers from gaming, from drinking, from wandring up & down, from town to town, from market to market, & from fair to fair . . .

"It is a great help for young Ministers & elder that have not been brought up in the Universities to hear & see the trade & method of the Learned; & it may well be maintained, in my opinion (under correction) that imitation doth more good sine arte, than art sine imitatione . . .

"The Profitablenesse of the said Exercise is thys. That whereas before the Exercise began, There was not in the whole Diocese three that were able to preach to any ordinary Audience, & the rest of the Ministers generally knew not the Principles of Religion. God be thanked now, viz. within the space of six years ther[e] be upon thirty well able to preach at Pawle's crosse, with great comenda[ti]on; & upon fourty or fifty more that make good & godly exhortations to the comon people with great edifying in their own parishes."

Altogether, eight bishops of the province of Canterbury agreed with the primate that prophesyings were "a thing profitable to the Church and therefore expedient to be continued".[1] This does not necessarily indicate that these prelates were radically inclined; they were only trying to remedy the scandal of clerical ignorance.

Elizabeth saw the potential danger to the royal supremacy in these exercises and she was determined to prevail. Once again she issued the order to Grindal to put an end to the prophesying but he replied that he would rather resign than carry out the

[1] Philip Hughes, *The Reformation in England*, III, 184.

queen's order. The result was that Elizabeth wrote directly to the bishops themselves. Since the government could not afford the scandal that the deprivation of Grindal would entail, he was instead confined to his house and suspended from the function of his office.[1]

Bishop Curteys would have received the queen's letter commanding the suppression of the exercises just a few days after he had conducted his famous visitation in Chichester Cathedral to which the better part of the Sussex gentry had been summoned. From that time on he was assailed from every quarter and was obliged to defend himself before the Privy Council on charges of misconduct in the exercise of both the spiritual and temporal magistracies.[2] It is improbable that he ever had a chance to carry out the queen's orders. Furthermore, there is evidence that the exercise conference meeting at Lewes not only survived, but by 1583 had reorganized as a presbyterian classis, comprising not only ministers but laymen as well.

This classis had begun to exercise a degree of discipline, excluding from their midst those more cautious ministers who felt that the precautions prescribed by Curteys and Grindal for the conduct of deanery exercises should still be preserved. Thus, the imparity of ministers, which Curteys had so carefully observed, was no longer maintained. What is more, it seems that the leaders of the Lewes classis had taken advantage of the fact that the see of Chichester was void (by the death of Curteys the year previous) to gain the ear of the lay judge of the archidiaconal court at Lewes, Giles Fletcher, LL.D., and to use this relationship to punish their opponents. Despite Puritan railing against church courts this was not the only instance where the archidiaconal courts deliberately failed to take notice of Puritan organizing, nor was this punishment of conservative opposition to a Puritan order at a deanery exercise unique.[3]

An example of the exercise of this discipline by the Lewes

[1] Knappen, op. cit., p. 257; Prothero, op. cit., pp. 205–6.
[2] See Chapters 4–6.
[3] Ronald Marchant, *Puritans and the Church Courts in the Diocese of York, 1560–1642* (London: 1960), chapter VI, especially pp. 132 and 134–5.

classis occurs in 1583. A controversy had broken out in the spring of that year when a group of Puritan clergymen and laymen, led by William Jackson, brought charges in the archidiaconal court against six ministers and sought to have their licences to preach revoked. One of the six, Henry Shales, had excited the Puritans' wrath by preaching a sermon at a deanery exercise conference in which Jackson and his friends were reproached as "The new brotherhood, the brotherhood of separation . . . private spirits, this new faction".[1] Because Shales had warned against the danger that uneducated persons encounter in trying to interpret sacred scriptures without using the fathers of the Church as a guide, his opponents felt constrained to charge that Shales must certainly be a seminary priest.[2] Shales, in a rebuttal to the charges preferred against him in the archidiaconal court at Lewes, stated that his opponents scorned the outward calling of holy orders, quoting Thomas Underdowne as having said in a public sermon that anyone might preach "if he had an inward [assurance] and perswasio[n] that he was called by god." Shales then cited instances of Jackson and another layman actually delivering sermons.[3]

Shales did not receive an impartial hearing in the archidiaconal court, because the judge, Giles Fletcher, LL.D.[4] seems

[1] S.P., Dom., Eliz., 159/14.

[2] Ibid., 159/14 and 16.

[3] Ibid., 159/16, 160/12. Jackson was a Marian exile who had been a member of the English congregation in Geneva; although a Cambridge M.A. and a former fellow of St John's, he was not in orders (Christina Garrett, The Marian Exiles (London: 1938), pp. 196–7; H. C. Porter, Reformation and Reaction in Tudor Cambridge (Cambridge: 1958), p. 96).

[4] Giles Fletcher, civilian lawyer and M.P. for Winchelsea in 1585, came from a very Protestant background, yet it is difficult to believe that he really was a Puritan. It is true that his brother Richard, bishop of Bristol and subsequently of London, was later to give great offence to the queen by his part in the Lambeth Articles; it is also true that their father Richard had been deprived of his vicarage in 1555 and that the younger Richard and his father had supplied John Foxe with an eye-witness account of a martyrdom. But in Elizabeth's reign, the father turned up as vicar of Cranbrook, where his son Richard and he became involved in a famous quarrel with the supporters of John Stroud, a deprived Puritan minister. The younger Richard Fletcher, who had once been granted one of those nebulous lectureships by Bishop Curteys, now had the audacity to attack Stroud because "he

to have been duped or unduly influenced by Shale's accusers. Fletcher's partiality is revealed by his tart notation next to Shales's rebuttal: "Make a scrybe sufficient for the Kingdome of heaven." Certainly, the whole incident smells of a Puritan attempt to purge the pulpits of east Sussex of all who did not share their advanced opinions.

When Shales appealed against the loss of his licence to preach to the Court of Arches, his accusers carried their case before the Privy Council.[1] The immediate sequel to this story, at least as far as Shales is concerned, remains a cipher; what we do know is that for the next 22 years the same group of Puritans successfully defied the efforts of the ecclesiastical authorities to discipline or remove them. Moreover, no effective action was taken against them until the next reign.

The death of Archbishop Grindal and his replacement with John Whitgift in September 1583 was taken to signify the beginning of a more vigorous enforcement of ecclesiastical discipline against Puritanism. Although Whitgift was the queen's personal choice for the primacy, the fact remained that nearly every member of the Privy Council was at variance with his determination to maintain episcopal rule in the face of Puritan efforts to abolish prelacy or at least turn the bishops into instruments of presbyterian government. Furthermore, Elizabeth preferred to leave the dirty work of enforcing unpopular policies to others; and, while she certainly stood up to Parliament when members of the House of Commons presumed to discuss matters touching the royal supremacy in religious affairs, instances of active royal intervention in the spiritual administration tend to be unusual. During the time of Grindal's sequestration, the Privy Council had become accustomed to treating the primate as an administrative subordinate,

---

hath noe lyvinge nor calling anywhere lawfull, [and] roveth and revelleth. . . ." Clearly Richard Fletcher and his son had proved a disappointment to those Puritans who remembered their early connection with the martyrologist (Cf. *D.N.B.*, *sub* Giles Fletcher the elder, and Richard Fletcher, D.D. and also *The Seconde Parte of a Register*, ed. Albert Peel (Cambridge: 1915), II, 116 ff. (I owe this reference to Dr Patrick Collinson).

[1] S.P., Dom., Eliz., 160/12.

and, unlike Whitgift and the queen, they regarded Catholicism as a greater danger than Puritanism.[1]

Yet despite the opposition of the Council, Whitgift began his archiepiscopate with a vigorous effort to tighten clerical discipline. Following confirmation in his authority as archbishop, he went after ministers who were irregular in dress and in the ministration of the sacraments according to the Book of Common Prayer. The three articles drawn up by Archbishop Parker in 1571 were revised to be used against Puritans who would not promise to use the Prayer Book exclusively.[2] Whitgift began his ministration of the articles in the diocese of Chichester, which being void at that time afforded a convenient place to conduct a metropolitical visitation.[3]

The visitation of the diocese of Chichester got under way promptly—"with much speede and more severitie", as the Puritan account lamented.[4] Archbishop Whitgift's articles were very strictly ministered in the archdeaconry of Chichester. All of those who refused to subscribe were suspended immediately.[5] In the archdeaconry of Lewes more leniency was used; the clergy were sent copies of the articles ahead of time and

[1] V. J. K. Brook, *Whitgift and the English Church* (London: 1957), pp. 79–80.

[2] Knappen, *op. cit.*, pp. 265–7. The articles used for the archiepiscopal visitation of the archdeaconry of Lewes are printed in Peel, *op. cit.*, II, 220.

[3] Bishop Curteys had died in 1582, and the queen allowed the see of Chichester to remain void until the election of Thomas Bickley on 30 December 1585. Whitgift issued the commission for the visitation of Chichester diocese in November 1583. The archbishop's commissary for the archdeaconry of Chichester was Henry Worley, LL.D., formerly Bishop Curteys's vicar general and at that time president of the cathedral chapter of Chichester; the visitation in the archdeaconry of Lewes was conducted by John Langworth, D.D., canon of Christchurch, Canterbury and archdeacon of Chichester (John Strype, *The Life and Acts of John Whitgift* (Oxford: 1822), I, 255–60).

[4] The following account of Archbishop Whitgift's visitation of the diocese of Chichester is based upon two separate sources: Peel, *op. cit.*, I, 209–20, presents an independent Puritan account, while the version in John Strype, *The Life and Acts of John Whitgift*, I, 255–60, is based upon the Archiepiscopal Register of Whitgift.

[5] For an explanation of the difference between major excommunication and minor excommunication or suspension *ab ingressu ecclesiae*, see Chapter 2, p. 28, note 3.

instructed to certify the fact that they had read them before attending the visitation.

When the archbishop's commissary began the formal tendering of the three articles at Lewes, he probably had a good idea of whom the Puritans were, since he chose to start with the deaneries of Lewes and Pevensey—the real hotbeds of Puritan activity. Most of the clerics of these two deaneries subscribed the articles, but several—almost all of them belonging to the Lewes group of Puritans—refused to sign the second article.[1] The archbishop's commissary promised Thomas Underdowne, who acted as the spokesman of the Puritan ministers on this and subsequent occasions, that he would proceed no further until turning the matter over to the archbishop; but after the commissary had taken the subscription in the other deaneries and found at least three more who also refused to subscribe, he then broke his promise and suspended the whole lot of them. Underdowne later stated that were "above twentie" ministers in Sussex suspended for failure to subscribe. The Puritans accused the archbishop's commissary of bad faith, but the suspensions did not come until after he was back at Canterbury, and it is quite possible that the suspensions were ordered by Whitgift.

When this news reached Sussex, the Puritans resolved to appeal to the archbishop, sending a delegation of three clergymen from each archdeaconry. They had two separate interviews with Whitgift himself—on 5 and 6 December 1583. The meeting on 5 December was very informal and the primate was at first very courteous, although he maintained that the suspensions would stand until unqualified subscription was made; none the less Whitgift made every attempt to satisfy Underdowne and his friends in their doubts (which chiefly concerned rubrics in the Book of Common Prayer), and no objection was raised to citing Calvin as an authority on baptism.

[1] This article required the clergy to adhere to everything in the Book of Common Prayer (including the rubrics) without qualification. It also required them to swear that they had ministered the sacraments according to the Prayer Book. The three articles are printed in P. M. Dawley, *John Whitgift and the English Reformation* (New York: 1954), pp. 162–3. See also S.P., Dom., Eliz., 163/68.

The Puritans, however, had not come merely to be satisfied concerning their unresolved consciences, but also to argue with the archbishop on any topic that entered the discussion. Whitgift's temper grew shorter as they continued to quibble, and he again called for their subscription, which they refused without appending a protestation. "I will allow no protestation", said the archbishop. "And you are not called to rule in this church of England . . ., nether shall you rule, but obey. And except you subscribe, you shall have no place in the ministrie." In the presence of more timid men this would have concluded the interview for the day, but Underdowne kept his composure and went on to dispute with Whitgift concerning the ministration of baptism, raising the question "as to whether baptism performed in jest, say by 'a turk', is efficacious".

At the second interview the archbishop was attended by three other bishops and a dean. The archbishop angrily attacked Underdowne and his associates for circulating a rumour "all the citie over that upon complainte of certaine ministers of Sussex, I should be sent for to the courte, and there charged not to proceede with these articles", which Whitgift was at pains to deny. Whitgift told them again that they must subscribe or face deprivation, adding that "because you are the first that have bene thus farr proceeded againste in this case you shalbe made an example to all others in this business". Yet he also tried to satisfy the Puritans with a sufficiently Calvinistic interpretation hoping thereby to avoid the scandal of such widespread deprivations, for as he explained to his fellow bishops, "if we call others out of Norfolke, they will as many doubtes, and not these. And if we have as many of Northamptonshire, they will other, and such as differ from both these". So, respite was given to the Sussex ministers, to allow them more time to consider. As they were crossing over the river from Lambeth Palace to Westminster, it was resolved that they would try once more to persuade the archbishop to allow them to qualify their subscription. Two of their number were selected to return to Lambeth Palace while the others waited in Westminster Abbey for an answer. After some further wrangling with the bishops the ministers' subscription was allowed with the qualifying limitation; they were even permitted to draw up the "protestation" themselves, though later they complained characteristically that it was "shorter then [than] we meant." They all returned to Lambeth Palace and subscribed, and at Underdowne's request the archbishop's suspension was to be lifted from the other ministers of Sussex if they signed in the same manner.[1]

Hardly had Whitgift's visitation of the diocese of Chichester got under way when resistance to the three articles was encountered elsewhere: in Kent, especially in the diocese of Rochester, Puritan clergyman had not only refused to subscribe the articles, but had actually demanded the substitution of elders for bishops; in Suffolk the leaders of the gentry had complained of Whitgift's tactics to the Privy Council.[2] Altogether, Whitgift was quite taken aback by the extent of clerical nonconformity and the enmity of the Privy Council.

It became obvious to Whitgift that he would have to move carefully. He still enjoyed the queen's confidence and stood closer to her in matters of religious policy than practically anyone else. Yet Elizabeth continued to cling to her preference for indirect rule through her Privy Council—a factor that did much

---

[1] There was an amusing sequel to these events that took place the next day, 7 December, when Underdowne and another colleague returned to Lambeth Palace to obtain individual copies of the order directing the archbishop's commissaries in the archdeaconries of Lewes and Chichester to lift their suspension. Whitgift was furious and withheld these letters because, "It hath bene signified unto me from the courte by a very honourable frende of mine, that there is a report given there that you have subscribed by protestation, and that it is ill taken. And indeed you have no protestation, but I have allowed you a declaration how farr your subscription shall extend". (Strype quotes the Archiepiscopal Register as stating that the ministers signed without protestation, a distinction which shows that Whitgift could split hairs with the best of Puritans.) It was noted by the archbishop that Underdowne had been conspicuously absent the previous day, and the latter was forced to admit that he "was indeed at the court . . . to speak with a very hon. personage . . .", but he denied having spread abroad the rumour that the archbishop had allowed them to subscribe with a protestation. Piqued by their defiant boldness Whitgift vowed he would "make better choise of men hereafter to be licensed", and he sent the Sussex ministers back home without the letters lifting their suspension—a sham display of indignation, for all the Sussex ministers were subsequently restored to their cures several days later.

[2] Brook, *Whitgift and the English Church*, pp. 83–5; Knappen, *op. cit.*, p. 269.

to weaken Whitgift's prestige. Under these circumstances wholesale deprivations might well bring about his own downfall. Well aware of the insufficiency of his own metropolitical power, Whitgift's solution to the Puritan problem afterwards was to undertake a strengthening and reorganization of the Ecclesiastical Commission and to transform it into a regular church court dominated by like-minded ecclesiastics and freed from the control of the Privy Council.[1]

Meanwhile, assured that the metropolitan dared not remove them from their benefices, the Lewes group of Puritans were encouraged to continue in their efforts to secure reform of the Sussex ministry. Their objective was to purge the parishes of east Sussex of unworthy and unlearned clerics. They soon began a survey of the clergy of east Sussex, deanery by deanery, which was forwarded to Edward Lewkenor, a Puritan layman who had long taken an interest in the welfare of his co-religionists in Sussex and elsewhere.[2] Edward Lewkenor sat for Shoreham in the 1585 Parliament, and on 15 February 1584/5 he offered to read to the House of Commons a petition concerning "abuses in the ministerie on behalf of the Inhabitants of the East parts of the countie of Sussex".[3]

The incidence of clerical nonconformity continued to rise into the 1590s In Sussex. Between 1583 and 1605 some 33 incumbents or curates in the diocese of Chichester are known to have been in trouble with the episcopal courts for nonconformity. Since there were something like 200 beneficed clergymen and curates in the diocese of Chichester in 1579,[4] this would represent one-sixth of the parish clergy. This figure represents those who were actually accused of Puritanism; it would not necessarily include those who were sympathetic to Puritan aims. Not one of these 33 Puritan clergymen was deprived by the episcopal courts of the diocese of Chichester between 1583 and 1605. While the paucity of High Commission records makes it difficult to make such a sweeping generalization about deprivations by that court, there is very

---

[1] Dawley, *op. cit.*, p. 164 ff.
[2] B.M., add. MS. 38,492, fos. 91–2. For a discussion of this document see Chapter 9.
[3] S.P., Dom., Eliz., 176/55.   [4] See Table III and Table II, Chapter 9.

little indication of activity on the part of the Ecclesiastical Commission in Sussex during this period.[1]

This high incidence of clerical nonconformity in certain areas of Sussex in the 1580s and 1590s plus the degree of co-ordination which the Puritans showed in circulating petitions throughout Sussex just prior to the Hampton Court Conference[2] provide evidence for the assertion that the attempt to break up the Puritan classical movement in Sussex was a failure. The existence of a presbyterian classis in Lewes, which had grown out of one of Bishop Curteys's deanery exercise conferences has been established beyond reasonable doubt. The evidence for the existence of classes in other deaneries is more indirect. An attempt to ascertain the geographical distribution of known Puritan ministers in Sussex (see Table III) suggests that besides

TABLE III

Geographical Distribution of Known Puritan Ministers by Deanery, Running from West to East

---

ARCHDEACONRY OF CHICHESTER
DEANERY OF BOXGROVE
Brian Lister, v. of Hunston, 1587–1605 (deprived).
Daniel Hanson, v. of Northmundham, occ. 1585–1603.
DEANERY OF CHICHESTER
None.
DEANERY OF MIDHURST
None.
DEANERY OF ARUNDEL
Anthony Hobson, v. of Lyminster, 1566–1605.
Henry Pitter, v. of Climping, occ. 1592.
Richard Whitaker, v. of Amberley, occ. 1577–85.
John German v. of Arundel, occ. 1583.
v. of Burpham, occ. 1584.
DEANERY OF STORRINGTON
Stephen Vinall, v. of Steyning, 1599–1605 (deprived).
Stephen Gough, v. of Bramber, 1603–1605 (deprived).
Beda Goodacres, r. of Ashurst, 1581–1605 (deprived).

[1] This is probably explained by the failure of Bishops Bickley and Watson to report suspected Puritans to the High Commission. See section ii of this chapter.   [2] S.P., Dom., Eliz., 173/15.

ARCHDEACONRY OF LEWES

DEANERY OF LEWES

Nicholas Chauntler, v. of Patcham, 1581–93.

John Batnor, r. of Westmeston, occ. 1595–1605.

Christopher Goldsmith, r. of Kingston-by-Sea, 1588–1605 (deprived).

John Postlethwaite, inst. 1605 r. of Kingston-by-Sea.

Samuel Norden, r. of Hamsey, 1582–1605 (deprived).

John Bingham, incumbent of West Hoathly, occ. 1583–4.

Thomas Underdowne of Lewes r. of St Mary Westout and
          St Peter, occ. 1580;
      r. of St John sub Castrum, 1582–92.

William Savidge, r. of Ovingdean, 1570–1619.
     r. of Rottingdean, occ. 1595.

Edmund Curteys, v. of Cuckfield, 1571–81 (deprived).

John Waterhouse, v. of Cuckfield, 1581–1607.

John Postlethwaite, v. of Portslade, c. 1598–1606.

DEANERY OF SOUTH MALLING (Peculiar to the Abp. of Canterbury.)

None.

DEANERY OF PEVENSEY

Stephen Turner, v. of Arlington, 1578–91.

William Knight, v. of Arlington, occ. 1603.

Maurice Sackville, r. of Withyham, 1589–c. 1596.

Roger Hall, r. of Horsted Keynes, occ. 1592.

John Boyse, r. of East Hoathly, deprived 1605.

—Warren, v. of Hellingly, deprived 1605.

William Clarke, v. of Laughton, c. 1583–1623.

John Jefferay, r. of Berwick, 1566–1618.

Edmund Spinkes, c. of South Heighton, occ. 1583.

John Bingham, incumbent of Chiddingly, occ. 1593–1603.

Thomas Underdowne, residing in Chiddingly, 1593.

DEANERY OF DALLINGTON

Thomas Healy, v. of Warbleton c. 1583–1605 (deprived).
    v. of Wartling, 1602–1605.

—Bell, v. of Dallington, occ. 1593–4.

John Frewen, v. of Northiam, 1582–1628.

William Hopkinson, v. of Salehurst, 1572–97.

—Morris, incumbent of Herstmonceux, occ. 1583.

DEANERY OF HASTINGS

None.

---

the Lewes classis there were, most likely, other classes existing in the deaneries of Pevensey and Dallington in east Sussex, and probably at least one classis in the western half of the diocese meeting in Arundel. Moreover, the fact that in 1583 the Puritans of east and west Sussex joined together in sending a delegation to see Archbishop Whitgift suggests a more than casual correspondence among these various classes.

Archbishop Whitgift's failure to suppress the Puritan classical movement in Sussex because of the opposition of the Privy Council helps to point out several weaknesses in the exercise of royal supremacy over the Church of England. As a result of the queen's preference for indirect rule the royal authority in ecclesiastical matters in actual practice was exercised by the Privy Council as well as by the bishops. Any conflict between agents of the royal supremacy could not but weaken that power and encourage those who were actively working to alter church government. Moreover, Parliament was, at this time, making a bid to gain legislative power over the Church. Since the leaders of clerical Puritanism had such highly placed friends in the Privy Council and in Parliament, Whitgift could not be sure that the queen would not sacrifice him if the outcry against him became too great. Because the next two bishops who succeeded Richard Curteys in the diocese of Chichester were weak and ineffective, it was not to be expected that they would be any more successful in disciplining the Puritan clergy of Sussex than Archbishop Whitgift.

(ii) *The Lack of Episcopal Leadership, 1578–1605*

In the first section of this chapter evidence has been presented to support the argument that the ecclesiastical authorities failed to suppress the Puritan classical movement in the 1580s and 1590s. The second and third sections will attempt to explain this situation in terms of the poor quality of episcopal leadership and the failure of the church courts to discipline the clerical leaders of this movement during the period from 1585 to 1605.

Many factors had combined to reduce the influence of the bishops of Chichester during the Tudor period. The conservatism of the Henrician and Edwardian bishops, the rural isolation of Sussex, the disruption of ecclesiastical administration, the want of a learned Protestant ministry had all conspired to delay the full enforcement of the Protestant religious settlement until the time of Bishop Curteys. Richard Curteys was the only effective Protestant bishop of Chichester in Tudor times, but his patronage of the prophesyings, the perennial quarrels with the cathedral chapter, his humiliation at the hands of the Sussex gentry and, finally, his suspension had further weakened episcopal authority.

Nearly four years passed from the time of Curteys's suspension in 1578 until his death in 1582. Having ascertained for himself the state of clerical discipline in the diocese of Chichester in 1583, Archbishop Whitgift had pointed out the necessity of filling up void sees.[1] The archbishop's plea failed to convey a sense of urgency to the queen who waited until December 1585 to appoint a successor to Curteys. Neither Thomas Bickley (episcopate 1585–96) nor Anthony Watson (episcopate 1596–1605), respectively the third and fourth Elizabethan bishops of Chichester, contributed anything to fill the void in episcopal leadership that had begun to manifest itself after the suspension of Bishop Curteys. They were both doubtless aware of the circumstances that had brought about the overthrow of Bishop Curteys and neither of them asserted his authority over the clergy in any way. Recusant affairs were now largely in the hands of special magistrates appointed for that purpose or were dealt with by the reconstituted Court of High Commission. Although the judges of the two episcopal courts were aware of the existence of Puritan conventicles and were informed of instances of clerical nonconformity the ecclesiastical courts failed to come to grips with the problem.

The man whom Elizabeth selected to be the successor to Bishop Curteys was Thomas Bickley, the archdeacon of Stafford and a royal chaplain.[2] Then in his seventy-eighth year, Bickley's

[1] S.P., Dom., Eliz., 173/15

[2] Born at Slough, Bucks., Bickley was educated at the Free School attached to Magdalen subsequently winning entrance to that college, and eventually rising to the vice-presidency in 1552. His reputed reforming zeal caused the members of the University of Oxford to elect him to preach before the young king at Windsor, for which office Bickley's lack of priest's orders did not seem to disqualify him. Bishop Gardiner's visitation of the university in 1553 resulted in his expulsion, but it is noteworthy that when he fled the realm, he went not to Geneva or Frankfort, but to Paris and Orleans to continue his studies, where it would have been dangerous to exhibit his Protestant views. With another change in the seasons of the religious climate,

reforming ardour had considerably cooled since that day in
1548 when, as a young fellow of Magdalen, he publicly trod
upon the Sacred Host in the college chapel.[1] The picture that
emerges of Bickley as bishop of Chichester is that of a tired old
man slumbering away in his diocese, except when occasionally
awakened by infrequent, but rude letters from the Privy
Council. There is nothing in Bickley's career to suggest that his
mitre was anything other than a reward for a long, but undis-
tinguished life of faithful service. At any rate there were few
able men from whom to choose.

Bickley had the reputation of being the most procrastinatory
bishop in England as is evident from a series of correspondence
in 1593–94 concerning lists of recusants and Puritans which the
bishops were ordered to send to the Privy Council. In a letter
of 24 October 1593 the Council complained that Bickley's list,
having omitted Christian names, social rank, and places of
residence, was "verye imperfect". In very sharp terms the
bishop was ordered to begin anew and to take sufficient pains in
his enquiries that he might not mistakenly include as recusant
Papists those whose absences from Church were lawful. Not
until the following 3 January did Bickley bestir himself to
write to his chancellor to order a new list to be drawn up,
adding "I have receaved lettres from her mag[es]ty['s] counsell
which signyfyeth unto me that all bishopps in England (saving
myself) have certifyed to them the Papists & puritans refusying
to come to the church". By 18 January the list was still incomplete.[2] Plainly, Whitgift had failed to get a vigorous prelate
appointed to the diocese of Chichester.

Part of the blame for this incredible inefficiency may be
ascribed to the discordant relations between the bishop and the
cathedral chapter. The vested interests of the Cathedral Close

---

he returned to England becoming a chaplain to Archbishop Parker, who
secured for him a place as canon residentiary of Lichfield Cathedral and the
wardenship of Merton College (D.N.B., sub Thomas Bickley); John Le
Neve, Fasti Ecclesiae Anglicanae (Oxford: 1854), I, 250; Anthony á Wood,
Athenae Oxoniensis, II, 839–41; Garrett, op. cit., p. 90.

[1] For a discussion of the evidence concerning this story, see Garrett, loc.
cit.

[2] DRO, Ep. I/37, nos. 7, 34, 37.

still, as in the time of Bishop Curteys, were extremely sensitive about episcopal attempts to pack the chapter. When Bickley tried to get one of his lieutenants, Henry Ball, admitted to residence in the Cathedral Close, the residentiaries took refuge behind the cathedral statutes which had been granted by Bishop Curteys.[1] Bickley tried to declare the statutes invalid "as concerning neither the good of the Church nor divine service".[2] The dispute smouldered on another three years before a vacancy among the residentiaries provided an opportunity for Bickley to get Ball admitted to the Close.[3] On the occasion when Ball was finally admitted to residence, the bishop tried to sneak another of his faction into the Close by having John Drury, judge of the episcopal court of Chichester, lodge in the same house with Ball. But the chapter would have none of this, and Drury wrote a trifle naively that he feared that "there is some conspiracie to kepe me out the cloase".[4] The intrigues of the cathedral clergy had distracted the bishops of Chichester ever since the beginning of the reign. Bickley would be dead before John Drury was finally admitted to the Cathedral Close.[5] The next Elizabethan bishop of Chichester did not even make the effort to keep his diocese in order.

For the first time since the beginning of her reign Elizabeth did not wait the usual couple of years to fill the void see of Chichester. A successor to Bickley was nominated within two months of Bickley's death.[6] The new bishop was Anthony Watson, dean of Bristol and chancellor of Wells, who can only be described as an inept timeserver and a pluralist.[7] Provincial

---

[1] See Chapter 4.

[2] Peckham, *Act Book A*, no. 906.

[3] *Ibid.*, nos. 918–19.

[4] DRO, Ep. I/37, no. 31.

[5] When Bishop Bickley died in April 1596 he was buried in the cathedral and a monument was erected in the Lady Chapel, which will perpetuate his fame if for no other reason than the fact—if the effigy is a good likeness—that he must have possessed the largest nose in recorded English history.

[6] Le Neve, *Fasti Ecclesiae Anglicanae*, I, 250.

[7] It is worth noting that Watson came recommended to Sir Robert Cecil by Lord Lumley, a devout Catholic peer, who had already helped Watson to previous preferment and who continued to plead his case with Cecil (Hist. MSS. Comm., *Salisbury MSS.*, vi, 199; v, 250). Watson was born about 1550 in the county of Durham, and matriculated at

life obviously did not appeal to Bishop Watson; he much preferred London where he could play the court bishop, as a later age would have called him. Among the reasons Watson gave the queen in his petition to hold the rectory of Cheam, Surrey *in commendam* was the proximity of that town to London, which would enable him to attend Parliament and carry out his duties as lord almoner—a position then largely concerned with the legal procedures involved in confiscating the estates of suicides for the Crown.[1] That Watson spent most of his time

---

Christ's College, Cambridge, where he was a student and a fellow after proceeding B.A. in 1572. He later went on to Oxford, where he graduated B.D. in 1582. By this time Watson had secured the friendship of Lord Lumley, who presented him to a pair of fat rectories, before obtaining his promotion to the bishopric of Chichester. After obtaining the see of Chichester, John Chamberlain wondered why Watson, who though a bachelor (as was the queen's preference in bishops) supported many relatives, was so rich "for so meane a living". The answer is that the bishop was an adept pluralist. The burden of first fruits due to the queen from the bishopric of Chichester amounted to £609 7s. 1½d., so Watson applied and apparently received permission to continue holding the deanery of Bristol *in commendam*. He continued to hold a prebend and two rectories, and he refused to leave Bristol until he had extracted the last penny of his tithes. Having assumed the temporalities of the bishopric Watson began bombarding Cecil and Sir John Stanhope, treasurer of the chamber, with letters beseeching the queen to remit payment of the first fruits of the bishopric, but the best deal that could be wrung from the tight-fisted Elizabeth was a delay of six years for payment of the first fruits. Despite pleas of utter insolvency Bishop Watson left a respectable estate providing generous bequests (Biographical information based upon: *D.N.B.*, *sub* Anthony Watson; F. O. White, *Lives of the Elizabethan Bishops of the Anglican Church* (London: 1898); Wood, *Athenae Oxoniensis*, II, 839–41; W. R. W. Stephens, *Memorials of the South Saxon See and the Cathedral Church of Chichester* (London: 1876), pp. 260–1; *Nugae Antiquae*, ed. Henry Harrington (London: 1804), II, 187; *Letters Written by John Chamberlain*, ed. Sarah Williams (London: Camden Society, 1861), I, 136, 209; B.M. Lansdowne MS. 983, fos. 79–80; B.M., Add. MS. 39,354, fo. 47; Hist. MSS. Comm., *Salisbury MSS.*, vi, 237; vii, 135; viii, 145; *Cal. S.P., Dom.*, 1595–1597, p. 454; B.M., Lansdowne MS. 1605, fos. 85–86v).

[1] In 1600 Bishop Watson granted a lease of Aldingbourne manor, the bishop's customary residence just outside of Chichester, so it is probable that the bishop was continuously absent from the diocese after that time. The lease was granted for three lives, which must have been an inconvenience for Watson's successors; however, the state of decay into which the bishop's

at court is further shown by the fact that he was present for ten out of the twelve consecrations that took place in Lambeth Palace during his episcopate. In May 1602 the gossipy John Chamberlain reported that it was rumoured that Watson was seeking translation to the bishopric of Hereford.[1] He was considered by Sir John Harrington to be "a verie good preacher",[2] who was always ready to preach at court; in attendance upon Elizabeth during her last illness, Watson uttered a pompous prayer—"Pull down, O Lord, the pride of those hateful Irishe Rebells that forget their obedience to thee . . .", which must have sorely tried the dying queen's patience.[3] Although always ready to offer prayers on special occasions, at the Hampton Court Conference Watson said nothing, perhaps embarrassed at the connection between the turn recent events had taken in his own diocese of Chichester and the boldness of the Puritan divines.

By 1603 the Puritan movement in Sussex had achieved a degree of organization unprecedented in the county.[4] The activities of the Puritans in the diocese of Chichester between the accession of James I and the Hampton Court Conference will further help to focus attention on the utter negligence of Bishop Watson. The inheritance of the English throne by James VI of Scotland had inspired the Puritans with visions of long-awaited reforms, for the Stuart king had the reputation of being a Christian prince, and so they began preparing their strategy forthwith. Intelligence concerning the king's ecclesiastical policies was forwarded to the English Puritan leaders by Patrick Galloway, a Scottish presbyterian minister who followed

residence had fallen is shown by the fact that the manor brought an annual rent of only £9. The house was finally demolished in 1606 by Bishop Andrewes, and the bishops of Chichester evidently had no suitable place to live until the present episcopal palace was built later in the century (Peckham *Act Book A*, no. 981; *V.C.H. Sussex*, IV, 134). That would explain why Lancelot Andrewes succeeded Watson in the rectory of Cheam as well as the bishopric of Chichester.

[1] Stephens, *op. cit.*, p. 260; Williams, *op. cit.*, I, 136.
[2] *Nugae Antiquae*, II, 187.
[3] S.P., Dom., Eliz., 287/57.
[4] Patrick Collinson, *The Elizabethan Puritan Movement* (London: 1967), pp. 453–4.

the royal court southward in the spring of 1603. The need for tact and restraint in dealing with James was seen, and the moderation urged upon the English Puritans by Galloway can be discerned in the Millenary Petition, alleged to reflect the aspirations of more than a thousand ministers, although without signatures. The Millenary Petition did not call for any drastic revision of episcopal government, but besought the king to grant a conference for the discussion of means to reform abuses within the existing system. If not inclined to any immediate change James was not adverse to a disputation with leading Puritan divines; indeed, just before the Hampton Court Conference, Galloway claimed to have received from James the promise "that all corruptions dissonant from the Word, or contrary thereto, should be amended". This only served to encourage the more radical Puritan leaders, such as the Brownist Henry Jacob of Kent, who proposed to revive the weapon of inundating the authorities with petitions differently worded to lend the appearance of spontaneity, but all singing the same tune.[1]

Jacob was busy organizing the petitions on a national scale by 30 June, when we find him writing from London to friends enclosing the form of petition and asking for their subscription.[2] For what reason we cannot determine, unless it was an absentee bishop, the Puritans decided to begin circulating their petitions in Sussex, when Jacob's activities were reported to the Privy Council in September by Lord Buckhurst. The circulation of petitions was so bold and open that even Bishop Watson finally heard of their activities.[3] Bishop Watson did not report this matter to the Privy Council until 15 October; by that time Archbishop Bancroft had already carried the alarm to the king, who promptly ordered the arrest of the Puritan leaders in Sussex.[4]

Separate petitions were to be submitted to the king by the gentry and the ministers, while nine different petitions were

[1] Knappen, *Tudor Puritanism*, pp. 321–2; S. B. Babbage, *Puritanism and Richard Bancroft* (London: 1962), p. 43 ff.

[2] B.M., Harley MS. 6849, fo. 271.

[3] B.M., Add. MS. 28,571, fo. 179.

[4] Hist. MSS. Comm., *Alnwick MSS.*, iii, 52; Knappen, *op. cit.*, p. 323.

circulated among the commonalty. For all their alleged spontaneity, Lord Buckhurst observed that all the petitions cried out against an unlearned ministry and called for reform of the church courts. One of the commonalty's petitions had come into the possession of Lord Buckhurst in September.[1] Another fell into the hands of Bishop Watson in October. Signatures were openly solicited at both public prayer, where the petitions were read to the congregation and served up with exhortative sermons, and at closed meetings of Puritan ministers and selected laymen; other petitions were carried throughout the country by leading Puritan laymen. In this manner 2285 signatures were affixed to the commonalty's petitions, which were to be presented at court by Patrick Galloway. But before that was accomplished the organizing activities of John Peerson, the lay author of the petitions, had so distracted Bishop Watson that he felt compelled to return to his diocese and make a personal investigation. He was then charged by the Privy Council to examine those who had been connected with the petitions.[2]

[1] The version that fell into the hands of Bishop Watson is preserved in the MSS. of the Duke of Northumberland at Alnwick Castle (cf. Hist. MSS. Comm., *Alnwick MSS.*, iii, 52). The ministers' petition is preserved in the Hatfield MSS., 103, fos. 64–64v; the gentry's petition and another version of the commonalty's petition are in "Extracts from the MSS. of Samuel Jeake", ed. T. W. W. Smart and W. D. Cooper, *S.A.C.*, IX (1847), 45–9.

[2] Assisted by Sir Thomas Bishop and Henry Shelley of Patcham, who himself had signed the gentry's petition, Bishop Watson examined some fourteen Puritans of whom he found Samuel Norden, John Frewen, Thomas Healy, Christopher Goldsmith, Stephen Gough, and one Erburie to be the "moste base agentes" among the ministers, while Peerson, Stephen and Thomas Collen were found most culpable among the laymen (Hatfield MS. 101, fos. 160–1). The gentry's petition was drawn up by Henry Apsley and William Newton of Lewes, and circulated by Apsley, Newton, John Peerson, and John Frewen. Lord De La Warr and 26 of the gentry signed, among them some of the most prominent men in county affairs: Sir Walter Covert, Sir Nicholas Parker, Sir Thomas Palmer of Angmering, and other prominent members of the Morley, Goring, Shirley, Shurley, Jefferay, Pelham, Bowyer, Culpepper and Sackville families. However, this was a great age for signing petitions and subscription cannot necessarily be taken as proof of Puritan leanings without corroborative evidence. For example, the presence of the signatures of Herbert Pelham of Michelham Priory and John Ashburnham III, both of whom had Catholic relatives living in their households,

In substance the gentry's petition asked for a learned ministry decently provided for, a reform of clerical abuses such as pluralism and non-residence, an end to forced subscription of ministers to rubrics in the Book of Common Prayer, a reform of church government in general, and a conference in the meantime where grievances might be discussed. The ministers' petition, drawn up by none other than the troublesome Samuel Norden, rector of Hamsey, and already carried to the court with 40 signatures by John Frewen and Daniel Hanson, vicar of Northmundham, sang the refrain to the same tune as the gentry; but in a special solo part written into their score, sang a song of clerical abuse, replete with statistics.[1] Just as Archbishop Whitgift had been alarmed to discover that the Puritans had connections at court, so Bishop Watson voiced his anger at similar Puritan circumventions, charging that Norden and his friends had sought to flee arrest by a royal servant and later perjured themselves before the lords of the Privy Council in denying complicity in the commonalty's petition, further compounding the offence by opening the Council's letters of dismission before delivering them to the bishop.[2]

It was now too late for Watson to take any action against the Puritan leaders in his diocese, since the king had already promised the Puritans a conference. Scarcely were the Twelfth Night revels over when there assembled at Hampton Court Palace a most impressive company of learned prelates and grave divines. Archbishop Whitgift, nearing the end of his last illness, was absent; but among the eight bishops present was Richard Bancroft, destined to replace the dying primate and hardly troubling to hide his impatience and scepticism regarding the outcome of the conference.[3]

Bancroft was made archbishop before the year was out, and

---

suggests the possibility that in some cases the motive for subscription may have been other than that of religious zeal. Cf my "Catholics and Local Office Holding in Elizabethan Sussex", *Bulletin of the Institute of Historical Research*, XXXV (May 1962), 47–61.

[1] Cf. Chapter 9 on the clergy.   [2] Hatfield MS. 101, fos. 160–1.

[3] Only four Puritan leaders actually were admitted to dispute with James and his eight bishops and eight deans, but the Puritans from the various counties sent delegates to advise the four disputants. Four came from Sussex: Samuel Norden, John Frewen, Christopher Goldsmith, and Mr

he did not wait many months to order the deprivation of ten of
the Puritan clergymen in the diocese of Chichester who had
been most notoriously active in the penning and circulation of
the petitions two years earlier.[1] The deprivations were decreed
the last of April 1605 in a private chamber of the "Ounce and
Ivy Bush" inn in East Grinstead—a setting that served to arouse
the indignation of a Puritan pamphleteer in 1606.[2]

Among those deprived were Samuel Norden, rector of
Hamsey, who had been in and out of trouble with the ecclesiastical authorities since the days of Bishop Curteys; the record
of the vicar of Wartling, Thomas Healy, stretches back almost
as far; all had been in trouble with the church courts or had
otherwise attracted attention to themselves (all had been
involved in the activities connected with the 1603 petitions),
yet of the four at the Hampton Court conference, two escaped
deprivation: John Frewen, who continued to hold his benefice
and, as his own patron, passed it on to his descendents, and the
elusive Mr Erburie, who was probably an unbeneficed extra-
parochial preacher. In assessing the era of Whitgift, Bickley,
and Watson, one fact that comes through very clearly is that
until 1605 Puritan clergymen in the diocese of Chichester,

Erburie. The Sussex delegation contained the same number as that of
Northamptonshire; both were the largest at the conference (Hist. MSS.
Comm., *Montagu of Beaulieu MSS.*, pp. 33–4).

[1] Dr S. B. Babbage, *op. cit.*, p. 193 states that the deprivations, pronounced
"ultimo Aprilis A.D. 1605", could not have been carried out by Bishop
Andrewes, since he was not consecrated bishop of Chichester until 3 Nov.
1605, and therefore must have been ordered by Archbishop Bancroft during
the vacancy of the see. However, the see did not become void until 10 September and if Bancroft had ordered the deprivations by his own authority while
the see was *sede vacante*, then the act would have been recorded in his own
archiepiscopal register. Dr Babbage's mistake seems to arise from the fact
that the episcopal registers of Bishops Watson, Andrewes, and two other
bishops are all found in the same volume. Although most certainly carried
out by the authority of Bishop Watson, the actual deprivations were most
likely pronounced by lieutenants of the metropolitan acting as commissaries
of the bishop of Chichester, since Sir John Harrington indicates that Watson
was invalided in the last months of his life (*Nugae Antiquae*, II, 187).

[2] Gabriel Powell, *A Myld and Ivst Defence of Certeyne Argvments, at the Last
Session of Parliament . . . in behalfe of the Ministers suspended and deprived & C.:
for not Subscribing and Conforming themselves . . .* (London: 1606), p. 82.

although perhaps occasionally harrassed by ecclesiastical officials, escaped with impunity in every case but one.

(iii) *The Puritans and the Church Courts*

Historians formerly asserted that the Puritan classical movement had failed to unite the English presbyterians and began breaking up in the late 1580s. Certainly the movement had lost its fire with the death of its organizer, John Field, in 1588 and the passing from the scene of the principal Puritan sympathizers in the Council, Leicester and Walsingham, but the classical organization remained intact in Sussex as well as in several other counties during the last decade of the queen's reign and sprang to life in 1603 in order to exploit the opportunities provided by the accession of James I.[1] The survival of the Sussex classes during this period was due not only to the lethargy and indifference of Bishops Bickley and Watson, but also to the failure of the church courts to remove the presbyterian leaders or even hinder their activities before 1605. The problem did not arise out of the failure to detect the activities of the presbyterian leaders; it was a failure to invoke ecclesiastical sanctions and make them stick. The Puritan clergymen from Sussex who presumed to dispute with Archbishop Whitgift in 1583 and who helped to circulate the petitions of 1603 were all in trouble with the church courts on at least one occasion.

The case of Samuel Norden provides an example of the continuity of leadership among the Sussex Puritan clergy from the time of Bishop Curteys down to the activities which preceded the Hampton Court Conference and beyond. Norden was ordained deacon and priest by Bishop Curteys in 1573, and described himself as an M.A. of Peterhouse, Cambridge. We next meet him as one of the signers of the testimonial to Bishop Curteys contained in the latter's *Truth of Christes naturall body*, which had been prompted by Curtey's dispute with the gentry. Since Norden did not secure a benefice until December 1582, it seems quite likely that Curteys employed Norden as an

[1] See Collinson, *The Elizabethan Puritan Movement*, part eight, chapter 5, but especially p. 453.

extra-parochial lecturer, as Curteys had done in the case of Richard Fletcher at Rye. When Norden was instituted to the rectory of Hamsey, it was on the presentation of Dorothy Lewkenor, wife of the well-known Puritan layman, Sir Edward Lewkenor. Lewkenor represented an important link between the Puritans in Sussex and influential presbyterian leaders in Parliament such as Peter Wentworth.[1] Although seated in Suffolk, Lewkenor had sat for New Shoreham in Sussex in the Parliament of 1572, and he owned several other advowsons in that county. Norden's prominence among the suspended Sussex ministers in 1583 and among the fomenters of the 1603 petitions has already been noted. When admonished in 1590 by the judge of the archidiaconal court of Lewes to observe the rubrics of the Book of Common Prayer and to pray for bishops, he scrupled, as in 1583, but conformed again. Not surprisingly, Hamsey was described in 1603 as a scene of conventicles. Norden continued to live in Hamsey after his deprivation in 1605 until his death in 1609.[2] Such a career is eloquent testimony to the failure of the church courts to deal with the problem of Elizabethan clerical Puritanism.

Indeed, for a time, the Lewes group of Puritans actually controlled one of the archidiaconal courts. It will be remembered that Thomas Underdowne, rector of St Mary Westout and St Peters and later rector of St John sub Castrum, had joined with Norden and the Marian exile, William Jackson, in their attempt to eliminate Henry Shales from the pulpit. In 1580 and 1581 their faction became so powerful that they controlled the archidiaconal court sitting in Lewes and Underdowne frequently sat as a deputy for the official principal, Giles Fletcher. With the death of Curteys, jurisdiction reverted to the metropolitan and Whitgift sent out his own judge in 1583 to Lewes, with the specific intention of finding out who the Puritans were. In November 1590 we find Underdowne himself before the archidiaconal court charged with the usual liturgical irregularities

---

[1] Cf. Neale, *Elizabeth and Her Parliaments, 1559–1581*, *passim*.

[2] D.R.O., Ep. II/9/2, fo. 118v, Ep. II/11/1, fo. 3v; W. C. Renshaw, "Some Clergy of the Archdeaconry of Lewes and South Malling Deanery", *S.A.C.*, LV, 220–77; Hatfield MS. 101, fos. 160–1; B.M., Add. MS. 39,447, fo. 30v; Babbage, *op. cit.*, pp. 194–5.

including a conspicuous inability to bring himself "to praie in all his sermons for Archbishops and Bishopps". Although ordered to certify that such omissions had been rectified Underdowne had still not complied by the following April; the judge then gave him until the following September to comply, but evidently no disciplinary action was taken, and Underdowne apparently was still beneficed when his will was proved in 1593.[1]

The case of the curate of Dallington, a certain Mr Bell, shows the lack of sanction that still existed in the archidiaconal court of Lewes even after Whitgift's commissary had replaced Giles Fletcher and Thomas Underdowne. Summoned before that court on 14 November 1583 upon presentation by six parishioners for failing to wear the surplice, Bell failed to send an apparitor and was excommunicated for contumacy. On the 27th of the same month an apparitor was sent, and through him Bell asked for the benefit of absolution, which was refused because he had not satisfied a monition about wearing the surplice. An apparitor was sent again on 11 December but still failing to satisfy the judge, Bell was suspended from office. Whitgift's commissary was apparently still under the impression that the archbishop intended to make an example of the non-subscribing Sussex ministers, but before Christmas all of that had changed. Whitgift had been forced to back down, restoring Underdowne, Norden and the others to their cures. Thus, when Bell appeared in person before the archidiaconal court on 7 Janurary 1584 to beg that he be absolved and restored, his plea was granted with the provision that the edict of the court would not take effect until Bell began wearing the surplice and subscribed the articles ministered by the archbishop's commissaries.[2] The case disappears from the records and probably Bell made a modified form of subscription similar to that which had been allowed by Whitgift to the eight Sussex ministers before Christmas.

Only in the case of Stephen Turner, vicar of Arlington, was the suspension made to stick for any length of time, the penalty

[1] B.M., Add. MS. 39,447, fos. 31–31v; Archdeaconry of Lewes, Registers of Wills, A9, 1591–6, B2, 255–186.
[2] D.R.O., Ep. II/9/2, fos. 118v–123.

being decreed because Turner would not even make the modified form of subscription agreed upon by the eight Sussex
ministers, which suggests that Turner may have leaned towards
congregationalism. Turner was ordained by Bishop Curteys in
1577. He appears to have been uneducated, for he had no
licence to preach, and in January 1585 was charged before the
archidiaconal court at Lewes with failure to provide someone
who was licensed to preach to give the quarter sermons, and in
general with serving his cure insufficiently.[1] It is not known
definitely whether Turner was among the forty-odd ministers
who had balked at subscription in the fall of 1583 or whether
he was at that time suspended, but a statement made by Turner
sometime later for inclusion in a piece of puritan propaganda
says as much by implication. In July 1585, when Turner was
again asked to subscribe, he was ready enough to affix his
signature to the first and third articles, but still could not
swallow the second, which would acknowledge the doctrinal
purity of the Book of Common Prayer. Although Turner stated
that he had already been under suspension for a year and a
quarter, a sentence of suspension was again decreed, and Turner's
vicarage was sequestered. The following November Turner
was given a third and last chance to subscribe, but still refused.
The suspension and sequestration was either subsequently
lifted or never enforced, since Turner was still vicar of Arlington at the archidiaconal visitation in April 1589.[2]

Although the strengthening of ecclesiastical discipline by
Archbishop Bancroft showed that Puritan clergymen could be
removed from their vicarage houses, the archbishop was unable
to devise the machinery to remove the recalcitrant minister
from the scene of his labours nor was he able to prevent a
determined patron from presenting another Puritan to replace
his deprived brother. Christopher Goldsmith, who obviously
was deprived in 1605 for the part he played in drawing up the
1603 petitions and for his subsequent selection by the Sussex
classes to attend the Hampton Court Conference, had been
presented to the rectory of Kingston-by-Sea by Sir Edward

[1] B.M., Add. MS. 39,447, fo. 30v; D.R.O., Ep. II/9/2, fo. 159v.
[2] Peel, *Seconde Parte of a Register*, I, 221; B.M., Add. MSS. 39,444, fos.
72v–73, 39,447, fo. 30v.

Lewkenor in 1588.[1] The void created by Goldsmith's deprivation was filled by Sir Edward Lewkenor's presentation to the
very same benefice of John Postlethwaite, who had helped to
circulate the commonalty's petition in 1603. Postlethwaite
also had held the vicarage of Portslade since 1598 of which he
was still in possession in 1606. Kingston-by-Sea became a
place where well-known Puritans from other parishes came to
have their children baptized.[2] The church machinery was
powerless to destroy a Puritan centre of worship when it
operated under conditions as favourable as those at Kingston-
by-Sea.

Of the four Sussex ministers at the Hampton Court Conference, Goldsmith and Norden were deprived, while Erburie
does not appear to have been possessed of a benefice from which
Bancroft could order him deprived, but John Frewen, rector of
Northiam, escaped scot free. Frewen was wealthy enough to
have his portrait painted by Mark Gheeraerts, who depicted
him with his right hand upon a Geneva Bible, opened at 2
Kings, chapter xxiii, which described Josiah's zeal for religious
reformation. Frewen was also the patron of his own rectory to
which Frewens presented Frewens until at least 1749. There
was little that could be done to prevent this since the common
law courts upheld the right of the patron to present where the
bishop refused to institute without canonical cause.[3]

The want of episcopal leadership and the failure of the archidiaconal courts to deal effectively with the problem of clerical
Puritanism only reinforces the argument that the ecclesiastical
machinery was too feeble to compel universal adherence to the
established church. By the time that clerical Puritanism became
a problem in Sussex it had already become obvious that the

[1] Babbage, op. cit., pp. 195–7; B.M. Add. MS. 39,447, fo. 32v; Renshaw,
op. cit., S.A.C., LV, 220–77.

[2] Ibid; S.A.C., XLIX, 47–65.

[3] Cf. Les Reports du Treserudite Edmund Anderson, . . . Seigniour Chief Justice
Del Common-Bank . . . (London: 1664), pp. 269–70.
The wealth that enabled John Frewen to found a county family that
survived into the present century also appears to have inculcated a feeling of
conservatism among his sons: Accepted Frewen became Charles II's archbishop of York, while Thankful Frewen was to suffer for his loyalty to
Charles I (D.N.B., sub John Frewen; Renshaw, op. cit., S.A.C., LV, 220–77).

ecclesiastical machinery in the diocese of Chichester was unequal to the task of enforcing conformity upon Catholic recusants, and the Elizabethan government was forced more and more to rely upon the temporal magistracy. But in the case of Puritanism the government could not turn to the temporal magistrates to carry out the suppression of a movement which so many of the local governors actively patronized or at least sympathized with. And, of course, there would always be a small number of hard-core Catholics and Puritans who would have suffered any fate before they would allow a secular government to dictate to their consciences.

PART IV

THE ENFORCEMENT OF THE RELIGIOUS SETTLEMENT AND THE TRANSFER OF SOCIAL POWER

II

THE NOBILITY AND THE LIEUTENANCY

AMONG THE CHIEF OBSTACLES to achieving religious uniformity in Sussex was a religiously disaffected nobility.
The exceptionally large number of noble families resident
in the county would have been a source of trouble for the
government regardless of other factors; the political frustra-
tions of ambitious peers when combined with religious discontent could only complicate the problem. Had the Sussex
nobility stood together, the government might well have faced
an uprising in Sussex of comparable magnitude to that of the
1569 rebellion of the northern earls. But they were hopelessly
divided among themselves and given over to factional rivalries.
The government was able to maintain political and social
stability in Sussex by effecting a gradual transfer of power from
the old Catholic nobility and their followers to the new
Protestant aristocracy that was spread over a period of 25 years.

Sussex was a county that was almost exclusively dominated
by landed interests.[1] This factor was sufficient to predispose
the rural society of the county to conservative tendencies, but
this resistance to change was reinforced by an over-abundance
of peers that was unique among English counties. During the
Elizabethan period there were five noble families that had their
principal seats in Sussex and actively participated in county
affairs. In the opinion of Bishop Curteys this was "more than
one shire can wel bear. Specially if ill affected or doubted &
agreeing all together & having often meetings".[2]

At the beginning of the reign all of the Sussex nobility were
Catholic: Thomas Sackville was not raised to the peerage until
1567, and the barony of De La Warr was in abeyance until

---

[1] See Chapter 1.

[2] S.P., Dom., Eliz., 165/22. There were also five noble families dominating
the West Riding of Yorkshire, although the Percies, who held the earldom
of Northumberland, were removed from the North after the 1569 rising and
exiled to Sussex. None of the West Riding peers were Protestants; all were
Catholics or had strong Catholic associations (Aveling, "The Catholic
Recusants of the West Riding of Yorkshire, 1558–1790", loc. cit., p. 206).

1570. In the early 1580s three peers, the earl of Arundel and Lords Lumley and Montague were Catholic; William West, the first Lord De La Warr of the restored barony, was thought to be indifferent,[1] while only Thomas Sackville, Lord Buckhurst could confidently be described as Protestant.[2]

The religious views of these five families of the Sussex nobility are an important consideration in discussing the enforcement of the religious settlement because the lords lieutenant were picked from among the peers who headed these families. The lords lieutenant were the key link between the Privy Council and the local magistrates, and the effectiveness with which they carried out their duties had a crucial bearing upon the exercise of the royal supremacy, especially since Parliamentary legislation and Privy Council administrative policy increasingly gave the temporal magistrates a more active role to play in enforcing religious uniformity.[3]

Since there were few among the Sussex gentry who did not attach themselves to the following of one peer or another, the maintenance of social and religious tranquillity required the government to deal with these magnates as delicately as possible. Elsewhere in England it was unusual for the lieutenancy of one county to be jointly shared by two or more magnates, but it was standard practice in Sussex where there were so many factions to be appeased. Thus, despite the attachment of the earl of Arundel and his son-in-law, Lord Lumley to the old order, they were allowed to dominate the lieutenancy until 1569, when the rising of the northern earls made it necessary to reduce the influence of the Arundel-Lumley faction with their many ties to the feudal families of the North. The new commission, issued to Lords Buckhurst and Montague and

[1] The 11th and 12th Lords De La Warr, the son and grandson of William West, were both Puritans. A decision of the House of Lords had restored the precedence of the ancient barony to the 11th Lord De La Warr (*G.E.C.*, IV, 159–60).

[2] There were other peers, such as the 8th and 9th earls of Northumberland and Henry, 4th Lord Bergavenny, who owned lands or had houses in Sussex. They are excluded from the present discussion because they were never in the commission of lieutenancy or else did not reside in the county for any appreciable length of time.

[3] See Chapter 7.

William West,[1] appears to have been drawn up with the idea of gradually weaning the Catholic gentry from the dangerous influence of the earl of Arundel by substituting Lord Montague as an alternative patron. The combination of Buckhurst, a moderate Protestant, and Montague, a Catholic who was absolutely loyal to the queen, was one that could command the largest following among both the Catholic and the Protestant gentry. Lords Buckhurst and Montague were cordial friends and they joined forces to manage county affairs until 1585. In that year Lord Montague was dropped from the commission— doubtless as a result of the threat of foreign invasion and the feeling that his continued presence in the commission would hinder a more stringent enforcement of anti-Catholic legislation. Thus, the transfer of social leadership from the old Catholic nobility to the Protestant nobility was not completed until 1585. After 1586 Lord Buckhurst shared the lieutenancy of Sussex and Surrey with Lord Howard of Effingham until the end of the reign.[2]

These three stages in the transition of power from the old Catholic nobility to the Protestant nobility as revealed in the various commissions of lieutenancy for Sussex correspond to three distinct periods in the enforcement of the religious settlement in Sussex. From 1559 to 1569, when the lieutenancy was in the hands of the earl of Arundel or Lord Lumley, the oath of supremacy was evaded by Catholic magistrates or false returns concerning the administration of the oath were made into Chancery. The stricter ministration of the oath of supremacy which began in 1569 was undoubtedly connected with the issuance of the new commission of lieutenancy in that year, but the retention of a Catholic peer joined with the politique Buckhurst inaugurates a second stage in the transition during which time Catholics were not wholly excluded from public office and the penal laws against recusants were laxly

[1] The barony of De La Warr was revived in his favour in 1570 by royal patent. William West was a man of small following and his inclusion in the commission of lieutenancy appears to have been a reward for informing against the earl of Arundel in 1569.

[2] A list of lords lieutenant of Sussex with references is found in Joyce E. Mousley, "Sussex Country Gentry in the Reign of Elizabeth" (London Ph.D. thesis, 1955), appendix 1, pp. 277–8.

enforced.[1] This was surely an important factor in keeping the Catholic gentry politically quiescent. The exclusion of Lord Montague from the lieutenancy of Sussex in 1585 was paralleled by a more strict policy towards recusants which begins in the 1580s with the appointment of specially selected commissioners for dealing with recusancy.

All evidence points to the fact that the dependence of the Sussex gentry on these five noble families was very pronounced. Sir John Neale has shown us how the nobility controlled the county parliamentary elections.[2] Bishop Curteys, who had good cause to fear the Sussex gentry when united to defend their interests, was always at great pains to stress the tendency of the Catholic gentry to follow the lead of the nobility. Curteys further observed that there were very few freeholders among the yeomanry; the members of that class were therefore in a position of economic dependence upon their social superiors. Consequently, "they are easier carried away, specially the countrey generally beeing ignoraunt & vngrounded in religion".[3]

The social preponderance of the Sussex nobility was based upon two main factors: landed wealth assured them of the goodwill of their tenants; the confidence of the monarch brought them influence at court, the tenure of high crown offices and the disposition of lesser offices.

Landed wealth was a source of social power common to all five families. All derived at least part of their wealth from monastic spoil. The ancient family of Fitzalan, who held the earldom of Arundel, had refounded their fortunes on monastic wealth,[4] while the Brownes and the Sackvilles were enabled to move up into the peerage as a result of their holdings of former monastic properties. Among the recipients of these monastic plums none fared so well as Lord Montague's father, Sir Anthony Browne, K.G., master of the horse and a personal favourite of Henry VIII, who acquired Battle Abbey and St Mary Overy, Southwark. Other monastic properties came to him from his half-brother, Sir William Fitzwilliam, earl of

[1] See Chapters 7 and 12, section i.
[2] *The Elizabethan House of Commons*, pp. 68–9.
[3] S.P., Dom., Eliz., 165/22.   [4] *G.E.C.*, I, 250–2.

Southampton, including Easebourne Priory near Midhurst, where he built Cowdray, which even in ruins is one of the finest houses of the Tudor age, and the monasteries of Waverly in Surrey, Calceto near Arundel, as well as lands formerly belonging to Newark Priory and Syon Abbey.[1] Sir Richard Sackville's enthusiasm for this game of spoliation earned him the name of "Sackfill" or "Fill-sack". He was in a favourable position to increase the family fortunes for two very good reasons: he was chancellor of the Court of Augmentations in 1548 when monastic wealth was still to be had, and he was a second cousin to Queen Elizabeth through Anne Boleyn, who was his first cousin.[2] The accession of Elizabeth brought new opportunities for alienation of church property and very little pressure was required to convince Bishop Barlow and the dean and chapter of the wisdom of yielding up to Sir Richard Sackville a few choice manors, impropriated rectories and advowsons.[3] The wealth that Sir Thomas Sackville inherited from his father and the substantial inheritance that his bride, Emily, the daughter of Sir Richard Baker, brought him, were sufficient to assure the Sackvilles of a prominent position in the county.

But, in explaining the decline of the Arundel-Lumley faction and the rise of the Buckhurst-Montague forces, it becomes obvious that the essential prerequisite for gaining and maintaining preponderance in county politics was possession of the confidence of the queen. Sir Thomas Sackville, raised to the peerage in 1567 as Lord Buckhurst, was a man whose outstanding talent, whose moderation, and whose enjoyment of wide respect among the Sussex gentry commended him to the queen. Elizabeth trusted Lord Buckhurst and Lord Montague; Arundel and Lumley, on the other hand, offered more than sufficient proof of disloyalty. The important thing to note is that although the White Horse, the Fitzalan badge, still commanded a following in Sussex, the source of Arundel's power was essentially royal service and not feudal loyalty. As

[1] J. A. E. Roundell, Cowdray: The History of a Great English House (London: 1884), p. 13; G.E.C., IX, 99.
[2] D.N.B., sub Sir Richard Sackville; Collins's Peerage of England, ed. Sir E. Brydges (London: 1812), II, 107–9.
[3] Cal. P.R., Eliz., III, 37–9.

soon as the earl of Arundel was cut off from the source of patronage, his social power began to decline.

Although Henry Fitzalan, nineteenth or twelfth earl of Arundel (1511?–1580) was doubtless influenced by his Henrician boyhood, there seems little reason to question his Catholic convictions. Queen Mary rewarded him for his invaluable support at the time of her accession with grants of the offices of lord steward of the royal household, lord high steward of Oxford, and finally the chancellorship of that university. Elizabeth confirmed Arundel in these offices upon her accession, allowed him to continue on the Privy Council, and commissioned him as lord lieutenant of Sussex and Surrey. Arundel harboured a scheme for marrying himself to Elizabeth and when he was finally rejected in 1564, he resigned all his offices and went out of favour. Subsequently he espoused the cause of his son-in-law, the ill-fated Thomas, duke of Norfolk. Together with Lord Lumley, his other son-in-law and staunchest supporter, Arundel went on to become involved in that complicated series of intrigues that included the Ridolfi plot and which sought the re-establishment of Catholicism and the marriage of Norfolk to the Queen of Scots.[1]

---

[1] *D.N.B.*, *sub* Henry Fitzalan; *G.E.C.*, I 250. In August of 1569 Lord Lumley and others intimated to the Spanish ambassador, Don Guerau de Spes, that they were ready to take up arms to forward the marriage project. They had already entered into negotiations with Mary and her agent, the bishop of Ross, when Lumley and Arundel were summoned before the Privy Council and confronted with damning evidence apparently supplied by William West, later Lord De La Warr, who appears to have been anxious to attract some favourable attention to himself (*A Collection of State Papers Relating to Affairs in the Reigns of King Henry VIII, King Edward VI, Queen Mary, and Queen Elizabeth*, ed. Samuel Haynes (London: 1760), pp. 529–37). By the end of November the names of Lumley and Arundel had been linked with those of the northern earls—Northumberland, Westmorland and Pembroke. Arundel was confined to his home at Nonesuch, Surrey until after the execution of the duke of Norfolk in 1572; Lumley was released from confinement towards the summer of 1570, when he again returned to plotting. He lost no time in communicating with his father-in-law or reopening negotiations with the Spanish ambassador, and he was also in indirect contact with William, Cardinal Allen. As a result of confessions extracted from followers of the duke of Norfolk, Lumley and Arundel were again implicated in plans to restore Mary Stuart to her throne; consequently Lumley was soon under confinement again—this time in the Marshalsea Prison (*Ibid.*, pp. 534–7;

The earl of Arundel was one of those overmighty subjects whose power Elizabeth was committed to weaken. Arundel was out of favour with Elizabeth almost from the very beginning of the reign, and he was removed as lord lieutenant in 1560 or 1561 and replaced by Lord Lumley. When the disgruntled Arundel left court in 1564, he began to attract to his faction other discontented old Catholic peers, who felt themselves wrongfully excluded from the royal counsels; the government sought to conciliate the earl, and after 1567 he either shared the lieutenancy with his son-in-law or acted in a similar capacity.[1] Of course, at the time of the Northern Rebellion in 1569, neither Arundel nor Lumley could be safely relied upon —it would have been surprising if the two Sussex peers with the strongest ties to the northern nobility, both in blood and religion, had remained disinterested. It was at this time— November 1569—that Lumley and Arundel were displaced and new commissions of lieutenancy for getting the county into a state of military readiness went out to Lords Buckhurst and Montague and William West.

The involvement of John, Lord Lumley (c. 1534–1609) in the complicated series of intrigues surrounding Mary, Queen of Scots would appear to have arisen out of the close relationship with his father-in-law, the earl of Arundel, as well as his own ties with the northern nobility.[2] It is difficult to believe that he had any real enthusiasm for plotting. Remembered as a noted scholar and patron of the arts—indeed a true Renaissance man —Lumley helped to found a lectureship in surgery at the Royal College of Physicians, and besides being the author or

---

Hist. MSS. Comm., *Salisbury MSS.*, I, 445–526; *The Letters and Memorials of William Cardinal Allen*, ed. T. F. Knox (London: 1882), p. 220; *A Collection of Papers Relating to Affairs in the Reign of Queen Elizabeth*, ed. William Murdin (London: 1759), pp. 121–2).

[1] Mousley, "Sussex Country Gentry in the Reign of Elizabeth", pp. 277–8.

[2] Lord Lumley's family background cannot but have influenced his religious and political outlook, for his father, George Lumley, was attainted of treason in 1537 for having taken part in Aske's insurrection and was executed at Tyburn. However, he became entitled to the family estates on the death of his grandfather, John, Lord Lumley (1493–1544), and after petitioning Parliament in 1547 he was restored in blood and created Baron Lumley of Lumley Castle in Yorkshire (*D.N.B.*, *sub* John, Lord Lumley).

translator of several learned treatises, he formed one of the finest libraries in Tudor England, parts of which now constitute portions of the collections at Lambeth Palace and the British Museum. In his old age he was admired as a pattern of true nobility: Camden thought him a person "of entire virtue, integrity, and innocence", and Bishop Hacket praised him for his attainments in learning. His universality was completed by a passion for collecting portraits, and he is thought to have had some skill in painting himself.[1]

Despite Lumley's exclusion from the lieutenancy after 1569, his political influence was not completely broken. He nominated one of the M.P.s for Chichester as late as 1593 when in response to pressures from Lumley, the Mayor of Chichester replied: "vppon the receipt of your L[ordship's] L[ett]res, we have elected chosen Mr. William Ashbie Esquire (whom it pleased your L[ordship] too nominate & recommende vnto our Election) a cyttezin of this Cyttie."[2]

After he was finally released from his imprisonment in 1573 Lord Lumley refused to countenance any of the plans to secure Mary Stuart's escape. Indeed, he actually sat on the special commission that tried the Scottish queen. But despite this apparent attempt to redeem himself in the eyes of the queen, he remained steadfast in his religion.[3]

The rebellion of the northern earls and the Ridolfi plot had discredited the old nobility in Sussex politics as elsewhere; thus the way had been cleared for the rise to ascendancy of Tudor parvenus such as Lord Buckhurst and Lord Montague.

Anthony Browne, first Viscount Montague (1526–1592) does not fit the stereotype of the Tudor upstart. His father was a Henrician who built his fortune on monastic spoil, but the son became a staunch Catholic. He always tried very hard to com-

---

[1] *Ibid.*   [2] B.M., Egerton MS. 2598, fo. 277.

[3] It was Lord Lumley who reconciled Philip Howard, earl of Arundel and Surrey to the Catholic Church after the latter had inherited the title and estates of his grandfather Henry Fitzalan, earl of Arundel (*The Lives of Philip Howard, Earl of Arundel, and of Anne Dacres, His Wife*, ed. Henry Fitzalan-Howard, 14th duke of Norfolk (London: 1857), p. 180). In the summer of 1587 Philip Howard and Lord Lumley were each sentenced to pay fines of £1000 by the Court of Star Chamber for harbouring seminary priests (B.M., Harley MS. 2143, fo. 12v).

bine devotion to his religion with a meticulous display of loyalty and he was said to have been distressed by Cardinal Allen's ultra-papalist views.[1] Since he was the only Catholic peer to whom Elizabeth showed favour, Lord Montague was in effect the spokesman for English Catholics at court. His services to Queen Mary in re-establishing the Catholic religion were well known (it was Mary who had raised him to the peerage), and he was one of the chief members of the embassy that Mary had sent to the Pope. Displaying singular courage, Montague was the only temporal peer who consistently opposed the ecclesiastical bills of 1559.[2] Taking advantage of the well-known fact of Montague's loyalty, Lord Burghley—ever an astute propagandist—wrote a pamphlet containing a description of Montague's role in defending England during the time of the Spanish Armada in the summer of 1588.

[1] Christopher Devlin, *The Life of Robert Southwell* (New York: 1956), pp. 91, 108–9. The duke of Norfolk's secretary said that the Florentine conspirator Ridolfi had included Lord Montague's name among those thought to be "well affected" to the proposed marriage of the duke of Norfolk to Mary Stuart, which was later confirmed by Lord Lumley; but Norfolk distrusted Montague because the latter had dissuaded his brother-in-law, Leonard Dacre, from coming to him for assistance during the Northern Rebellion. Although his son, George Browne, and his son-in-law, the earl of Southampton, were both imprisoned for complicity in the Norfolk-Queen of Scots marriage plans, Lord Montague himself had avoided all such intrigues. Yet not only did the government trust Lord Montague sufficiently to release Southampton into his father-in-law's custody, he was even included in the commission of lieutenancy during the Northern Rebellion of 1569 (Loseley MSS., vol. IV, nos. 6–21, printed St G. K. Hyland, *A Century of Persecution under Tudor and Stuart Sovereigns from Contemporary Records* (London: 1920), p. 139 ff. ; S.P., Dom., Eliz., 85/64; Hist. MSS. Comm., *Salisbury MSS.*, I, 773).

[2] Lord Montague's speech against the royal ecclesiastical supremacy has survived and gives proof of his moderate views. Montague did not argue that Protestantism was false; rather he viewed it as a novel doctrine which should not be forced on a people who had not resolved the truth of that doctrine in their consciences. In an explicit plea for toleration of Catholics he asked what "man is there so without courage and stomach, or void of all honour that can consent or agree to receive an opinion and new religion by force and compulsion, or will swear that he thinketh the contrary to what he thinketh. To be still and dissemble may be borne and suffered for a time; to keep his reckoning with God alone; but to be compelled to lie and swear, or else to die therefore, are things that no man ought to suffer and endure" (Printed in John Strype, *Annals of the Reformation* (Oxford: 1824), I, 442).

According to Burghley, the first man to appear at Tilbury was Lord Montague, who now aged and sick, vowed that "he would hazard his life, his children, his land and his goods" as a token of loyalty. When the queen held her famous review at Tilbury Lord Montague "came personally himself before the Queen, with his band of horseman, being almost two hundred; the same being led by his own sons, and with a young child, very comely, seated on horseback".[1] The story may or may not have been true. Certainly, Burghley knew that it was plausible.

The dominant member of the commission of lieutenancy that was issued in 1569 was Thomas Sackville, Lord Buckhurst and later first earl of Dorset (1536–1608). By reason of his membership in the Privy Council he was to become the chief link between the government and the Sussex magistracy. His character had many facets: he was a major poet in his youth and a pioneer in blank verse,[2] but he devoted his later life to the game of politics seemingly achieving only mediocrity despite his very considerable talents. However, it must be remembered that he was overshadowed by Lord Burghley during most of his career; perhaps in less olympian company he might have stood out as a great statesman.[3]

Lord Buckhurst's political career was not without its vicissi-

[1] The pamphlet, entitled *The Copy of a Letter sent out of France to don Bernadino Mendoza, ambassador in France for the King of Spain, declaring the state of England* (1588), has been asserted to be a clever forgery by Conyers Read. Cf. "William Cecil and Elizabethan Public Relations", *Elizabethan Government and Society: Essays Presented to Sir John Neale*, ed. S. T. Bindoff *et al.* (London: 1961), p. 45 ff. The part of the pamphlet dealing with Montague is printed in " 'A Booke of Orders and Rules' of Anthony Viscount Montague in 1595", *S.A.C.*, VII, 180–1.

[2] For a study of Buckhurst's literary significance cf. J. Swart, *Thomas Sackville: A Study in Sixteenth-century Poetry* (Groningen, 1949).

[3] Buckhurst earned a reputation as a Latin and English poet while still an undergraduate at Oxford. He helped compose *The Tragedy of Gorboduc*, which was first presented at the Inner Temple as part of the Christmas festivities in 1561 and, a few days later, was performed before the queen at Whitehall. His entry into a political career was facilitated by the position of his father as chancellor of the Court of Augmentations and privy councillor to both Mary and Elizabeth. He first entered the House of Commons in the Parliament of 4 and 5 Philip and Mary as a member for Westmorland county, but when the first Parliament of Elizabeth assembled he was sitting for East Grinstead. In June of 1566 Elizabeth presented him with Knole in Kent but, because the

tudes. In 1587, after his return from a diplomatic mission to the Netherlands, Buckhurst incurred the earl of Leicester's displeasure and was confined to his house for nine months. He was not completely idle during this time and used his flair for vigorous English prose as a vehicle for royal flattery. In a petition to the queen he implored that he might "behold that rare and royal face, the only sight whereof hath power to raise up and recomfort my woeful heart, which hath so long mourned and languished for lack thereof".[1] The letter was delivered by his cousin and Elizabeth allowed him to appear personally, but the sight of "that rare and royal face" brought only a new rehearsal of the objections against his conduct which had been insinuated by Leicester. In a letter to Lord Burghley, Buckhurst fell to musing on the vagaries of court life: "But lo! what is the faith and fortune of this world, where neither state nor friends are certain, nor Prince's favours may be made freehold".[2] However, the next year Buckhurst regained his sovereign's favour, and if he did not possess a freehold, he certainly enjoyed an advantageous leasehold, for he was made a knight of the Garter, and on the death of Lord Burghley he succeeded as lord treasurer. He was instrumental in discovering the Essex plot and passed sentence on the conspirators as lord high steward.[3]

Lord Buckhurst's struggle with the earl of Leicester for influence and position at court was accompanied by the use of his power as lord lieutenant to consolidate his position in county affairs. Assisted by the second member of the commission of lieutenancy, Lord Montague, he sought to gain control of Sussex county elections, which, it would seem, were usually decided without contest by general agreement among the gentry.[4] The location of their lands, in both east and west

---

house was let and sublet, it was 1603 before he was ever able to take possession, and until that time Buckhurst, near Withyham, remained his principal seat (*Collins's Peerage*, II, 110–13; V. Sackville-West, *Knole and the Sackvilles* (London: 1922), p. 38).

[1] Hist. MSS. Comm., *Salisbury MSS.*, III, 280–1.
[2] *Ibid.*, III, 283–4.   [3] *Collins's Peerage*, II, 116–17.
[4] Sir John Neale, *The Elizabethan House of Commons*, p. 29.

Sussex, enabled Buckhurst and Montague to exert their influence among the gentry throughout the whole county. For example, in October 1584 Buckhurst nominated his son Robert Sackville and Sir Thomas Shirley of Wiston to be knights of the shire. However, this election was not to go uncontested because Herbert Pelham of Michelham Priory and George Goring attempted to oppose Buckhurst's choices. Buckhurst set about to rally his followers by writing to Walter Covert, a prominent magistrate and several times sheriff of Sussex, to remind Covert that he had offered to help him: "you frendle offered me your furtherance if nede so now though I doubt not of anie great nede yet wold I be glad to use the help of my frends in this cause for Sir Thomas Sherilie and my sonne".[1] In a few days Lord Montague followed up with another letter making it known "that sondrie noble men and gentlemen with me selfe" also approved of Lord Buckhurst's two choices. Choosing to ignore the opposition of Goring and Pelham, Lord Montague added: "I praie you to make known to the free-holders there as I thinck most fitt and to whom I have given my consent and earnestlie request my frends to do the same".[2] Buckhurst's son was elected to the senior seat for Sussex in 1584, but when Buckhurst was removed from the lieutenancy between July 1585 and August 1586—most likely due to the efforts of his rival Leicester—his prestige and influence seem to have suffered despite the fact that he regained the confidence of the queen and was restored to the lieutenancy.[3] At the next election in 1588 the best that Buckhurst could do for his son Robert was the borough seat of Lewes, and it was not until 1593 that Buckhurst could get his son elected to the county seat again.[4]

[1] B.M., Harley MS. 703, fo. 19v. The fact that Michelham Priory had originally been granted to the earl of Arundel suggests that Pelham and Goring represented what was left of the old Arundel-Lumley faction.

[2] *Ibid.*, fo. 17v.

[3] However, Buckhurst was compelled to share the lieutenancy with the lord admiral, Charles, Lord Howard of Effingham, later earl of Nottingham.

[4] Neale, *The Elizabethan House of Commons*, pp. 68–9. Buckhurst's troubles with both Leicester and the freeholders of Sussex may have been connected with his opposition to the increased harassment of recusants after 1585 and might well explain his temporary removal from the commission of lieuten-

This political alliance between the politique Buckhurst[1] and a Catholic peer must surely be unique. It was an alliance built upon Buckhurst's ambition and the necessity of destroying the influence of the earl of Arundel and Lord Lumley, which task Buckhurst could not accomplish by himself; but it also rested upon a cordial relationship between the Sackvilles and the Brownes. That this relationship was more than a political alliance can be seen in the marriage of Buckhurst's daughter, Jane Sackville, to Lord Montague's grandson and heir,

---

ancy (See Chapter 7). Moreover, Buckhurst's own household had become tainted with Catholicism. His daughter-in-law, the sister of Philip Howard, earl of Arundel, was in the Tower of London in 1585 (S.P., Dom., Eliz., 164/58). On the death of Lady Margaret Sackville, Robert Southwell, the Jesuit poet, praised her character in his *Triumphs Over Death* (London: 1595), a volume dedicated by the publisher "to the Worshipful Mr Richard Sackville, Cecily Sackville, and Anne Sackville, [and] the hopeful issues of the honourable Master Robert Sackville, Esquire" (Reginald Sackville, 7th Earl De La Warr, *Historical Notices of the Parish of Withyham in the County of Sussex* (London: 1857), pp. 66–7 n.).

[1] Despite Puritan overtones in some of Buckhurst's writings, he has been said by several authorities to have become a secret Catholic. One Catholic historian states that, although Buckhurst was compelled to enforce recusancy laws against Catholics because of pressure from higher quarters, Catholics "continued perseveringly to repose a certain trust in him" (Devlin, *op. cit.*, p. 231). Another story that has persisted about Buckhurst says that Fr Richard Blount, S.J. converted him shortly before "he died *anno* 1608 of an apoplexy, as he sat at the council table. . ." (John Morris, *The Troubles of Our Catholic Forefathers Related by Themselves* (London: 1872), I, 197). Yet Thomas Morgan, a zealous adherent of the Scottish queen's cause, wrote to Mary in 1586 that "some hold Buckhurst for a Catholic in his harte; but if he be, he dissembleth the matter egregiouslye" (*The Ven. Philip Howard, Earl of Arundel, 1557–1595*, ed. J. H. Pollen and W. MacMahon (London: C.R.S., 1919), p. 149).

While it is not completely unlikely that *agents-provocateurs* could have planted such ideas in Catholic minds, there is too much evidence to be discounted out of hand. In the diplomatic preparation for the Somerset House Peace Conference of 1604 between England and Spain, Juan de Tassis wrote from Brussels to Philip III that Buckhurst was one of the peace commissioners who favoured toleration for Catholics. From Rome the duke of Sessa had written to the same monarch that he had "had interviews with Thomas Sackville, who had now become a Catholic with his father's consent on condition that it was not known" (A. J. Loomie, "Spain and the English Catholic Exiles, 1580–1604" (London Ph.D. thesis, 1957) pp. 534–7).

Anthony Maria, which occured some time after Lord Montague had been removed as lord lieutenant in 1585.[1]

Naturally, Lord Buckhurst incurred obligations for Lord Montague's support. Lord Montague was allowed to share patronage with Buckhurst and even Catholics sometimes were allowed to benefit from the distribution of offices. For example, on 4 November 1576 Montague wrote to William More of Loseley recommending William Dawtrey, a known Catholic, for the office of undersheriff of Sussex and Surrey; a year later the same recommendation was made by Buckhurst.[2] All of this changed in the 1580s. As a result of the increasing militancy of the Catholic Reformation overseas the dominant voice in the government decided on a tougher policy towards English Catholics, which brought a more effective enforcement of the laws against recusants. The easygoing tolerance of the 1570s when Catholics were still permitted a voice in county affairs came to an end in 1585 when Lord Montague's name was omitted from the new commission of lieutenancy. Seeking to curb the power that Lord Montague still wielded, the Privy Council attempted to destroy what remained of his patronage. Yet such an overturn could not be effected all at once, and even in the troubled times of 1588 the Privy Council found it necessary to give assurance that Adam Ashburnham, one of Montague's followers, would continue as captain of the rape of Hastings. Lord Buckhurst, who had been restored to the lieutenancy by this time, told the Privy Council that it would not do to treat Montague in such cavalier fashion, to which the Privy Council replied on 27 July 1588,

"that their Lordship's late letter touching the Lord Montague's servantes and reteyners was not to withdrawe any principall officer heretofore employed in the countrye, and that therefore Adam Ashburnham may, not withstanding the said letter, continew one of the Capteines of the Rape of Hastings as heretofore he had done, wherewith their Lordships thought Lord Montague wold not be discontented."[3]

[1] For a Sackville genealogy see *The Works of Thomas Sackville, Lord Buckhurst*, ed. R. W. Sackville-West (London: 1859), p. v.
[2] Hist. MSS. Comm., [Loseley MSS.] vii, 630–1.
[3] *Acts P.C.*, XVI, 194.

Thus were the Privy Council forced to recognize Montague's position as the most important landowner in the rape of Hastings, where his second seat, Battle Abbey, was situated;[1] but he was never restored to the lieutenancy of Sussex.

Just how much influence was exercised by the third member of the commission of lieutenancy of 1569, William West, remains shrouded with mystery. That he had an evil reputation and was widely distrusted can clearly be inferred from the facts, but whether this reduced him to a cipher in local politics is another matter. West had been adopted as heir by his uncle, the ninth Lord De La Warr, but "being not content to stay till his uncle's natural death, prepared poison to dispatch him quickly".[2] By an Act of Parliament of 4 Edward VI he was disabled from all honours and though restored in blood in 1563 he could hardly have gained much respect among the gentry of Sussex, for Elizabethans—violent as they were—abhorred poisoning as a despicable Italian crime. His part in the plot against Queen Mary in April 1556 probably reflected a desire to gain power rather than a sincere religious conviction. The barony of De La Warr remained in abeyance until February 1570 when it was revived in West's favour by royal patent. It would appear that the government was desperately looking for noblemen not tinged with conspiracy. West sat on the commissions set up for the trials of the duke of Norfolk and the Scottish queen, but outside of his lieutenancy the only significant political reward that he ever secured was the election of his son, Sir Thomas West, as an M.P. for Chichester in 1571. Recognizing that one of the Chichester seats was usually controlled by the Arundel-Lumley faction, Professor Neale suggests that Sir Thomas West may have been selected in response to a nomination by the earl of Arundel.[3] But two facts argue against this: firstly, Arundel and Lumley were either confined or under close surveillance at this time; secondly, it was William West who had denounced Arundel and Lumley to the government. The answer to the question must be sought elsewhere; Sir Thomas West was more successful socially than his father, marrying Anne,

[1] See also Chapters 8 and 11, Section ii.
[2] G.E.C., IV, 158.
[3] The Elizabethan House of Commons, pp. 262-3.

the daughter of Sir Francis Knollys. Thus the nomination may have come from the Privy Council.

William, the first of the restored barony, died in 1595 and was succeeded by his son Sir Thomas who, by a dubious decision of the House of Lords, was placed in the precedence of the ancient barony and thus reckoned the eleventh Baron De La Warr. The eleventh lord was connected with the Puritan classical movement and its Parliamentary leadership through his son Sir Thomas and his son-in-law, Richard Blount, both members of the 1593 Parliament.[1] Sir Thomas, when he succeeded as twelfth baron in 1602, also assumed the nominal leadership of the Puritan movement in Sussex and his name appeared first on the petition of the Puritan gentry in March 1603/4. Perhaps the twelfth baron is best remembered as governor and captain general of Virginia, which he actually visited in 1610 and 1611, and for the fact the state of Delaware is named after him.[2]

Of all the social classes of Sussex which the government sought to bind to the Protestant settlement, the nobility presented the greatest problem. In the absence of an effective centralized bureaucracy the Elizabethan government was less able to ignore special interests than more modern governments. County factions and local influence simply had to be taken into consideration; and, since Lord Montague had shown himself a man of moderation, it must have seemed impolitic to withhold from him the small amount of patronage that he felt was his due. Until after the defeat of the Spanish Armada there lurked around every corner the possibility of violent resistance from a disgruntled nobility: among other reasons, the duke of Norfolk and many of the Ridolfi plotters were driven into conspiracy because they were disappointed in the rewards that they received.[3] The gains from monastic lands did not sufficiently balance the loss of favour and influence that the old nobility had suffered at court.

[1] Neale, *Elizabeth I and Her Parliaments, 1584–1601*, pp. 257–9.

[2] *G.E.C.*, IV, 158–61; "Extracts from the MSS. of Samuel Jeake", ed. T. W. W. Smart and W. D. Cooper, *S.A.C.*, IX, 45–9.

[3] W. T. MacCaffrey, "Place and Patronage in Elizabethan Politics", *Elizabethan Government and Society: Essays Presented to Sir John Neale*, ed. S. T. Bindoff *et al.* (London: 1961), p. 98.

With the evidence of discontent among the Fitzalan faction in 1569, it may have seemed that the best thing to do was to balance the older Catholic nobility with Buckhurst, Montague, and William West, representing those who would have liked to displace the Fitzalan party in the management of county affairs. Lord Buckhurst's absence from the lieutenancy in 1585–86 was only a temporary setback and may be tentatively explained by the intrigues of jealous courtiers anxious to exploit the existence of embarrassing relatives. This lacuna in Buckhurst's career will probably only be fully explained when he finds a competent biographer. As for Lord Montague, his commission as lord lieutenant could hardly be considered permanent when other courtiers had better claims for reward. Whatever the evidence of his own personal loyalty, he was still a Catholic, and around his person and his household there inevitably hovered a cloud of suspicion.

12

THE GENTRY AND THE COMMISSION
OF THE PEACE

THE GROWING POWER of the gentry in the time of Elizabeth I was to have a vital influence upon the success of the Protestant settlement of religion. Considering the loss in power of the old nobility, the unpopularity of the bishops and the subservience of a clergy caught up in an economic struggle for survival, it could not have been otherwise. Lay participation in religious affairs was spreading. Not only was the central government completely dependent upon the gentry as magistrates for the local enforcement of laws of a temporal nature; the execution of later statutes buttressing the original parliamentary settlement of 1559 also was placed increasingly in the hands of the gentry. As the House of Commons, exhorted by its Puritan conscience, began to assume the legislative initiative in religious matters, it was only natural that the execution of these laws should be placed increasingly in the hands of the deputy lieutenants, justices of the peace or special lay commissioners for dealing with recusants and seminary priests, rather than in the hands of the bishops. The whole feeling of the Tudor period was against giving the clergy or the church courts any more power. The Protestant gentry showed a pronounced predilection for managing their own affairs, religious or otherwise.

In Sussex, however, the untitled gentry could not hope to dominate the scene entirely in the county. This situation was perceived by Bishop Curteys in a report on "The General State of Sussex" written sometime in 1581 or 1582. In this survey Curteys complained, with some exaggeration, that most of the more substantial Sussex gentry were "ill affected", while many others were weak and indifferent and easily swayed by the nobility.[1] Actually, the power of the more uncompromising recusants had been broken by the Court of High Commission in the early 1580s, but other Catholics were more flexible and circumspect in the profession of their religion, and did not

[1] S.P., Dom., Eliz., 164/22.

hesitate to make an occasional demonstration of conformity to retain public office.

Otherwise, no other class was in a position to challenge the social hegemony of the Sussex gentry. The citizens of Chichester, the only town in Sussex that had a viable civic life or a reasonably sound economy, chose to identify their interests with those of the gentry. There were very few freeholders among the yeomanry; as tenants they remained economically dependent upon the gentry.

Thus many of the social and economic factors which retarded the spread of the popular reformation in Lancashire and the more remote parts of Yorkshire were also present in Elizabethan Sussex. But this fact also offers a key to understanding the weakness of Elizabethan Catholicism: it survived only where there were conservative social institutions to support it. In Sussex the survival of Catholicism is most noticeable in those areas where the social and economic influence of Catholic peers remained strongest. The decline of Catholicism was most pronounced in those parts of the county where a well-organized Puritan movement existed.

Before the Protestant gentry could play their role in the enforcement of the religious settlement and the spread of the popular reformation, the power of the Catholic gentry had to be broken. While the Act of Supremacy placed legal obstacles in the way of Catholics seeking local office, the full force of this exclusion was delayed for at least a decade and then was not fully effective. Sussex presented special problems not found elsewhere in England. Catholics were more numerous than in most other counties, and some of them were among the wealthiest landowners in the county at the beginning of the reign, although all but a couple appear to have suffered economically as a result of their recusancy. The most intransigent of the recusant gentry chose to withdraw from county affairs and to exercise social influence no further than the limits of their households; others were forcibly removed from the scene by imprisonment. But there were others among the Catholic gentry who were not so easily removed. By evading legal disabilities and through the connivance of Protestant friends and relatives they were able to remain in office. This latter group of crypto-Catholics refused to accept the position of being a caste set apart. No legislative enactment nor administrative decree coming down from Westminster could ignore these realities.

It was neither prudent nor practical to purge the Catholic gentry from the magistracy all at once. As lord lieutenant, Lord Buckhurst had realized that. He fought very hard to build up his power in the county and he did not scruple to ally himself with Lord Montague as long as such an alliance contributed to the realization of his ambitions. Lord Buckhurst did not believe in denying his patronage to Catholics any more than the earl of Essex did. Thus when Lord Buckhurst's moderating influence is seen restraining over-zealous commissioners seeking out recusants and missionary priests, or, when he is found trying to secure a minor position for a Catholic squire, he is simply remembering political realities and the need for goodwill wherever it can be found.[1]

To offset the slowness with which Catholics were removed from the commission of the peace and the reluctance of many Protestant J.P.s to persecute their Catholic neighbours and relatives, the Sussex commission of the peace usually included two or three ecclesiastics: the bishop of Chichester, one of his chancellors, and perhaps a canon residentiary. The Privy Council had relied very heavily on Bishop Curteys as a temporal magistrate; besides serving as a J.P. he was often found executing special commissions and sending intelligence to the Privy Council until the more moderate faction among the gentry succeeded in having his name removed from the commission of the peace in 1577. In 1570 Bishop Curteys had thought it imperative to have several ecclesiastics among the justices to offset those who displayed such a lack of enthusiasm in "causes ecclesiastical".[2] Lord Buckhurst also realized this need. When he wrote to the lord keeper requesting that John Drury, LL.D., a commissary of the bishop of Chichester, be included in the commission of the peace, he explained that it would "geve quiett furtherans to the servis of the church and her majestie".[3]

---

[1] See the case of William Dawtrey, below, pp. 244–5.
[2] S.P., Dom., Eliz., 74/44.   [3] B.M., Harley MS. 6996, fo. 167.

Lord Buckhurst's action in softening somewhat the persecution of Catholics while, at the same time, being careful to place the execution of the recusancy laws in the hands of trusted Protestants, could indicate a conscious policy of easing the transference of political and social power from the Catholic to the Protestant gentry. Such a policy, reflecting an awareness of the special conditions of Sussex, would have been consistent with the known desire on the part of the local governors to maintain social stability in the commonwealth.

(i) Catholics and Local Office Holding

For several years after the passing of the Elizabethan Act of Supremacy, it was common knowledge that the oath of supremacy was being evaded. J. B. Black has attributed this to the laxity of sheriffs and other officials responsible for administering the oath and to the fact that the ecclesiastical penalty of excommunication no longer carried any secular sanction.[1] Parliament attempted to close up these loopholes by passing a statute in 1563 entitled, *An act for the assurance of the Queen's Majesty's royal power over all estates and subjects within her Highness's dominions*,[2] which included several new classes of people among those who had to swear an oath recognizing the queen's ecclesiastical supremacy. Besides members of the House of Commons, lawyers and sheriffs, the act clearly included all justices of the peace and other holders of local office—"all persons whatsoever who have or shall be admitted to any ministry or office belonging to common law or any other law within the realm". Some historians have argued that there could be no avowed Catholics in office after this act went into effect —provided the oath was ministered as specified. The fact is that the oath continued to be evaded, and where it could not be evaded, the swearing of such an oath under pressure often did little to change a man's beliefs or alter the course of his action. The term "avowed Catholic" is rather a narrow classification that excludes the Catholic who might momentarily succumb to weakness or extreme pressure from above, or the Catholic

[1] *The Reign of Elizabeth* (Oxford: 1936), p. 20.
[2] 5 Eliz. I, c. 1.

ambitious for the power, influence and prestige that public office can bring. Human nature is frail and "avowed Catholics" constitute a minority in troubled times. It is not the weakness displayed in a difficult moment, but rather the pattern of a lifetime that gives the best indication of a man's religious views.

Desiring complete conformity in religion, the Privy Council were always ready to go to great lengths to persuade just one Catholic to accept the religious settlement. Obviously they were bound by law to extract the oath of supremacy from all office-holders. At least that was the policy in London. On the local scene there might be other considerations: there were few members of the Sussex gentry who had no Catholic relatives except perhaps the Morleys of Glyn and the Jefferays of Chiddingly; even the Pelhams had their Catholic branch. The Privy Council themselves were aware that false returns of the oaths of supremacy were being made into Chancery as late as 1592;[1] earlier in the reign the returns were often not made at all. This could not have come about without at least some connivance on the part of Protestant relatives or friends.

In 1564 all the bishops of England were required to make surveys of the gentry in their dioceses evaluating the religious attitudes of both the justices of the peace and the important local gentry who might be eligible for a commission of the peace. Bishop Barlow found the situation quite unfavourable, although not without hope if the commission of the peace could be extensively revised. Altogether, his letter to the Privy Council conveys a sense of relief that things were not worse:

". . . thanks be to almightie god, through the Quenes most gracious government assisted by your lordships providente circumspections this Countye of Sussex . . . is free from all violent attemptes eyther to affli[c]te the godlye or to distourbe the stablisshed good orders of this Realme. Notwithstandinge I doubte of secrett practices which perhappes myght breake oute into open violence, were yt not for feare of your Lordshippes vigilante Aucthorite".[2]

---

[1] B.M., Harley MS. 703, fos. 70–70v.

[2] "A Collection of Original Letters from the Bishops to the Privy Council", ed. Mary Bateson, *Camden Society Miscellany*, IX, 8–11.

Bishop Barlow's survey of the justices and the important gentry in Sussex begins with the western half of the county. He considered five of the justices reliable, although he had reservations about Sir Thomas Palmer of Parham. There were also three Catholic recusants in the commission: William Shelley of Michelgrove, William Dawtrey of More House, and Edmund Forde of Chartinge, who was "extremely perverse". Among the gentry of West Sussex who were not magistrates three were "favourers of godlie procedinges"; six were not. The situation in east Sussex was worse because the Catholics were still entrenched in the commission from Queen Mary's time, while rising Protestant families, such as the Morleys and Pelhams, had not yet made their way into power, although they would soon have the opportunity. Protestantism was to make great gains in east Sussex and would be coloured by Puritanism; Catholicism though much diminished was never rooted out of west Sussex. The Protestant magistrates in east Sussex numbered five including two important lawyers, John Jefferay of Chiddingly and George Goring of Ovingdean, who probably were absent during legal terms; there were nine justices who were considered unreliable, one of whom was Sir Edward Gage of Firle. Of the rural gentry in the eastern half of Sussex, Barlow lists seven who were favourable to the religious settlement and four who were not.

East Sussex had a tradition of Protestantism going back to the reign of Edward VI, which is illustrated by the fact that a total of 27 convicted heretics were burned at the stake during Queen Mary's reign in the towns of Lewes, Mayfield, East Grinstead, and Steyning.[1] Protestantism was strongest in the towns: Rye, Hastings, Lewes, and Brighton "ar governed with suche officers as be faythfull favourers of goddes worde and earnestly given to mainteyn godly orders", said Bishop Barlow.[2] However, the towns of west Sussex were filled with aldermen and magistrates whom Barlow variously described as "notorious obstinate aduersaries" or "frowardly supersticious". Among them was Ralph Chauntler, alderman of Chichester, who survived to harass Bishop Curteys.[3]

---

[1] Philip Hughes, *The Reformation in England* (London: 1954), III, 128.
[2] Bateson, *op. cit.*, pp. 8–11.   [3] DRO, Ep. I/15, Box A 2 (1).

The Privy Council apparently were unable to get the whole commission of the peace to swear the oath of supremacy until late in 1569. In accordance with instructions from the Privy Council the sheriff and justices assembled at Steyning in December of that year to witness the signatures of all justices and former justices. Although summoned, William Shelley of Michelgrove and William Scott of Iden refused to appear, and are not known to have subsequently subscribed. William Dawtrey of More House and James Gage of Bentley did appear, but refused to subscribe, "yet with suche humblenes as it semed to vs not to be of stobbovrnes, but as they said there contiencis [were] not yet satysfyd".[1] None the less, bonds were taken of Gage and Dawtrey as a guarantee of their good behaviour and their appearance before the lords of the Privy Council should they be summoned there. Several other Catholics did sign including John Apsley of Pulborough, the sheriff that year, John Gage of Firle, and Richard Covert of Slaugham, who were justices, as well as Henry Poole, who had been dropped from the commission.[2]

A year later, no Catholics, open or suspected, remained on the commission except Sir Thomas Palmer of Parham and William Dawtrey, both of whom had powerful friends, and Richard Covert who appears to have been converted to a Protestant attitude. Bishop Curteys tells us that the religious dispositions of all the gentry had been well known to the late Bishop Barlow, yet the churchwardens could not be brought to present recusants. Recusants among the Sussex gentry were

"concealed for favor or feare as shoulde seeme by the saied churche wardens and syde men for the most parte beinge but tenants to the chiefe offenders, beinge a verie evill and perilouse example if it should be suffered."[3]

Bishop Curteys made a survey in 1570 for the Privy Council of the whole Sussex magistracy in which he said that some justices were very industrious and could be trusted with temporal affairs. But he proposed to withdraw recusancy cases from the jurisdiction of the justices of the peace and entrust them only to special "commissioners for causes ecclesiastical". In other

[1] S.P., Dom., Eliz., 60/18.   [2] Ibid., 60/18. I.   [3] Ibid., 74/44.

words, Bishop Curteys was suggesting that all cases with a religious bearing should be tried only before a special branch of the ecclesiastical commission sitting in Sussex.[1] This bold attempt to establish a prerogative court in Sussex was doubtless one of the factors that brought about the downfall of Bishop Curteys.

At the end of his episcopate in 1582, Bishop Curteys complained that some of the magistrates were under suspicion for their own religious beliefs or else were known to be very lax in punishing others for recusancy. Magistrates accused of such liberality towards recusants included Thomas Bishop, a relative of Thomas Stapleton, the Catholic controversialist, John Culpepper, and Thomas Parker. This Bishop Curteys blamed primarily on the influence of local noblemen, and he singled out as a special example of their influence and power the fact that the earl of Arundel's steward, Edward Caryll, had lately been restored to the commission of the peace "being a knowen papist".[2] As in 1570, so in 1582; the gentlemen that Bishop Curteys trusted the most were William Morley of Glyn, Thomas May of Burwash, and John Pelham of Laughton. Otherwise, most of the Sussex gentry were personal enemies of Bishop Curteys, which increased his personal distrust of them; he felt that the religious statutes would be better enforced if townsmen from the Protestant Cinque Ports were brought into rural areas to serve in the magistracy.[3]

Another evaluation of the magistracy was made in 1587.[4] Except possibly for Herbert Pelham of Michelham Priory, there were no J.P.s who could be classified as Catholics. But several were under suspicion because of friends or relatives. The mother-in-law of Nicholas Parker, who was sheriff in 1587, was a known recusant. Thomas and Richard Lewkenor, both justices who to all intents and purposes dominated the Chichester rape, had a brother, George Lewkenor of Exton, Hants, who was a civilian. George was a recusant residing in Chichester with his family, knowing that his brothers would not convict him for nonconformity. George Lewkenor's son was a Catholic exile living at the court of the prince of Parma. In Hastings rape

[1] *Ibid.*   [2] *Ibid.*, 165/22.   [3] *Ibid.*
[4] B.M., Lansdowne MS. 53, no. 80, printed *S.A.C.*, II, 58–62.

the J.P.s included Sir Thomas Vaen, John Culpepper, John Wyldgoose, and Edmund Pelham, all of whom were counted "cold professors of religion". Sir Thomas Vaen lived in Kent; Edmund Pelham, a lawyer, spent most of his time in London.

"Mr. Culpeppir and Mr. Wyldgoose dwell in one towne at the northe border of Sussex; and Mr. Wyldgoose is most abidynge in Waells, lettyng his howse to Mr. Turwhit, a notable recusant. It is therefor thought convenyant that some other zelous in religion were appoynted with them to be justysses nearer the sea sowthward, as well for ease of the contre as for furderans of religion."[1]

The backbone of the magistracy was still provided by the Morleys, Mays, and Pelhams of Laughton. Other substantial families were now in the commission: the Shurleys, Bowyers, Marvyns; the Shirleys of Wiston were already well established.

The number of sheriffs of Sussex and Surrey with Catholic backgrounds and associations presents a contrast to the reasonably successful attempt to purge Catholics from the commission of the peace after 1570. It is apparent that the risk of having a Catholic in the office of sheriff was not considered as great as the presence of a Catholic in the commission of the peace. Really dependable Protestant gentry were not so numerous that they alone could bear the burden of serving as sheriffs. Nor could such men be spared when they were needed elsewhere as J.P.s and deputy lieutenants, because a man was dropped from the commission of the peace when he became sheriff.

The sheriff had once been the most important shire official; but because the crown found difficulty in controlling sheriffs the bulk of their duties had been gradually transferred to the J.P.s during the fifteenth century. Under the Tudors the lord lieutenant had replaced the sheriff as the principal official in county affairs. The duties of the sheriff entailed responsibility for certain local revenues, for executing writs from local and royal courts of justice, supervising parliamentary elections, and maintaining the county gaol. The office was still granted only to knights and esquires as in former times, but dubious

[1] Ibid.

honour that it was, it brought a whole year of unwanted burdens and expenses.[1] However, in the opinion of Dr Elton, although the office of sheriff was much reduced in powers, it still "retained intermittent weight in the administration".[2] Dr Elton says that the office came only once in a lifetime, but a glance at the P.R.O. *List of Sheriffs* reveals that it could and sometimes did come twice, as in the case of Sir Walter Covert of Slaugham or Herbert Pelham of Michelham Priory.[3] Herbert Pelham had been sheriff of Sussex and Surrey in 1576. When an attempt was made to allow him to enjoy that office again in 1582, he tried to evade the responsibility by claiming that, as an inhabitant of Winchelsea, he was exempted from that duty by virtue of liberties contained in the charters of the Cinque Ports. A month and two days in the Marshalsea prison persuaded Herbert Pelham that perhaps these exemptions did not apply in his case, and he confessed himself ready to submit to better legal judgment. His cousin, Edmund Pelham, a student at Gray's Inn, was found to be the author of this novel interpretation of the ancient liberties of the Cinque Ports; Edmund was committed to the Fleet for his rash counsel.[4] Yet despite Catholic relatives living in his household, Herbert Pelham was appointed sheriff for a second term from November 1590 to November of the following year.[5]

Admittedly not every sheriff held the office twice, but it is hard to explain the presence of so many Catholic gentlemen among the holders of the sheriffdom of Sussex and Surrey during the reign of Elizabeth. Altogether, the office of sheriff of Sussex (and of Surrey for part of the reign) was held by members of the Catholic gentry of Sussex in 1558, 1560, 1565, 1567,

[1] For two examples of the financial risks that sheriffs incurred, cf. A. L. Rowse, *The England of Elizabeth* (London: 1959), p. 358.

[2] G. R. Elton, *The Tudor Constitution* (Cambridge: 1960), p. 451.

[3] *List of Sheriffs for England and Wales* (London: P.R.O. Lists and Indexes no. 9, 1898), *passim*.

[4] Hist. MSS. Comm., *Salisbury MSS*,. ii, 502; Hatfield MS. 1151, printed in *A Collection of State Papers Relating to Affairs in the Reign of Queen Elizabeth*, ed. W. Murdin (London: 1759), pp. 371–2.

[5] In 1592, the Privy Council instructed Lord Buckhurst, the lord lieutenant to remove J.P.s who had recusants residing under the same roof. B.M., Harley MS. 703, fos. 70–70v.

1568, 1569, 1571, 1576, 1589, 1591 and 1603—eleven times.[1]
Could not a Catholic sheriff have helped his fellow recusants by
removing names from the lists turned over to the Exchequer?
Could he not have refused to execute writs against a harried
recusant? Probably not. In the first place affairs concerning
recusants and missionary priests were increasingly being turned
over to special commissioners, and these commissioners were
always trusted Protestants.[2] Furthermore, local officials were
under close scrutiny by the Privy Council and the justices of
assize; only the bravest would risk the wrath of these vigilant
overseers. On the other hand a sheriff may have been able to
relieve Catholics from persecution in small ways, which the
government may have realized but dismissed as no great source
of danger. The fact is that in a county such as Sussex the most
reliable supporters of Protestantism were better employed
elsewhere. This was doubly true in the years before 1570,
when there were still so many Catholics in the commission of
the peace who bore watching.

A couple of detailed examples will serve to illustrate the
difficulty that the government encountered in trying to remove
Catholics from the magistracy where such individuals felt that
they should be counted among the local governors. Gentry of
this type were willing to conform occasionally to hold local
office and to spare their families the inconvenience of harassment by the government. In the two cases to be discussed, both
individuals were able to survive the periodic purges of the
magistracy because of the patronage of a peer.[3]

An extremely interesting case is that of William Dawtrey of
More House and Chichester, who married Margaret Roper of
Eltham, Kent, a granddaughter of Sir Thomas More.[4] Reputedly
of Norman descent, the Dawtreys were well established among
the gentry of Sussex: both the father and the grandfather of

---

[1] For detailed examples, see my "Catholics and Local Office Holding in
Elizabethan Sussex", *Bulletin of the Institute of Historical Research*, XXXV
(May 1962), 47–61.

[2] Sir Walter Covert's letter-book (B.M., Harley MS. 703) is full of such
commissions.

[3] More detailed examples will be found in my article cited above.

[4] D. G. Elwes, *A History of the Castles and Mansions of Western Sussex* (London
1876), p. 173.

William Dawtrey had held the sheriffdom of Sussex; he himself sat as a knight of the shire in the second Parliament of Elizabeth despite the fact that he was a recusant. In his report on the religious attitudes of the J.P.s, Barlow said that William Dawtrey was not only unfavourable to "godly proceedings", he was also "verye supersticious".[1] If Dawtrey subscribed the oath of supremacy during his term as sheriff from November 1566 to the following November, no record of it has survived. But when the magistrates were commanded to assemble at Steyning in 1569 to swear the oath of supremacy, Dawtrey appeared, but refused to sign.[2] Dawtrey's name appeared on the commission of the peace in November 1570, but appears to have been removed shortly thereafter. In 1573 Dawtrey and his wife were presented for not having received communion at Easter.[3] Yet he still had powerful friends: on 4 November 1576 Lord Montague wrote to William More of Loseley recommending Dawtrey for the office of under-sheriff of Sussex and Surrey; and in the following November Lord Buckhurst also wrote a letter to More making the same recommendation.[4] But the picture is complicated by the fact that William Dawtrey had a son with the same name who was a lawyer of Lincoln's Inn. It was presumably this William Dawtrey, "Mr. Dawtrey of Petworth", who was summoned to appear before Bishop Curteys in August 1580 for recusancy and who, in the same month, subsequently conformed and came to church.[5] The elder William Dawtrey's will was proved on 23 November 1591;[6] his son predeceased him in September 1589 and was buried at St Dunstan's, Stepney.[7] Elwes states that it was the younger William Dawtrey who was reported in 1587 to have lost his commission because he was a recusant.[8] The survey of J.P.s made in that year stated that he had recently married[9] and

[1] Bateson, op. cit., pp. 8–11.
[2] S.P., Dom., Eliz., 60/18.
[3] DRO, Ep. I/23/4, fo. 21.
[4] Hist. MSS. Comm. [Loseley MSS.], vii, 630–1.
[5] DRO, Ep. I/37, 58 and 3.
[6] P.C.C. 85 Sainherbe.   [7] Elwes, op. cit., p. 173.
[8] B.M., Lansdowne MS. 53, no. 80, printed S.A.C., II, 58–62.
[9] The younger William Dawtrey's marriage licence was dated 20 Aug. 1574. He married Dorothy, d. of Richard Stanley of Warwick, a teller to the

since that time had conformed and publicly received the sacrament, "wherfor yf he was restored to iustys office, I take it a means to encorrage hym to procead, and to allure other recusants for to do their dewghty to God and their prinse".[1] Dawtrey is not known to have been restored to the commission of the peace, but a pattern is beginning to form: except in the case of the most stubborn and open recusants like the Shelleys and the Gages, who were barred from all offices if not imprisoned, a slight show of conformity could open up the possibility of local office. But such families as were moved by the unquenchable desire of power and influence often show an ebbing of Catholic fervour from generation to generation.

The Caryll family affords an outstanding and well-documented example of a recusant family maintaining influence in local affairs quite late in the reign of Elizabeth. As leaders of the Catholic gentry they took second place only to the Shelleys and the Gages; that they were able to hold public office at all shows how much more flexible they were than their more stubborn cousins. The Carylls were an old Sussex family that had refounded their fortunes through the law and the tenure of Crown offices. Sir John Caryll was attorney-general to Henry VII; his son, also named Sir John, was attorney-general for the duchy of Lancaster and inherited his father's stewardship of the rape of Bramber. As attorney for the Court of First Fruits and Tenths in 1539, the younger Sir John administered revenues confiscated from the church by Henry VIII, yet he refused to subscribe to the Prayer-book of 1549.[2] The younger Sir John's son, Edward Caryll of Harting, also prepared for his father's profession by entering the Inner Temple at the age of nineteen in the autumn of 1556. Edward Caryll was sheriff of Sussex and Surrey from February to December 1571, although he is not known to have sworn the oath of supremacy. Almost all the Carylls were linked by marriage with other prominent Catholic families in Sussex: Edward was married to Philippa, the daughter of James Gage of Bentley in the parish of Framfield, who was a

---

Exchequer. J. Dallaway, *A History of the Western Division of the County of Sussex* (London: 1815–1830), II, i, 332; Elwes, *op. cit.*, p. 173.

[1] B.M., Lansdowne MS. 53, no. 80, printed *S.A.C.*, II, 58–62.

[2] Max de Trenqualéon, *West-Grinstead et les Caryll* (Paris: 1893), I, 350–1.

recusant.[1] In October 1577 Bishop Curteys assessed Edward Caryll's lands at four hundred marks per year, but later in the reign of Elizabeth, Caryll turned his lands at Washington, West Grinstead, and Shipley over to his eldest son Thomas and removed himself to a new seat at Ladyholt Park in West Harting.[2] In the next century a descendant, John Caryll, was secretary of state to James, the Old Pretender, and was created the titular Baron Caryll.[3] The whole family appeared to be well off; Edward's nephew John Caryll of Warnham was worth a thousand marks per year in 1577.

Edward Caryll is first described as a recusant by Bishop Curteys in 1577.[4] In 1580 Bishop Curteys was placing pressure upon recusants to conform, and in an undated letter to the Privy Council he states that he had persuaded Caryll to come to prayers at the episcopal residence, but he was unable to ascertain whether or not Caryll was attending his parish church. He therefore recommended that Caryll be summoned before the Privy Council for examination.[5] In August 1580 Caryll and his wife were presented for recusancy along with two servants, one of whom was suspected of being a schoolmaster.[6] In the same month Bishop Curteys summoned Caryll to appear before him at the episcopal residence at Aldingbourne, and Caryll began to conform.[7] The alternative was imprisonment, the fate that most of the Shelleys and Gages chose. Apparently, Caryll was never again cited as a recusant, but it certainly appears that he continued to be religiously disaffected. He was suspected of being involved with Philip Howard, earl of Arundel, in helping Lord Paget flee overseas in 1583 after the Throgmorton conspiracy. He and his servant, John Mitchell, were examined about the matter; although Caryll admitted having met the individuals in question, he denied any complicity.[8] Caryll suffered imprisonment in the Tower as one of the earl of

---

[1] Elwes, op. cit., p. 253.

[2] S.P., Dom., Eliz., 117/15, printed C.R.S., Miscellanea XII, pp. 80–1; Elwes, op. cit., pp. 113–14; V.C.H. Sussex, IV, 11.

[3] D.N.B., sub. John Caryll (1625–1711).

[4] C.R.S., Miscellanea XII, pp. 80–1.

[5] DRO Ep. I/37, no. 29.

[6] Ibid., no. 38.   [7] Ibid., no. 3.

[8] S.P., Dom., Eliz., 164/23.

Arundel's followers; it was only subsequent to his imprisonment that he was dropped from the commission of the peace.[1] In 1587 Caryll was said to have been removed from the magistracy because he was "an active wysman, my lord of Arondell, his steward and doer of thys contre";[2] and the earl had specified in his will that Caryll was to administer his property after his death.[3] Despite his involvement with the earl of Arundel, Caryll had sufficiently recovered the good graces of the government to be restored to the commission of the peace in January 1591, remaining on the commission until the end of the reign.[4] He was knighted in May 1603 along with his son Thomas and survived until 1609.

Sir Edward Caryll was a very flexible man, but his associations were Catholic. His daughter Mary was a nun, and his son Sir Thomas was known to have kept a chaplain. In 1614 that chaplain was Fr Henry More, S. J.[5] Two of Sir Edward's houses, Benton's Place in Shipley and Ladyholt at Harting, had several priest holes each.[6]

Although the second half of the sixteenth century has been characterized as an age of religious fanaticism, it must be remembered that fanatics by their very nature attract more attention than is due to them. The undoubted existence of many fanatics at this time has too often led historians to assume that everyone took an ideological stand and never compromised that position. However, it does not necessarily follow that a person who has once taken up a position will never afterwards modify his actions even for the give and take of local politics. This is attributing rather more consistency to human nature than is warranted by historical fact.

Bishop Barlow had complained about the strength that the Catholic gentry wielded in the commission of the peace, and Bishop Curteys also found himself faced with the problem of

[1] Mousley, "Sussex Country Gentry in the Reign of Elizabeth", pp. 456–8.
[2] B.M., Lansdowne MS. 53, no. 80, printed *S.A.C.*, II, 58–62.
[3] *The Ven. Philip Howard, Earl of Arundel*, ed. J. H. Pollen (London: C.R.S., 1919), XXI, 368–9, 380.
[4] Mousley, *op. cit.*, pp. 456–8.
[5] Trenqualéon, *op. cit.*, II, 368, 373.
[6] H. Foley, *Records of the English Province of the Society of Jesus* (London: 1875–83), III, 538.

proving guilt against recusants when their neighbours would not or dared not accuse them. Yet someone had to enforce the laws until a new generation of Protestants could be brought up to take over the magistracy. There is evidence that the government had no desire to exclude any but the most uncompromising Catholic from local offices, for the lure of public office might well be the deciding factor in a person's allegiance. And it certainly must have occurred to Elizabethan statesmen that time was on the side of a government that was satisfied with an occasional show of outward conformity. Yet whatever the attitude of politicians in London, it seems most likely that the decisive factors which permitted Catholics to hold local public office were administrative inefficiency in detecting nonconformity and the continuing importance of local factions arising from the patronage of some great magnate and sometimes resting on kinship and economic influence.

(ii) *The Decline of Catholicism among the Gentry*

The counting of Catholics (or Protestants) is an approach to Reformation social history that is fraught with even greater dangers than the attempt to measure the wealth of the gentry by the counting of manors.[1] Any attempt to make a quantitative estimate for the decline of Catholicism in post-Reformation England inevitably raises several problems: (1) the administrative inefficiency in detecting recusancy, and especially the difficulty for the historian in discovering crypto-Catholicism where it is covered over with outward and occasional displays of religious conformity; (2) the incompleteness of records; (3) the difficulty in delineating a sociological group for purposes of study; (4) the dangers encountered in trying to make religious distinctions within such a sociological group.

In utilizing the various varieties of recusant lists to ascertain the extent of Catholicism, one must be aware of the administrative problems that were involved in detecting recusancy,

---

[1] For a criticism of the debate over the rise of the gentry and the danger of using manors as the units of measuring wealth, see J. H. Hexter, "Storm over the Gentry", *Reappraisals in History* (New York: Harper Torchbook edition, 1963), pp. 117–62.

such as sheer inefficiency, the conflict of jurisdictions in cases of religious dissidence, the sympathy sometimes displayed towards Catholic neighbours or relatives by a magistrate, or the rather common practice of occasional conformity by the head of the family.

Individual recusant lists, whether one is speaking of church-wardens' presentments, bishops' returns, the reports of government spies, or the Recusant Rolls of the Exchequer very rarely give any idea of the extent of recusancy in a particular county. Unless laboriously compared one with another, they give no idea of the problem of crypto-Catholics. Of all of these various types of recusancy returns the churchwardens' present-ments are the least satisfactory and most incomplete.[1] The returns made by the bishops to the Privy Council or to the Ecclesiastical Commission generally include only the chief recusants with whom the bishop felt himself unable to deal. It was official policy to leave such cases to the former two authorities. The Recusant Rolls of the Exchequer are also unsatisfactory. They list only of those intransigent recusants who were considered wealthy enough to pay the fine of £20 per lunar month. These lists generally omit recusants currently incarcerated by the court of High Commission. Although no quarter-sessions records dealing with cases of recusancy sur-vive for Sussex from the Elizabethan period, there is sufficient indirect evidence to indicate that little faith was reposed by the government or the bishops of Chichester in the average J.P. dealing with the problem. Reference has already been made in this chapter to cases of connivance on the part of temporal magistrates. The most effective agents for dealing with recu-sancy were the special commissioners appointed for that pur-pose in the 1580s and 1590s and selected from among the more zealous and trustworthy Protestants on the commission of the peace. Such men were usually Puritans.[2]

[1] See Chapter 7.

[2] One of the few lists that really approaches completeness is the one drawn up in Feb. 1585 by Sir Thomas Palmer of Angmering, Thomas Shirley, Thomas Pelham and Walter Covert, which specifies recusants to be disarmed. Several of these men are known to have inclined towards Puritanism. Palmer and Covert were among the most competent of the local governors during this period. The list (B.M., Harley MS. 703, fo. 20) gives the names of 45

Taken together, all of the sources for determining the extent of Elizabethan Catholicism can give a fairly accurate picture if the researcher is ambitious enough to undertake what Dr G. R. Elton calls "a broad-fronted attack on the vast resources of public and private archives".[1] This more ambitious approach is better conducted on the county level rather than the national level. One must particularly be wary of attempting an arbitrary sampling of a large number of families spread over a geographical area too extensive for a single researcher to become familiar with.[2]

The important criterion in selecting a sociological group among the gentry to be studied in order to determine its religious complexion is the wielding of political and social power or the potential for wielding such power. In order to obtain valid results it is also important that the families of the gentry to be analysed statistically should be chosen on the basis of possessing roughly the same potential for political and social power. It is more meaningful to study that portion of the gentry that held local political office at some time during the reign of Elizabeth rather than to try dissecting that amorphous group that included not only knights and esquires but also those who, whether rightfully or presumptiously, called themselves gentlemen. It is very difficult to tell just where the lesser gentry fade into the yeomanry.

The problem of evidence is also involved in the selection of a sociological group for study. Lack of contemporary evidence makes it impracticable to study the lesser gentry. But the greater gentry, as a group, do possess the merit of being easily defined and set off. There do exist sufficient lists of major local office holders during this period to indicate quite accurately the members of the county magistracy. In the case of this

---

recusants among the Sussex gentry who were to be disarmed, of whom at least 41 were heads of households. Some idea of the extent of recusancy among the lesser gentry can be gained if it is remembered that only six of these gentlemen are among the heads of families selected in Table VI for statistical study. Moreover, other names could be added from other sources.

[1] "The Problems and Significance of Administrative History in the Tudor Period", *The Journal of British Studies*, IV (May 1965), 18–28.

[2] I am thinking particularly of W. R. Trimble's *The Catholic Laity in Elizabethan England, 1558–1603* (Cambridge, Mass.: 1964).

present study, the religious views of the various families who were numbered among the local governors can be established with reasonable certainty in three quarters of the cases selected.[1]

Probably the most perplexing problem is making religious distinctions within the sociological group which has been selected for study. The distinction between "Catholic" and "Protestant" was not very precise in the 1560s. The whole idea behind the Elizabethan religious settlement from the government's point of view was to construct a church that would accommodate everyone. It was, of course, the papal bull of 1570 excommunicating the queen and holding out the threat of actual deposition that ultimately forced Catholics to draw the line somewhere and to make a personal decision. But, in Sussex such a decision could have been delayed until late in the 1570s. It is true that an effort was made by the government beginning in the 1560s to purge the commission of the peace, but it seems more likely that it was Bishop Curteys's determined attempt to root out Catholicism in 1577 that ultimately forced Catholics remaining among the local governors to make their choice. Both the papal bull of 1570 and the attempt to enforce the swearing of the oath of supremacy as a prerequisite for office holding tended to reduce the issue to one of papal supremacy *versus* royal supremacy. Yet, as Dr G. W. O. Woodward reminds us, if we assign a broader definition to the word "Catholic" and include within that category those who were conservative in their religious attitudes, we must conclude that most "Catholics" were not actively concerned about the issue of papal supremacy—whether in its spiritual or political sense.[2] Certainly, Cardinal Allen allowed the pope more political authority in his *A True Sincere, and Modest Defense of English Catholics* (1584)[3] then most English Catholics who thought about the problem were willing to concede. In the end, Allen and the extreme papalists failed to sway the English Catholic

---

[1] See Table VI at the end of this chapter.

[2] *A Short History of 16th Century England, 1485–1603* (New York: New American Library, 1963), pp. 114–15.

[3] The best modern edition is that prepared by R. M. Kingdon (Ithaca, N.Y.: 1965).

laity and a good portion of the Catholic secular clergy, the vast majority of whom preferred Elizabeth to any foreign ruler.

The danger to be avoided is that of viewing Catholicism or even recusancy too narrowly in terms of specific acts of non-conformity. When the head of a family, which had hitherto been recusant, is discovered to have conformed, one must probe deeper and determine if the head of the household subsequently relapses into recusancy, or if, notwithstanding a temporary conformity, a pattern of recusancy still persists among the members of his household. The case of Sir Edward Caryll of Harting illustrates the danger of assuming that a man is a Protestant because he has conformed and remains in the commission of the peace, yet maintains massing priests as chaplains and educates his daughter as a nun.[1]

My own definition of the term "Catholic" is broader than that generally held, but I believe it to be more realistic, especially when applied to the period before about 1580. This can be contrasted with the rigidly narrow definition of Catholicism employed by Professor W. R. Trimble in his *The Catholic Laity in Elizabethan England, 1558–1603.*

While the title of Professor Trimble's book and his opening argument lead one to believe that he is studying a cross section of the Catholic laity, he has in fact excluded from his social and economic analysis in Chapter IV all but the most intransigent recusants. His method of classifying individuals as recusants is at once haphazard and arbitrary. In one place[2] he asks if they have "recognizably Catholic names", or in choosing his "representative sampling" in Chapter IV of 128 cases in 22 counties his criterion is that they were still uncompromised as late as 1586. Presumably, Professor Trimble equates the temporary conformity of a harassed Catholic with patent proof of insincerity.[3]

In attempting to analyse the religious complexion of the

---

[1] See Section i of this chapter.

[2] Trimble, *op. cit.*, p. 86.

[3] As an example of the severity with which Professor Trimble renders his judgments, he concludes that in all of Elizabethan England the Vauxes of Harrowden were "perhaps the only sincerely Catholic family in the peerage". *Ibid.*, pp. 30, 136.

gentry of Elizabethan Sussex I have been fortunate in being able to draw upon the important economic and social study of the Sussex country gentry done by Dr Joyce E. Mousley.[1] Dr Mousley has studied certain families of the gentry in order to ascertain whether they were prospering or decaying. These families were selected on the basis of office-holding, meaning that sometime during the reign of Elizabeth a member of the family must have held the office of either deputy lieutenant, sheriff or justice of the peace. Further considerations were that the family was primarily seated in Sussex and had a member alive in 1580. By excluding seven families of the peerage and two cadet families related to peers Dr Mousley arrived at the figure of 78 families to be studied. I have added these nine families to my list, plus one more family that properly belongs to this same group, thus coming up with a total of 88 families to be analysed statistically.[2] By marshalling all available evidence (using contemporary sources only), the religious disposition of the families in this group can be determined at some point during the Elizabethan period in 65 out of the 88 cases.

In classifying the religious attitudes of the families selected, an attempt has been made, where the evidence would permit, to use terms more precise than "Catholic", "recusant" or "Protestant".[3] Where the evidence exists, the religious attitudes for each family are classified in Table VI for each of three different chronological periods, the 1560s, c. 1580 and the 1590s, in order to indicate any changes in these attitudes. Table IV gives the total number for each category in each of the three chronological periods in order to visualize quantitatively the decline of Catholicism.

Part I of Table IV will afford an idea of the difficulties that faced Bishop Barlow and the government in trying to enforce the religious settlement in the Sussex of the 1560s. In the 51 cases where the religious views are known, Catholic families

[1] "Sussex Country Gentry in the Reign of Elizabeth" (London Ph.D. thesis, 1955). Dr Mousley's conclusions concerning the economic status of the Sussex gentry have been reported in her article, "The Fortunes of Some Gentry Families of Elizabethan Sussex", *Economic History Review*, 2nd ser., XI (April 1959), 467–83.

[2] See Table VI at the end of this chapter.

[3] See the explanation of abbreviations used in Table VI.

TABLE IV

Statistical Evidence of the Decline of Catholicism among the Office-Holding Gentry during the Elizabethan Period, based on Table VI

I. *The 1560s.*
1. Total number of Catholic families. 33
2. Total number of Protestant families. 18
3. Total number of families where the religious views are not known. 34

II. *Circa 1580.*
1. Total number of Catholic families. 25
   Categories:
   a. Recusant families. (15)
   b. Heads of Catholic families not returned as recusants. (3)
   c. Crypto-Catholics or Catholic sympathizers (excluding those who are labelled as Protestants) who are heads of families. (7)
2. Total number of Protestant families. 27
3. Total number of families where the religious views are not known. 34

III. *The 1590s.*
1. Total number of recusant families. 16
2. Total number of families where the head of the house harbours recusants or the head of the house is a Catholic sympathizer. 3
3. Total number of Protestant families. 22
4. Total number of families where the religious views are not known (which would include those families where the line has become extinct). 45

outnumber Protestant families almost 2 to 1.[1] These figures do not really illustrate the magnitude of the problem at the very beginning of the reign because the evidence used for the 1560s is largely drawn from the years 1564 to 1570. These figures substantially agree with the estimate made in Chapter 3, section i, based on Sussex wills from 1552 to 1560, that at least

[1] See Section i of this chapter for a discussion of the problem of Catholics in the commission of the peace.

Of the 34 families whose religious attitudes during the 1560s are not known, I would assume that a good many were "Catholic" or conservative in outlook. Of the 34 families in the same category *c.* 1580 or the 45 in the 1590s one would have to presume that all conformed to the established church, although a few could have been crypto-Catholics.

half of the property-owning families in Sussex at the very beginning of the reign were Catholic (with reference to belief in purgatory and the efficacy of praying for dead, rather than the more remote and academic issue of papal supremacy).

Taken together, parts I and II of Table IV indicate that the total number of heads of families classified as Catholic has declined from 33 to 25, but only 15 of these have emerged as recusant by 1580. During the same period, which approximates the episcopate of Bishop Curteys (1570–1582), the number of known Protestant families has increased from 18 to 27. These figures help to support my argument that the full impact of the popular reformation was not felt in Sussex until Bishop Curteys brought learned Protestant preachers into the diocese in the 1570s.

The third part of Table IV shows that the number of recusant families, among those of the gentry who were at one time wealthy enough to hold local office, has not significantly changed from the period c. 1580 to the 1590s. These were the uncompromising recusants whom the penal laws, fines, imprisonment and other forms of persecution could not deter from nonconformity. But if the efforts of the government or the Protestant clergy to enforce the Elizabethan religious settlement did not sway this group, it would also appear that the ministrations of the missionary priests did very little to increase the incidence of recusancy.

A comparison of my classification of the religious attitudes of the 88 families selected for study with Dr Mousley's conclusions concerning prosperity and decay among roughly the same group of families also seems to indicate that the attempt to establish a connection between recusancy and economic decay is valid. Looking at the whole Elizabethan period, nine of the families whom Dr Mousley classifies as either decaying or not prospering, were recusant. Only two recusant families, the Scotts of Iden and the Gunters of Racton, were actually prospering.[1] Whether such economic decline is to be attributed to penalties imposed by the recusancy laws or to bad management or both is a problem that remains to be worked out.

[1] The evidence in the case of four other recusant families is inconclusive.

Elizabethan Catholicism survived best where there were social institutions to support it.[1] This was because the country gentry could provide the facilities for sheltering missionary

TABLE V

Geographical Distribution of the Catholic Gentry in Sussex during the Elizabethan Period, based on Table VI

	1560s	c. 1580	1590s
West Sussex			
I. Rape of Chichester			
1. Peers	2	2	2
2. Untitled Gentry	7	6	5
II. Rape of Arundel			
1. Peers	1	2	1
2. Untitled Gentry	4	3	1
III. Rape of Bramber			
1. Peers	—	—	—
2. Untitled Gentry	4	4	2
East Sussex			
IV. Rape of Lewes			
1. Peers	—	—	—
2. Untitled Gentry	5	1	—
V. Rape of Pevensey			
1. Peers	—	—	—
2. Untitled Gentry	5	2	2
VI. Rape of Hastings			
1. Peers	1	1	1
2. Untitled Gentry	5	5	5
West Sussex			
1. Total Peers	3	4	3
2. Total Untitled Gentry	15	13	8
East Sussex			
1. Total Peers	1	1	1
2. Total Untitled Gentry	15	8	8

priests more readily than lesser folk. Moreover, it was hopeless and dangerous to try to convert the commonalty in parishes where the local gentry were Protestant since tenants usually

[1] See Chapter 8 for a discussion of the pattern of social institutions among the recusant gentry of Sussex. See also John Bossy, "The Character of Elizabethan Catholicism", *Crisis in Europe, 1560–1660* (London: 1965), p. 223.

conformed to the religious pattern established by their squires. Since the houses of peers were considered privileged, they could usually maintain permanent chaplains. Table V, which shows the geographical distribution of the Catholic gentry, broken down into the figures for each of the rapes, illustrates the connection between the social influence of certain Catholic peers and the continuing strength of Catholicism in the spheres of their influence. In the 1560s Catholic families among the untitled gentry are about evenly distributed among the six rapes, except for the greater concentration of both Catholic peers and untitled gentry in the rape of Chichester. The number of Catholic untitled gentry remains constant in the rape of Hastings from the 1560s to the 1590s, and decreases only from seven to five in the rape of Chichester during the same period. One does not have to look far for a probable explanation: a combination of the spiritual fervour and the quasi-feudal influence of Lord Lumley and the first and second viscounts Montague in the rape of Chichester and the first Lord Montague and his widow Magdalen, the dowager Lady Montague at Battle Abbey in the rape of Hastings helped to stiffen Catholic resistance. At the same time, it would appear that neither Philip Howard, earl of Arundel nor the earls of Northumberland ever succeeded in filling the void left in the rape of Arundel by the death in 1580 of Henry, the last of the Fitzalan earls of Arundel. The virtual disappearance of Catholicism from the rape of Lewes and its pronounced decline in the rape of Pevensey is, perhaps, not unrelated to the presence of vigorous Puritan classical movements in the deaneries of Pevensey and Lewes in the 1580s and 1590s.[1]

(iii) The Spread of Protestantism among the Gentry

As the Catholic gentry were squeezed out of important local offices, several families of the Protestant gentry are seen making their way up in county affairs. A strong desire to be counted among the local governors was often a motive for adherence to the new religion, but this did not necessarily preclude enthusiasm for Protestantism. The Coverts of Slaugham, near

[1] See Table I, p. 175.

Horsham, offer the pattern of a family shifting from religious disaffection to not mere conformity, but abundant fervour. Richard Covert was one of the J.P.s in east Sussex whom Bishop Barlow classified in 1564 as "Myslykers of religion and godly procedinges".[1] Despite Bishop Barlow's opinion of him, Richard Covert remained on the commission of the peace as late as 1579, a year before his death. When the justices of Sussex were called upon to swear the oath of supremacy in 1569, Covert's name was among the subscribers.[2] From the time of Richard Covert's death until the reign of Charles I, his son, Sir Walter Covert, was the "active and trusted representative of the government in Sussex".[3] Sir Walter was twice sheriff in the 1590s, a deputy lieutenant after 1569; he also sat in four different parliaments as a knight of the shire.[4] Of Puritan leanings, Sir Walter was the second person to sign the Puritan petition presented by the Sussex gentry to James I on 5 March 1603/4.[5]

Dr Mousley's investigations of the economic trends among the Sussex gentry show that the names of such well-known Protestant families as the Coverts, the Pelhams of Laughton, both branches of the Bowyers and both branches of the Mays, stand out among those families that were waxing richer during the reign of Elizabeth.[6] Without doubt, their improved economic status helps to explain the increasing prominence of such families in county affairs, but another important factor was their unquestioned Protestantism. Bishops Barlow and Curteys had repeatedly stressed the importance of placing such men in the commission of the peace.[7] In the case of John Pelham of Laughton, his absence from the commission had been lamented by Bishop Barlow in 1564, but he does not seem to have made his way into the magistracy until about 1569.

[1] Bateson, op. cit., IX, 8–11.   [2] S.P., Dom., Eliz., 60/18, I.
[3] J. H. Cooper, "The Coverts", S.A.C., XLVII, 137.
[4] Mousley, "Sussex Country Gentry in the Reign of Elizabeth" (London Ph.D. thesis, 1955), pp. 3–4.
[5] "Extracts from the MSS. of Samuel Jeake", ed. T. W. W. Smart and W. D. Cooper, S.A.C., IX, 45–9.
[6] Mousley, "The Fortunes of Some Gentry Families of Elizabethan Sussex", loc. cit.
[7] Bateson, op. cit., IX, 10; S.P., Dom., Eliz., 165/22.

In view of the prominence of the Pelhams, their absence from the magistracy at the beginning of the reign is difficult to explain. The Pelhams were no mere parvenus; they had been well-established among the Sussex gentry since at least the fifteenth century. But it is in the Tudor age that the family fortunes began to climb to the pinnacle reached in the eighteenth century under the famous duke of Newcastle and his brother Henry Pelham.

Because of their associations the Pelhams must be accounted one of the mainstays of the Protestant movement in east Sussex. Evidently converted to Protestantism while they were students at Queen's College, Cambridge in the late 1540s John Pelham and his cousin, William Morley of Glyn, were exiles in Queen Mary's time.[1] John Pelham's father, Sir Nicholas, was a soldier and a member of Parliament who died in 1560 never doubting that he would be "received amongst his [Christ's] electe."[2] His uncle, Sir William Pelham, later lord justice of Ireland, had been imprisoned in connection with Wyatt's rebellion in 1554, but later made his escape, possibly overseas. Sir Nicholas Pelham and another uncle, Thomas Morley, were in the Fleet in July 1558 for failure to make a contribution of demilances to the Crown.[3] The Pelhams were allied to some of the most important Protestant families in Elizabethan England: John's grandmother was a Carew, his mother a Sackville, while he himself was to marry Judith, the daughter of Lord St John of Bletsho. It hardly comes as any surprise that two Pelhams and a Morley were among the signers of the Puritan petition presented to King James in 1604 by the Sussex gentry, and it seems only natural that another Morley should play a notable part in

[1] After escaping from prison in England, John Pelham made his way to the University of Padua, where he joined William Morley. While at Padua, they must have known Sir Francis Walsingham, whom Morley and Pelham each in turn succeeded as *consiliarius* of the English students. A younger brother, John Morley, is known to have been licensed to bear arms by the Signory of Venice in 1555 and may also have been with his brother and cousin at Padua. In 1557 John Pelham and William Morley decided to go to Geneva, where they were received into John Knox's congregation on 26 Nov. (Christina Garrett, *The Marian Exiles* (Cambridge: 1938), pp. 23, 247–8).

[2] P.C.C., 9 Streat.

[3] Garrett, *op. cit.*, pp. 247–8, 23.

the Civil War both as an M.P. and a colonel in the parliamentary army and that Pelhams should be connected with both the execution of Charles I and the founding of Massachusetts.

Details concerning the early spread of Protestantism among the Sussex gentry are all too few, but the Bowyers of Leythorne and Northmundham are a well-documented exception. Thomas Bowyer I (d. 1558) was of gentle birth, his family having been established in Sussex since the fifteenth century. He had been apprenticed as a boy to a grocer and by 1534 had risen to the wardenship of the Grocers' Company, but had no desire to remain a London merchant. In 1540 he bought the manors and rectories of Northmundham and Runcton, formerly belonging to Bruton Priory, Somerset, from Henry VIII for the price of £660. Appropriately enough, when he died in September 1558 his tomb was covered with a marble slab which had formerly served as an altar. Re-entry into the Sussex gentry did not mean that the Bowyers had turned their backs on London life; Thomas II (d. 1594) was admitted to the Middle Temple after coming down from Oxford. In London he came under the strong influence of Alexander Nowell, later to become the Calvinist dean of St Paul's, whom Elizabeth once felt compelled to rebuke publicly for departing from the text of his sermon. Following the death of Bowyer's father, Nowell married his mother, thus becoming his stepfather. The efforts of Thomas Bowyer II to give warning to Protestant friends against whom Mary's government had issued writs soon necessitated his own flight from the country. At Frankfurt Thomas ran into Bartholomew Traheron, sometime friar and deprived dean of Chichester, whose daughter Maudelyn he married. Upon his return to England he resided mostly in London and became a prominent lawyer. In the 1572 Parliament he was an M.P. for Midhurst. Whether because of his legal career or for other reasons he was a very old man before his name appeared on the commission of the peace. He was active in the commission of the peace in the last year of his life, but his position in Sussex does not seem to have been commensurate with his legal prominence.[1]

[1] J. H. Cooper, "Cuckfield Families". *S.A.C.*, XLII, 19–53; WSCRO, Q/R, W1/1; Mousley, "Sussex Country Gentry in the Reign of Elizabeth", pp. 391–2.

Neither the exclusion of the Catholic gentry from the local government of Sussex nor the ascendancy of their Protestant counterparts was accomplished overnight. Both the individual cases that have been considered and the survey of the J.P.s made in 1564[1] tend to support this argument. Some further calculations based upon Tables V and VI will help to illustrate the difficulty that the government had in finding reliable magistrates. In the 1560s it was only in the rape of Pevensey that known Protestants constituted a majority of that portion of the gentry considered eligible for local office holding. In this particular case eight families can be classified as Protestant; five were definitely Catholic. If those of the same class, whose religions are not known, were to be considered in these calculations, then the possibility exists that religious conservatism still predominated even in this rape.

In every other rape during the 1560s the number of known Catholic gentry is greater than the number of known Protestant gentry.[2] Looking at these statistics for the period *circa* 1580 and for the 1590s we can observe a generally slow diminution in the numbers of known Catholic gentry and a slow rise in the number of known Protestant gentry. Inclusion of the families whose religious views are unknown and their classification as Protestant would show a more rapid diffusion of Protestant attitudes, especially in the rapes of Chichester, Arundel and Hastings.

The relative strength of Protestant gentry in the rape of Pevensey is clearly an Edwardian survival. In this rape were concentrated a number of the most important Protestant gentry; the Sackvilles of Buckhurst, the Morleys, the Pelhams of Laughton and the Spelmans.

Both the numerical increase in the known Protestant gentry in the rape of Lewes and the decline of the known Catholic gentry are striking and unique. The proportion of Protestant to

---

[1] See Section i of this chapter.

[2] In each of the rapes of Arundel and Bramber there were four Catholic families and two Protestant families among those of the gentry considered eligible for local office. In the rape of Lewes the comparable figures were five to two; the rape of Hastings five to one; and in the rape of Chichester seven to two if the two Catholic peers are excluded.

Catholic gentry changes from two to five to five to one in the period from the late 1560s to *circa* 1580. By the 1590s no families of Catholic gentry of the office-holding class remain in this rape. The rape of Lewes seems to be the one area of Sussex where the numerical increase in the Protestant gentry and the numerical decline of the Catholic gentry can be explained by changes of religious attitudes within the same family. The Bellinghams of Hangleton made the transition to Protestantism in the first generation.[1] The conversion of the Coverts from Catholicism to Puritanism in two generations has already been described. Henry Bowyer of Cuckfield was an upstart iron master who certainly underwent a change of heart about Puritanism.[2] The Shelleys of Patcham, a younger branch of a staunchly Catholic family, are also known to have changed to Protestantism sometime between the 1560s and *c.* 1580. Three of these families are known to have become Puritan by the beginning of James I's reign.[3]

The remarkable success of the Protestant movement in east Sussex would appear to be attributable to several factors. Little pockets of vigorous Protestantism had survived since Edwardian times, especially among the country gentry in the rape of Pevensey and among the burgesses of several east Sussex towns, especially Rye and Lewes.[4] Encouragement and spiritual succour for the Protestant movement came from the institution of Puritan lectureships, such as the one at Rye which was held by Richard Fletcher, and from Bishop Curteys's warm support for the "exercises" which were a regular feature in every deanery in the 1570s and which re-appeared as presbyterian classes in the 1580s.[5] The patronage of Bishop Curteys and later of such laymen as Edward Lewkenor brought eager young ministers,

[1] See my "Catholics and Local Office Holding in Elizabethan Sussex", *Bulletin of the Institute of Historical Research*, XXXV (May 1962), 47–61.

[2] See Chapter 6.

[3] "Extracts from the MSS. of Samuel Jeake", ed. T. W. W. Smart and W. P. Cooper, *S.A.C.*, IX, 45-9.

[4] See Chapter 3, Section i. These two towns were also places where English Protestants could hear firsthand accounts of the persecution of Huguenots in France from the refugees who passed through or settled in these towns.

[5] See Chapter 10.

fresh from Cambridge, into the pulpits of village churches where they imparted to the movement a zeal for reform. But what seems fairly clear is that the spread of Protestantism among the gentry in Sussex was most evident in those areas which were later the scenes of well-organized presbyterian classes. The body of laws that constituted the Elizabethan religious settlement compelled men to go to church, but it took something with more spiritual animation to turn Elizabethans into fervent Protestants. If east Sussex is at all typical of Elizabethan England it would certainly appear that Puritanism was the spiritual force—indeed, the only vigorous force—that animated the popular reformation.

TABLE VI

Religious Classification of Sussex Families of the Office-Holding Class during the Elizabethan Period

Family name and residence	1560s	c. 1580	1590s
1. Agmondesham of Petworth	?	?	?
2. Apsley of Thackham	Pr	Pr	?
3. Apsley of Pulborough	C	R	R
4. Ashburnham of Ashburnham	(C)	R	R
5. Ashburnham of Guestling	Pr	?	?
6. Barentyne of Horsted Keynes	C	?	?
7. Barkeley of Bolney	?	?	?
8. Bartellot of Stopham	Pr	Pr	?
9. Bellingham of Hangleton	C	Pr	?
10. Bishop of Henfield and later Parham	(C)	S	?
11. Blount of Dedisham	?	?	?
12. Bowyer of North Mundham	ME	Pr	Pr
13. Bowyer of Cuckfield	?	Pr	P
14. Browne, viscounts Montague, at Cowdray and Battle	C	R	R
15. Caryll of Warnham	C	R	R
16. Caryll of Shipley, near West Grinstead and later of Harting	(C)	R	R/CE
17. Casie of Roughton	?	?	?
18. Churcher of —	?	?	?
19. Colbrand of Warminghurst and later Chichester	?	?	P
20. Covert of Slaugham	C	Pr	P
21. Cowper of Harting	?	?	?
22. Culpepper of Wigshill	?	?	Pr
23. Culpepper of Wakehurst	C	S	?

24. Darell of Scotney Castle	C	R	R
25. Dawtrey of More House, near Petworth	C	R	?
26. Drew of Funtingdon	?	?	?
27. Ernley of Ernley	(C)	S	?
28. Eversfield of Worth and later Horsham	?	?	?
29. Fenner of Crawley	Pr	Pr	?
30. Fitzalan, earl of Arundel at Arundel Castle	C	C	_1
31. Ford of Harting	C	?	?
32. Fortescue of Harting	C	R	R
33. Gage of Firle	C	R/CE	R
34. Gage of Bentley, in Framfield	C	R	R
35. Garton of Woolavington	?	?	?
36. Goring of Burton	Pr	Pr	?
37. Goring of Ovingdean	Pr	Pr	Pr
38. Gunter of Racton	C	R	R
39. Howard, earl of Arundel at Arundel Castle	–	–	R
40. Hussey of Cuckfield	Pr	Pr	Pr
41. Jefferay of Chiddingly	Pr	Pr	Pr
42. Leech of Fletching	?	?	?
43. Levett of Hollington	?	?	?
44. Lewkenor of Selsey	C	CC/S	S
45. Lewkenor of Trotton	C	S	?
46. Lewkenor of West Dean	?	?	Pr
47. Lumley, baron Lumley at Stanstead	C	C	R
48. Lumsford of East Hoathly	Pr	Pr	Pr
49. Marvyn of Durford	Pr	Pr	?
50. May of Burwash	?	Pr	?
51. May of Ticehurst	?	?	?
52. Michell of Cuckfield	?	P	?
53. Morley of Glyn	ME	Pr	Pr
54. Nevell of Chichester	?	?	?
55. Onley of Pulborough	?	?	?
56. Palmer of Angmering	?	Pr	Pr
57. Palmer of Parham	C/CE	CC	?
58. Parker of Ratton	C	Pr/S	Pr
59. Pelham of Buckstepe	C	?	?
60. Pelham of Laughton	ME	Pr	P
61. Pelham of Michelham Priory and Winchelsea	?	S	S
62. Percy, earls of Northumberland at Petworth	–	C	Pr
63. Pole of Ditching	C	?	?
64. Pole of Racton	C	R	R/CE
65. Porter of Cuckfield	?	?	?
66. Roberts of Ticehurst	C	?	?
67. Sackville, baron Buckhurst at Witham	Pr	Pr	Pr/S
68. Sackville of Chiddingly	?	?	?
69. Sackville of Seddlescombe	?	?	?
70. Scott of Iden	C	R	R

71. Selwyn of Friston	Pr	Pr	Pr
72. Sharpe of Northiam	?	?	?
73. Shelley of Michelgrove	C	R	R/CE
74. Shelley of Patcham	C	Pr	Pr
75. Sheppard of Peasmarsh	?	?	?
76. Shirley of West Grinstead	?	?	?
77. Shirley of Wiston	Pr	Pr	Pr
78. Shurley of Isfield	?	?	Pr
79. Shurley of Lewes	?	?	Pr
80. Spelman of Hartfield	Pr	Pr	?
81. Stanley of Fittleworth	?	?	?
82. Stannye of Wittering and Eston	?	Pr	?
83. Stapley of Framfield	Pr	Pr	?
84. Stoughton of Stanstead Lodge and later West Stoke	C	?	?
85. Thatcher of Priest Hawes, in Westham	C	R	R
86. Threele of Bexhill	?	?	?
87. West, barons de la Warr at Offington, near Broadwater	—[2]	Pr[3]	P
88. Wyldgoose of Salehurst	?	?	S

[1] The Fitzalans became extinct in 1580.

[2] I have not classified William, 1st/11th baron de la Warr because the only contemporary opinion concerning his religion was that he had none.

[3] The 1st/11th Lord de la Warr's son, Sir Thomas West, an accepted leader of the Protestant faction in Sussex.

Abbreviations for Table VI

C   Heads of families described as Catholics by contemporary sources although not known to have been indicted or convicted for recusancy.

Pr   Heads of families referred to explicitly or implicitly as being Protestant by contemporary sources.

R   Families in which the head of the household was either presented by the churchwardens, or indicted and convicted of recusancy, or accused of recusancy by a magistrate or a bishop. Temporary conformity is ignored if followed by a relapse into recusancy.

P   Families explicitly or implicitly referred to as Puritans by contemporary sources.

CC   Instances where I have classified the head of the family, being the holder of an important local office, as a crypto-Catholic. All such cases are discussed either in Chapters 4 and 11. i, or in my article in the *Bulletin of the Institute of Historical Research*, XXXV (May 1962), 47–61.

ME   Instances where the head of the household or a son is known to have been a Protestant exile during the reign of Mary I.

CE   Instances in which a son or daughter by blood or marriage is known to have been a Catholic exile during the reign of Elizabeth I.

S   Families which harboured and protected recusants, or instances where the head of the family either had a recusant wife or was considered sympathetic towards Catholics.

(C) In three cases I have decided to classify families as Catholic during the 1560s even though direct evidence is lacking, because they later manifested pronounced patterns of recusancy.

?   Cases where there is no evidence or insufficient evidence concerning the religious views of a family. In most cases where the head of the family is magistrate after 1570 or so, it may be presumed that the family is conforming to the established church.

Sources for Table VI

PRO. Chancery 202/Box 144 (I owe this reference to Professor S. T. Bindoff).

S.P., Dom., Eliz., 60/18; 74/44; 117/15, printed C.R.S., *Misc. XII*, pp. 80–1; 165/22; 183/38; 184/45; 248/116.

Chichester DRO. Ep. I/15; I/37; I/17/4, 10; I/23/1, 6, 7; Ep. II/9/2; II/24/1.

British Museum. Add MSS. 11,402; 33,410; 39,454.

Harley MSS. 360; 703 (Letter Book of Sir Walter Covert); 5702; 7042.

Landsowne MSS. 50, fos. 39–40v., 53, no. 80 and 55, no. 58, printed in *S.A.C.* II, 58–62; 82, fos. 103–103v.

Hatfield MSS. 138, fos. 237–52; 238.

Lambeth Palace Library, MS. Carta Misc. IV.

"A Collection of Original Letters from the Bishops to the Privy Council", ed. Mary Bateson, *Camden Society Miscellany*, IX.

C.R.S. *Miscellanea XII*, passim.

Recusant Roll, no. 1, 1592–93, vol. XVIII.

"Extracts from the MSS, of Samuel Jeake", ed. T. W. W. Smart and W. D. Cooper, *S.A.C.*, IX, 45–9.

Christina Garrett, *The Marian Exiles* (Cambridge: 1938).

Mousley, "Sussex Country Gentry in the Reign of Elizabeth" (London Ph.D. thesis, 1955).

13

CONCLUSION

WHETHER ONE LOOKS at it from the national level or from the local level, compromises and opportunism pervaded every aspect of the Elizabethan religious settlement. The guiding principle of the Elizabethan religious settlement was the determination to preserve the unity of England against the threat of foreign invasion and against the corrosive effect of transcendental ideologies. From the queen's point of view this necessitated a comprehensive national church. When the queen submitted her proposal to Parliament, a vocal Puritan minority forced a more radical religious settlement upon the government.

Particular local circumstances modified the religious settlement even further. When the Elizabethan government took up the task of enforcing the Acts of Supremacy and Uniformity in Sussex, it gave priority to social stability among the local governors rather than to religious conformity. Maintaining a realistic and flexible approach to the problem of entrenched social and religious conservatism, the government effected a gradual and orderly transfer of social power from the old Catholic nobility and their followers to the new Protestant aristocracy that was spread over a quarter of a century. This policy of opportunism brought success in so far as the unity of England was maintained. But it also weakened royal control of the church and failed to secure religious uniformity.

Although Elizabeth consistently maintained that her power to make ecclesiastical policy was vested in her royal person, the fact remains that her supremacy was essentially Parliamentary.[1] From both the legal and the constitutional point of view this was the prelude to lay control of the Church of England. The power of executing the laws constituting the religious settlement theoretically still belonged to the queen, to be enforced through her agents. However, the decline in the influence of

[1] Elton, *The Tudor Constitution*, p. 335 f.

the bishops and the clergy, the decay of church courts, and the increasing participation of the gentry in local government—especially in the execution of recusancy statutes—hastened the actual lay domination of the church. The attempt by Archbishops Bancroft and Laud to revive episcopal power temporarily reversed the process, but the direction in which events were moving was already clear in Elizabethan Sussex. Ultimately, the gentry would not only determine national religious policy through Parliament, they would indirectly control the Church on the local level through the powers of patronage and local government which they possessed.

Because of its relative geographical isolation and conservative social structure, the county of Sussex in the Elizabethan period bore a closer resemblance to some of the more distant counties of the North and West of England than to what we think of as a typical southern county. The decline of the Cinque Ports, the numerous quasi-feudal nobility with their ties to the northern magnates, and the tendency of those economic activities in the hands of the landed aristocracy to prosper rather than those connected with the urban middle class emphasized these conservative aspects of Sussex society.

The conservative social structure of Sussex greatly complicated the problem of enforcing religious uniformity during the earlier part of Elizabeth's reign. This was particularly true of the rather numerous families of the nobility. Their households remained privileged and constituted little islands of Catholic worship. Their presence emboldened Catholic members of the gentry to resist Bishops Barlow and Curteys in the latters' attempts to destroy Catholicism and especially to purge the commission of the peace. The social stature of the Catholic peers of Sussex remained formidable, even though their political power became increasingly illusory. No bishop of Chichester ever dared risk a direct encounter with one of them, and indeed these prelates, whose humble origins are often shrouded with mystery, were not even equal to the task of imposing conformity upon the gentry. As a consequence the interference of the Privy Council in the ecclesiastical affairs of the diocese of Chichester became more and more frequent as the reign of Elizabeth progressed and by the end of Richard

Curteys's episcopate in 1582, the bishops of Chichester were reduced to mere functionaries.

For these reasons it took Elizabeth's government a quarter of a century to reconstitute a local magistracy in Sussex that could be counted upon to execute the laws against Catholics. During this period of time three distinct stages in the transfer of social power are discernible. A combination of factors frustrated Bishop Barlow's efforts at religious reform. The Arundel-Lumley faction held the commission of lieutenancy. The Catholic gentry dominated the commission of the peace. There was a lack of educated Protestant clergymen. Episcopal administration was in chaos. The second stage in this transference of social power coincides with the young and vigorous Richard Curteys's tenure of the bishopric of Chichester. During this period the influx of learned and enthusiastic Protestant missionaries into Sussex did much to fill the spiritual vacuum that in some parishes dated back a generation and more. Together, Curteys and his followers among the clergy were able to lead a party of reform that, for the first time, united the official and the popular reformations into one movement. That movement received a very severe setback because Curteys had proceeded too vigorously against a small but influential group of crypto-Catholic magistrates, who apparently enjoyed the protection of Lords Buckhurst and Montague, the joint lords lieutenant in the 1570s. Curteys's excessive zeal in religious matters threatened to upset that precarious balance of social and political power which had been worked out during this second stage of transition when the lieutenancy of Sussex was shared by a politique Protestant and a moderate Catholic. The last stage in the transfer of social power was reached by the middle of the 1580s when both the commission of lieutenancy and the commission of the peace had been completely purged of Catholics and the power of lay magistrates in ecclesiastical affairs was increased at the expense of the bishops of Chichester.

If the assertion that a desire to preserve the social order guided the enforcement of the religious settlement in Elizabethan Sussex is accepted, it should not seem surprising that, except for a brief period during the episcopate of Richard Curteys, the official doctrine of the Anglican church had remarkably little influence upon popular religious attitudes. Although pockets of Protestantism had existed in Sussex since the days of Henry VIII and Edward VI, their existence appears to be attributable to London and continental influences rather than to any attempt by the government to impose an official brand of Protestantism. Certainly, what we know about the spread of Protestantism among the Sussex gentry tends to confirm this. Other recent research lends additional support to the view that the Henrician and Edwardian churches had failed to come anywhere near achieving religious uniformity. Professor A. G. Dickens has discovered that the Lollards and Protestants in the early Tudor diocese of York were "oddly oblivious to royal and episcopal propaganda, Protestant, Catholic, and Erastian".[1] At least half of the people of Sussex—gentry and commonalty alike—were still Catholic when Elizabeth ascended the throne in 1558. The mingling of attitudes and practices which shaped the English Protestant tradition took place largely during the reign of Elizabeth[2] and was, more than any other factor, the work of a Puritan minority working within the Church.

During the 1570s—the episcopate of Richard Curteys—the official Reformation coincided with the popular Reformation. But the suspension of Curteys and the failure of episcopal leadership brought about a crisis of leadership that led to a divergence of those two movements. The leadership of the popular Reformation fell to the Puritan minority and manifested itself in the Puritan classical movement of the 1580s, while the enforcement of the laws, which sought to impose religious uniformity upon the laity, was placed largely in the hands of a select few of the gentry, who were also mostly Puritans. Only the regulation of the clergy remained in the hands of the bishops and the church courts and their power was much diminished. This was the situation that prevailed in Sussex until Archbishop Bancroft's reconstruction of the Anglican Church began to make itself felt in 1605 with the deprivation of the ten Puritan ministers and the appointment of Lancelot Andrewes to the see of Chichester.

[1] *Lollards and Protestants in the Diocese of York, 1509–1558* (London: 1959), pp. 250–1. [2] *Ibid.*, p. 251.

The basic reason for Richard Curtey's downfall and the subsequent divergence of the official and the popular Reformations is that Curteys's concept of reform represented a threat to social stability. Like the Laudians who came after him, Curteys realized that a religious reformation, if it were to be meaningful, must be accompanied by a clean sweep of the corruption in church and society alike. This involved a broad attack not only upon lingering traces of Catholicism but also upon those who used their offices in the cathedral close or the temporal magistracy for purposes of private gain. But such a concept of reform produced convulsions that threatened to disturb the social stability that both the local governors and the queen's government believed essential to national unity in the face of threats of foreign invasion. Curteys's tactlessness and disregard of vested interests aside, a concept of reform so thorough-going as this could not be allowed to prevail when the kingdom was threatened by foreign invasion.

Curteys's concept of reform was defeated because it was too narrowly conceived; it rested upon the leadership of a predominantly clerical party and failed to secure the support of the local governors. The success of such a concept of reform would have necessitated the strengthening of the church courts and clerical power at a time when Parliament increasingly was placing the enforcement of religious uniformity in the hands of the temporal magistrates.

One cannot say that the reform movement which Curteys had led in the 1570s completely failed, although it was modified so as not to be offensive to the property-owning classes. It was only his all-encompassing concept of reform that went down to defeat, while the reform movement itself passed from episcopal leadership into the hands of the presbyterian classes of the 1580s. The Puritan classes continued to press for reformation of clerical abuses such as ignorance and non-residence, while the specially-selected commissioners for recusant affairs implemented a more stringent persecution of Catholics. But social reform was forgotten and vested interests were safe.

The tendency to transfer recusant affairs from the jurisdiction of the bishops and the episcopal courts to commissioners specially chosen from among the gentry is but one symptom of the weakening of the royal supremacy over the church by the growth of lay power in ecclesiastical affairs. The queen's preference for indirect rule in religious matters increasingly led to the actual exercise of the powers of the royal supremacy by the Privy Council and the Court of High Commission to the detriment of the ordinary authority of the bishops. The resulting confusion of jurisdictions, the many conflicts between the Privy Council and prelates such as Curteys and Whitgift, and the aggressiveness of Parliament in introducing religious legislation further weakened royal control over the church.

The increasingly prominent role that the Privy Council and the Court of High Commission played in enforcing the religious settlement is itself evidence of the weakening of episcopal authority. Until the end of the 1580s the membership of the Privy Council was made up to a considerable degree of men of Puritan sympathies who were contemptuous of prelates and did not hesitate to interfere in episcopal affairs. Moreover, it was common knowledge in Sussex that a country gentleman of any standing could appeal to the Council over the head of his ordinary and win a sympathetic hearing. At the same time the bishops themselves, by the frequent use of their authority as ecclesiastical commissioners, made tacit admission that a bishop's ordinary authority commanded little respect. John Whitgift, who was a very judicious prelate, stands out as the sole exception to the decline in influence among Elizabethan bishops;[1] not only was he respected by the gentry as bishop of Worcester, even the Privy Council reposed a degree of confidence in his abilities—something that body rarely conceded to bishops. Yet bishops such as Richard Curteys or John Whitgift were trustworthy and enthusiastic agents of the royal will in both secular and religious matters. Their power derived from royal authority and not local influence or divine-right concepts of episcopal authority, and as such they were the nearest thing that the Tudors had to the French *Intendants*. By their treatment of the Elizabethan bishops, the Privy Council not only weakened the royal supremacy, they added to the power of the gentry and insured that they, and not the bishops, would increasingly set the tone of religious life. By the time that the Bancroftian and,

[1] V. J. K. Brook, *Whitgift and the English Church* (London: 1957), p. 53 ff.

later, the Laudian revivals of episcopal power began, too much water had passed under the bridge to allow the Stuarts and their bishops to reverse the trend. Lay influence in the Church of England had become a permanent feature of English religious life.

No sooner had it become clear that the bishops and their episcopal courts were unequal to the task of enforcing conformity upon Catholic recusants, than the spread of Puritanism placed a further burden upon them. Recusancy was a public act of which a majority of the local governors disapproved, but Puritanism did not necessarily involve a public act and it was an attitude that commanded widespread sympathy. When it became obvious that the episcopal courts could not deal with this problem, there was no other recourse but to the High Commission. This not only further weakened the authority of the bishops of Chichester, it failed to remove any of the clerical Puritan offenders from their benefices.

If the bishops could not root out Puritanism among the clergy, there was no hope of stopping its spread among the laity. The growth of clerical Puritanism, which remained unchecked during the early part of Elizabeth's reign (and throughout the whole period in the diocese of Chichester) can be partly attributed to the first generation of Elizabethan bishops such as Richard Curteys, who admitted many Puritans to the ministry and encouraged the exercise conferences with their prophesyings. Yet while there was latitude in doctrinal matters (since many of these prelates were themselves Calvinists), matters pertaining to discipline or liturgy were viewed more narrowly. This inconsistency in episcopal administration became more pronounced under the primacy of Whitgift. Because ecclesiastical canons and injunctions became increasingly impractical to administer, an even wider divergence appeared in policy from one diocese to another, eventually giving rise to what Ronald Marchant has called "episcopal anarchy".[1]

Another factor that tended to weaken the influence of the bishops of Chichester was the growing amount of ecclesiastical patronage that laymen—especially courtiers and privy coun-

[1] *The Puritans and the Church Courts in the Diocese of York, 1560–1642* (London: 1960), pp. 205–6.

cillors—dispensed. Insufficient control over the disposition of cathedral canonries had delayed the reforming efforts of Bishop Curteys, and the stubborn resistance of the canons residentiary was certainly one of the reasons for the inactivity of Bishops Bickley and Watson. Only a few of the Elizabethan canons of Chichester Cathedral owed their livings to the bishops. Most looked to some great courtier such as the earl of Leicester or the earl of Sussex for patronage. Even a canon residentiary such as William Overton, who was confident that he would get a see of his own some day, could undermine the bishop's influence and build up a following of his own by promise of future preferment.

Much the same can be said for the Bishop's relations with the parochial clergy. A great many lesser advowsons had come into the hands of the gentry with the distribution of monastic spoils, and the Elizabethan and Jacobean periods saw a continued increase of lay patronage. Moreover, the common-law courts made it a practice to favour the patronage rights of the gentry in any dispute that arose with the ecclesiastical authorities. Just as contempt for the sentence of excommunication had weakened the influence of the ecclesiastical authorities over the laity, so also the growing proportion of ecclesiastical patronage in lay hands lessened the control of the bishops over the clergy. But what the clergy may have gained in independence from the bishops they lost in further dependence upon the squirearchy.

Sussex was not a county of extremes. It is true that Puritanism had become a potent force among the Sussex gentry by the end of the sixteenth century. But my analysis of Bishop Curteys's attempts to clear Catholics out of the commission of the peace and to clean up the west Sussex grain trade argues that during earlier part of the Elizabethan period the predominant group among the gentry were more interested in protecting their political and economic interests than in carrying through a religious revolution. If, as Dr Lucy Sutherland suggested in the Raleigh Lecture to the British Academy for 1962, R. H. Tawney and Sir Lewis Namier accomplished the medievalization of modern history through their emphasis upon "patronage as an expedient of government and a means of social climbing",[1]

[1] Quoted in *History Today*, XIII (December 1963), 809.

then they have only restored to the study of history a more balanced view of human nature itself. The flexible pragmatism of Sussex magnates such as Lord Buckhurst or Sir Thomas Palmer or Sir Edward Caryll towards the inter-relationship between religion and politics argues the emergence of a practical tolerance comparable to that more usually associated with the French "politiques". Professor W. T. MacCaffrey also has noted the existence of this same attitude of practical tolerance among the merchants of Exeter: the Marian reaction brought little active persecution in Exeter, and the restrictions on office-holding are known to have been evaded under both Mary and Elizabeth. While religious issues were a cause for disagreement among the citizens of Exeter, it was felt that these issues should be resolved on a personal basis and should not be allowed to "impair the working unity of the community in other matters"—a conviction based upon the firm determination to protect their material interests.[1]

There can be no doubt that the government's desire to maintain social stability found wide support among the local governors of Sussex towns as well as the gentry of Sussex. In Chichester, James Colbrand, a firebrand with Puritan associations and a following among the commonalty, failed in his attempt to challenge the oligarchy that controlled the municipal corporation;[2] while at Rye, although the jurats actively supported religious reform, they were careful to keep the artificers in their place.[3] Whether squire or prosperous merchant, one senses that the local governors were motivated more by an obsessive fear of popular tumults than by any affinity for particular brands of Protestantism. Thus they were disposed to acquiesce in the religious policy of a regime that could maintain order and protect property, but they were at the same time very sensitive about any manifestation of absolutism that threatened to disturb their preponderance in local affairs, their patronage or economic interests.

The enforcement of the Elizabethan religious settlement

---

[1] *Exeter, 1540–1640: The Growth of an English Country Town* (Cambridge, Mass.: 1958), pp. 189–90, 202.

[2] Neale, *The Elizabethan House of Commons*, pp. 263–72.

[3] Hist. MSS. Comm., [Rye MSS.] xiii (4), 98–100.

followed the middle road (although this was not a straight road), because the primary aim of Elizabeth's government was the preservation of national unity at all costs. As a result, the queen's ecclesiastical policy lacked consistency, but it was a policy that came to enjoy wider and wider support from among the governing classes of town and county society, who, although they had religious differences, shared the queen's earnest desire to preserve political and social stability and to prevent England from becoming an arena for internecine religious war. It remained for the Stuarts and their bishops to undo the policy of a comprehensive national church as a basis of national unity and to permit the contagion of civil war to spread into England.

BIBLIOGRAPHICAL ESSAY

PRIMARY SOURCES

THE MSS. USED AS SOURCES for this study are largely of an official nature. These fall into four main categories: (1) those pertaining to the central temporal administration, (2) those dealing with the metropolitical administration of the archbishop of Canterbury, (3) the records of county government, and, (4) diocesan records. In the first category the most important administrative body was the Privy Council which not only exercised oversight over county government but also was the main link between the diocesan ordinaries and the queen. Since the queen rarely issued orders directly, the Privy Council became the most important instrument in the exercise of the royal supremacy. By far the most important MS. source in this category is the State Papers, Domestic Series for the Reign of Elizabeth, housed in the Public Record Office. The State Papers for the Elizabethan period are summarized in the Printed Calendars published by the P.R.O. The summaries are brief in the earlier volumes, but rather more full in the latter volumes. The Hatfield MSS. of Lord Burghley and his son Sir Robert Cecil are available on microfilm in the British Museum and the Folger Library. The Acts of the Privy Council have been printed in full. The records of the Court of Star Chamber in the P.R.O. can be a very rewarding source of information, but their accessibility is limited by the lack of an adequate catalogue—the MS. index in the P.R.O. lists only the names of litigants and not the subject matter. The records of the Court of High Commission, another extremely important instrument in the enforcement of the religious settlement, have perished except where they have survived by accident in other collections or series of documents such as the State Papers or among episcopal records.

Metropolitical authority came into direct play only when the diocese of Chichester was *sede vacante*. Reports of metropolitical visitations are to be found in Lambeth Palace Library and among the State Papers. However, the archbishop corresponded frequently with his suffragans, and most of the letters of this kind that have survived have been printed in the volumes of the Parker Society or in the works of John Strype. The wills of those who owned property in more than one diocese were proved in the archbishop's prerogative court and are now deposited in Somerset House. They shed much light upon the property and connections of both the gentry and the clergy, and sometimes give a clue as to their religious views. Excerpts from the wills of those who owned property only in the diocese of Chichester have been printed in the volumes edited by R. G. Rice for the Sussex Record Society.

The records of county government in Sussex are lamentably sparse for the Tudor period. Nothing significant concerning the execution of the recusancy statutes was found among the few remaining quarter-sessions rolls, and there are no great family collections among the gentry seated in Sussex dating from this period. The Gage MSS. in the possession of the Sussex Archaeological Trust in Lewes, for example, begin to bear abundant fruit only in the seventeenth century. However, the Loseley MSS. are helpful (See the Hist. MSS. Comm. Calendar; St G. K. Hyland, *op. cit.*; and Kempe's selection of the Loseley MSS., *op. cit.* Some of the Losley MSS. are now in the Folger Library.) and Sir Walter Covert's letter-book (B.M., Harley MS. 703) is particularly valuable. The County Councils of West and East Sussex have published *A Descriptive Report on the Quarter Sessions, Other Official and Ecclesiastical Records* (Chichester: 1954).

The records of the diocese of Chichester are more fully described in chapter 2. They are very useful for observing the ecclesiastical machinery from the churchwardens' presentments through the archidiaconal courts, but they leave a lot of questions unanswered concerning the problems of episcopal administration. Here the most useful sources have been the State Papers and W. D. Peckham's excellent edition of the Capitular Act Book 1545–1642, published by the Sussex Record Society, which has thrown much light upon the strained relations between the bishops of Chichester on the one hand and the dean and chapter and the Sussex gentry on the other.

The bulk of the unofficial manuscript sources were found in

the various collections of the British Museum. These collections, such as the Lansdowne and Harley MSS., were originally in private hands. Since they have no organic unity, it is impossible to give a brief account of their contents, and the reader is referred to the printed catalogues published by the British Museum.

Contemporary biographies are rare in the late sixteenth century, and it is therefore unusual that we possess three such accounts: *The Lives of Philip Howard, Earl of Arundel, and of Anne Dacres, His Wife*, ed. 14th Duke of Norfolk (London: 1857), written by an anonymous Jesuit, probably between 1630 and 1642, and Bishop Richard Smith's *Life of the Lady Magdalen, Viscountess Montague*, ed. A. C. Southern (London: 1954), written somewhat earlier. Useful material on the recusant gentry will be found in the volumes of the Catholic Record Society and in Henry Foley's *Records of the English Province, S.J.* (London: 1876). The most important single source of information concerning Puritan activities in Sussex was *The Seconde Parte of a Register*, ed. Albert Peel (2 vols., Cambridge: 1915).

SECONDARY SOURCES

The only scholarly monograph dealing with the history of Sussex is Charles Thomas-Stanford's *Sussex in the Great Civil War and the Interregnum, 1642–1660* (London: 1910), which provides a great fund of information on the county during the middle of the seventeenth century, but which emphasizes the military activity of the opposing armies to the neglect of social history. The most complete survey of Sussex history is, of course, the *Victoria County History of Sussex*, which has reached seven volumes. Volume II contains an uncritical, chronological history of religious events in Sussex from ancient to modern times by L. F. Salzman. Still useful is James Dallaway's *A History of the Western Division of the County of Sussex. Including the Rapes of Chichester, Arundel, and Bramber, with the City and Diocese of Chichester* (2 vols., London: 1815). This work is highly disorganized and contains many mistakes, but is none the less valuable because of the many documents it prints.

W. R. W. Stephens in his *Memorials of the South Saxon See and the Cathedral Church of Chichester* (London: 1876) and *The South Saxon Diocese—Selsey-Chichester* (London: 1881) was the first historian to use the Chapter Act Book and the Episcopal Register, although he used few other sources and was apparently unaware of the Churchwardens' Presentments or the Detection Books.

Professional historians are too often wont to look down their noses at local historians and antiquarians, but studies such as this present one would not have been feasible but for the patient gathering of factual information and the printing of documents that have been undertaken over the last century and a half. For over a hundred years Sussex has had one of the most active historical and archaeological societies in England, and in recent years the volumes of the *Sussex Archaeological Collections* along with *Sussex Notes and Queries* have contained many articles of a very high calibre by both amateur and professional historians. W. D. Peckham's many articles on the archaeology and ecclesiastical history of Sussex are very well done and cover the medieval and modern periods. Most of the articles for the Tudor and Stuart periods deal with the economic and social history of the county: especially notable are the articles by Julian Cornwall and G. E. Fussell on Sussex agriculture. The conclusions of Joyce E. Mousley's London Ph. D. thesis on the Sussex gentry appear in her "The Fortunes of Some Gentry Families of Elizabethan Sussex", *Economic History Review*, 2nd ser., XI, 477.

John Comber's *Sussex Genealogies* (4 vols., Cambridge: 1931), which is the most complete and accurate authority on the relationships among the Sussex gentry, proved to be very helpful in compiling information on the gentry. It contains references to wills, chancery cases, and inquisitions post mortem. In addition there are numerous family histories and articles on this subject in the *S.A.C.*

There have been too few attempts to do local studies of the Reformation in England. A. L. Rowse tells us that he started out to do this in his *Tudor Cornwall* (London: 1941), but he decided that a broader approach would be more interesting. His book is both learned and colourful, but it still begs the question as to how the Reformation was actually carried out. A. G. Dickens's *Lollards and Protestants in the Diocese of York, 1509–1558* (London: 1959) has convincingly revived the argument about the survival of Lollardy and has shown the contribution that members of the gentry made to the spread of the popular Reformation. Ronald Marchant demonstrates how hopelessly inefficacious the York diocesan courts were in maintaining discipline against Puritan clerics in his *The Puritans and the Church Courts in the Diocese of York, 1560–1642* (London: 1960). Dr Marchant also promises us an administrative history of the diocese of York during the same period.

The writing of Elizabethan religious history in the past has been over concerned with the spread of ideas among eminent divines or zealous Puritans. Yet only a minority of Elizabethans fell into those categories. A more fruitful line of investigation into the spread of Protestantism in Tudor England would be to look more closely at the actual exercise of the royal supremacy. R. G. Usher's *The Rise and Fall of the High Commission* (Oxford: 1913), points in this direction, but his study could be profitably revised. J. V. P. Thompson's *Supreme Governor. A Study of Elizabethan Policy and Circumstance* (London: 1940), is a good essay on the administrative conditions and religious problems surrounding the maintenance of the Elizabethan supremacy, but contributes no new research. Henry Gee, *The Elizabethan Clergy and the Settlement of Religion, 1558–1564* (Oxford: (1898), and H. N. Birt, *The Elizabethan Religious Settlement* (London: 1907), both view the problem too narrowly in terms of the deprivation of a few Marian priests. This certainly is not what brought about the firm establishment of Protestantism in Elizabethan England.

BIBLIOGRAPHY

I. UNPUBLISHED MANUSCRIPTS

British Museum
  Additional MSS.
  Egerton MSS.
  Harleian MSS.
  Landsowne MSS.
  Royal MS. 18 D.III, fos. 17–18.
Chichester Diocesan Record Office
  Archdeaconry of Chichester
    Detection Books, DRO, Ep. I/17/3–10.
    Original Wills, STC 2.
    Registers of Churchwardens' Presentments, DRO, Ep.
      I/23/1–7.
    Registers of Wills, STC 1.
  Archdeaconry of Lewes
    Detection Books, DRO, Ep. II/9/2–9.
    Nonconformists' Returns, 1603, DRO, Ep. II/24/1.
    Registers of Orders, DRO, Ep. II/11/1.
  Diocese and Archdeaconry of Chichester
    Miscellaneous Court Proceedings, DRO, Ep. I/15.
    Return of Nonconformists, DRO, Ep. I/37.
    Valors, DRO, Ep. I/44/1–7.
East Sussex County Record Office, Lewes
  Archdeaconry of Lewes
    Registers of Wills, A9, B2.
Folger Library, Washington, D.C.
  Bagot MSS., L.a. 240–1.
  Loseley MSS.
  Miscellaneous MSS., X.d. 317(1).
  Microfilm copy of the MSS. of the Marquess of Salisbury at
    Hatfield House.
Lambeth Palace Library
  MSS. Cartae Miscellaneae, IV, VI, XII, & XIII.
Public Record Office
  Chancery 202/144.

Proceedings of the Court of Star Chamber, Elizabeth, Star
Cha 5/C43/10.
State Papers, Domestic, Elizabeth.
Somerset House, London
Prerogative Court of Canterbury
Registers of Wills.
Westminster Cathedral Archives
Thatcher-Gage MSS.
West Sussex County Record Office, Chichester
Quarter Sessions Rolls, Michaelmas 1594, Q/R, W.1.
Comber Papers, Ac. 542, vol. XVIII.

II. PRINTED CALENDARS OF DOCUMENTS AND DOCUMENTS PUBLISHED OFFICIALLY

The Acts of the Dean and Chapter of the Cathedral Church of Chichester, 1545–1642, ed. W. D. Peckham (Lewes: S.R.S., 1959).
Acts of the Privy Council, volumes VII–XXXII.
The Ashburnham Archives, A Catalogue, ed. F. W. Steer (Lewes: East Sussex County Council, 1958).
Calendar of the Patent Rolls, Elizabeth, volumes I–V.
Calendar of State Papers, Domestic Series of the reigns of Edward VI, Mary I, Elizabeth, volumes I–VII.
A Descriptive Report on the Quarter Sessions, Other Official, and Ecclesiastical Records in the Custody of the County Councils of West and East Sussex (Chichester, 1954).
Historical Manuscripts Commission, *Appendix to the Third Report of the Royal Commission on Historical Manuscripts*.
Historical Manuscripts Commission, *Appendix to the Seventh Report of the Royal Commission on Historical Manuscripts*.
Historical Manuscripts Commission, *Appendix to the Thirteenth Report of the Royal Commission on Historical Manuscripts*.
Historical Manuscripts Commission, *Calendar of the Manuscripts of the Hon. the Marquis of Salisbury, K.G., Preserved at Hatfield House, Hertfordshire*, 15 volumes.
Historical Manuscripts Commission, *Report on the Manuscripts Of Lord Montagu of Beaulieu*.
Lists of Sheriffs for England and Wales, from Earliest Times to A.D.

1831, Compiled from Documents in the Public Record Office.
Volume IX of the P.R.O. *Lists and Indexes* Series.

Sussex Archaeological Trust (Barbican House, Lewes), "Calendar of Sussex Deeds Relating to Midhurst and the Montague Family." A typescript in the Library of the Sussex Archaeological Trust.

Sussex Archaeological Trust, "Calendar of the Sussex Muniments of Viscount Gage in the Custody of the Trust." Typescript, 1931.

Valor Ecclesiasticus, Temp. Henr. VIII Autoritate Regia Institutus, volume I (London, 1810).

III. DOCUMENTS PUBLISHED OTHERWISE THAN OFFICIALLY

Articles Ministered by . . . Anthony, Bishop of Chichester, at the visitation begun there the 6 of September 1600, and to be enquired of quarterly within the seide Diocesse (London: 1600).

The Book of John Rowe, Steward of the Manors of Lord Bergavenny, 1597–1622, ed. W. H. Godfrey (Lewes: S.R.S., 1928).

"'A Booke of Orders and Rules' of Anthony Viscount Montague in 1595", ed. Sir S. D. Scott, *Sussex Archaeological Collections*, VII, 173–212.

The Book of Robert Southwell, Priest, Poet, Prisoner, ed. Christobel Hood (Oxford: 1926).

Catholic Record Society, *Miscellanea*, volume XII (London: 1921).

"A Certificate Concerning the Justices of Peace in Sussex in 1587 . . . from MS. Lansdowne 53, art. 80. Also Documents relating to the Papists and Recusants of Sussex in 1597", ed. Sir Henry Ellis and W. D. Cooper, *Sussex Archaeological Collections*, II, 58–62.

Challoner, Richard, *Memoirs of Missionary Priests*, ed. J. H. Pollen (New York: 1924).

The Chronicle of the English Augustinian Canonesses Regular of the Lateran, at St Monica's in Louvain, 1548–1644, ed. Adam Hamilton, 2 volumes (Edinburgh: 1904).

A Collection of Letters from the Original Manuscripts of Many

Princes, Great Personages and Statesmen, ed. Leonard Howard (London: 1753).

"A Collection of Original Letters from the Bishops to the Privy Council, 1564", ed. Mary Bateson, *Camden Society Miscellany*, IX, 8–11.

A Collection of State Papers Relating to Affairs in the Reigns of King Henry VIII, King Edward VI, Queen Mary and Queen Elizabeth, ed. Samuel Haynes (London: 1760). Transcripts from the Salisbury MSS. at Hatfield.

A Collection of State Papers Relating to Affairs in the Reign of Queen Elizabeth, from the Year 1571 to 1596, ed. William Murdin (London: 1759). Also transcripts from the Salisbury MSS.

Correspondence of Matthew Parker, D. D. Archbishop of Canterbury, ed. John Bruce (Cambridge: Parker Society, 1853).

The Diary of Henry Machyn, ed. J. G. Nichols, Camden Society Publications, XLII (1848).

Documentary Annals of the Reformed Church of England: Being a Collection of Injunctions, Declarations, Orders, Articles of Inquiry, &c., ed. Edward Cardwell, volume II (Oxford: 1844).

Documents Illustrative of English Church History, ed. Henry Gee and W. J. Hardy (London: 1896).

Drayton, Michael, *Polyolbion*, in *Complete Works*, ed. R. Hooper, 2 volumes (London: 1876).

"Ecclesiastical Returns in East Sussex in 1603", *Miscellaneous Records*, volume IV (Lewes: S.R.S., 1905).

Edwards, Edward, *The Life of Sir Walter Raleigh*, volume II: "Letters of Sir Walter Raleigh" (London: 1868).

English Protestants Plea, and Petition for English Priests and Papists, to the Present Court of Parliament, and all persecutors of them ([Douai]: 1621).

"Extracts from the MSS. of Samuel Jeake", ed. T. W. W. Smart and W. D. Cooper, *Sussex Archaeological Collections*, IX, 45–9.

The First and Second Diaries of the English College, Douay, ed. T. F. Knox (London: 1878).

Gage, Thomas, *The English-American . . . A New Survey of the West Indies, 1648*, ed. A. P. Newton (London: 1946).

Godwin, Francis *A Catalogue of the Bishops of England* (London: 1615).

Harrison, William, *A Description of England*, ed. F. J. Furnivall (London: 1877).

Haweis, J. O. W., *Sketches of the Reformation and the Elizabethan Age Taken from the Contemporary Pulpit* (London: 1884).

Holinshed, Raphael, *Chronicles of England, Scotland, and Ireland*, 6 volumes (London: 1808).

Kennedy, W. P. M., *Elizabethan Episcopal Administration: An Essay in Sociology and Politics*, volume III: "Visitation Articles and Injunctions, 1583–1603" (London: 1925).

Letters and Memorials of Fr. Robert Persons, S.J., volume I, ed. Leo Hicks (London: C.R.S., 1942).

The Letters and Memorials of William Cardinal Allen (1532–1594), ed. T. F. Knox (London: 1882).

The Letters of Sir Thomas Copley, ed. R. C. Christie (London: Roxburghe Club, 1897).

"Letters of Thomas Wood, 1566–1577", ed. Patrick Collinson. *Bulletin of the Institute of Historical Research Special Supplement No. 5* (London: 1960).

Letters Written by John Chamberlain during the Reign of Queen Elizabeth, ed. Sarah Williams (London: Camden Society, 1861).

"The Life of the Right Honourable Lady the Lady Anne Countesse of Arundell and Surrey, Foundresse of the English College of the Society of Jesvs in Gant [Ghent]", *The Lives of Philip Howard, Earl of Arundel, and of Anne Dacres, His Wife*, ed. 14th Duke of Norfolk (London: 1857). Written by an anonymous Jesuit.

The Losely Manuscripts, ed. A. J. Kempe (London: 1835).

Mosse, George L., *Calvinism: Authoritarian or Democratic?* (New York: 1961).

Nugae Antiquae: Being a Miscellaneous Collection of Original Papers in Prose and Verse; Written during the Reigns of Henry VIII, Edward VI, Queen Mary, Elizabeth, and King James by Sir John Harrington, Knt. and by others who lived in those times, ed. Henry Harington, 2 volumes (London: J. Wright, 1804).

"Official Lists of Prisoners for Religion, 1562–1580", ed. J. H. Pollen, *Miscellanea I* (London: C.R.S., 1905).

Original Letters Illustrative of English History, ed. Sir Henry Ellis, 3 volumes (London: 1824).

The Presbyterian Movement in the Reign of Queen Elizabeth as Illustrated by the Minute Book of the Dedham Classis, 1582–1589, ed. R. G. Usher, Camden Society Publications, 3rd series, volume VIII.

Puritan Manifestoes: A Study of the Origin of the Puritan Revolt. With a Reprint of the Admonition to Parliament and Kindred Documents, ed. W. H. Ferre and C. E. Douglas (London: 1954).

Renshaw, W. C., "Notes from the Act Books of the Archdeaconry Court of Lewes", *Sussex Archaeological Collections*, XLIX, 47–65.

Les Reports du Treserudite Edmund Anderson, Chivalier, Nadgairs, Seigniour Chief Justice del Common-Bank . . . (London: 1664).

Rymer, Thomas, *Foedera, Conventiones, Literae, Et Cujuscunque Generis Acta Publica, Inter Reges Angliae, Et alios quosvis Imperatores, Reges, Pontifices, Principes, vel Communitates . . .* volume XV (London: 1713).

The Seconde Parte of a Register, ed. Albert Peel, 2 volumes (Cambridge: 1915).

Select Statutes and Other Constitutional Documents Illustrative of the Reigns of Elizabeth and James I, ed. Sir G. W. Prothero, 4th ed. (Oxford: 1913).

The Remains of Edmund Grindel, ed. William Nicholson (Cambridge: Parker Society, 1843).

Shelley, Sir Richard, *Letters of Sir Richard Shelley, Who Was the Last English Grand-Prior of the Order of St. John of Jerusalem* (N.p.: 1774).

Smith, Richard, *An Elizabethan Recusant House, Comprising the Life of the Lady Magdalen Viscountess Montague (1538–1608). Translated from the Original Latin of Dr. Richard Smith . . . by Cuthbert Fursdon, O.S.B., in the Year 1627*, ed. A. C. Southern (London: 1954).

Sparrow, Anthony, *A Collection of Articles, Injunctions, Canons, Orders, Ordinances, & Constitutions Ecclesiastical, With Other*

Publick Records of the Church of England, Chiefly in the Times of K. Edward VI. Q. Elizabeth, K. James, and K. Charles I (London: 1684).

Statutes and Constitutions of the Cathedral Church of Chichester, ed. F. G. Bennett *et al.* (Chichester: 1904).

"Sussex Religious Houses and Recusants, Temp. Hen. VIII and Elizabeth", *Sussex Archaeological Collections*, XIII. 197–202.

Sussex Chantry Records, ed. John E. Ray. Lewes: S.R.S., 1930.

The Town Book of Lewes, 1542–1701, ed. L. F. Salzman (Lewes: S.R.S., 1946).

Transcripts of Sussex Wills as Far as They Relate to Ecclesiological and Parochial Subjects, Up to the Year 1560, ed. R. G. Rice, 4 volumes (Lewes: 1935).

The Troubles of Our Catholic Forefathers Related by Themselves, ed. John Morris, 3 volumes (London: 1872).

The Truth of Christes naturall body. By Richard Coortesse, Doctor of Diuinitie, and Bishop of Chichester (London: 1577).

Two Sermons Preached by the reverend father in God the Bishop of Chichester, the first at Paules Crosse on Sunday beeing the fourth day of March. And the second at Westminster before ye Queenes maiestie the iij Sunday in Lent last past (London: 1576).

Unpublished Documents Relating to the English Martyrs, 1584–1603, ed. J. H. Pollen (London: C.R.S., 1908).

The Ven. Philip Howard, Earl of Arundel, 1557–1595, ed. J. H. Pollen (London: C.R.S., 1919).

Wilkins, David, *Concilia Magnae Britaniae et Hiberniae*, Vol. IV (London: 1737).

The Works of Thomas Sackville, Lord Buckhurst, ed. R. W. Sackville-West (London: 1859).

IV. SECONDARY SOURCES

Allen, J. W., *A History of Political Thought in the Sixteenth Century* (London: 1960).

Attree, F. W. T., "Lists of Sussex Gentry at Various Dates", *Sussex Archaeological Collections*, XXXIX, 99–133.

Attree, F. W. T., and J. Booker, "The Sussex Colepeppers, Part II", *Sussex Archaeological Collections*, XLVIII, 65–98.

Aveling, Hugh, "The Catholic Recusants of the West Riding of Yorkshire, 1558–1790", *Proceedings of the Leeds Philosophical and Literary Society*, Literary and Historical Section, X. vi (1963), 191–306.

Babbage, S. B., *Puritanism and Richard Bancroft* (London: 1962).

Baines, J. M., "The Ships of the Cinque Ports in 1586/7", *Sussex Notes and Queries*, XIII, 241–4.

Barnes, A. S., *Bishop Barlow and Anglican Orders* (London: 1922).

Bayne, C. G., "Visitation of the Province of Canterbury, 1559", *English Historical Review*, XXIII, 636–7.

Birt, H. N., *The Elizabethan Religious Settlement* (London: 1907).

Black, J. B., *The Reign of Elizabeth* (Oxford: 1936).

Bossy, John, "The Character of Elizabethan Catholicism", *Crisis in Europe, 1560–1660*, ed. Trevor Aston (London: 1965).

Brenan, Gerald, *A History of the House of Percy from Earliest Times down to the Present Century*, ed. W. A. Lindsay, 2 volumes (London: 1902).

Brook, V. J. K., *A Life of Archbishop Parker* (Oxford: 1962).

Brook, V. J. K., *Whitgift and the English Church* (London: 1957).

Brydges, Sir Egerton, *Collins's Peerage of England*, Vol. II (London: 1812).

Burrage, Champlin, *The Early English Dissenters in the Light of Recent Research (1560–1641)*, 2 volumes (Cambridge: 1912).

Burrows, Montagu, *The Cinque Ports* (London: 1888).

Challen, W. H., "Henry Blaxton, D.D.", *Sussex Notes and Queries*, XIV, 221–5.

The Chichester Customary. The Rites of the Church as Observed throughout the Year in Chichester Cathedral (London: 1948).

Churton, Ralph, *The Life of Alexander Nowell, Dean of St. Paul's* (Oxford: 1809).

Collinson, Patrick, *The Elizabethan Puritan Movement* (London: 1967).

Collinson, Patrick, "The 'nott conformyte' of the Young John Whitgift", *Journal of Ecclesiastical History*, XV, 192–200.

Collinson, Patrick, "The Puritan Classical Movement in the Reign of Elizabeth I" (London Ph.D. thesis, 1957).

Comber, John, *Sussex Genealogies*, 4 volumes (Cambridge: 1931).

Cooper, C. H. and T., *Athenae Cantabrigienses*, 3 volumes (Cambridge: 1858).

Cooper, J. H., "The Coverts, Part III", *Sussex Archaeological Collections*, XLVIII, 1–15.

Cooper, J. H., "Cuckfield Families, II", *Sussex Archaeological Collections*, XLII, 19–53.

Cooper, J. H., "The Elizabethan Vicars of Cuckfield", *Sussex Archaeological Collections*, XLIV, 11–27.

Cooper, J. H., *A History of the Parish of Cuckfield* (Haywards Heath, Sussex: 1912).

Cooper, W. D. and Thomas Ross, "Notices of Hastings, and Its Municipal Rights", *Sussex Archaeological Collections*, XIV, 65–118.

Cooper, W. D., "Protestant Refugees in Sussex", *Sussex Archaeological Collections*, XIII, 180–208.

Cornwall, Julian, "Agricultural Improvement, 1560–1640", *Sussex Archaeological Collections*, XCVIII, 118–32.

Cornwall, Julian, "English Country Towns in the Fifteen Twenties", *Economic History Review*, 2nd ser., XV, 54–69.

Cornwall, Julian, "Farming in Sussex, 1560–1640", *Sussex Archaeological Collections*, XCII, 48–92.

Cornwall, Julian, "Forestry and the Timber Trade in Sussex, 1560–1640", *Sussex Notes and Queries*, XIV, 85–91.

Curtis, Mark, "The Alienated Intellectuals of Early Stuart England", *Crisis in Europe, 1560–1660*, ed. Trevor Aston (London: 1965).

Daeley, J. I., "Pluralism in the Diocese of Canterbury during the Administration of Matthew Parker, 1559–1575", *Journal of Ecclesiastical History*, XVIII (April 1967), 33–49

Dallaway, James, *A History of the Western Division of the County of Sussex*, 2 volumes (London: 1815).

Dawley, P. M., *John Whitgift and the English Reformation* (New York: 1954).

Devlin, Christopher, *The Life of Robert Southwell. Poet and Martyr* (New York: 1956).

Dickens, A. G., "The Extent and Character of Recusancy in Yorkshire, 1604", *Yorkshire Archaeological Journal*, XXXVII (1951), 24–8.

Dickens, A. G., *Lollards and Protestants in the Diocese of York, 1509–1558* (London: 1959).

Elizabethan Government and Society: Essays Presented to Sir John Neale, ed. S. T. Bindoff *et al.* (London: 1961).

Ellis, Sir Henry, "Notices of Richard Curteys, Bishop of Chichester, 1570–1582", *Sussex Archaeological Collections*, X, 52–8.

Elton, G. R., *England Under the Tudors* (London: 1962).

Elton, G. R., "The Problems and Significance of Administrative History in the Tudor Period", *Journal of British Studies*, IV (1965), 18–28.

Elton, G. R., *The Tudor Constitution* (Cambridge: 1960).

Elwes, D. G., *A History of the Castles and Mansions of Western Sussex* (London: 1876).

Fitzwilliam, J. W., *Parham in Sussex* (London: 1947).

Foley, Henry, *Records of the English Province of the Society of Jesus*, Vol. III (London: 1876).

Fuller, Thomas, *The History of the Worthies of England*, vol. III (London: 1840).

Fussell, G. E., "Four Centuries of Farming Systems in Sussex, 1500–1900", *Sussex Archaeological Collections*, XC, 60–101.

Gage, John, *The History and Antiquities of Hengrave in Suffolk* (London: 1822).

Garrett, C. H., *The Marian Exiles: A Study in the Origins of Elizabethan Puritanism* (Cambridge: 1938).

Gasquet, Aidan, *Parish Life in Medieval England*, 5th ed. (London: 1922).

Gee, Henry, *The Elizabethan Clergy and the Settlement of Religion, 1558–1564* (Oxford: 1898).

Grove, Henry, *Alienated Tithes in Impropriated Parishes, Commuted or Merged under Local Statutes and the Tithe Acts: Together with all Crown Grants of Tithes, Henry VIII to William III* (London: 1896).

Head, R. E., *Royal Supremacy and the Trials of the Bishops, 1558–1725* (London: 1962).

Hennesy, George, *Chichester Diocese Clergy Lists: Clergy Succession from the Earliest Time to the Year 1900* (London: 1900).

Hill, Christopher, *Economic Problems of the Church from Archbishop Whitgift to the Long Parliament* (Oxford: 1956).

Hill, Christopher, *Intellectual Origins of the English Revolution* (Oxford: 1965).

Hill, Christopher, *Society and Puritanism in Pre-Revolutionary England* (London: 1966).

Holloway, William, *The History and Antiquities of the Ancient Town and Port of Rye in the County of Sussex* (London: 1847).

Hope, Sir W. St J., *Cowdray and Eastebourne Priory in the County of Sussex* (London: 1919).

Hughes, Philip, *The Reformation in England*. Volume III: "True Religion Now Established" (London: 1954).

Hurstfield, Joel, *The Queen's Wards: Wardship and Marriage under Elizabeth I* (London: 1958).

Hurstfield, Joel, *Liberty and Authority under Queen Elizabeth I* (London: 1960).

Hyland, St G. K., *A Century of Persecution under Tudor and Stuart Sovereigns from Contemporary Records* (London: 1920).

Jenkins, Claude, "Bishop Barlow's Consecration and Archbishop Parker's Register: With Some New Documents", *Journal of Theological Studies*, XXIV, 1–32.

Kennedy, W. P. M., "Visitation Articles and Injunctions, 1576–1603", *English Historical Review*, XXXII, 273–6.

Kenyon, G. H., "Wealden Iron", *Sussex Notes and Queries*, XIII, 234–41.

Knappen, M. M., *Tudor Puritanism: A Chapter in the History of Idealism* (Chicago: 1939).

Koszul, A., "Was Bishop William Barlow Friar Jerome?", *Review of English Studies*, IV (1928), 24–5.

Le Neve, John, *Fasti Ecclesiae Anglicanae*, 3 volumes (Oxford: 1854).

Lives of the English Martyrs, ed. E. H. Burton and J. H. Pollen, 2nd ser., vol. I (London: 1914).

Lloyd, Eleanor, "Leedes of Wappingthorne", *Sussex Archaeological Collections*, LIV, 37.

Loomie, A. J., "Spain and the English Catholic Exiles, 1580–1604" (London: Ph.D. thesis, 1957).

Lower, M. A., *Historical and Genealogical Notices of the Pelham Family* (N.p.: 1873).

Lower, M. A., *The Worthies of Sussex* (Lewes: 1865).

The Lumley Library: The Catalogue of 1609, ed. Sears Jayne and F. R. Johnson (London: 1956).

MacCaffrey, W. T., *Exeter, 1540–1640: The Growth of an English County Town* (Cambridge, Mass.: 1958).

McDermott, Eric, "The Life of Thomas Stapleton, 1535–1598" (London M.A. thesis, 1950).

Magee, Brian, *The English Recusants: A Study of the Post-Reformation Catholic Survival and the Operation of the Recusancy Laws* (London: 1938).

Manning, Roger B., "Catholics and Local Office Holding in Elizabethan Sussex", *Bulletin of the Institute of Historical Research*, XXXV, 47–61.

Manning, Roger B., "Richard Shelley of Warminghurst and the Catholic Petition for Toleration of 1585", *Recusant History*, VI, 265–74.

Mantoux, Paul, *The Industrial Revolution in the Eighteenth Century*, rev. ed. (New York: 1962).

Marchant, Ronald, *The Puritans and the Church Courts in the Diocese of York, 1560–1642* (London: 1960).

Marshall, Edward, "Bishop William Barlow", *Sussex Notes and Queries*, 6th ser., VIII, 31–3.

Mousley, Joyce E., "The Fortunes of Some Gentry Families of Elizabethan Sussex", *Economic History Review*, 2nd ser., XI, 477.

Mousley, Joyce E., "Sussex Country Gentry in the Reign of Elizabeth" (London Ph.D. thesis, 1955).

Neale, Sir John, "The Elizabethan Acts of Supremacy and Uniformity", *English Historical Review*, LX, 304–32.

Neale, Sir John, *The Elizabethan House of Commons* (London: 1949).

Neale, Sir John, *Elizabeth I and her Parliaments, 1559–1581* (London: 1953).

Neale, Sir John, *Elizabeth I and her Parliaments, 1584–1601* (London: 1957).

Neale, Sir John, *Elizabethan Essays* (London: 1958).

O'Dwyer, Michael, "Catholic Recusants in Essex, c. 1580–c. 1600" (London M.A. thesis, 1960).

O'Dwyer, Michael, "Recusant Fines in Essex", *The Month*, July 1958.

Owen, H. G., "The Episcopal Visitation: Its Limits and Limitations in Elizabethan London", *Journal of Ecclesiastical History*, XI, 179–85.

Owen, H. G., "The London Parish Clergy in the Reign of Elizabeth I" (London Ph.D. thesis, 1967).

Porter, H. C., *Reformation and Reaction in Tudor Cambridge* (Cambridge: 1958).

Peckham, W. D., "The Vicars Choral of Chichester Cathedral", *Sussex Archaeological Collections*, LXXVIII, 126–59.

Peckham, W. D., "The Parishes of the City of Chichester", *Sussex Archaeological Collections*, LXXIV, 65–97.

Peters, Robert, *Oculus Episcopi: Administration in the Archdeaconry of St. Albans, 1580–1625* (Manchester: 1963).

Powicke, Sir Maurice, *The Reformation in England* (London: 1961).

Price, F. D., "The Abuses of Excommunication and the Decline of Ecclesiastical Discipline under Queen Elizabeth", *English Historical Review*, LVII, 106–15.

Price, F. D., "The Commission for Ecclesiastical Causes in the Dioceses of Bristol and Gloucester, 1574", *Transactions of the Bristol and Gloucestershire Archaeological Society*, LIX, 61–181.

Price, F. D., "Elizabethan Apparitors in the Diocese of Gloucester", *Church Quarterly Review*, CXXIV (1942), 37–55.

Price, F. D., "An Elizabethan Church Official—Thomas Powell, Chancellor of Gloucester Diocese", *Church History Review*, CXXVIII (1939), 94–112.

Read, Conyers, *Lord Burghley and Queen Elizabeth* (London: 1960).

Reed, Michael, "The Keeping of Sessions of the Peace in the Borough of Hastings", *Sussex Archaeological Collections*, C. 46–59.

Renshaw, Walter C., "Some Clergy of the Archdeaconry of

Lewes and South Malling Deanery", *Sussex Archaeological Collections*, LV, 220–77.

Revill, Philippa, and F. W. Steer, "George Gage I and George Gage II", *Bulletin of the Institute of Historical Research*, XXXI, 141–53.

Roundell, J. A. E., *Cowdray: The History of a Great English House* (London: 1884).

Rowse, A. L., *The England of Elizabeth: The Structure of Society* (New York: 1951).

Rowse, A. L., *Tudor Cornwall: Portrait of a Society* (London: 1941).

Rupp. E. G., "The Early Career of Bishop Barlow", *Studies in the Making of the English Protestant Tradition* (Cambridge: 1949).

Sackville, Reginald, 7th Earl De La Warr, *Historical Notices of the Parish of Withyham in the County of Sussex* (London: 1857).

Sackville-West, Victoria, *Knole and the Sackvilles* (London: 1922).

Smith, L. B., *Tudor Prelates and Politics, 1536–1538* (Princeton: 1953).

Smith, Sir Thomas, *De Republica Anglorum*, ed. L. Alston (Cambridge: 1906).

Stenning, Alan H., "A Return of the Members of Parliament for the County and Boroughs of Sussex", *Sussex Archaeological Collections*, XXXIII, 69–100.

Stephens, W. R. W., *Memorials of the South Saxon See and the Cathedral Church of Chichester* (London: 1876).

Stephens, W. R. W., *The South Saxon Diocese, Selsey-Chichester* (London: 1881).

Strype, John, *Annals of the Reformation* (Oxford: 1824).

Strype, John, *The Life and Acts of Edmund Grindal* (Oxford: 1824).

Strype, John, *The Life and Acts of John Whitgift* (Oxford: 1822).

Swart, J., *Thomas Sackville: A Study in Sixteenth-Century Poetry* (Groningen, the Netherlands: 1949).

Thomas-Stanford, Charles, *Sussex in the Great Civil War and the Interregnum, 1642–1660* (London: 1910).

Thompson, A. H., *The English Clergy and their Organization in the Later Middle Ages* (Oxford: 1947).

Thompson, J. V. P., *Supreme Governor: A Study of Elizabethan Policy and Circumstance* (London: 1940).

Tierney, M. A., *The History and Antiquities of the Castle and Town of Arundel* (London: 1834).

Torr, V. J. B., "An Elizabethan Return of the State of the Diocese of Chichester", *Sussex Archaeological Collections*, LXI, 92–124.

Trenqualéon, Max de, *West Grinstead et les Caryll*, 2 volumes (Paris: 1893).

Trevor-Roper, H. R., *Archbishop Laud, 1573–1645*, 2nd ed. (London: 1962).

Trimble, W. R. *The Catholic Laity in Elizabethan England, 1558–1603* (Cambridge, Mass.: 1964).

The Victoria History of the County of Sussex, ed. William Page, vol. II (London: 1907).

Wadey, J. E., "Schools and Schooling in Sussex, 1548–1607", *Sussex Notes and Queries*, XIV, 217–21.

Walker, F. X., "The Implementation of the Elizabethan Statutes against Recusants, 1581–1603" (London Ph.D. thesis, 1961).

White, F. O., *Lives of the Elizabethan Bishops of the Anglican Church* (London: 1898).

Wood, Anthony á, *Anthanae Oxoniensis*, 6 volumes (Oxford: 1813).

Woodward, G. W. O., *A Short History of 16th Century England* (New York: 1963).

INDEX